THE 2001 FILE

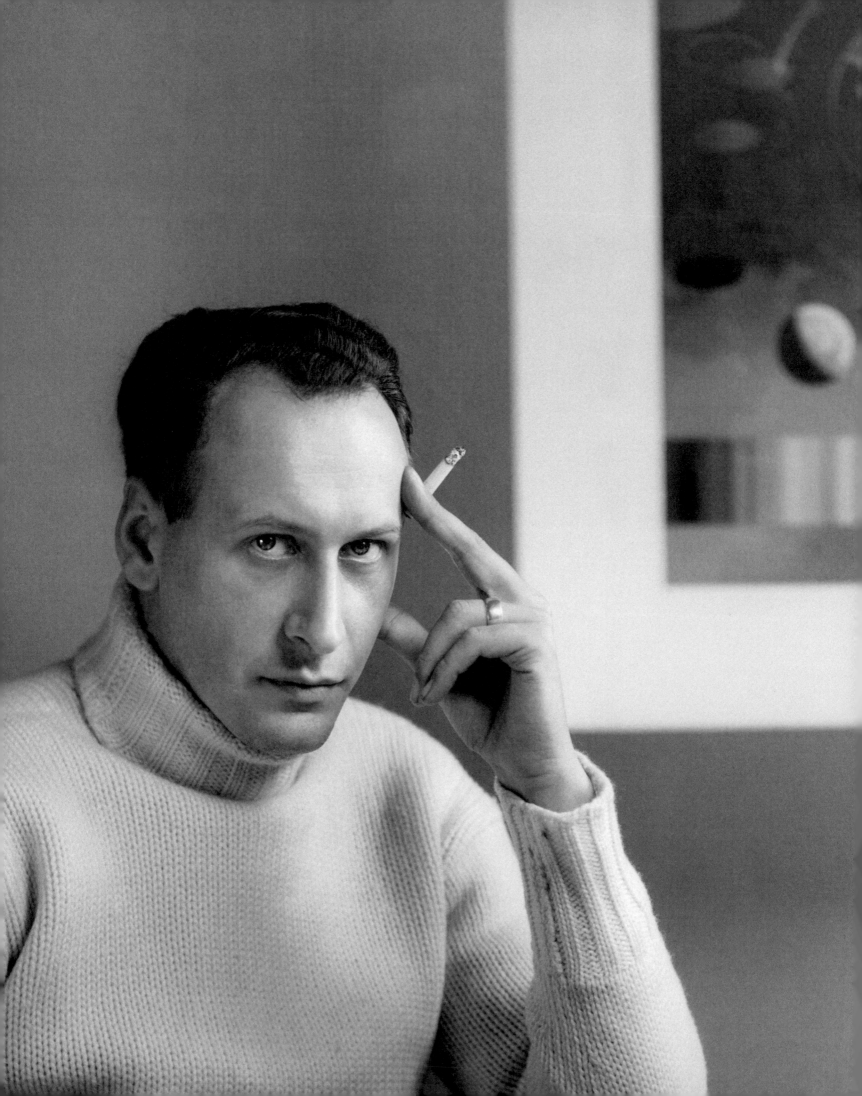

THE 2001 FILE

HARRY LANGE AND THE DESIGN OF THE LANDMARK SCIENCE FICTION FILM

CHRISTOPHER FRAYLING

REEL ART PRESS

ANKS TO JAN HARLAN, THE KUBRICK FAMILY AND PIERS BIZONY FOR GIVING THEIR
PERSONAL SUPPORT TO THIS PUBLICATION.

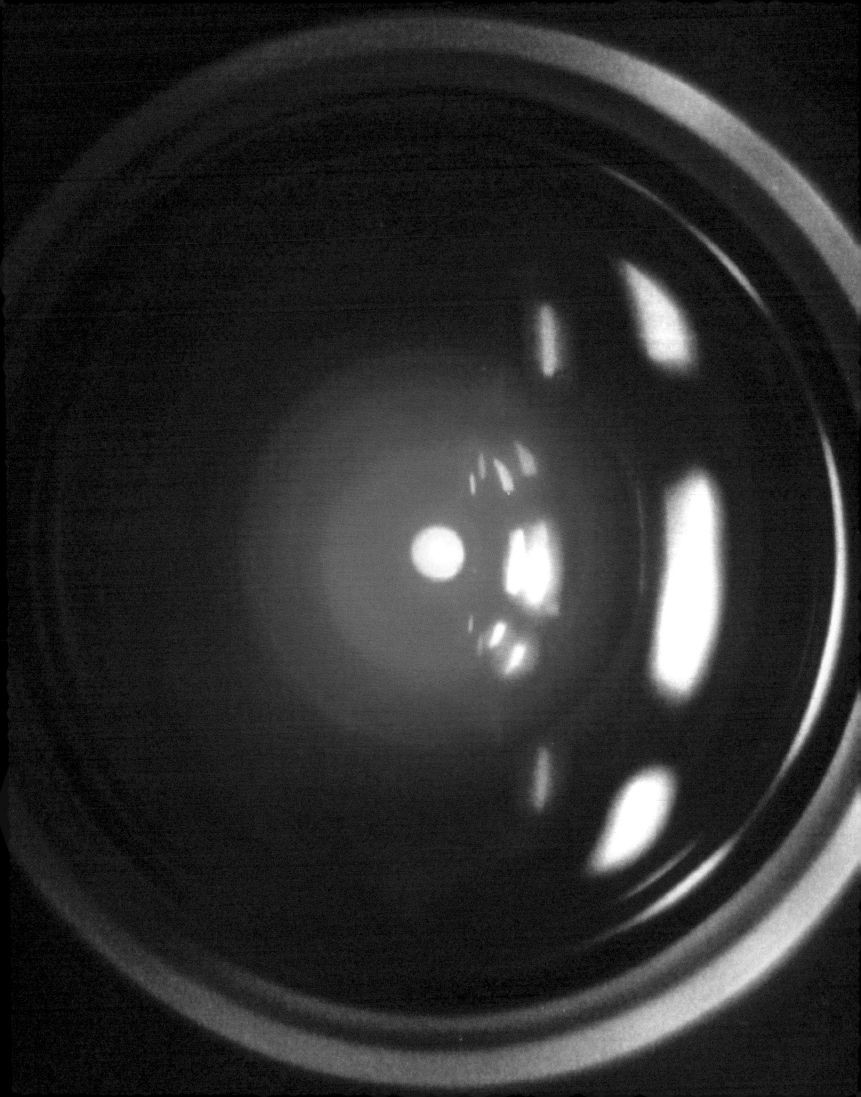

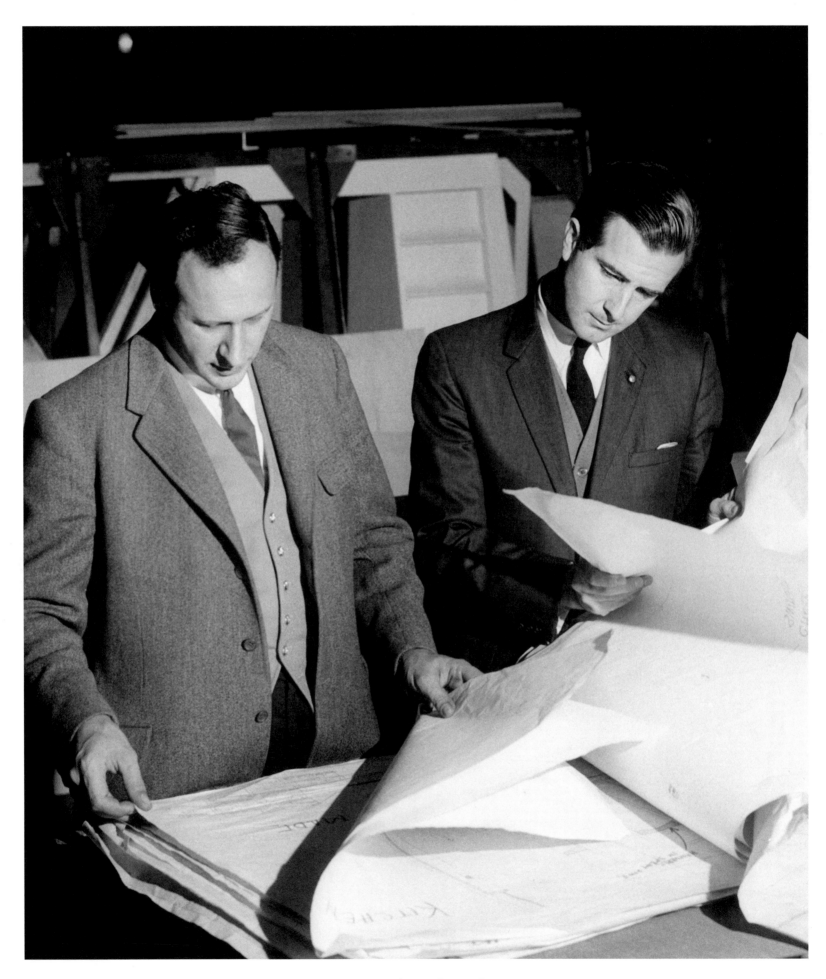

Harry (Hans–Kurt) Lange and Frederick I. Ordway III, checking designs at MGM studios, Borehamwood.

FOR

HARRY LANGE (1930–2008) AND **FREDERICK I. ORDWAY III** (1927–2014)
TWO GREAT EXPLORERS OF YESTERDAY'S TOMORROWS

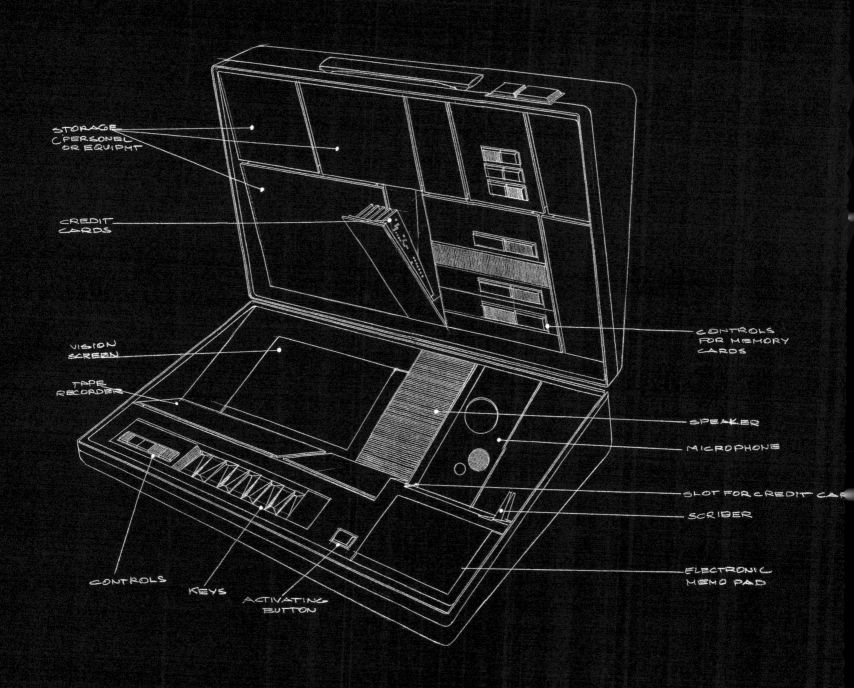

STORAGE
(PERSONL
OR EQUIPMT

CREDIT
CARDS

VISION
SCREEN

TAPE
RECORDER

CONTROLS
FOR MEMORY
CARDS

SPEAKER

MICROPHONE

SLOT FOR CREDIT CAR

SCRIBER

ELECTRONIC
MEMO PAD

CONTROLS

KEYS

ACTIVATING
BUTTON

Harry Lange's drawing of a miniature computer/tape recorder/newsreader/data display unit/telephone and 'automatic writing storage area', all inside an attaché case: this 'beautifully laid out and finished interior' was described in detail in production notes, developed with industrial help from Honeywell—and never used in the finished film, where Floyd on Aries simply uses a standard zip-up document briefcase.

CONTENTS

THE 2001 FILE **11**

THE NOVEL **40**

THE SCREENPLAY **46**

THE HARRY LANGE ARCHIVE **87**

Odyssey I Into Space **99**

Odyssey II To The Moon **151**

Odyssey III Towards Jupiter **209**

ODYSSEY'S END **329**

ACKNOWLEDGEMENTS **332**

BIBLIOGRAPHY **334**

CREDITS **336**

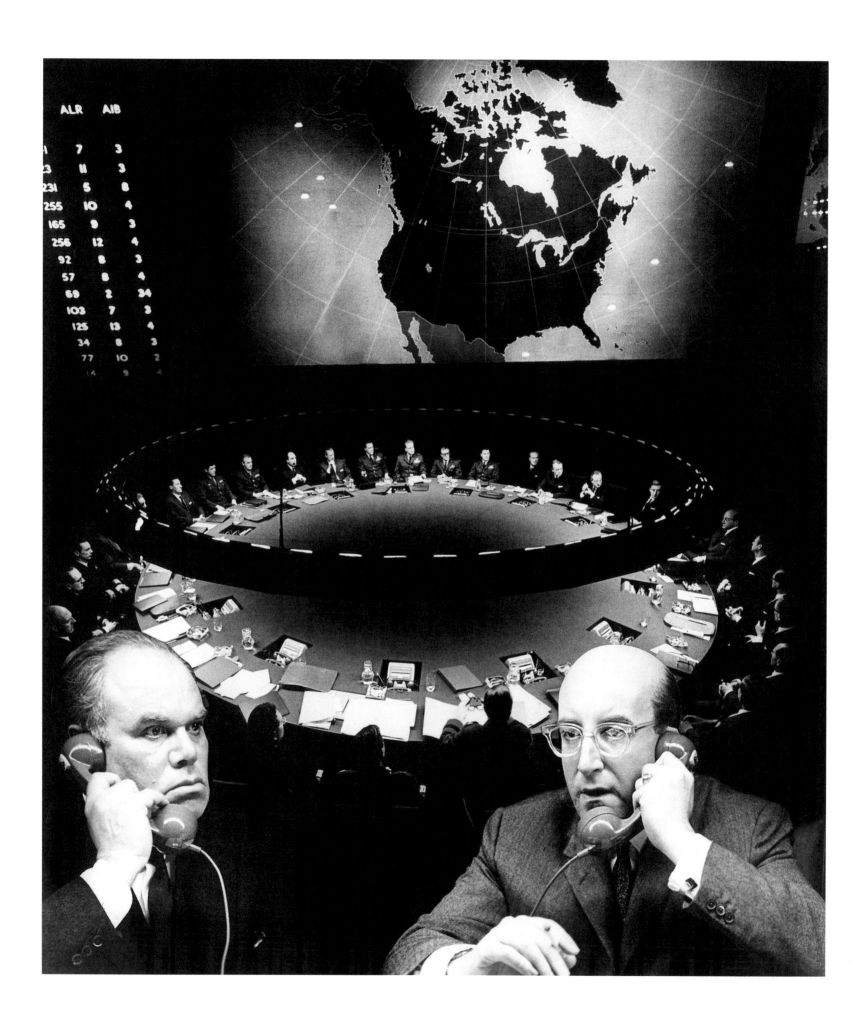

THE 2001 FILE

On 26th July 1964 Stanley Kubrick wrote to Ken Adam—his production designer on Dr Strangelove—from New York, to ask in a handwritten letter if he would consider designing his next film project called Journey Beyond the Stars.

Ken Adam lived in Knightsbridge, London, and his letters from Kubrick were always delivered from a chauffeur-driven car, to make sure they arrived safely. Adam had developed a very close, intense working relationship with Kubrick on **Dr Strangelove**—which had been released six months earlier—and his set design for the Pentagon War Room, built at Shepperton Studios, had already attracted a lot of critical attention: one part concrete bomb-shelter, one part oval light-ring illuminating a giant green baize poker game, one part animated map or scoreboard showing the flight-paths of bombers carrying nuclear weapons, three parts paranoia, the War Room set had been an inspired visualisation of the film's atmosphere of surreal, over-the-top black comedy. This, in contrast to the documentary-style treatment of the aircraft cockpit of the fateful B-52 bomber, 'in its minutest detail', which had been based on a comparison between the real cockpit of a B-29, and some photos 'from aeronautical magazines' of the still-classified B-52. 'Stanley,' Adam was to recall, 'was like a Boy Scout because he adored switches and dials. He'd sit on the set for hours playing with the switches. And the Air Force jargon; he loved the way people talked with no emotion in their voices.' Some

American Air Force personnel had been invited to Shepperton to see the results and were surprised to discover that so many secret details were 'very near the mark'.

'I got a memo from Stanley, who hoped I could justify all my research (legally) because we could well be investigated by the CIA!'

So Ken Adam could do documentary and hyper-realism as well as expressionism. Would he be interested in designing Kubrick's *next* project?

'… *I'm working*' wrote Stanley Kubrick, '*on what I think will be a good (I won't sound immodest and say great) script—the only problem is that it will almost certainly have to be made in Hollywood. It's hard for me to predict a start date but I'd say sometime around March 1965, with preparation starting about Octoberish-Novemberish. Are you allowed to work in Hollywood? Are you enslaved by the Great Saltzman?*'

Kubrick added that he had recently purchased a penthouse on East 84th Street ('two together') in a newly built air-conditioned building off Lexington Avenue a couple of blocks from the park. Ken Adam replied on 22nd August, after he had returned from a

*Opposite: The Pentagon War Room, designed by Ken Adam for Stanley Kubrick's **Dr Strangelove** and built at Shepperton Studios in 1963.*

four-week motoring holiday and location recce in his 'E' type Jaguar with his wife Letizia, from Sicily via Rome to Switzerland. His letter was handwritten:

'I am naturally delighted that you are working on another subject, instead of being office bound in the Columbia empire watching box-office receipts, but at the same time I wish'd you would start shooting 2-3 months later, since it goes without saying that I would love to work with you old rompe scatole (transl. "ball-breaker") again. In principle, there should be nothing against my working in Hollywood.'

The problem was that Adam had just signed a contract 'with the great Harry' to design the next James Bond film **Thunderball**—which was scheduled to be filmed from February to April 1965, most of it in the Bahamas—had recently completed **Woman of Straw** and **Goldfinger**, was 'casing London locations interior and exterior' for **The Ipcress File**, and 'if you had written to me two weeks earlier I would have consulted you prior to committing myself'. So if Stanley Kubrick really *was* set on starting **Journey Beyond the Stars** in spring rather than summer ('around March 1965'), the answer had to be no. But:

'Hate to admit it, that even with all the long shots [of the War Room] cut, the sets must have made some impact [... had a lot of personal publicity lately in National & Trade press]. Kidding apart, Stanley, I am proud to have been connected with **Strangelove**... I know I must be a masochist but... you somehow became part of our life and it seems ridiculous that we now function in different cities. I also miss the stimulus of your company, though it could be trying at times.'

About the new 'penthouse apartment', Adam added that he 'can't believe it yet': after all, since 1961 Kubrick had made a point of living in England.

'How does your intellect justify such a step? Am sure with... your insatiable thirst for switches and mechanics it should be most interesting and I cannot wait to see it.'

On 2nd February 1965, Stanley Kubrick wrote again, this time from his New York office at Polaris Productions. If he could not have Ken Adam as his production designer on **Journey Beyond the Stars**, then perhaps Ken could recommend someone else?

'You were going to send me a list of several British art directors you would recommend for my picture. Very good on technical, trick and cost factors but also creative. If the stress must be on creative or the other elements, I think I would prefer the technical side. I am doing a tremendous amount of research and will also probably have a number of artists do some conceptual drawings of the extra-terrestrial world...

The people you recommend should be available starting May 1, or possibly April, though anyone top-notch should be given [sic] even if

their dates create a minor problem... Keep in mind the personality of the old maestro and how it might mesh with your choices.

Things are starting to happen and I need this information.'

Ken Adam replied on 28th February with 'names of all the people' and in the same letter enquired whether he could perhaps see a script of **Journey**—hinting in the process that there might, after all, be just a chance of his involvement in some capacity. Stanley Kubrick replied, sharply, in an uncharacteristic typewritten letter on 12th March that 'it would be out of the question' for him 'to submit a script to you for your approval'. The key question remained as before: was Adam 'willing to do' the project or not?

'I know that you are very busy and apparently besieged with possibilities and offers, and I can appreciate how ambivalent your feelings may be towards my mystery film. I hope, however, that you understand my position and understand how impossible it is for me to, as it were, submit a script for your approval before you give an indication of whether or not you can, or are willing to, do my film. I would suggest, therefore, that we drop all further discussions about it and I will seek divine guidance elsewhere.'

Four days later, on 16th March, Ken Adam made clear—also in a typed letter this time—that he had *not* asked for script approval, of course he hadn't, but had merely requested sight of an 'outline or book or Script'. He had hoped to meet Stanley Kubrick in New York the previous week to talk things through—en route to Miami—but for some reason this had not worked out:

'I cannot be expected to accept blindly a very important position on a most difficult project, which I know would require all my resources and ingenuity.'

The most sensible thing was to agree to 'drop all further discussions in this matter'.

'Dear Stanley,
    Let's get one thing straight, I did not ever ask you for Script approval.
    In my last letter to you, I asked you:
    (a) To let me have more time to consider your offer, since I am overworked at this moment and therefore in a somewhat confused state of mind.
    (b) If possible and not out of lack of respect or confidence in you to let me have an outline or book or Script of your subject.
    (c) I was willing to arrange my flight to Miami a week ago in such a way to enable us, if possible, to meet for Dinner in New York. (Reason, I wanted to discuss the film with you and was hoping that you would give me some indication as to what it was all about.) I also asked you to phone me confirmation re the Dinner appointment.

*Opposite: Harry Lange and Frederick Ordway, behind the scenes of **2001** at MGM studios, Borehamwood. They had both worked for NASA, and could ensure that the film would look 'realistic and detailed'.*

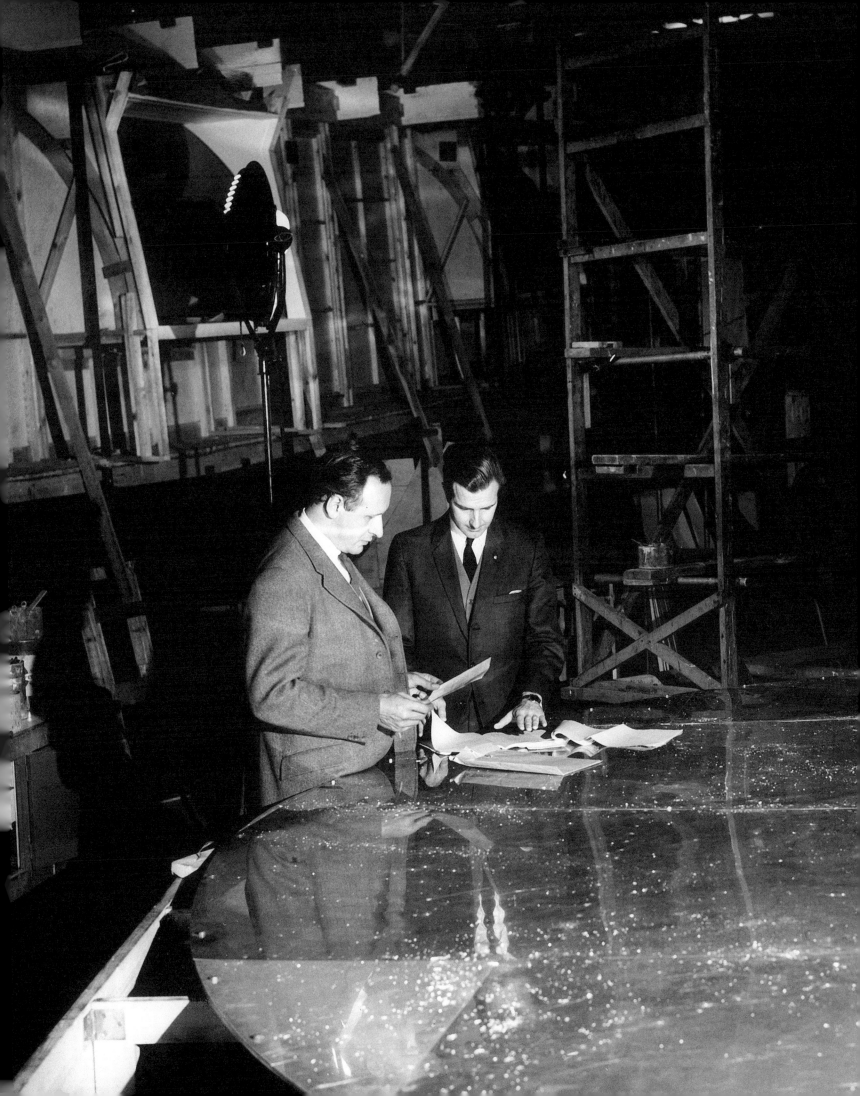

Apparently, you did not consider it necessary to call me and I therefore had to phone you, only to be told that on the evening in question you were otherwise engaged. I am only bringing all this up, since surely it must have indicated my interest and keenness in your proposal and film.

After having worked with you for 8 months I am fully aware of your desire for perfectionisme (sic), the high standard of work you demand and your various idiosyncrasies and however much I may respect and admire you, I cannot be expected to accept blindly a very important position on a most difficult project, which I know would require all my resources and ingenuity. You have worked on this subject for over a year with all kinds of research at your disposal. I would have to digest all this in a relatively short period and for the time being I am up to the hilt in "Thunderball". Also remember Stanley that you sometimes take months or even years to make up your mind before embarking on your next project.

You ask me in your letter to understand your position, which frankly and under the circumstances I do not understand at all. —However, be that as it may, as you suggested we will drop all further discussions in this matter.
Kindest regards, Ken'

And that was the end of Ken Adam's involvement in **2001**. When I asked him what he remembered about being approached by Kubrick to design **Journey Beyond the Stars**, he recalled that 'however much I liked to be in his company—he was, after all, a fascinating person—I didn't feel it was worth going through that period, emotionally, on another film'. The letter of 22nd August, in reply to Kubrick's original offer, was trying to turn him down, gently, while at the same time expressing his strong admiration for him. Adam had been driven almost to distraction by the director's relentless logical questioning—standing over him while he tried to get on with his design work—but he had also loved an experience which resulted in 'the best design I ever did'. In the same letter, Ken Adam had written that he 'cannot wait to see' the Kubricks' new apartment on the Upper East Side. When eventually he *did* manage to see it, while passing through New York in spring 1965, Adam recalls that 'we discussed balconies, and how dangerous they were—he thought that someone could take a shot at you from across the street'. They also discussed the science-fiction novel and film that Kubrick was in the process of brainstorming with the British author Arthur C. Clarke, by now with advice from the space specialists working on 'some conceptual drawings of the extra-terrestrial world':

*'I went to his New York apartment, where he had been working with some experts from NASA. One of them, Harry Lange, later worked for me on the spacecraft and spacesuits for **Moonraker**. And Stanley knew as much about space as the experts. He certainly knew more*

than I did. And I thought to myself, "I couldn't do that." Because if I did it and Stanley knew more about it, every time I designed something that was intuitive, like my idea for a space station, he would say "It isn't what NASA says."

*I said that there wouldn't be any room left for my imagination. And honestly I'd had enough problems on **Dr Strangelove**.'*

Ken Adam recalls that Stanley Kubrick persisted for a while:

'I got letters from him on two occasions. One was handwritten [and] it said: "The fact that you have become a star should not cause you to act like one." You don't forget a letter like that.'

In fact, the letter in question was dated 24th June 1968, two and a half months *after* **2001: A Space Odyssey** was released. It seems to have been intended as Stanley Kubrick's summary of what had transpired when Ken Adam was offered the project. His recollection was that it was *Adam* who kept wanting to keep the door open, rather than vice versa, as he had on 28th February. Kubrick's letter certainly reveals how very prickly their creative partnership had become:

'1. I don't want to have a quarrel with you about the matter of what was said and what one should have said or done.

2. The fact is that you were not available, you said Spiegle had first call on your services, but that if something had either gone wrong, or he had changed his mind, then you would be delighted to work for me.

3. To then tell me I had done an unfriendly thing by going elsewhere is unrealistic and, may I say, expecting a degree of Risk-taking by me that is not reciprocated by you.

4. Let's not allow this to become an "issue". The fact that you have become a "star" should not cause you to act like one. You should know that an offer rejected goes stale in minutes.
Sincerely, Stanley

PS. This is especially ridiculous because the chances of you not being wanted by Big S after he had asked you to do it were nill.'

When he wrote 'Spiegle' [Sam Spiegel], Kubrick must really have meant producer Harry Saltzman—to whom Ken Adam referred several times in his letter of 22nd August. Adam did not work with Sam Spiegel until 1973. Between the time he received Kubrick's first letter about **Journey Beyond the Stars** and his last, he had designed five major films, four of them for Harry Saltzman. But there were evidently no long-term hard feelings. On 20th April 1970, Stanley Kubrick offered Adam a follow-up project—perhaps **A Clockwork Orange**—but by then could not afford his services on the meagre production budget: 'though it goes without saying that there are no other Ken Adams.' And after **A Clockwork Orange**, Ken Adam went on to design **Barry Lyndon** for him—starting

January 1973—a protracted and stressful experience which led to a serious nervous breakdown and a period in hospital as well as an Academy Award.

In the end—whatever the ins and outs of who said what when—Ken Adam realised, even in the absence of an 'outline or book or script', that this was going to be a very different film to **Dr Strangelove**—a *realistic* myth based on the latest researches from NASA; a fictional documentary set in space and on a colossal scale, to be shown on just about the widest screen there was. The wild expressionism, the satire, the exaggerations, the improvisation on set, of the earlier film could scarcely be further from Stanley Kubrick's intentions. The model of a B-52, wobbling against rear projection plates of the Arctic Circle, was now a thing of the past. There would, though, still be a nod towards **Dr Strangelove** in the original treatment (or 'film story') of **Journey Beyond the Stars**. Part II, in space, would begin with the thought that there were by now thirty-five nuclear nations, and 'it was estimated that the world stockpile was now sufficient to move the entire crust of the earth'. This survived into the 'production notes' of 1st June 1965: 'An Orion III spacecraft is making its way from Earth to Space Station-1. It passes two orbiting nuclear Space bombs—one belonging to the USA, one to the USSR—circling the Earth' at an altitude of 250 miles. And even into the screenplay of **2001** dated October-December 1965, just before shooting began. 'Part II Year 2001' begins with a shot of Earth from 200 miles up, then of an orbiting thousand-megaton nuclear bomb, with Russian insignia and CCCP markings. Over successive shots of 'American thousand megaton bomb', then French, then German, then Chinese; the narrator spoke of 'the absolute and utter perfection of the weapon':

'Hundreds of giant bombs had been placed in perpetual orbit above the Earth. They were capable of incinerating the entire earth's surface from an altitude of 100 miles. Matters were further complicated by the presence of twenty-seven nations in the nuclear club. There had been no deliberate or accidental use of nuclear weapons since World War II and some people felt secure in this knowledge. But to others, the situation seemed comparable to an airline with a perfect safety record; it showed admirable care and skill but no-one expected it to last forever.'

The reference to an airline's safety record was, of course, a sly reference to Stanley Kubrick's own anxieties about flying. But the narration, so similar to that in **Dr Strangelove**, and nearly all—not all—the shots of the orbiting bombs, were to be deleted from the finished film version. Just two unexplained pieces of equipment in space. As Arthur C. Clarke was to put it, in the end, 'this was not really spelled out in the film': the celebrated cut from bone to orbiting bomb platform still represented some four million years of weapons development and showed that the human race had not advanced that much. The movement from bone to bomb—from four million years ago to early in the twenty-first century—was

one of redescent not ascent. But Stanley Kubrick had decided not to make 'an issue' of it.

Ken Adam recalls that he did make one significant contribution to **2001**:

*'... there was one person I brought to Stanley's film and he was Wally Veevers, the special effects specialist who had come in on **Dr Strangelove**, working for me and solving some of my technical problems. He had worked with me before that, on **Sodom and Gomorrah**. I remember recommending him to Stanley as someone who was very good on the technical side.'*

Did Ken Adam remember recommending Tony Masters, also, as head of the art department on **2001**—and perhaps as a man who in Kubrick's words was stronger on the 'technical' side than the 'creative'? Masters had worked (uncredited) on the design logistics of **Lawrence of Arabia** with David Lean—so he had a proven track-record in organising a complex production, running a large budget and understanding the latest technologies of film-making. Kubrick had thanked Ken for his list on 12th March 1965, Adam had worked with Masters in his early days in the film industry, and Tony Masters arrived in New York from England in mid-April, with his associate on day-to-day matters John Hoesli.

'I can't remember if his name was on my list, and I don't any more have a copy of my letter to Stanley. Just his reply. It could have been. You have to remember that Tony Masters, John Box and I all came out of the forces at much the same time, at the end of the Second World War. Tony had been a Major in the Royal Artillery, and had trained as an architect. He was a very good organiser—he needed to be—he had a real ability to get on with people, and a charm.'

Stanley Kubrick had been collaborating with author Arthur C. Clarke, in New York, since 22nd April 1964. He had contacted Clarke at his home in Colombo, Ceylon (later Sri Lanka), on 31st March, saying that he had been 'a great admirer of your books for quite a time' and that he was interested in discussing 'with you the possibility of doing the proverbial "really good" science-fiction movie'—implying that none of the others had been up to his exacting standards. His main interests, he added, were 'the reasons for believing in the existence of intelligent extra-terrestrial life' and 'the impact (and perhaps even the lack of impact in some quarters) such a discovery would have on Earth in the near future'. Also, 'a space probe with a landing and exploration of the Moon and Mars'. Perhaps during the discussions 'an idea might exist or arise'—and they could as a result 'collaborate on a screenplay'. Kubrick's letter finished with an enquiry about the best long-range stargazing telescope, for home use. The two men met at Trader Vic's in the Plaza Hotel, New York, for an eight-hour brainstormer. By coincidence, this was also the day the New York World's Fair opened, and, in the pre-production phase of the film, **Journey** would make full use of several of the companies and products represented in the Fair.

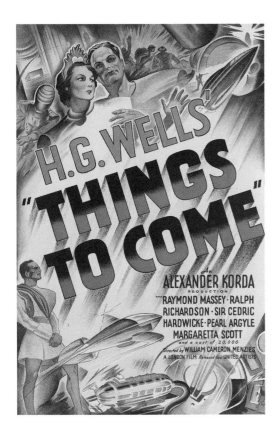
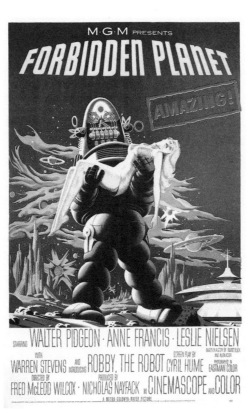
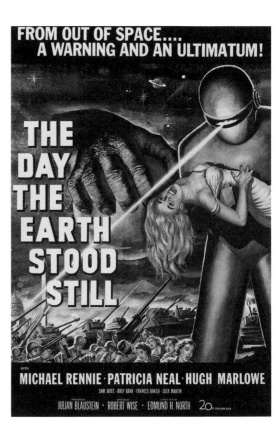

Clarke was in town to complete editorial work on his picture-book for Time-Life, **Man and Space**. He and Kubrick agreed, unusually, to write a complete novel together and *then* derive a screenplay from it—although the boundaries between the two would become blurred towards the end of this protracted process. Clarke formally agreed on 17th May 1964. He was to recall:

'When I met Stanley Kubrick for the first time... he had already absorbed an immense amount of science fact and science fiction, and was in some danger of believing in flying saucers; I felt I had arrived just in time to save him from this gruesome fate. Even from the beginning, he had a very clear idea of his ultimate goal and was searching for the best way to approach it. He wanted to make a movie about Man's relation to the universe... Of course, there had been innumerable "space" movies, most of them trash. Even the few that had been made with some skill and accuracy had been rather simpleminded, concerned more with the schoolboy excitement of space flight than its profound implications for society, philosophy and religion. Stanley was fully aware of this...'

Not just 'Man's relationship to the universe' but his relationship with technology *and* material culture and the future of evolution: far from 'simpleminded'.

By early May—'after various false starts and twelve-hour talkathons'—it had been agreed that Clarke's short story **The Sentinel**, written over Christmas 1948 and published in 1951 as **Sentinel of Eternity**, would provide the starting-point. It had been entered for a BBC short story contest, and it had not won. The climax of the story was the discovery of an alien artefact, a cosmic fire-alarm on the moon—and this remained the climax of the novel/film for the next few months. At that early stage, the proposed schedule was, according to Clarke, 'hilariously optimistic'—with scriptwriting and revisions from June-October 1964, closing the deal with a studio in October-November, pre-production November-March and filming from March 1965 for five months. This was the timetable offered to Ken Adam. In the event, the project was to take four years rather than eighteen months. And it was to be filmed at MGM Borehamwood, north of London, rather than in Hollywood.

As part of his early preparations, Stanley Kubrick viewed as many 'space movies' as he could lay his hands on. Later in 1964, Clarke noted in his log that 'Stanley calls after screening H.G. Wells's **Things to Come** and says he'll *never* see another movie I recommend'. The huge space-gun with its bullet-shaped projectile, which propels the winsome astronauts towards the moon, at the climax of that film, was of no interest to him. None at all. As had been pointed out at the time, the concussion would have exerted a force of about 435 tons on each of the astronauts and immediately reduced the young couple to raspberry jam. This was the sort of mistake which really annoyed the logically-minded Stanley Kubrick, whatever Wells's symbolism was intended to convey. They also viewed, among other

*Above & Opposite: Posters of some of the science fiction films viewed by Stanley Kubrick and Arthur C. Clarke in New York during 1964, as preparation for **2001**: none of the films reached Kubrick's exacting standards, but parts of **Destination Moon** intrigued him.*

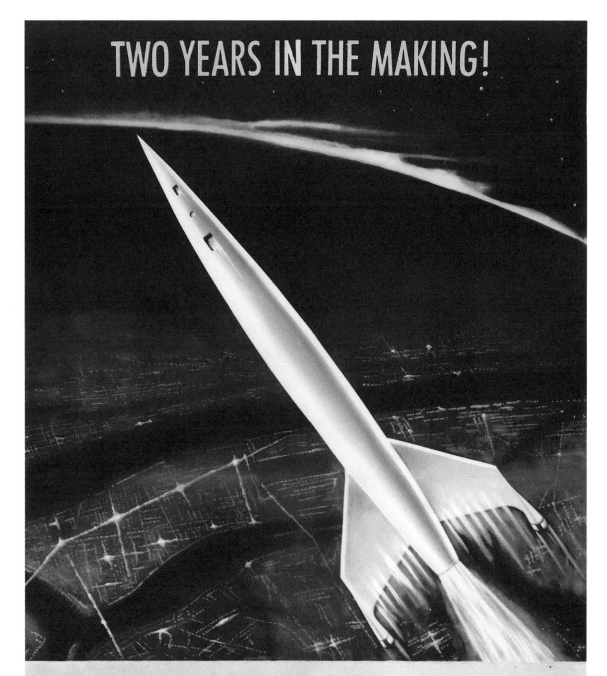

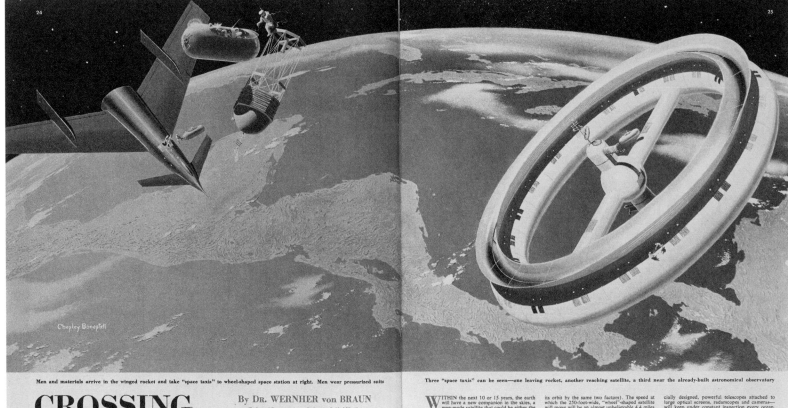

Men and materials arrive in the winged rocket and take "space taxis" to wheel-shaped space station at right. Men wear pressurized suits

Three "space taxis" can be seen—one leaving rocket, another reaching satellite, a third near the already-built astronomical observatory

CROSSING THE LAST FRONTIER

By Dr. WERNHER von BRAUN

Technical Director, Army Ordnance Guided Missiles
Development Group, Huntsville, Alabama

Scientists and engineers now know how to build a station in space that would circle the earth 1,075 miles up. The job would take 10 years, and cost twice as much as the atom bomb. If we do it, we can not only preserve the peace but we can take a long step toward uniting mankind

Collier's for March 22, 1952

WITHIN the next 10 or 15 years, the earth will have a new companion in the skies, a man-made satellite that could be either the greatest force for peace ever devised, or one of the most terrible weapons of war—depending on who makes and controls it. Inhabited by humans, and visible from the ground as a fast-moving star, it will sweep around the earth at an incredible rate of speed in that dark void beyond the atmosphere which is known as "space."

In the opinion of many top experts, this artificial moon—which will be carried into space, piece by piece, by rocket ships—will travel along a celestial route 1,075 miles above the earth, completing a trip around the globe every two hours. Nature will provide the motive power; a neat balance between its speed and the earth's gravitational pull will keep it on course (just as the moon is fixed in its orbit by the same two factors). The speed at which the 250-foot-wide, "wheel"-shaped satellite will move will be an almost unbelievable 4.4 miles per second, or 15,840 miles per hour—20 times the speed of sound. However, this terrific velocity will not be apparent to its occupants. To them, the space station will appear to be a perfectly steady platform.

From this platform, a trip to the moon itself will be just a step, as scientists reckon distance in space.

The choice of the so-called "two-hour" orbit—in preference to a faster one, closer to the earth, or a slower one like the 29-day orbit of the moon—has one major advantage: although far enough up to avoid the hazards of the earth's atmosphere, it is close enough to afford a superb observation post.

Technicians in this space station—using specially designed, powerful telescopes attached to large optical screens, radarscopes and cameras—will keep under constant inspection every ocean, continent, country and city. Even small towns will be clearly visible through optical instruments that will give the watchers in space the same vantage point enjoyed by a man in an observation plane only 5,000 feet off the ground.

Nothing will go unobserved. Within each two-hour period, as the earth revolves inside the satellite's orbit, one twelfth of the globe's territory will pass into the view of the space station's occupants; within each 24-hour period, the entire surface of the earth will have been visible.

Over North America, for example, the space station might pass over the East Coast at, say 10:00 A.M., and, after having completed a full revolution around the earth, would—because the

PAINTING BY CHESLEY BONESTELL

films, **War of the Worlds**, **Forbidden Planet**, **Them!** and **The Day the Earth Stood Still**. During these screenings, most of which took place in April-May 1964 according to Clarke, Kubrick was 'highly critical of everything', always noting the poor quality of the design and special effects. But one film, **Destination Moon**, made in 1950 and based on a 1947 novel for children by Robert Heinlein (who also contributed to the screenplay), does seem to have attracted his attention.

In the novel, three boys and their uncle build a do-it-yourself spaceship in their backyard and use it to travel to the moon—only to discover when they get there that the Nazis have beaten them to it: the Nazi angle was quietly dropped from the film, perhaps because so many ex-Nazis were in real life working for the Guided Missile Development Group of the U.S. Army; it had become tactless to mention the war. Besides, it made a much more uplifting story if the Americans got there first. **Destination Moon** was shot in pseudo-documentary style: the technical advisor was the veteran German expert Hermann Oberth, author of the classic **Rocket into**

Planetary Space, who in 1929 had also advised on the first serious space travel film, Fritz Lang's **Die Frau im Mond**, the film which invented the countdown as a dramatic device. Oberth had been fascinated by space travel since submitting his doctoral thesis on the subject in 1922: he had already by the late 1920s designed a rotating space station, a spacesuit and a lunar vehicle. Although the script of **Destination Moon** had been somewhat earthbound, its authentic-looking production design did set new standards of verisimilitude. The rocket ship was a scaled-up sleek and silver version of the single-staged pencil-shaped A4/V2, the world's first supersonic ballistic missile dating from the Second World War: a pencil with fins at the back. But it was the lunar landscape, in full colour, that propelled the film into a different league.

This was designed by Chesley Bonestell, the Hollywood matte painter and illustrator, trained as an architect, who was soon to create most of the sharp-edged visual images of hardware and space landscapes for a very influential eight-part series of articles for **Collier's** magazine, beginning in March 1952, on the possibilities

*Above & Opposite: Chesley Bonestell's very influential illustrations of space exploration, for a series of articles in the wide circulation **Collier's** magazine (1952), several written by Dr. Wernher von Braun. They were intended to boost public interest in space research.*

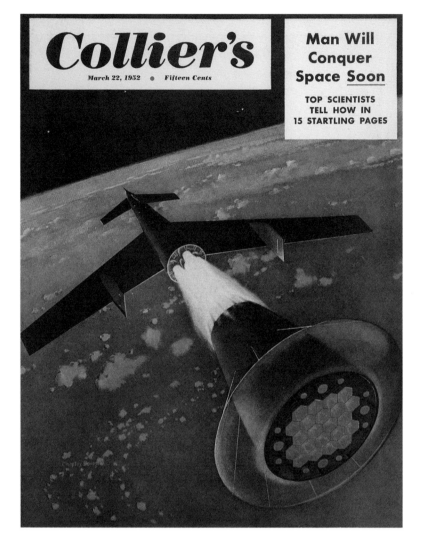

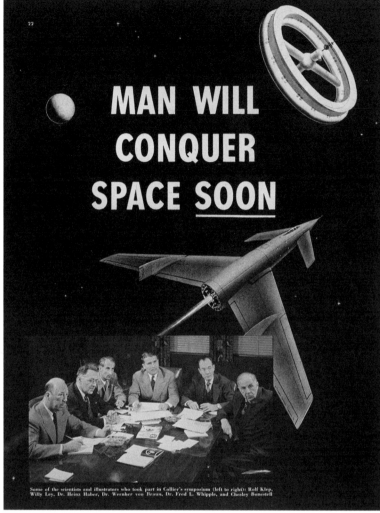

Some of the scientists and illustrators who took part in Collier's symposium (left to right): Rolf Klep, Willy Ley, Dr. Heinz Haber, Dr. Wernher von Braun, Dr. Fred L. Whipple, and Chesley Bonestell.

of space exploration or rather 'the conquest of space' as it was then called. These articles established him as the Maxfield Parrish of outer space. Much of the text was written by Dr. Wernher von Braun, and the paintings/illustrations were based on his technical specifications—like the illustrations he used in his pitches to research funders in Washington. As Bonestell was to explain:

'Von Braun would send me sketches drawn on engineer's graph paper, which I converted into working drawings and then into perspective. The courses I had had at Columbia University [as an architecture student] enabled me to handle some very complicated problems and my courses in structural engineering helped me to understand the mechanics of space machinery.'

Bonestell had also illustrated Willy Ley's classic book **The Conquest of Space** in 1949. Sharp-edged, detailed, with velvet shadows. It has been written of his visuals:

'No artist had more impact on the emerging popular culture of space in America than Chesley Bonestell. Bonestell did for space what Albert Bierstadt and Thomas Moran accomplished for the American Western frontier. Like Bierstadt and Moran, Bonestell's paintings took viewers to places they had never been before... Through his visual images, he stimulated the interest of a generation

of Americans and showed how space travel would be accomplished. Many readers remembered the paintings of planets and spaceships more than the words in the articles that accompanied them.'

One key difference between Bonestell and nineteenth-century landscape painters of the West, the promised land, was that Bonestell had never had a close-up view of the landscapes he was painting— or even a close-up photograph. He knew much more about the hardware than the moon itself. But he knew enough to be plausible. For **Destination Moon**, he chose as the actual destination a crater on the northern latitudes of the moon, from which the earth could be seen near the horizon—the classic view. The pioneer animator Georges Méliès had first shown this effect at the turn of the century in his **Le voyage dans la lune** (1902), a twenty-minute send-up of Jules Verne's **From the Earth to the Moon** (1865), and the more recent H.G. Wells's **First Men in the Moon** (1901). Since then, it had become *the* view. Verne's novel, incidentally, had rightly predicted that the first rocket to the moon would take off from the coast of Florida. But Bonestell made the costly studio moon set for **Destination Moon** look hyper-real for the first time, with jagged mountains and a cracked, parched mudflat lunar surface like a vanished sea—resembling his dust-jacket for the book

The Conquest of Space.

Destination Moon won an Academy Award for special effects. Following its box-office success, Bonestell designed **Conquest of Space** in 1955 for the same producer George Pal—based partly on the Willy Ley book and partly on von Braun's fictional **The Mars Project** and especially its non-fictional appendices. Ley and von Braun had worked together on the V2 project, in Peenemünde. **Conquest** turned out to be a turgid disaster, but its opening sequences—of a huge, shiny white circular space station in low earth orbit with a shuttle approaching it and astronauts in spacesuits performing construction duties against a velvet-black sky—were impressively conceived, given the technical constraints of the time. The trouble was that the sequences were badly lit and there were obvious fuzzy matte lines showing around the edge of the space station. And the interior of the station resembled a submarine more than anything else. Its fate at the box-office had put Hollywood off attempting serious space travel movies—as distinct from bug-eyed-monster movies—ever since.

On 14th May 1964, Stanley Kubrick wrote from his New York office at Polaris Films to Chesley Bonestell in Berkeley, California:

'I am presently working with Arthur Clarke on an idea for a science-fiction film, which might prove to be the definitive attempt. I am, as you might well imagine, enormously impressed by the imagination and quality of your work. This is just a note to say hello and find out how to get in touch with you when the time comes.'

Bonestell replied enthusiastically six days later:

'If anything should develop along the lines you mention, I would be glad to discuss it with you at any time.'

He followed this up on 21st July with a letter enclosing some 'colour clips' of his work and referring to a conversation he'd had in the meantime with Kubrick about the potential of 'the travelling matte' and how far it had developed as a visual technique since the early 1950s; apparently, although 'it was not good then' it had since become something 'wonderful and, as I suspected, much of the processing is [now] done in the optical printer'. Bonestell had asked an old friend in Hollywood for advice about this—but he hastened to add, 'I didn't mention your name or tell him what the picture was.'

'Am enclosing some astronomical shots from Paramount, I think from **When Worlds Collide** [1951, which also won an Academy Award for special effects]. Mars was a hypothetical city at the intersection of the canals. The clouds (on glass) moved across Saturn's rings. The foreground pinnacle (miniature) on Mercury moved across the painted background. Jupiter was a pan shot, and I think we had some vapour introduced... I think our trouble with the stars on the pan shot in **Destination Moon** was that the

proper equipment was not available to pour on enough light. On the set, the electricians stuck little automobile headlight bulbs into the sky, all of the same candle-power, no sense of constellations. The result was bad.'

On 11th August, Kubrick replied that 'Arthur Clarke and I are still pounding it out on the story and nothing definite can yet be discussed.' And there the correspondence ended.

Kubrick did keep reproductions of paintings by Chesley Bonestell from the book **The Conquest of Space** among his pre-production notes, and a used 35mm print of **Destination Moon** was shipped over to the MGM Studios at Borehamwood, at his request, on 24th September 1965 ('the purpose of the loan is so that Mr Kubrick may study some of the special effects used in the motion picture'), but by then he had decided to adopt a very different approach to the design of his film—which unlike **Frau im Mond** and **Destination Moon** would not be about persuading viewers of the necessity of space research; it would be about taking space travel as a given, and starting from there. And he would be improving on the matte-effects in **Conquest of Space**—when he used them—frame by meticulous frame. By the time Kubrick set about preparing his film, manned space flights had been happening—really—since 1961. 'We were interested in starting where **Destination Moon** finished,' Clarke wrote.

Another film which intrigued Kubrick at this time—also because of the special effects—was a low-budget twenty-nine-minute short animated educational documentary from Canada called **Universe** (1960), about a journey into the immensity of deep space. It had taken three years to complete and, among other visual techniques, used chemical agents to break surface tension, agents which could be injected into water over a black-velvet background to represent gases and dust in the vastness of deep space. This looked effective, and Kubrick hired the special effects supervisor on the film, Wally Gentleman (director of special effects at the National Film Board of Canada), to do some preparatory work for **Journey** on revolving planets—according to Gentleman he 'sucked information like a sponge'—but he left early in production. Gentleman had mixed feelings about the experience. The chemical agents idea was used for the second section of 'Beyond the Infinite'. Kubrick also eventually cast the uncredited narrator of **Universe**, Douglas Rain, as the voice of the computer HAL. Several shots in **2001** mirror those in **Universe**—including the opening of the moon landing station, and an asteroid spinning in space—and Kubrick screened this short film many times.

Shortly after the time Stanley Kubrick was writing to Ken Adam and Chesley Bonestell, on 7th September 1964, according to Clarke's log, he produced 'a 100-item questionnaire about our

*Opposite: Caricature of Stanley Kubrick, accompanying an article about the background research for **Journey Beyond the Stars** (as it was then called) in **The New Yorker** magazine, April 1965.*

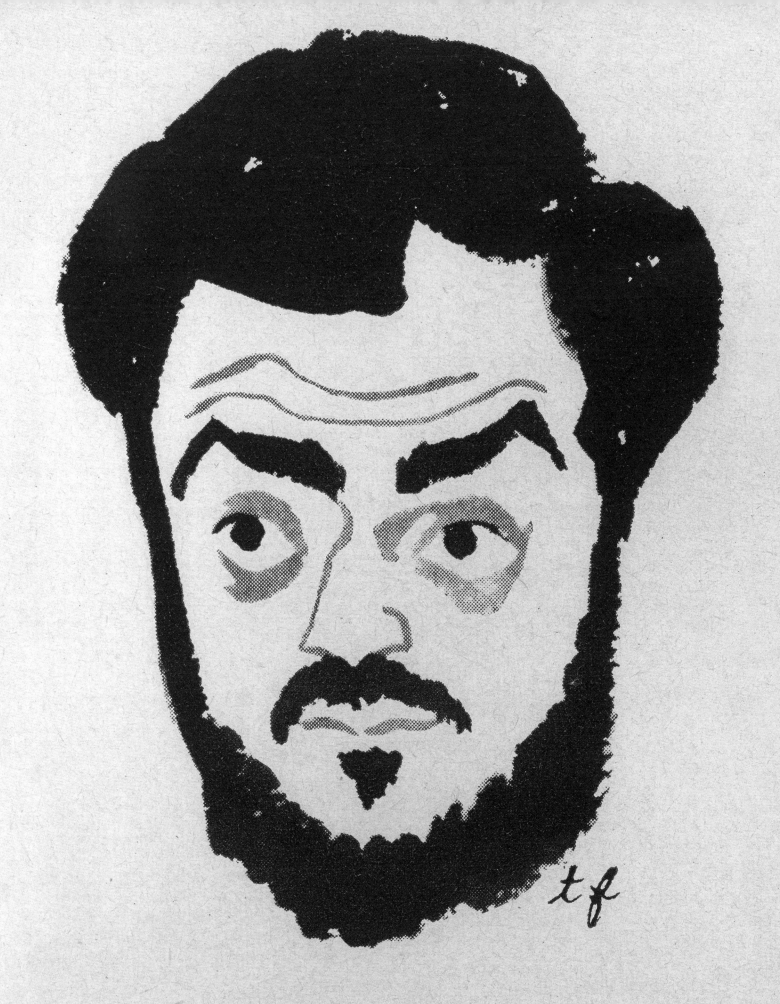

Stanley Kubrick

astronauts, e.g. do they sleep in their pyjamas, what do they eat for breakfast, etc.'. **Journey Beyond the Stars** would represent a decisive break with the usual Hollywood way of doing these things. It would present technological and scientific change within conceivable limits—designing a plausible future for filmgoers who could well live to see it—and would have to work punishingly hard to do so. But unlike earlier science-fiction fictions, it would not attempt to break the continuity of history: on the contrary, it would deliberately mix the familiar with the speculative. It would be obsessively detailed—not with scientific verisimilitude as an end in itself, but as an aesthetic strategy. It would create a visual world out of material things that had never been seen in public quite like this before (except, occasionally, at World's Fairs): a kind of semi-documentary about things that had not happened yet. Instead of jagged mountains and a parched mudflat surface, it would feature rounded mountains and rubble—which is what they really looked like.

There would still be Kubrick's love-hate relationship with modern technology, as there had been in **Dr Strangelove**: Clarke's boyish optimism about future science and its possibilities would be tempered by the director's anxieties about the wider implications of technological change. The astronaut would only become a fully-rounded human being when he cut loose from **Discovery**'s techno-environment and took over control of the space-pod. But Wernher von Braun and his researchers would no longer be the butt of slapstick jokes. Arthur C. Clarke later reminisced about his working partnership with Stanley Kubrick at this time. He had started writing in May 1964 at the Polaris office, with Stanley Kubrick hovering close by but 'after one day' sensibly moved to Suite 1008 at the Chelsea Hotel, 222 West 23rd Street:

*'Every other day Stanley and I would get together and compare notes; during this period we went down endless blind alleys and threw away tens of thousands of words. The scope of the story steadily expanded [beyond **The Sentinel**], both in time and space... Our brainstorming sessions usually took place in the Kubrick Eastside penthouse off Lexington...'*

Clarke was to recall of Stanley Kubrick himself at the start of their creative odyssey together:

'He had a night-person pallor, and one of our minor problems was that he functions best in the small hours of the morning... Another characteristic that struck me at once was that of pure intelligence; Kubrick grasps new ideas, however complex, almost instantly.'

Enter Frederick Ordway III and Harry (Hans-Kurt) Lange, who from 22nd January 1965 happened to be in New York for talks with publishers and for a conference of the American Institute of Aeronautics and Astronautics in the New York Hilton. Ordway

(1927-2014) had been on the staff of the Army Ballistic Missile Agency and was currently with the NASA George C. Marshall Space Flight Center, Huntsville, Alabama; in addition to editing the journal **Aeronautics**, he had published widely on space science and technology, and on the possibility of life in other solar systems. He could write popular books and specialised technical articles, and he was a very persuasive communicator. He understood the science *and* the public relations. Part of his job was to liaise between the predominantly German rocket scientists, business and government. His book **Intelligence in the Universe** (1966) was to become one of Kubrick's favourites on the subject of extra-terrestrial life. Harry Lange (1930-2008) had been born and educated in Eisenach, Thuringia (the birthplace of J.S. Bach and the place where Martin Luther translated the Bible), which after the Second World War came within the Soviet-occupied zone of East Germany. In 1949, he had escaped under cover of darkness to Hamburg and Munich, where he studied art and design, and had moved to New York City in 1951 to work in advertising. During the Korean War, he had been drafted into the U.S. Air Force, at Craig Base near Selma, Alabama, where he spent three years producing graphics for flight training manuals. As an 'alien', he was not sent into combat. After that he had joined the U.S. Army Ordnance Guided Missile Agency in Huntsville, Alabama (later the Army Ballistic Missile Agency) as an illustrator of advanced spacecraft concepts, space platforms, new propulsion systems, proposed missions to other planets, 'even though I did not have a scientific background'—eventually becoming head of Future Projects Graphics at NASA, in charge of a team of ten or twelve illustrators working on promotional visuals or 'space boosters' under Wernher von Braun. 'Harry,' said von Braun, who used Lange's visualisations to elicit funding from Washington, 'Your work makes money where everybody else spends it.' As Lange himself was to put it, 'I made them as dramatic as possible ... to take to Washington to appropriation committees.' His spaceships existed on paper before the technology was available to build them. NASA (the National Aeronautics and Space Administration) had been set up in October 1958, and two years later ABMA was absorbed within it. Ordway's ABMA office had been 'very close' to Lange's, and in 1954 they had set up with a couple of colleagues the grand-sounding 'General Aeronautics Research Corporation' 'to do some consultancy on the side'—mainly producing publications together. Ordway provided the words, Lange the pictures. I asked Frederick Ordway how he first came to meet Harry Lange:

'Well, Harry worked very closely with me in Huntsville, Alabama. He was in the section The Future Projects Graphics Group, which did all the illustrations, all the drawings and so forth. Von Braun was very keen on having beautiful drawings—technical layouts of

---

Opposite: An early collaboration between Frederick Ordway and Harry Lange, through their company 'General Aeronautics': Ordway supplied the words, Lange the illustrations. This book, intended for high school-level students, was about exploration of the solar system, and was published in January 1963.

CONQUERING THE SUN'S EMPIRE

FREDERICK I. ORDWAY, III

RONALD C. WAKEFORD

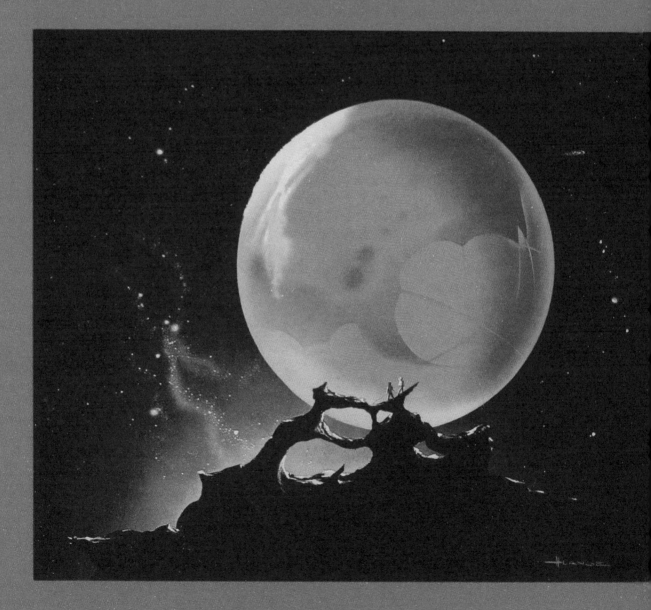

Illustrations by HARRY H–K LANGE

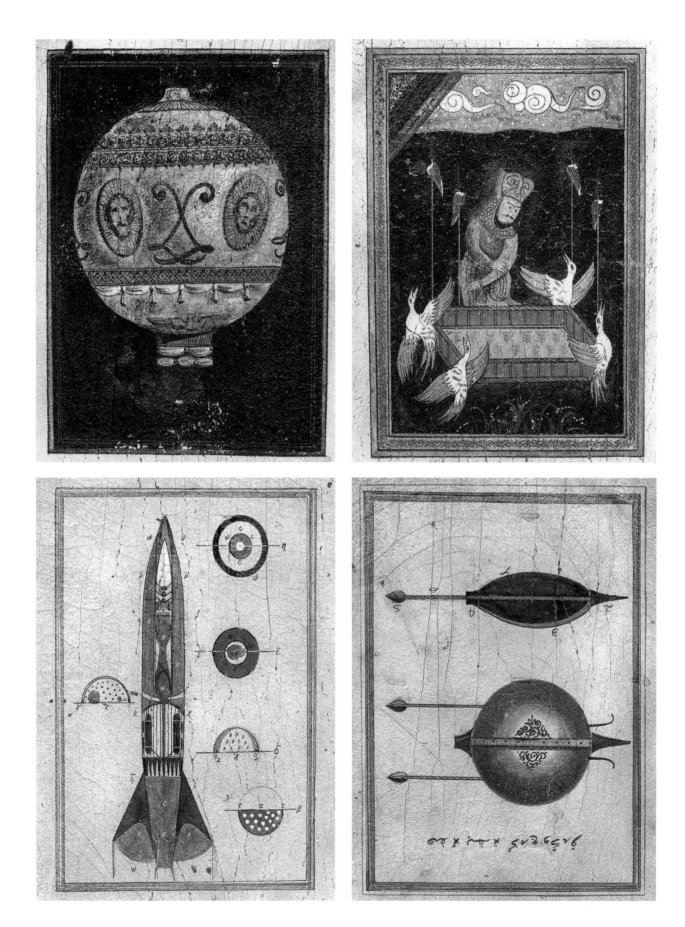

Some of Harry Lange's illustrations, derived from traditional sources, for **The History of Rocketry and Space Travel** *written by Dr. Wernher von Braun and Frederick Ordway and published in January 1966.*

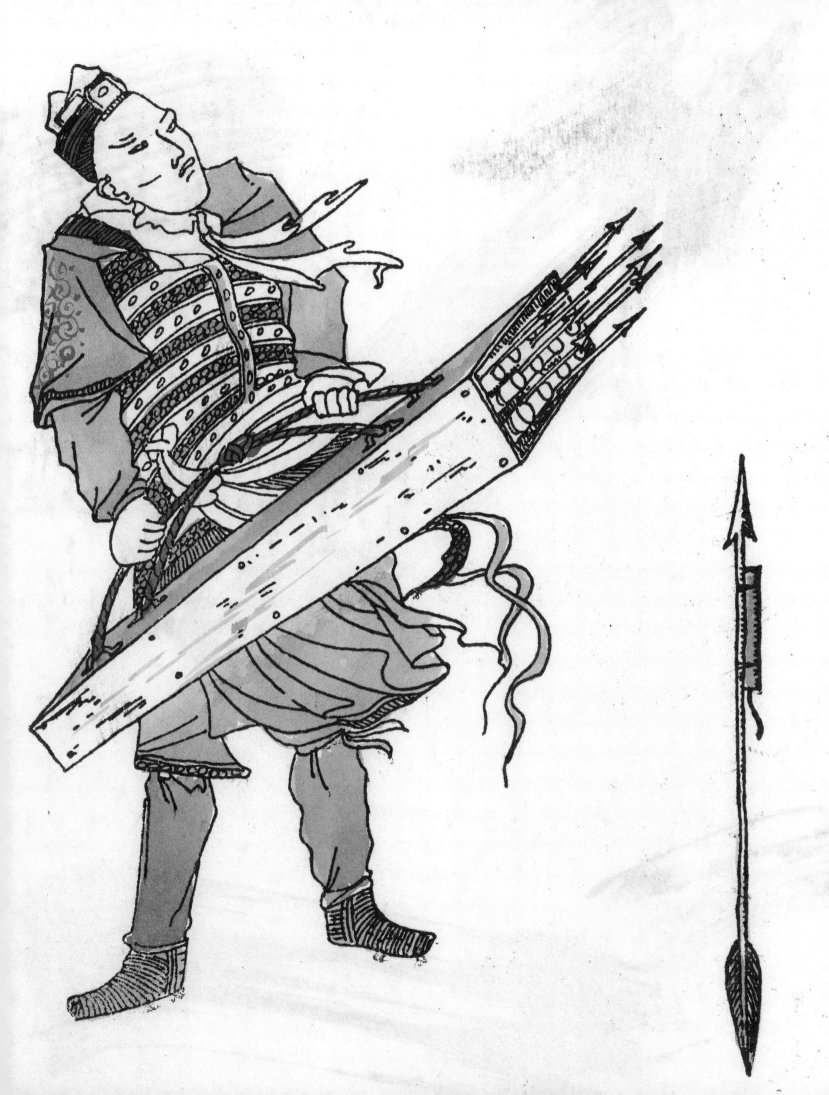

what things might look like, then artists' renditions of them—which he could use for presentations, and we would put these onto lantern slides—big 3 x 5—for his presentations at NASA, in Washington and to the defence people. He wanted drawings and illustrations based on what might happen in the future—the future potential of space travel. And von Braun was often criticised for this. He said when he was visualising his pitches in those days, "don't do things small". And I remember [the physicist] Fred Singer, who had come up with his early MOUSE Satellite (Miniature Orbital Unmanned Satellite, Earth)—while von Braun was doing his great big launch vehicle and so forth—and Fred finally had to admit, "Wernher, you were correct—that's the way to get the attention of the people." For our company General Aeronautics, Harry illustrated many of my books as well—we did three volumes of **The History of Rocketry and Space Travel** co-written by von Braun with illustrations by Harry [Kubrick had a copy among his pre-production sources], **Intelligence in the Universe, Life in other Solar Systems**, textbooks and magazine articles, and other publications. We were good friends too.'

Did Ordway already know him well, back in Army Ballistic Missile Agency days?

'Yes. You see, von Braun was like a pied piper to second-generation Germans. Some Germans just wanted to work with the master—so they applied. We had a number of younger Germans come over after World War Two and join the team. They weren't the original "Operation Paperclip" Germans—they weren't the generation who worked at Peenemünde—these were young students. The first generation who came before had been approved at the end of the war: they were categorised as "Nazi" or "very Nazi"! The next generation was different...'

Harry Lange had contributed to a two-man exhibition of space art in Washington DC, with Chesley Bonestell, in the heyday of space-boosterism. Did Ordway recall going to this?

'I didn't see that, but I met Chesley through Wernher von Braun, back in October 1951 at a symposium on space travel at the Hayden Planetarium, part of New York's American Museum of Natural History. There were three symposia, and the last of them, in 1954, was co-ordinated by Arthur C. Clarke. And in that same period, as I'm sure you know, Chesley was doing a series of eight **Collier's** magazines—with Rolf Klep and other artists. Fred Freeman too. So I met Chesley Bonestell through the Wernher von Braun connection—going way back.'

Which brought us up to 22nd January 1965 in New York:

'The main reason I was there—was sent up from Huntsville—was as a delegate to the big Aeronautics and Astronautics meeting. But being in New York, we also had a series of meetings with our publishers—Academic Press, Dutton, Prentice-Hall. And during the day, somebody mentioned "by the way, I heard your old friend Arthur C. Clarke was in town"—we were a real closed community—and I knew that he always stayed in the Chelsea Hotel down on West 23rd, so I rang him and sure enough there he was. I'd known Arthur since 1950, when I met him in Paris at an international astronomical conference—took place in the Sorbonne—at which I was the only American there, and he gave me a copy of his book **Interplanetary Flight**, which had just been published. And we were kindred spirits. Also did you know that von Braun was a great admirer of Arthur and vice versa? I don't think many people know that. Anyway, we met Arthur at the Harvard Club, where I always stayed, around six that same evening. We talked about the various space programmes at the Marshall Flight Center and how they were going. And about Wernher von Braun and how he was. And why were we in New York? That's when he mentioned that, as well as completing his latest book, for Time-Life Space Library, **Man and Space**, he was working with the film director Stanley Kubrick on a film which aimed to be the space fiction film, one which would be serious, scientifically plausible and big-budget. It would involve other intelligences in space. And Harry said, "Well, it just so happens that we have just published a children's book for Dutton on **Life in Other Solar Systems**, and we are working on a big Prentice-Hall book, a professional work, to be called **Intelligence in the Universe**, and we are delivering galleys to them and a lot of my artwork—and the book is on the very subject you and Stanley Kubrick are planning." Harry then went upstairs to his room at the club, and brought some of his artwork down, and showed it to Arthur, and I showed him some of the galleys and the text we were working on—we talked for about half an hour—and he said, "That's extraordinary—I'm on the same kind of project." And that was it. We didn't think anything further about it. Harry had to go to some kind of evening and I had a dinner-party up in Park Avenue at eight. And Arthur obviously went out, and immediately went to the first callbox he could find on Sixth Avenue and called Kubrick and, when I was just about to leave for dinner, I went up to get my topcoat because it was snowing heavily that day and cold—and as the front-doorman was hailing a cab for me, another employee of the club rushed out and said I had a telephone call. I thought it might be my host or hostess wondering if I was having trouble getting to Park Avenue, but the voice on the other end of the telephone said, "My name is Stanley Kubrick." And I said, "How do you do" and so forth...'

Did you know much about Stanley Kubrick before this?

'I knew of him—Arthur had told me about his connection with him. And I'd seen **Paths of Glory** and **Dr Strangelove** and one of my favourites, **Spartacus**. Kubrick said that he'd just been talking to Arthur, who suggested he get in touch with Harry and me before we went to our dinners. Would we be available for a meeting? He seemed most anxious to meet us both. He had some thoughts he'd

Opposite: Dr. Wernher von Braun behind his desk at the Marshall Space Flight Center in Huntsville, Alabama, with 'space booster' art work—probably by Harry Lange—behind him, and assorted rocket models on display as well.

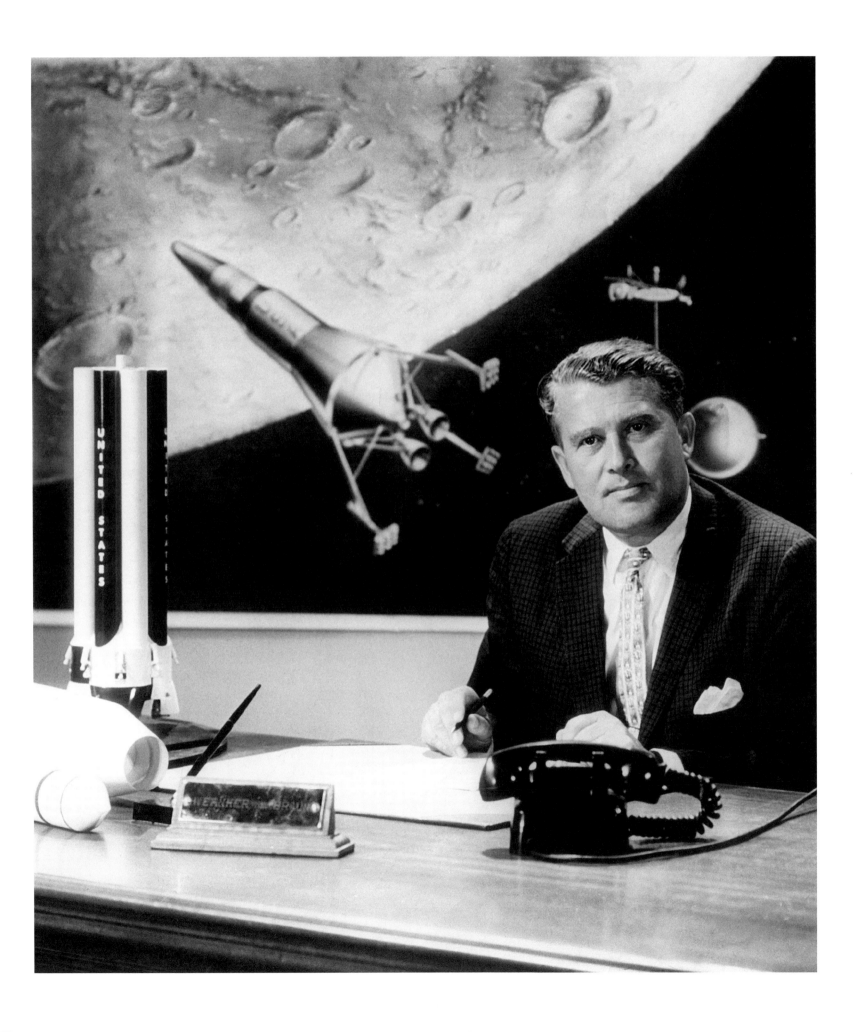

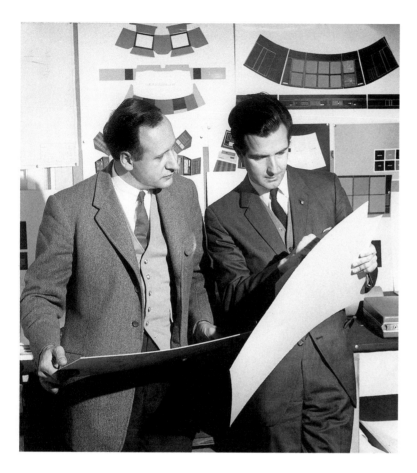

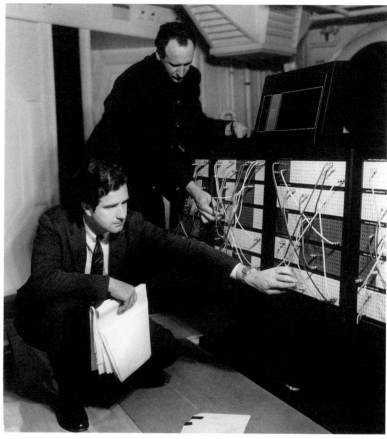

*like to share with us. So we set up a meeting for the next afternoon, the 23rd of January, in his penthouse near Central Park. We went up there, after our morning commitments—Harry, Arthur and myself—and Kubrick was very interested in the work Harry and I had been involved with for von Braun. We took along the galleys and the pictures and I told him that I'd been working with von Braun at ABMA and NASA and that this was a little sideline here. Also about the **Jupiter** intermediate-range ballistic missiles, which were in competition with the Air Force missiles. There was inter-service rivalry, you see. And we also had the **Juno** version of it, a multi-stage rocket which could push past the moon. So I told him I was working on these projects. We also talked about the problems of intelligence beyond our solar system as well as our work on Mars exploration craft, and their possible payload requirements. Then Harry told him about NASA Future Projects, and how supplying that office was the Future Projects Graphics Group, and how they would prepare all the presentations. It was, I remember, a mentally exhilarating afternoon. Kubrick told us about what had been achieved so far—if we might be interested in working with him. And we thought, "Yeah, we could fly up on weekends"—anything with Arthur, who was such an old friend. He said, "Well, I'll send you a letter to Huntsville with some concrete details." We returned there on the 28th January, and*

*we read Arthur's story treatment of **Journey Beyond the Stars**.'*

By January 1965, Arthur C. Clarke had in fact delivered to Kubrick 'the first version of the novel'—a fifty-thousand-word draft treatment which already (since August 1964) included the Odyssey parallel and a hero called Bowman (originally Alex, then Dave), but which had turned out to be 'a rough draft of the first two-thirds of the book, stopping at the most exciting point'—when Bowman converses with the computer, and then enters the Stargate, a shortcut through space and time which leads to another universe. Visited by **New Yorker** science essayist and physicist Jeremy Bernstein, for a **Talk of the Town** piece published on 24th April 1965, Kubrick and Clarke were again to stress the Odyssey angle. Kubrick was to keep a copy of Bernstein's article on **Great Ideas Today** (1965) for Encyclopaedia Britannica in his files, and he evidently respected the man. The interview took place in the living room of the new Kubrick penthouse:

'Mr Kubrick and Mr Clarke sat down side by side on a sofa, and we asked them about their joint venture. Mr Clarke said that one of the basic problems they've had to deal with is how to describe what they are trying to do. "Science-fiction films have always meant monsters and sex, so we have tried to find another term for our film," said Mr C. "About the best we've been able to come up with is a

Above & Opposite: Harry Lange and Frederick Ordway discussing drawings and examining equipment at MGM Borehamwood, during pre-production and production of **2001**, *and (far right) standing on the bare bones of the Centrifuge, on one of the seven sound stages.*

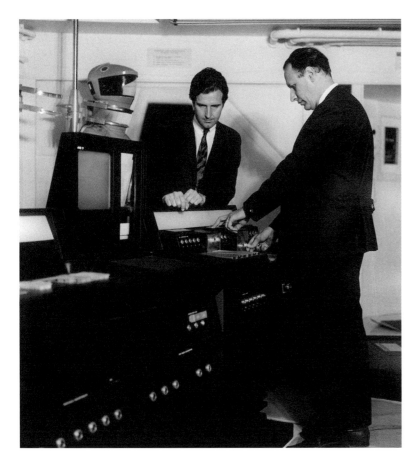

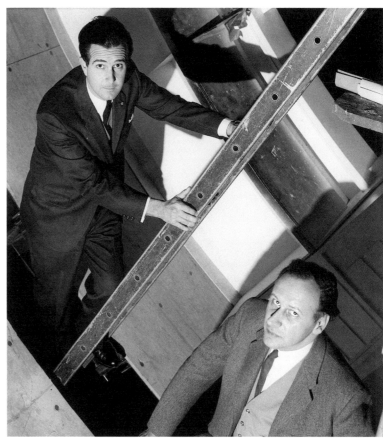

Space Odyssey—comparable in some ways to the Homeric Odyssey," said Mr K. "It occurred to us that for the Greeks the vast stretches of the sea must have had the same sort of mystery and remoteness that space has for our generation, and that the far-flung islands Homer's wonderful characters visited were no less remote to them than the planets our spacemen will soon be landing on are to us..."

Mr Clarke agreed, and went on to tell us that the new film is set in the near future, at a time when the moon will have been colonised and space travel... will have become commonplace.'

It was not until around the time of this interview that Kubrick selected **2001: A Space Odyssey** as his new title, and abandoned **Journey Beyond the Stars** which Clarke 'always disliked' because there had been so many comic-book-style movie voyages and journeys in the past. **Odyssey** rather than **Journey** sounded much more upmarket and seemed to give the project literary credentials as well. Fred Ordway remembers Kubrick 'sitting down with me' and discussing whether the practicalities of the **2001** concept would work:

'Kubrick said, "I don't like **Journey Beyond the Stars**—I'd like something more serious." And he suggested **2001**. I said, "Okay, let's look at where we are today and where we will be thirty-five years in the future". Remember we were still four years from 1969 and the successful landing on the moon. I was involved also in the Marshall Center working on post-Apollo programmes. In those days we thought we were having twenty Apollo missions, and Congress

in 1972 cancelled three of them because of the Vietnam War and race riots and so forth; the budgets. But in 1965, we were convinced that maybe even lunar bases would have started. And orbiting space stations. And I was also working on a programme called "EMPIRE"— Early Manned Planetary-Interplanetary Round-trip Expeditions— for manned trips to Mars. In 1965 we were already working on that at Marshall. And I worked that all up in technical journals and so forth. And this was key to my thinking while working with Kubrick. And we thought that at the end of the Apollo programme there would be a strong nuclear rocket programme going on—with the Atomic Energy Commission—and it was called the NERVA programme— Nuclear Energy Rocket Vehicle Applications—and that was doing very well even back then in 1965. So I projected forward: "Okay, we'll be successful on the moon—after the Apollo flights—and we'll be ready to develop temporary bases on the moon." And then we thought: "By the middle 1980s, we could succeed with 'EMPIRE', which would be a round-trip expedition out there, to encircle planets, not land on them, and come back." So I said to myself, "Okay, that's going to be the 1983-85-87 period, then if we're successful there, with a major effort might we not be able to think of Jupiter"—not a landing, you can't land on Jupiter anyway—but a Jupiter inspection, research, and then return. But all that was completely dashed in 1972, when Congress cancelled Apollos 18, 19 and 20—cancelled the second of the space stations, cancelled production of the Saturn V—all of which was absolutely insane. They were gone. So we can't do today

'We'd often work into the night on designs and discussions about the film plot.'

what we could do in the 1960s. And Congress cancelled any mention of Mars. So "EMPIRE" was scotched in 1972. But in 1965, it looked as though it was all going to happen, even if the picture was hazy. So with Kubrick, I did some thinking about where we might be, based on where we were. I thought we would be patted on the back after Apollo, and we would go on from there. We all thought that, naïvely. **2001** was made within a framework of the year 1965 and the first half of 1966. Thinking about thirty-five years in the future.'

According to Clarke, 'the Odyssean parallel was clear in our minds from the very beginning, way before the title of the film was chosen'. The Odyssey—Bowman—the single, all-seeing 180° fish-eye lens of the computer (originally friendly, female and called 'Athena', Kubrick's idea, after Odysseus's goddess-protectress)—spaceships rather than the unnamed black flagship of the eighth century BC—all these or their equivalents were already present in Clarke's 'early treatments', even if they were not yet reflected in the title. In the novel, Bowman passes the time on **Discovery** by reading **The Odyssey**, 'which of all books spoke to him most vividly across time'. **Discovery** wasn't named after **The Odyssey**, though; it was named 'after the most famous of polar-exploration ships'. There were references to **Moby Dick** as well, this time about the hunt for a black alien artefact rather than a great white whale—one reason why Stanley Kubrick needed so much specialist advice about the vehicles and spacesuits which were likely to carry these latter-day warrior-adventurers to the moon and beyond. Ordway continues:

'Two days after we got back to Huntsville from New York, an airmail, special delivery, arrived confirming that Kubrick wanted to collaborate with Harry and me and asking for a proposal. So we said, "Yeah, we could supply some help—flying up there at weekends," and then he said, "We're going to need more of your time." And one thing led to another and by February it was clear that it would involve about 80 percent of our time, and then we thought that would be over in about six months and we had no idea at all at that stage about going to England. So we signed for six months. It became more than full-time. In June 1965 we still assumed we would be returning to our Huntsville, Alabama base. After all, we had only contracted

for work in New York. But Kubrick and Clarke thought otherwise. Would we accompany them, with our families, to Borehamwood? And we agreed.'

The six months became two years plus...

What did Wernher von Braun, their boss, think of all this?

'Well, of course we asked him if it was okay to get involved. And he said, "anything to promote the space programme".'

By 'more than full-time', was Ordway perhaps referring to Stanley Kubrick's eccentric lifestyle, and to working at night in New York?

'Yeah, sure. We'd often work into the night on designs and discussions about the film plot.'

I wondered what Stanley Kubrick felt about working with such close associates of Wernher von Braun, one of whom was German. After all, the character of Dr Strangelove, as played so memorably by Peter Sellers, had in many ways been a wheelchair-using caricature of Dr von Braun, his excitable German-American accent partly based on viewings of the rocket scientist's star performance in the three-part series of Walt Disney television documentaries **Man in Space** (1955-57), partly (it has been suggested) on the accent of the photographer Weegee, who was on the set for part of the filming. In an early draft of the screenplay, Strangelove was named 'von Klutz'. Peter George's novelisation of the screenplay was in no doubt about who the doctor was meant to be:

Dr Strangelove... had long exerted an influence on United States defence policy. He was a recluse and perhaps had been made so by the effects of the British bombing of Peenemünde, where he was working on the German V2 rocket. His black-gloved right hand was a memento of this. He was not sure whether he disliked the British more than the Russians. He gazed out through myopic eyes, which were assisted by frameless bifocals...

In the film, he is presented as a combination of mad scientist (**Frankenstein**-style), prosthetic scientist (who has lost touch with his humanity—an old cliché), corporate scientist (working for the 'BLAND Corporation') and genius-specialist working for the military who is not at all concerned about the implications of his research—one of the great composite negative images of the scientist. Others have suggested as candidates for the title 'the real Dr Strangelove'

Opposite: Harry Lange and Frederick Ordway—always smartly dressed in their different ways—looking at blueprints at MGM Borehamwood, with part of the Centrifuge in the background.

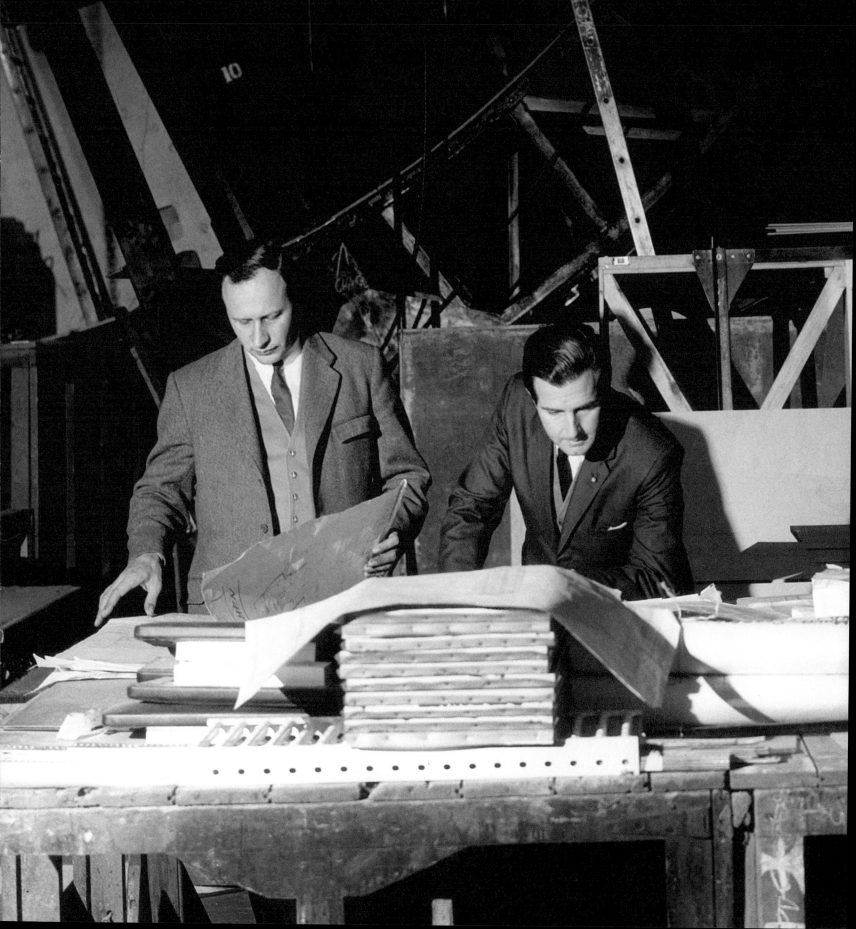

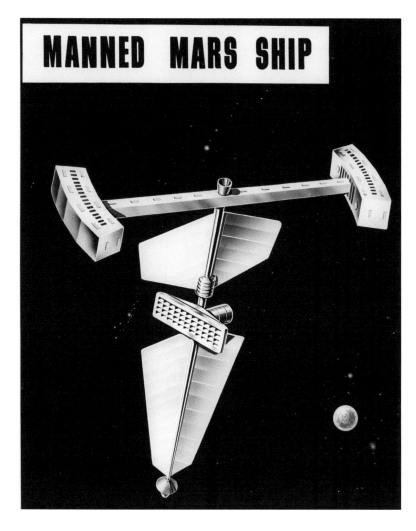

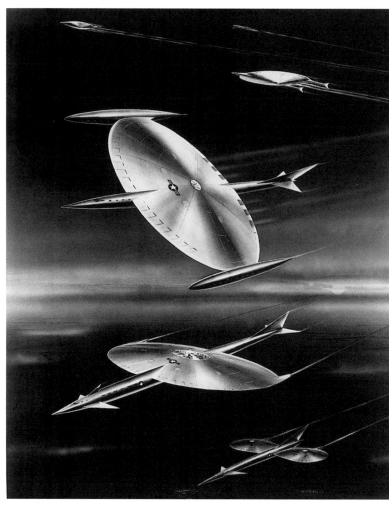

Edward Teller—unlikely, since Kubrick would *never* have turned a victim of anti-Semitism into an unreconstructed Nazi—and Henry Kissinger, even though neither Kubrick nor Sellers had even *seen* Kissinger before the film was shot. Also Herman Kahn, strategist for the RAND Corporation. Ken Adam, though, remembers clearly that Dr Strangelove was modelled by Sellers on von Braun. 'Peter Sellers had to base his performance on satirising somebody'—and that somebody 'was Wernher von Braun'. Sellers, for his part, stated categorically, 'it was *always* Wernher von Braun'. And Adam should know: the two men both went to the same school in Berlin in the 1920s. So, what did Stanley Kubrick think about working closely with a German protégé of von Braun?

'Well, Kubrick was fascinated and enchanted by Harry, in the sense that he was German… Of course, Kubrick was Jewish and Harry would come in with Germanic clothes sometimes. There was a time when he wore Bavarian jackets! But they got along fine. Harry wasn't a "Paperclip" Nazi, after all, and this was long after the war and we were all friends with the Germans. Kubrick did sometimes say, "Well, I don't think I ever imagined I'd be working this close to a German".'

1965 was also the year when Wernher von Braun was satirised by Tom Lehrer in his song '"Once the rockets are up, who cares where they come down? / That's not my department," says Wernher von Braun'—and by Jean-Luc Godard in **Alphaville**, where Prof. von Braun is responsible for the soulless 'Alpha 60 super-computer' which rules the metropolis. Stanley Kubrick must surely have been aware of these. Especially when Harry Lange turned up for work in a traditional tailored green woollen 'Janker' jacket, with its rows of buttons, much favoured in the Austrian and Bavarian Alps—and prominently featured, from March 1965 onwards, in **The Sound of Music**. This 'Tracht' garment was in the process of being redefined as a men's fashion item, as worn for example by Christopher Plummer as von Trapp. But it still had strong connotations of pre-war South German culture. By making a joke of it, Harry Lange was perhaps subtly trying to 'lay the ghost' where Kubrick was concerned, by bringing the culture-clash out into the open. If so, it certainly worked. Besides, for obvious reasons, Kubrick was now keen to disassociate himself from jokes about Wernher von Braun and involuntary Nazi salutes: von Braun was friendly with his writer, and employed his two key consultants…

Above: Early 1960s concepts of space transportation, commissioned by NASA and kept for reference in Harry Lange's files. Opposite: 'Ion-propelled' spaceship, illustrated by Lange.

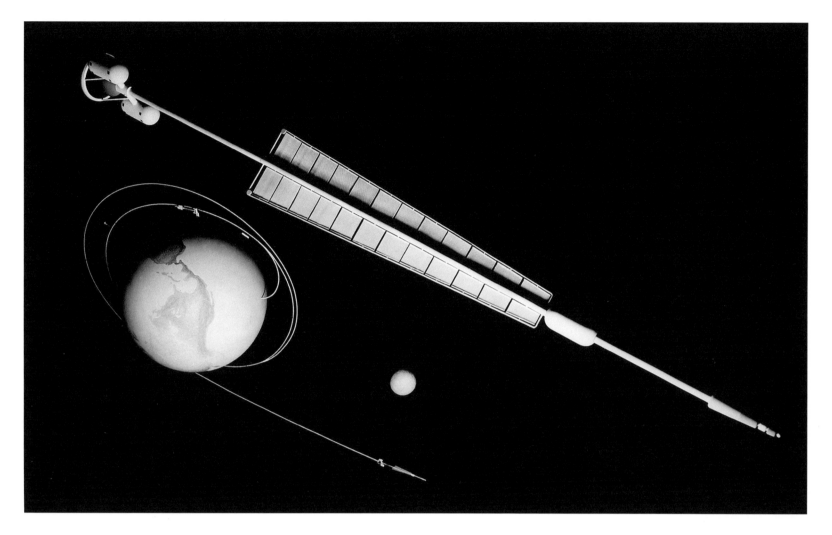

Harry Lange liked to recall that, just as he was leaving that first meeting in Kubrick's apartment, after the director had studied his illustrations, he looked Harry in the eye and announced, 'Well, I can get better illustrators in New York City a dime a dozen, but they don't have your NASA background, your combination. That's what I need. You've been around rockets of all shapes and sizes, you know what they look like.' And that was what clinched it. Harry, luckily, did not take offence. Was this true, I asked Frederick Ordway?

'Yeah, that could well be. That's why he wanted to get me too; working for Wernher von Braun, that probably had a lot to do with it in both our cases. He wanted the film to be realistic, you see. Realistic and detailed. His relationship was with our company General Aeronautics, that's what Kubrick wanted to deal with. So together we had a contract with Polaris Films in New York—and then, when we had agreed to go over to England, with Hawk Films Ltd. The cheque would go to the company and then I'd pay Harry and myself. He wanted us both.'

Jeremy Bernstein described the working atmosphere at this time, in his **New Yorker** piece:

'[Mr Clarke] was carrying several manila envelopes, which, it turned out, contained parts of **Journey Beyond the Stars**. Mr Kubrick then came into the room carrying a thick pile of diagrams and charts, and looking like the popular conception of a nuclear physicist who has been interrupted in the middle of some difficult calculations... [He added emphatically that everything possible would be done to make each scene completely authentic and to make it conform to what is known to physicists and astronomers.]'

Did Frederick Ordway recognise this description?

'Well, we soon discovered that Kubrick had read voraciously—science fiction and space science—and had developed a way of talking about them. He'd talk about a "systems" approach, "what are your parameters?" and so forth. And as we proceeded, a month or two in, he then became fascinated with computers which had voice input-outputs. He'd talk about "neural nets", "heuristic systems", "logic elements"—he had quite a lingo!'

In the film—as distinct from in Arthur C. Clarke's novel—this 'lingo' was to morph into the jargon used by all the characters, the only means of expression they seem to possess. The dialogue was to become deliberately flat, with the implication that the emotions lying behind it were becoming deadened by prolonged exposure to new technologies—and especially display technologies, all surface with no cables or plugs or evidence of manual skill to be seen. When astronaut Poole (Gary Lockwood) receives a long-distance happy birthday greeting from his parents back on Earth, his only

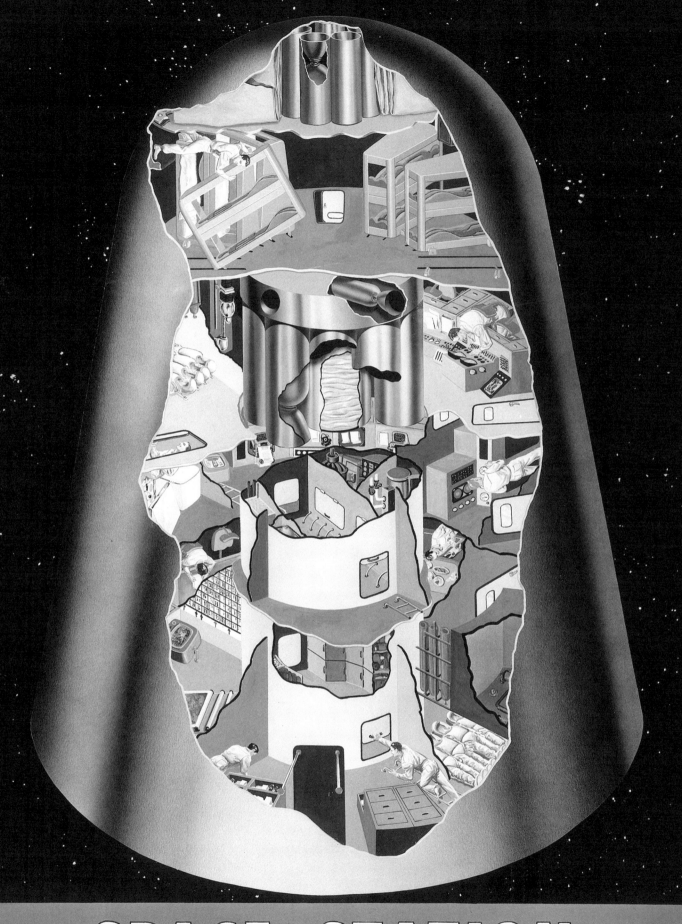

SPACE STATION
QUARTERS AND LABORATORIES

'It is a scientifically-based yet dramatic attempt to explore the infinite possibilities that space travel now opens to mankind...'

reaction is to instruct HAL to make his headrest more comfortable: 'a bit flatter please'. While the audience experiences the beauty of the visuals, the characters seem to have lost the ability to respond to it except at the level of jargon, 'the lingo'—a mix of computer-speak, space jargon, air-traffic control and vacuous clichés. In the novel, as in Clarke's stories, the characters use jargon when conversing with fellow-specialists, but use ordinary language when communicating with everyone else. In early drafts of the screenplay, this remained the case—especially through the character of Dr Heywood Floyd, in conversation with the flight-crew, space station receptionists, the female Russian scientists and his five-year-old daughter; and through the conversations of the astronauts aboard **Discovery**. Also, there was florid Clarkean voice-over narration throughout. In the finished film, the voice-over had been removed, dialogue was pared down to a minimum, and in the docking sequences radio communications or 'typical cockpit chatter' between pilot and ground control (lengthy in the novel) had become purely visual—with graphic displays which were more easily seen by the viewer than by the two pilots. Kubrick had been fascinated by 'the Air Force jargon' in **Dr Strangelove**—with what technology does to the language. He enhanced this theme in the 'lingo' of **2001**, and Ordway remembers him practising for it. During filming, he ruthlessly cut out any language which betrayed emotion. As early as the 'film story' of **Journey Beyond the Stars**, Kubrick was writing in the margin 'too wordy', or—of a long technical description by Floyd of hibernation in space—'this can be explained to the press'. This pruning continued through to the shooting of the film, and even beyond. Harry Lange, for his part, also remembered total immersion in the latest data:

'*You see, this film was generally not called a science-fiction film, it was called a science-fact film, because we totally—virtually totally— projected space travel to the year 2001, and this nobody had ever done before. **The War of the Worlds** envisioned it with wonderful*

creatures, a pure fantasy, and we stayed totally away from all that. So an awful lot of time was spent on the preparation, to get it as accurate as possible, projected to the year 2001. I mean, we didn't even know what the surface of the moon was like... But, you know, we actually did get it right, but it took time.'

By 23rd February 1965, Kubrick felt ready to approve a press release announcing 'STANLEY KUBRICK TO FILM **JOURNEY BEYOND THE STARS** IN CINERAMA FOR MGM'. It stated, very optimistically, that production would begin 'on August 16th with a cast of international importance', and that the novel would be 'published this winter by Arthur C. Clarke and Stanley Kubrick'. Location filming would apparently take place in Britain, Switzerland, Africa, Germany and the United States, with interiors shot at the MGM Studios in Borehamwood, London. (At this stage, and up to summer 1965, it was planned that parts of the Space Station interior would feature actual locations 'such as the hold of a ship or car ferry, or an establishment like Farnborough', and the Tycho Research Base on the moon could in part be 'De Havilland Aircraft Establishment, Hatfield—room with ISORA translucent ceilings...'. Other locations were also mooted). Kubrick was quoted as stating:

'*It is a scientifically-based yet dramatic attempt to explore the infinite possibilities that space travel now opens to mankind... Space is one of the great themes of our age, yet, it is still almost untouched in serious art and literature. Now that the first man-carrying spaceships are actually being built, and the United States is spending over $10 million a day to reach the moon, and robot probes have already been landed on Mars and Venus, it is time to break away from the clichés of Monsters and Madmen... The story of **Journey Beyond the Stars** opens in the year 2001, when permanent bases have been established on the moon, manned expeditions have visited Mars, and automatic probes have been sent to all the major planets of the Solar System...*'

The announcement at the beginning of the release was made

Opposite: Early 1960s concept of a 'Space Station', commissioned by NASA: illustrations such as this would have been used in presentations to raise funds in Washington DC. Harry Lange kept them in his files, and was responsible for drawing several of them.

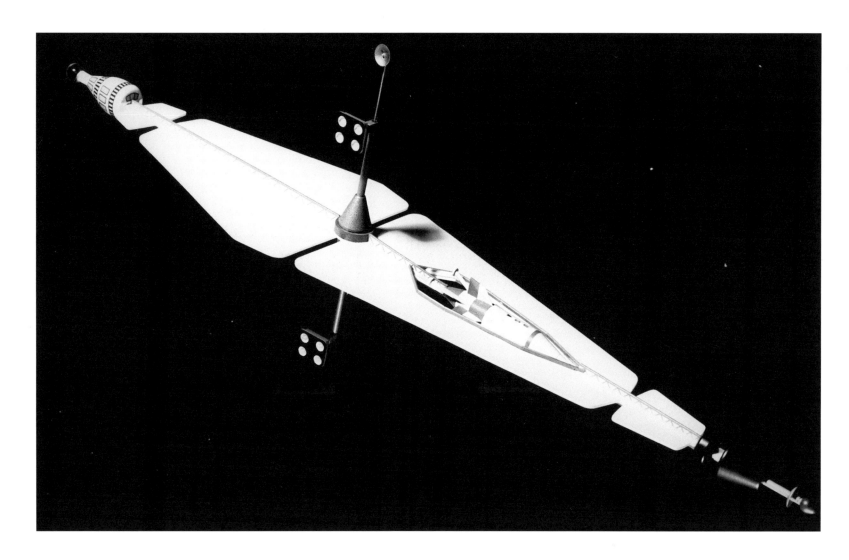

by MGM President Robert H. O'Brien. No mention was made of Ordway and Lange, even though they had been signed up for their initial six months on the 13th February. Only on 4th October 1965 would a press release announce their formal participation. But it was clear from Kubrick's quoted remarks that he had been listening carefully to their accounts of work-in-progress at NASA. The release made **Journey Beyond the Stars** sound like a futuristic version of **Cinerama Holiday**. Since there was to be a prologue, shot in black and white and featuring key thinkers in science, astronomy, biology, religion and philosophy—discussing the possibility and implications of extra-terrestrial life, and establishing that extra-terrestrial life was a fit subject for scientists to investigate, giving the film some heavyweight academic credentials—there was even to be a parallel moment to Lowell Thomas saying at the beginning of the first triple-screen-presentation 'This is **Cinerama**'. The screen would open up, black and white would make way for colour, 35mm for Cinerama, and **2001** would begin with 'an animated section, similar in type to the film **Universe**'. The interviews were all to be filmed and

transcribed by Roger Caras in 1966, Clarke presenting the prologue and Ordway the epilogue, but the idea was abandoned late in the day. When the press release was issued, the screenplay—and the pre-production design work—were nowhere near ready. Ken Adam was to ask for sight of an 'outline or book or script' later that month. Kubrick replied indignantly to his request, but the fact was that no workable script yet existed.

Arthur C. Clarke and Stanley Kubrick were still animatedly brainstorming about the precise nature of the computer's role, and what should happen after astronaut Bowman (and maybe fellow members of the crew) enter the Stargate. But Clarke's treatment, which *seemed* complete though it wasn't, and Kubrick's brand of intense showmanship, had successfully sold the project to MGM and Cinerama. Meanwhile, real-life events had to be incorporated into the novel/screenplay as it evolved. On 1st August 1964, Clarke watched on television the first close-up of pictures of the moon—taken by Ranger VII before it crashed. Ten days later Kubrick wrote his letter to Chesley Bonestell, letting him know that 'nothing

*Above & Opposite: More NASA concept designs from the Lange files, dating from when Harry Lange was working at Future Projects Graphics: they were re-used as part of the research for **2001**.*

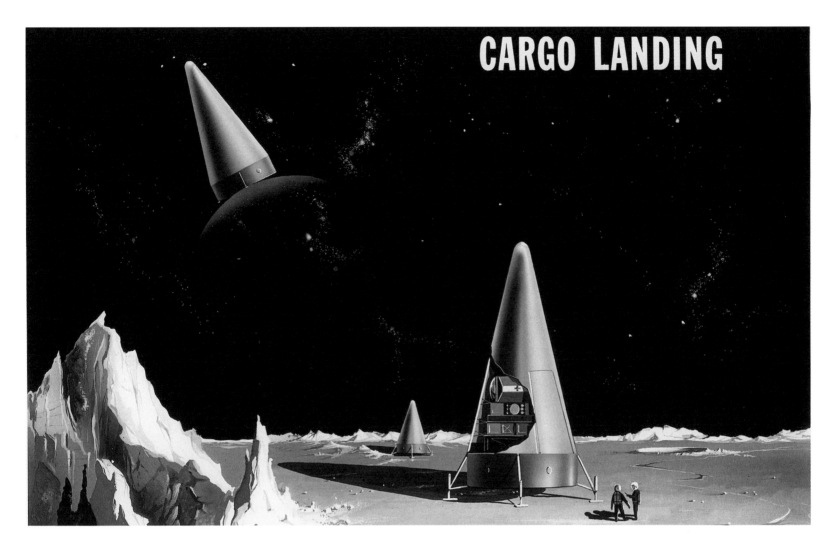

CARGO LANDING

definite can yet be discussed'. There would no longer be any need for Bonestell's imaginative paintings with their velvet shadows. Photographs of the lunar surface would eventually be supplied by the Department of Astronomy at the University of Manchester ('photography of the moon from Pic du Midi sources; large-scale photos of Tycho and Clavius craters—consultations on surface characteristics of the moon') and by the Soviet science attaché at the Soviet Embassy in London ('stills of lunar photography'). These were the best available images, before the successful moon landing in 1969. On 18th March 1965, a Russian astronaut called Aleksei Leonov became the first human being to 'walk' in space, followed on 6th April by the launch of the first commercially-operated satellite (Early Bird) from Cape Kennedy: Clarke was watching this from COMSAT headquarters in Washington. And on 3rd June, American astronaut Ed White took a longer 'walk' in space. On 15th July, 22 photographs of the ancient craters of Mars—taken from only 9,846 kilometers away—were beamed from the flyby space probe Mariner IV, finally proving that there were no oceans there (it had been launched in November 1964). Such developments confirmed that the film was on the right track—but they also made Stanley Kubrick nervous. He apparently got in touch with Lloyd's of London for a

quotation on an insurance policy against life on Mars being proven beyond doubt before the film was ready for release. 'Stanley starts to worry about the forthcoming Mars probes. Suppose they show something that shoots down our storyline?' He honestly believed that evidence of extra-terrestrial life might actually come to light at any moment. And as Clarke was to put it, 'We knew that the film would be released when man had either reached the moon or had failed to reach the moon—either scenario could affect the reception of the movie.'

Through the spring of 1965 [wrote Clarke], we continued to revise and extend the novel, and threw away—again and yet again—whole sections which we had once imagined to be final and complete. All this time, Stanley was also hiring staff, checking designs, negotiating with actors and technicians, and coping with the millions of other problems which arise in the production of even the most straightforward movie...

Through 1965, he gathered around him the armies of artists, technicians, actors, accountants, and secretaries without which no movie can be made; in this case, there were endless additional complications, as we also needed scientific advisors, engineers, genuine space hardware, and whole libraries of reference material.

This certainly was not 'the most straightforward movie'. It was to be shot in Hertfordshire but prepared from New York by a man who flatly refused to travel by air, even though he had a pilot's licence. Actually *because* he had a pilot's licence: his first experience of flying solo had apparently been traumatic. The project was already digesting an unprecedented amount of advice from a range of specialists—from companies, agencies, universities, research institutes—and this would only increase after the move to Borehamwood. Ordway brought with him to New York from Huntsville his very extensive network of contacts with people engaged in space and computer research, while publicity director/Vice-President of Polaris Roger Caras (ex-ten years at Columbia Pictures) helped to liaise with commercial companies about the products, technologies and corporate logos to be featured in the film. The Kubrick Archive contains 300 files on 'product development' alone.

As early as 19th April, according to Clarke's log, 'the walls [of the Polaris office] are getting covered with impressive pictures and I already feel quite a minor cog in the works'. By June, Clarke was reading a set of 'production notes', based on a series of conferences held in May and on a synopsis dated 23rd March, which in turn was based on the original treatment, all compiled by associate producer Victor Lyndon, and dated 1st June. These 'left me completely overwhelmed. Glad that's not *my* job'. The level of detail was mind-blowing. Harry Lange recalled:

'Every single panel, for example, in the big centrifuge [aboard the **Discovery***], the big wheel, was totally studied, the purpose of the panel, whether it was geophysical, or whether it was a life support system or whatever. And each one of them was thoroughly thought out, and the whole sequence was worked out so that you could actually look at that panel and there was how the whole ship could run if it is operated properly, the hibernation chamber and so forth. And this took a lot of time. You see, a lot of other people would have thought, "Well, we'll just have a little black panel there and paint it black, and then stick some blue squares on it, that's it, you make one or two of them light up." But that's for television, and they can get away with it because it's a little bitty screen; but this was Cinerama, the wraparound, 75 mil negative and you don't get away with it. [It had to be absolutely perfect.] And Stanley was a great stickler for detail...'*

Kubrick would constantly be asking questions about the finer details of spacecraft 'that had to be designed as if they could touch the edge of the solar system and beyond'. How would they be powered? What exactly would their control decks contain? What would a deep-space vehicle which was never intended to enter an atmosphere look like? Would it have supply and power units bolted on? Would it have an 'additive' look? It certainly wouldn't look like the traditional pencil with fins. Kubrick was always

probing the latest ideas on space flight, exploration in deep space, interplanetary research—'learning everything about everything'. He seemed to have an inexhaustible hunger for knowledge which was observable, describable or imaginable—and he had no time at all for woolly thinking. If NASA did not have the answers, what would be the most rational *speculations*?

Meanwhile, Clarke's novel was lagging behind the advice, which begged the biggest question of all: what to do after entering the Stargate? What would happen to Bowman, and maybe his colleagues too? It was clear that 'a smashing theme of mythic grandeur' was called for, but what? In October 1964, there had been the idea of 'people we meet on the other star systems' being 'humans who were collected from Earth a hundred thousand years ago...' or perhaps some 'slightly fag robots who create a Victorian environment to put our heroes at their ease'. In May 1965, Kubrick was attracted by the idea of a 'floating island' of rock, from another of Clarke's stories, where **Discovery** encounters the immortal alien Clindar surrounded by 'souvenirs of a thousand worlds and a hundred civilisations', and where the alien finds much of the astronauts' equipment surprisingly crude as if 'bolted on as an afterthought'. Or maybe the 'Devil theme' from Clarke's novel **Childhood's End** which had launched his idea of Man evolving into pure energy after contact with a redeeming alien force. Or maybe Bowman—the sole survivor—should descend in a pod deep into a Stargate or 'time-slot' on Jupiter V, travelling towards his destiny, and eventually fly over a cosmopolis inhabited by elongated aliens who have 'two arms and two legs and stand upright' before encountering non-human intelligences resembling 'squat cones with tube-like legs' and then finding himself in a replica of an anonymous Washington hotel room with no windows or doors. The cosmopolis would somehow be 'as strange and wonderful as New York City would have seemed to Neanderthal Man'. In another suggestion, the aliens have skin resembling shiny flexible metal, perhaps with faces dominated by a curled-up trunk or proboscis 'where the nose should have been'. In yet another, they were 'elegant silvery metal crabs, supported on four jointed legs'. Some design concepts and even models for extra-terrestrials were developed—and at least one of them did indeed have 'tube-like legs'. Harry Lange recalled that 'at one time Stanley wanted to use visually extra-terrestrials', with 'everybody fighting' about what they should look like. Kubrick's wife Christiane, an artist, contributed some visual ideas, Lange continued. In the end, though, they all had to agree:

'... So why does it have to be visible? We always felt that half the audience would accept it and the other half would mind—but nobody would be very impressed.'

In an early draft of **Dr Strangelove**, too, Kubrick had wanted to frame the story with aliens looking down on Earth at the idiotic behaviour of pompous, self-destructive humans after World War 3

Opposite: Painting of two astronauts in their cockpit, approaching another space craft, made during his NASA period.

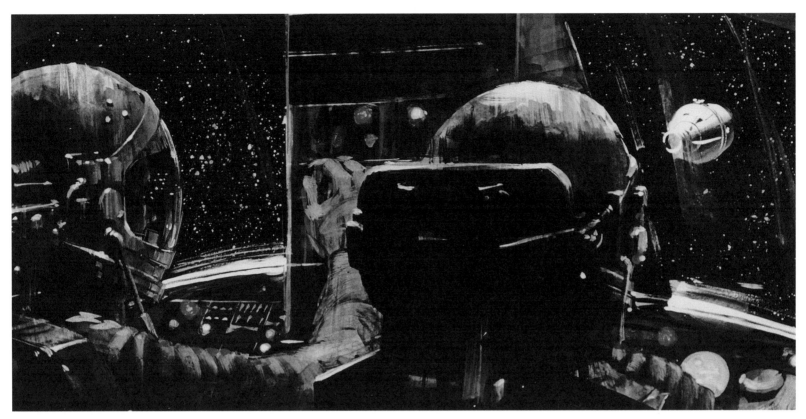

and saying the equivalent of, 'Lord, what fools these mortals be'. But he soon thought better of it, as he did with **Journey**. The conversation about the ending seems from the evidence to have been between Clarke's wish to have Bowman become a new kind of superior being—like in **Childhood's End**—as a result of some apocalyptic climax or other, perhaps involving an incomprehensibly advanced alien city—and Kubrick's intention to create a less literal, more *visual* experience—a big finish of 'mythic grandeur'—one in which contact with extra-terrestrials would not necessarily turn him into a better person. It would be another stage in evolution. Clarke likened the conversation to 'a sculptor' chipping 'down through the stone toward the figure concealed within.'

'... *We certainly had to show something, though there were moments of despair when I feared we had painted ourselves into a corner from which there was no possible escape—except perhaps a "Lady or the Tiger" ending... That would be a lazy way out, and would have started people queuing at the box office to get their money back.*'

'... *We spent months imagining strange worlds and cities and creatures, in the hope of finding something that would produce the right shock of recognition. All this material was abandoned, but... it contained the alternatives that had to be eliminated, and therefore first had to be created.*'

'... *it was just as well that the problem of creating explicit super-civilisations was bypassed. They are things that are better left to the imagination—which is why so many "horror" movies collapse when some pathetic papier-mâché monster is finally revealed.*'

In the end, extra-terrestrials, and their cities, were deemed 'unfilmable'. The designers were pleased to concur. Only on 3rd October did they settle on the idea that 'Bowman will regress to infancy, and we'll see him at the end as a baby in orbit. Stanley called again later, still very enthusiastic...' Bowman would seem to see himself as a man who ages and dies to become a baby, who is then transported back to the solar system to gaze down on Earth. The screenplay would continue to contain explicit references to aliens 'tinkering with the destiny of many species on land and in the oceans', or to 'Lords of the Galaxy', until filming was actually in progress. In the version dated 9th December 1965 it would end with the not-very-helpful words:

'*In a moment of time, too short to be measured, space turned and twisted upon itself.*'

Meanwhile, where scientific verisimilitude was concerned, Harry Lange did not have much in the way of physical descriptions of space hardware to go on, in **The Sentinel** or even in the treatment or related screenplay as they progressed. **The Sentinel**, set on the moon, refers to 'two heavy freighters which had flown our supplies and equipment from the main lunar base' and to 'three small rockets which were intended for short-range transport over regions which our surface vehicles couldn't cross'; also to 'our powerful caterpillar tractors' (resembling metal insects) which 'would have no difficulty in taking us wherever we wished to go'. These, plus a couple of mentions of 'spacesuits' with built-in refrigeration units, were all there was. Visual clues were almost entirely missing.

The final version of the novel, published after the film was released but written before and during the screenplay, was not much help to the designers either.

THE NOVEL

The Space Station revolves 'once a minute, and the centrifugal force generated by this slow spin produced an artificial gravity equal to the Moon's'.

The **Orion III Spaceplane**, capable of carrying twenty passengers on the fifty-five minute transit from Cape Kennedy to **Space Station One**, 'must have been two hundred feet across the narrow V of its wings'. The 'swept-back' wings blaze like 'white-hot metal in the reflected sunlight'; 'the empty lower stage would glide down into the atmosphere, trading speed for distance as it homed in on Kennedy'. The sunlight also floats on 'the polished metal surfaces of the slowly revolving, three-hundred-yard dramatic disc [of **Space Station One**]. Not far away, drifting in the same orbit, was a swept-back **Titov-V** Spaceplane and close to that an almost spherical **Aries-1B**, the workhorse of space, with the four stubby legs of its lunar-landing shock-absorbers jutting from one pole'.

The Space Station revolves 'once a minute, and the centrifugal force generated by this slow spin produced an artificial gravity equal to the Moon's'.

Inside the Station,

the lounge had been redecorated since [Dr Heywood Floyd's] last visit, and had acquired several new facilities. Besides the usual chairs, small tables, restaurant and post office, there was now a barber shop, drugstore, movie theater and a souvenir shop selling photographs and slides of lunar and planetary landings.

Floyd makes a quick phone call to Washington, dropping 'his plastic all-purpose credit-card' into the pay slot.

The **Aries-1B** lunar carrier, for the twenty-four-hour trip from the Space Station to the moon, is designed to carry thirty passengers; it is powered for take-off by 'low-thrust plasma jets' which blast 'their electrified streams into space'.

Once on board:

A whole generation of research by heroic but unsung volunteers had gone into the design of the washroom, and it was now considered

to be more or less foolproof... [It consists of] a little cubicle with all the fittings of an ordinary airline toilet, but illuminated with a red light that was very harsh and unpleasant to the eye...

Floyd follows the complex instructions and presses the START button, at which point the whole toilet compartment goes into a 'carousel-like spin' ensuring that 'everything moved in the right direction'.

Safely back in the passenger cabin, Floyd 'would plug his foolscap-sized Newspad into the ship's information circuit and scan the latest reports from Earth. One by one he would conjure up the world's major electronic papers...'

On the pilot's panel, lights flashed above radar screens, numbers came and went on computer displays, clocking off the distance of the approaching Moon...

'Clavius Control to Special 14, you are coming in nicely. Please make manual check of landing-gear lock, hydraulic pressure, shock-pad inflation.'

The pilot pressed sundry switches, green lights flashed, and he called back, 'All manual checks completed. Landing-gear lock, hydraulic pressure, shock-pad OK.'

'Confirmed,' said the Moon, and the descent continued wordlessly...

Clavius Crater is 150 miles in diameter, in the centre of the southern highlands of the moon. The Lunar Base there is like 'an underground empire':

The Base was a closed system, like a tiny working model of Earth itself, recycling all the chemicals of life. The atmosphere was purified in a vast 'hothouse'—a large, circular room just below the lunar surface. Under blazing lamps by night, and filtered sunlight by day, acres of stubby green plants grew in a warm, moist atmosphere. They were special mutations... More food was produced by chemical processing systems and algae culture. Although the green scum

*Opposite: Author Arthur C. Clarke looking cautious on the set of **2001** at MGM Borehamwood, with two of the completed spherical 'space pods' in the background.*

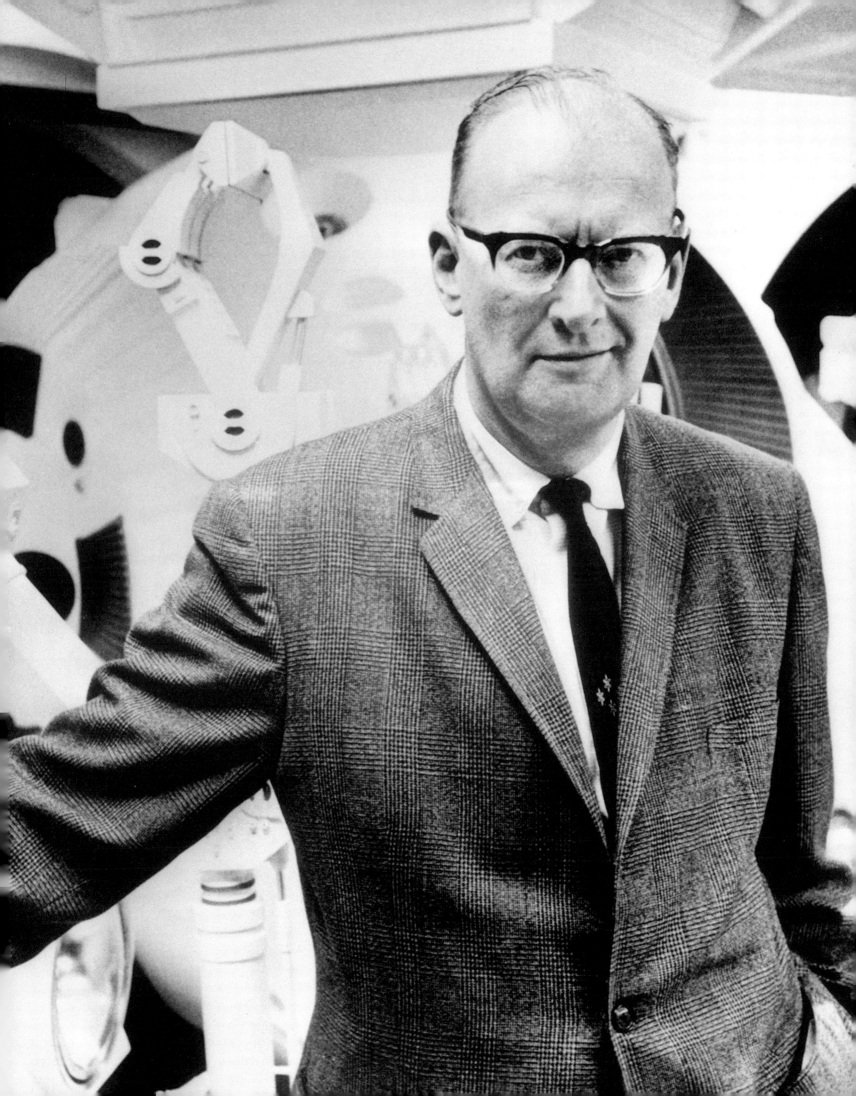

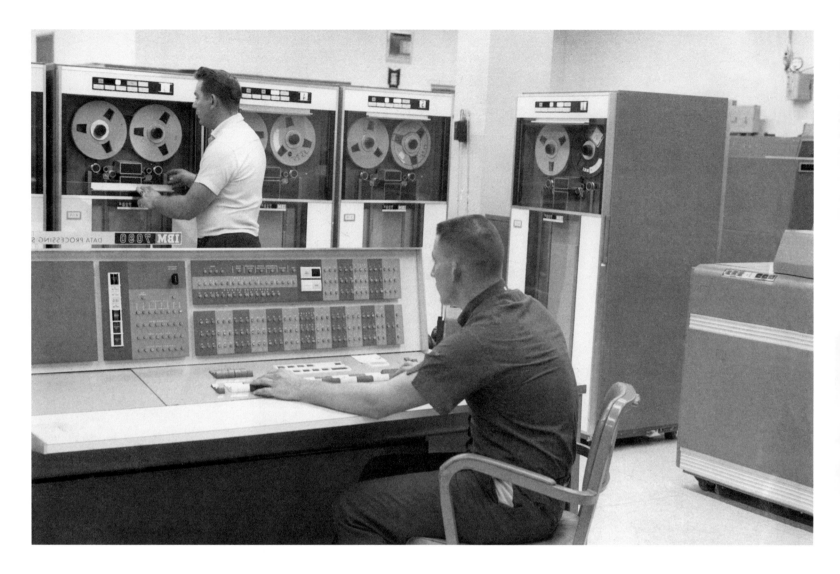

circulating through yards of transparent tubing would scarcely have appealed to the gourmet, the biochemists could convert it into chops and steaks only an expert could distinguish from the real thing. The eleven hundred men and six hundred women who made up the personnel of the Base were all highly trained scientists or technicians... Each room was attractively furnished and looked very much like a good motel suite... Clavius Base was a mini-world in itself.

After **Aries-1B** has successfully docked,

several very odd vehicles were rolling up to [it]—cranes, hoists, servicing trucks—some automatic, some operated by a driver in a small pressure cabin. Most of them moved on balloon tires... but one tanker rolled on the peculiar flex-wheels which had provided one of the best all-purpose ways of getting around the Moon... A series of flatplates arranged in a circle, each plate independently mounted and sprung, the flex-wheel had many of the advantages of the caterpillar truck from which it had evolved.

A small bus with an extension-tube like a stubby elephant trunk was now nuzzling affectionately up against the spacecraft. A few

seconds later, there were bangings and bumpings from outside, followed by the sound of hissing air...

This bus travels the thousand feet from the docking site to Clavius Base. After a short walk through a tunnel 'packed with pipes and cables', Floyd reaches 'executive territory'—'the familiar environment of typewriters, office computers, girl assistants, wall charts and ringing telephones'. An earth office in space (surprisingly indistinguishable, it has to be said, from its mid-1960s predecessor).

A photograph of **Tycho Magnetic Anomaly-One** (TMA-1), which has been discovered within the crater ring of Tycho, fifty-four miles in diameter, shows 'a man in a light-red-and-yellow spacesuit standing at the bottom of an excavation and supporting a surveyor's rod marked off in tenths of a meter'.

Floyd traverses the two-hundred-mile moonscape from **Clavius** to **Tycho** in a 'mobile lab':

... rolling across the crater plane at fifty miles an hour [it] looked rather like an outsized trailer mounted on eight flex-wheels. But it was very much more than this... virtually a land-going spaceship... If it came to a crevice or canyon which was too large to detour, and too

Above & Opposite: Reference photographs of mid-1960s computers and communications systems, from Harry Lange's research files.

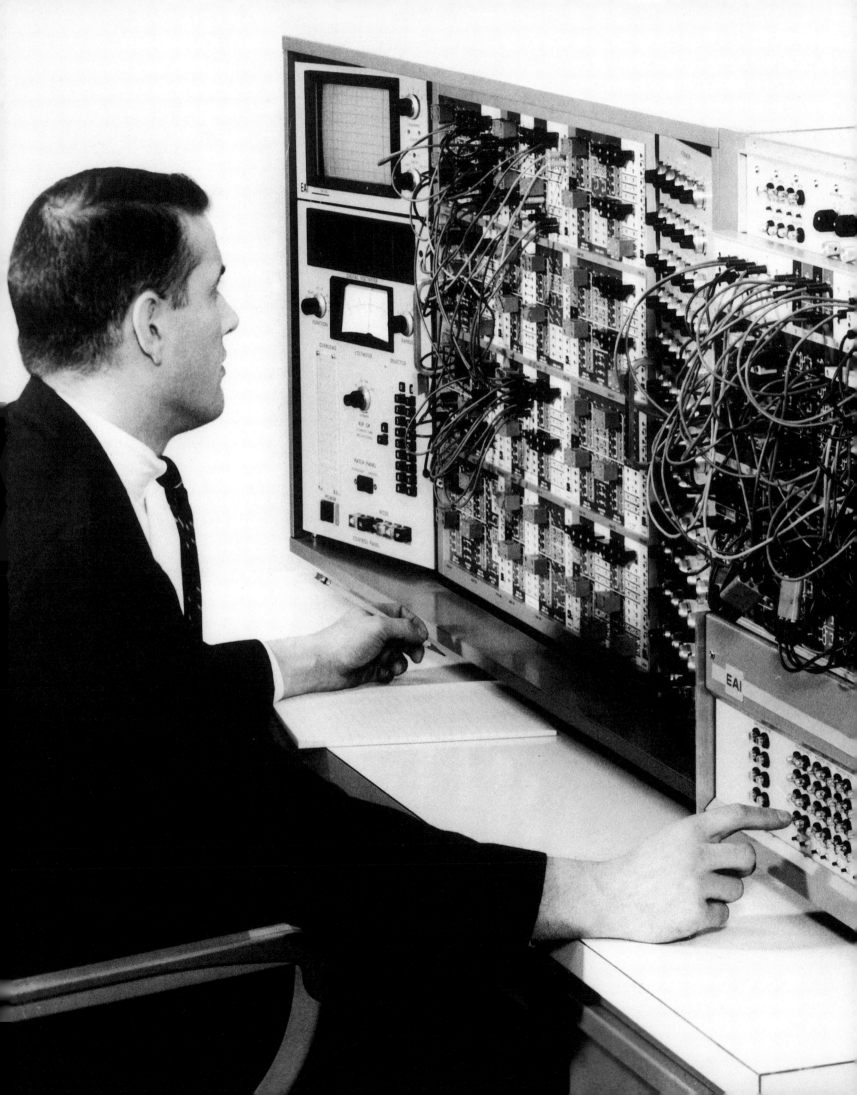

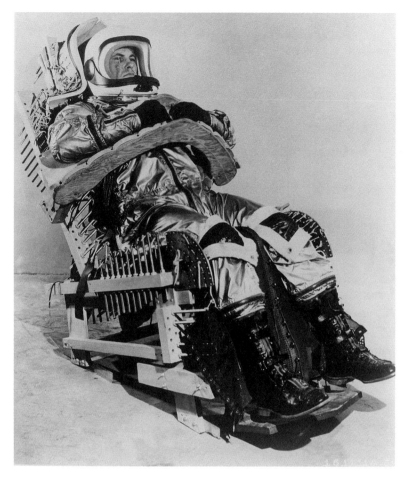

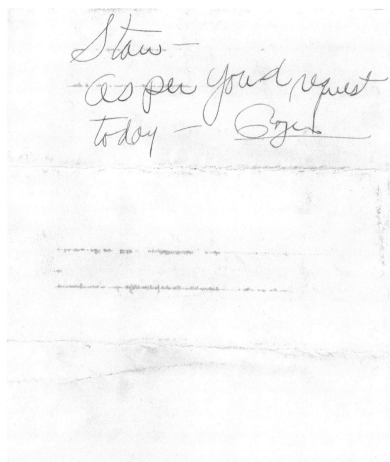

steep to enter, it could hop across the obstacle on its four underjets.

At TMA-1, Floyd can see:

Glistening like silver bubbles in the earthlight, a group of pressure domes—the temporary shelters housing the workers on the site. Near there was a radio tower, a drilling rig, a group of parked vehicles, and a large pile of broken rocks, presumably the material that had been excavated to reveal the monolith.

The main pressure dome at TMA-1 is only twenty feet across, a hemispherical double-walled balloon, which houses six scientists and technicians as well as their equipment and instruments. It is cramped. Floyd leaves the dome in a spacesuit which has 'dials and gauges on the outside':

... the latest models were infinitely more comfortable than the clumsy suits of armor worn by the first lunar explorers. They could be put on in less than a minute, even without help, and were quite automatic. The Mk V into which Floyd was now carefully sealed would protect him from the worst that the Moon could do...

The **Discovery** spacecraft, with David Bowman as its First Captain, overseen by 'the Ship's tireless electronic brain', is on its ten-month odyssey to Jupiter and thence to Saturn.

[She] was still coasting with her slender arrow-like body pointing

away from Earth, and all her high-powered optical gear was oriented towards the outer planets, where her destiny lay... There was one telescope, however, that was permanently aimed at Earth: it was mounted like a gun-sight on the rim of the Ship's long-range antenna, and checked that the great parabolic bowl was rigidly locked upon its distant target...

Discovery *measured about four [later five] hundred feet from end to end, but the little universe occupied by her crew lay entirely inside the forty-foot sphere of the pressure hull. Here were all the life-support systems and the Control Deck which was the operational heart of the ship. Below this was a small 'space-garage' fitted with three airlocks, through which powered capsules, just large enough to hold a man, could sail out into the void if the need arose for extravehicular activity... The equatorial region of the pressure sphere... enclosed a slowly rotating drum, ninety-five feet in diameter. As it made one revolution every ten seconds, this carousel or centrifuge produced artificial gravity equal to that of the Moon... The carousel contained the kitchen, dining, working and toilet facilities...*

(The galley—a 'tiny lounge-cum-dining-room'—is the place where the crew can eat freeze-dried packet food cooked quickly in a 'tiny auto-galley which beeped for attention when the job was done'.)

Above: Reference photograph of seated astronaut, requested by 'Stan' during pre-production in New York. Opposite: The latest, mid-1960s, research into astronauts' food—here approximating 'bacon & eggs' and 'beef pot roast'—was used in preparing the screenplay and novel.

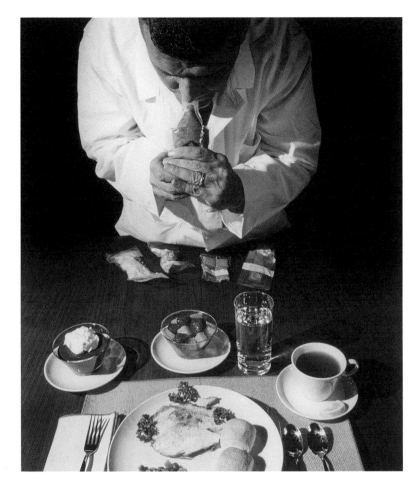

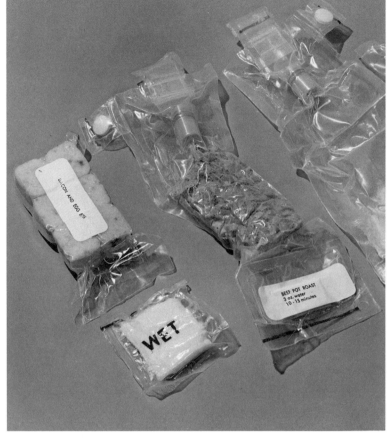

The spherical pressure hull formed the head of a flimsy, arrow-shaped structure more than a hundred yards long. **Discovery**, *like all vehicles intended for deep space penetration, was too fragile and unstreamlined ever to enter an atmosphere, or to defy the full gravitational field of any planet... She was a creature of pure space—and she looked it. Immediately behind the pressure hull was grouped a cluster of four large liquid hydrogen tanks—and beyond them, forming a long, slender V, were the radiating fins that dissipated the waste heat of the nuclear reactor... they were like the wings of some vast dragonfly, and from certain angles gave* **Discovery** *a fleeting resemblance to an old-time sailing ship.*

Various sensors and booms project from the hull 'at unlikely places'. Also aboard **Discovery** is a 'Hibernaculum' for induced human hibernation. The three-member survey team of scientists is sleeping 'in frozen peace', each with a separate display screen on the Control Deck and 'constellations of tiny green lights' announcing that 'everything is well'. The Hibernaculum is described in some detail.

The sixth member of the crew—with Bowman, Frank Poole and the surveyors—is 'not human':

It was a highly advanced HAL 9000 computer, the brain and nervous system of the Ship. HAL (for Heuristically Programmed Algorithmic Computer, no less) was a masterwork of the third computer breakthrough, an artificial intelligence machine which reproduced, or maybe mimicked, the human brain... it was clear that artificial intelligences at least as powerful as Man's need be no larger than office desks...

The first generation of computers had received their inputs through glorified typewriter keyboards, and had replied through high-speed printers and visual displays. HAL could do this when necessary, but most of his communication with his shipmates was by means of the spoken word... Whether HAL could actually think was a question which had been settled by the British mathematician Alan Turing back in the 1940s... HAL could pass the Turing test with ease.

The Turing test was about whether a computer was/is aware of itself. This one clearly was. It could interact and it could think. But it wasn't very good at lying.

Discovery's *extravehicular capsules or 'space pods' were spheres about nine feet in diameter, and the operator sat behind a bay window which gave him a splendid view. The main rocket driver produced an acceleration of one-fifth of gravity... while small altitude-control nozzles allowed for steering. From an area immediately beneath the window sprouted two sets of articulated metal arms or 'waldoes', one for heavy duty, the other for delicate manipulations... Space pods were not the most elegant means of transport devised by man, but they were absolutely essential for construction and maintenance work in vacuum...*

THE SCREENPLAY

The draft screenplay of 2001: A Space Odyssey by Kubrick and Clarke, dated October-December 1965 (and often revised after that date), was even less precise about design details.

4th October 1965

ORION-III SPACECRAFT IN FLIGHT AWAY FROM EARTH. 200 MILES ALTITUDE...

Orion-III Passenger Area. Dr Heywood Floyd is the only passenger in the elegant cabin designed for 30 people. He is asleep. His pen floats near his hand...

Orion-III cockpit. Pilot, co-pilot. Floyd can be seen asleep on a small TV monitor. Stewardess is putting on lipstick. She sees pen...

Space Station-5. The raw sunlight of space dazzles from the polished metal surfaces of the slowly revolving, thousand-foot diameter space station. Drifting in the same orbit, we see swept-back Titov-V spacecraft. Also the almost spherical Aries-IB...

The Orion-III spacecraft in docking approach. The earth is seen in breathtaking view in b.g...

From Docking Port we see the Orion-III inching in to complete its docking. We see various windowed booths inside docking port. We see the pilot and co-pilot inside the Orion-III cockpit...

ARIES-1B IN SPACE. EARTH MUCH SMALLER THAN AS SEEN FROM THE SPACE STATION.

NARRATOR: 'The Aries-1B has become the standard Space-Station-to-Lunar surface vehicle. It was powered by low-thrust plasma jets which would continue the mild acceleration for fifteen minutes. Then the ship would break the bonds of gravity and be a free and independent planet orbiting the Sun in an orbit of its own.'

ARIES PASSENGER AREA. FLOYD IS ASLEEP, STRETCHED OUT IN A CHAIR, COVERED WITH BLANKETS WHICH ARE HELD SECURE BY STRAPS... THE ELEVATOR ENTRANCE DOOR OPENS AND A SECOND STEWARDESS ENTERS CARRYING A TRAY OF FOOD...

Aries-1B closer to Moon. Floyd goes to Aries-1B washroom and looks at the very long list of complicated instructions.

Aries-1B closer to Moon.
Dissolve:
Floyd visiting Aries-1B cockpit. Weightless trick entrance.
Aries-1B orbiting Moon.
NARRATOR: 'The laws of Earthly aesthetics did not apply here, this world had been shaped and moulded by other than terrestrial forms, operating over aeons of Time unknown to the young, verdant Earth, with its fleeting Ice-Ages, its swiftly rising and falling seas, its mountain ranges dissolving like mists before dawn. Here was age inconceivable—but not death, for the Moon had never lived until now.'

ARIES-1B COCKPIT—THE CREW AND DOCKING CONTROL PEOPLE ON THE MOON GO THROUGH THEIR DOCKING ROUTINE. THIS HAS THE RITUALISTIC TONE AND CADENCE OF PRESENT-DAY JET LANDING PROCEDURES.

Aries 1B descending. See air view of base...
NARRATOR: 'The Base at Clavius was the first American lunar settlement that could, in an
emergency, be entirely self-supporting. Water and all the necessities of life for its
eleven hundred men, women and children were produced from the lunar rocks, after they
had been crushed, heated and chemically processed.'

Several scenic views of moon rocket bus skimming over surface of the Moon. Inside rocket
bus, Floyd [and colleagues] all in spacesuits minus helmets... He looks out of the
window thoughtfully.

The photographes [sic] of TMA-1 are taken from a satellite of the moon's surface, and
have numbered optical borders, like recent Mars photos. A few seats away, Michaels and
Halvorsen carry out a very banal administrative conversation in low tones. It should
revolve around something utterly irrelevant.

19th November 1965

Part III   14 months later. Discovery 1,000,000 miles from earth. See earth and
moon small. We see a blinding flash every 5 seconds from its nuclear pulse propulsion.
It strikes against the ship's thick ablative tail plate. Several cuts of this.

[Clarke had written in his log on 26th October: 'Had a discussion with Stanley over his latest idea—that Discovery should be nuclear-pulse-driven. Read a recently declassified report on this and was quite impressed—but design staff rather upset.' The theoretical idea of using a series of nuclear explosions pushing against a drive-plate as a source of propulsion in outer space, for very long-distance travel, had been around since the late 1950s and 'it works in principle'. The idea was called Project Orion. Ordway consulted the Department of the Air Force at the Pentagon, the General Atomic-Division of the General Dynamic Corporation and the Institute of Advanced Study, School of Mathematics, Princeton, about it. But the idea was eventually deleted from 2001 by Kubrick because, in Clarke's words, he 'decided that putt-putting away from Earth at the rate of 20 atom bombs per minute was just a little too comic'. Besides, 'After Dr Strangelove, I think he didn't want to have anything more to do with nuclear bombs, so he dropped the idea. I'm very glad we did.' So sometimes at least the latest declassified scientific researchers had to make way for visual and dramatic considerations—and audience expectations. The 'design staff' were relieved when Project Orion was finally put aside, even though it survived into the November screenplay. The name Orion, however, remained.]

ANOTHER CLOSER VIEW OF DISCOVERY. SEE BOWMAN THROUGH COMMAND MODULE WINDOW.

Bowman inside Discovery command module. He is looking for something. Computer readout
display showing an ever-shifting assortment of color-coded linear projections. We see
Poole in background in computer brain center area. After a few seconds he exits.
The elapsed mission timer reads 'Day 003, Hour 14, Minute 12, Second 10'.

Bowman exits to Access-Link airlock, bright color-coded doors lead to centrifuge and pod
bay. Large illuminated printed warnings and instructions governing link operations are
seen. He presses recess buttons to operate airlock door to pod bay. Bowman enters pod
bay and continues his search. Suddenly he finds it—his electronic newspad. He exits pod
bay. In the Airlock-link, Bowman operates buttons to open door marked 'Centrifuge'...

... We get a good look at the three men in their hibernaculum. Poole is seated at a
table reading his electronic newspad...

Bowman operates artificial food unit, takes his tray and sits down. Keys on his electronic
newspad and begins to eat. Both men eat in a friendly and relaxed silence...

Discovery in space, still nuclear pulsing. Earth and Moon can be seen in background...

24th November 1965

Documentary sequence illustrating the following activities. Split-screen technique and
superimpose clock to give sense of simultaneous action and the feeling of a typical day.
In the course of these activities we shall see the computer used in all its functions.
NARRATOR: 'Bowman and Poole settled down to the peaceful monotony of the voyage, and the
next three months passed without incident.'

[The screenplay then divides into two parallel columns, hour by hour. Bowman goes to sleep in the morning with 'instant electronarcosis and ear plugs', while Poole has breakfast, visits the gymnasium, inspects the ship, engages in 'household duties', has lunch, 'experiments with astronomy', goes back to the gymnasium and then has dinner, as Bowman wakes up and has breakfast.

The subsequent Pod Bay sequences are dated 1st December and 14th December—and include such unfinished stage directions as 'narration to explain tenuous and essential link to earth. Also what tracking telescope does'; revival procedures for the hibernators, 'details of which still have to be worked out'.]

14th December 1965

... Poole walks to the HAL 9000 computer.
Poole: 'HAL... Dave and I believe that there's something about the mission that we
weren't told'...

The Computer Brain consists of hundreds of transparent perspex rectangles, half an inch
thick, four inches long and two and a half inches high. Each rectangle contains a centre
of a very fine grid of wires upon which the information is processed. Bowman begins
pulling these memory blocks out. They float in the weightless condition of the brain
room. Bowman works swiftly...

These solid-state memory units—similar to computer discs but rectilinear—are clearly intended to be small echoes of the alien sharp-edged rectangular black monolith. They share the modernist logic of pure geometry. This solution had been the subject of 'considerable' discussion throughout 1965, according to Clarke. The alien artefact started out, in **The Sentinel** and the treatment, as a 'black tetrahedron' and 'the art department constructed models of various sizes'. But these never looked right and besides resembled a pyramid which might lead to irrelevant speculations about the chariots of the gods. Then Kubrick considered using a large see-through cube, perhaps with visual images projected onto it. But this proved impracticable. Eventually, he settled on a tall matt black rectangular shape. Harry Lange's drawings show some 'geological' versions—round or diamond-like, or a tetrahedron—sometimes *in situ* at Tycho. Clarke was to recall: 'I frantically followed—and

occasionally anticipated—all these changes on my typewriter, but must admit that I had a considerably easier job than the Props Department.' On the first day of shooting, 29th December 1965, Clarke noticed that 'someone had smeared the black finish [of the monolith] and Stanley went on a rampage when I pointed it out to him.'

Harry Lange thought this design solution was 'beautiful, because it made a high-tech contrast, stark reality, it was wonderful. And a very, very simple and basic idea... in perfect proportion: 4 x 1 x 12'. He also recalled that a graphite mixture was added to the black paint, to achieve a smooth but not shiny finish. Kubrick would sometimes have his designers work for several days on ideas he was almost sure he did *not* want—just to reassure himself: an *iterative* process of design, and one that 'took a lot of time'.

'You see, a lot of the time, Stanley, this is a very clever way of doing

things—he would have you design for days, in order to show him that this is not what he wants to do. So it's a process of elimination.'

The monolith was, as Clarke wittily admitted, just such an 'end product of considerable evolution'.

[The climax of the screenplay, also dated 1st December and 9th December, was still unresolved, just three weeks before filming had to begin. There is a lot of narration about alien intelligence and at the fadeout space 'twisted upon itself'.]

Clearly, the design briefing of Harry Lange and team must have taken place in conversations with Kubrick, Clarke and Masters, especially Kubrick; with a variety of corporate, government and university contacts; with his colleagues at NASA and his business partner Fred Ordway. The 'production notes' dated 1st June 1965 and based on meetings in May, reveal just how much the project depended on such design briefings. The 'Technical Advisers' or 'Technical Consultants' referred to in the notes were evidently Ordway and Lange.

On the cockpit set of **Orion III**, 'a lot of instrumentation for set dressing, to be detailed by Technical Advisers'.

On the interiors of the **Space Station**, 'the range of set dressing props is almost infinite, so they cannot be completely listed. Many items will have to be specially made, or adapted. Some suitable for the 2001 period can perhaps be found existing—these wil (sic) have to be carefully sought and collected with intelligence and imagination'.

On the passenger section of **Aries IB**, 'toilet, galley, crew lounge and Cockpit Area are still subject to design'; 'Cockpit Instrumentation to be discussed with Technical Advisers when requirements are known'.

Photographs of the lunar landscape 'are being obtained by the Technical Advisers'.

Costumes for the **Tycho Moon Base** 'to be researched and designed as required, and according to locations'.

At **TMA-1**, 'Floyd, Halvorsen and four others don Space Suits in this sequence. These suits are designed for the lunar environment and should be different from those worn later by the Astronauts … The Set will be in accordance with the approved design … Plenty of monitoring gear of every kind, real if possible—to be obtained (Technical Advisers to arrange)'.

For the **Lunar Surface Vehicle**, 'it may be possible to obtain an actual prototype Lunar Vehicle (Technical Advisers to investigate), otherwise a Snowcat or similar tractor vehicle could be adapted with a fibre-glass body'.

On the four main elements of the **Discovery** interior—the Command Module, the entry to the Centrifuge, the Centrifuge itself and the Space-Pod Bay—'a number of design drawings have been made, but the final version had not been arrived at when these notes were made'.

'Means must be found to retain the Astronauts comfortably in their command positions in the Cockpit. This depends on the design of the seats, upside-down couches, or whatever is finally decided upon…'

Where the Command Module, the Centrifuge and the Pod Bay were concerned, there was much to 'check with Technical Advisers' and 'a detailed list of action requirements and set dressings [needed to] be prepared in consultation with Technical Advisers, in accordance with the requirements of the script'. 'Basic design drawings' had already been made.

As for the ending, **Space Probes** 'will have to be designed—discuss with Technical Advisers', and the miniature landscapes of 'Jupiter V, Stargate, Final Journey etc. … to be discussed further in the light of script and storyboard requirements.'

In the replica hotel suite, 'Bowman is led by an Extra-terrestrial into the "Room with a Cube" where we see, once again, the strange transparent cube from which "Moonwatcher" learned the lesson which set man on his path to civilization … Whatever form this "Cube" finally takes will be the same here as in the "Dawn of Man" sequence'.

No wonder Arthur C. Clarke wrote gratefully, after reading these notes, 'that's not *my* job'.

Essential to this process was Lange's long experience as an illustrator of advanced space concepts, which enabled him to produce not just visual images of the hardware but logical explanations of all the details as well. Kubrick insisted on both. According to Lange:

'Stanley was an absolute stickler for detail, and a good taskmaster—which was fine with me, because I was new to filmmaking.'

'I was not a professional, I was a spacecraft designer, visualisation expert, whatever you want to call it. But I certainly knew nothing [at the start] about how to put that into practice and make it into film sets.'

When 'people like [fellow production designers] Ernie Archer and Tony Masters came over', they were very helpful in guiding him through this new world:

'But then I got more and more involved, of course… and I would take over this, and I'd take over that, so I learned an awful lot in a very short time.'

The design cycle during pre-production went from script to 'small thumbnails' or rough sketches which Lange would discuss with Stanley Kubrick, then more sketches, then semi-developed drawings—still with plenty of options—and finally or almost finally detailed technical specifications and in some cases paintings which were submitted through Tony Masters.

'And with Stanley you had a lot of small thumbnails'—part of that

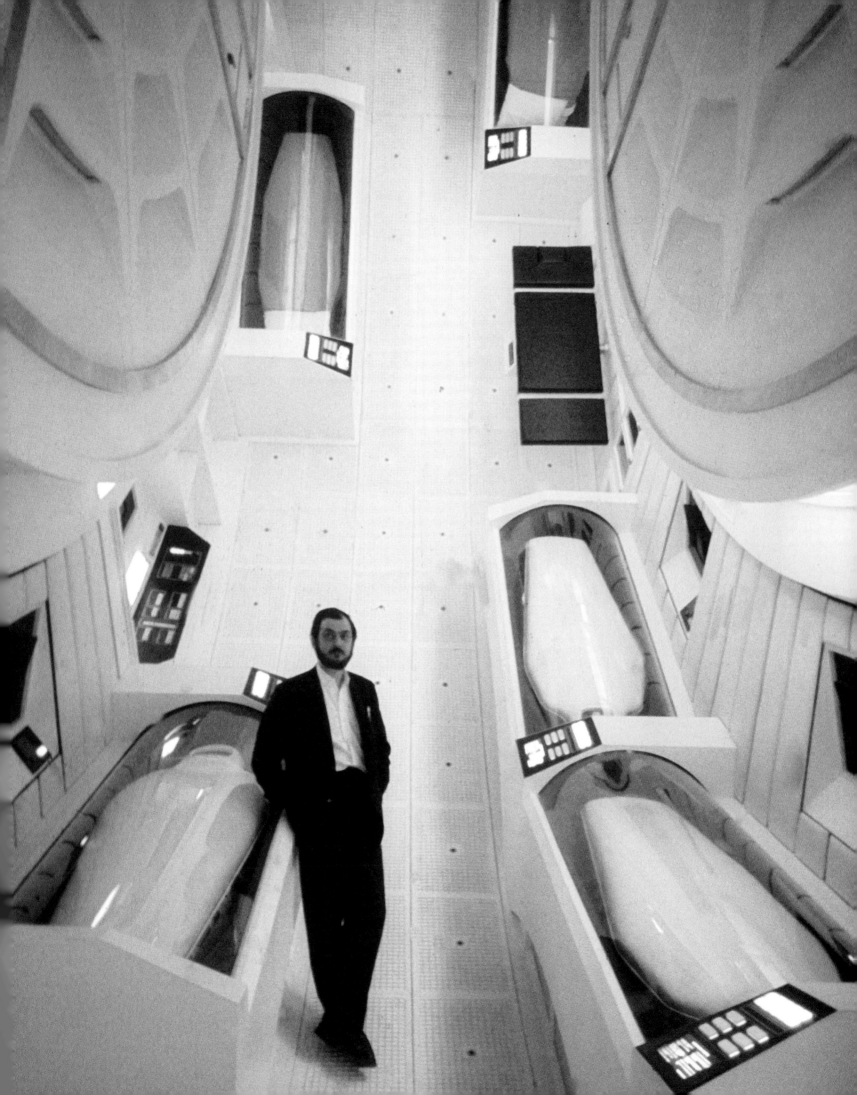

iterative process again. Lange was expert at producing these quick thumbnail sketches. As the key to this cycle, he liked to see himself, modestly, as 'a designer and craftsman' rather than any kind of artist. Maybe at a pinch a 'technological artist', but he was happier with 'craftsman':

'Design in space films, I always believe, is purely based on its purpose and its function, and out of that comes a design style of its own...'

'I think it is exciting to do it factual... I love to do research, to go back to knowledge and then project that into the future.'

'[I did not read design magazines for the latest ideas], because that wouldn't have done any good at all. Because then I would have been drifting and drifting. Pure design, or too much meaning to the design, forgetting the basic function—that you must not do; everything in that film had a purpose...'

When asked about the *functionalism* of the film's design, Kubrick expressed himself in a slightly different way:

'I think there were two problems with the design of anything. One was, is there anything about it that would be logically inconsistent with what people felt would actually exist; and the other one was, would it be interesting? Would it look nice?'

A third was whether it would fit into the story they were telling. Sometimes—as with the nuclear propulsion—looking 'nice' or at least acceptable took precedence.

So, I asked Frederick Ordway, what was the division of labour—where the design work was concerned—in the crucial period February/March to August 1965, when pre-production was still based in Kubrick's New York penthouse and the Polaris offices at 239 Central Park West:

'What I had to do was to work with all these companies, sixty-five of them in total, and work with individuals that would come out there to help us. "How would you talk to a computer?" We worked with IBM, General Electric, Honeywell—even to the extent of working with **Paris Match**. They did that cover in the film [on the counter of the security check—in **Space Station-5**]. I took advantage of my connections. I worked with RCA/Whirlpool on that kitchen and toilet, for example. I had to fly out to Benton Harbor, Michigan, where they were located. They were all very helpful. I flew all over the place during those months up to August. Here's a list:

I visited General Electric's Missile and Space Vehicle Division near Philadelphia—on **Discovery**'s propulsion method and spacecraft instruments; Bell Telephone Labs in Murray Hill, New Jersey—on deep-space communications; Whirlpool, the subsidiary of RCA, at Benton Harbor on food equipment and eating routines on **Orion-III** and **Aries-13**—I've mentioned them; Honeywell, Inc. in Minneapolis on instruments and vehicle controls—they even wrote a hundred-page report for us at my request, "A Prospectus for 2001 Interplanetary Flight"; and IBM in Armonk, New York—and its Eliot Noyes industrial design contractors in New Canaan, Connecticut—for all the computer sequences, the panels and consoles and displays and even the computer jargon. Harry worked with IBM as well, for some time. But while I was busy handling all of that part, Harry was doing a lot of the design work. Some of the design work was done by him alone. Some was done by the contractors. Some was done by us then built by the contractors. It was a mish-mash.'

How much latitude did Harry Lange have? After all, he was designing space vehicles, environments and spacesuits—from his own experience at NASA—with all these companies giving him advice as well. For the space vehicles alone, there were detailed consultations with Aero-Jet General Corporation, Boeing Aerospace Division, Douglas Aircraft Co., Flight Research Center NASA (Edwards), Goddard Space Flight Center, General Electric's Missile and Space Division, George C. Marshall Space Flight Center NASA (Huntsville), Grumman Aircraft Engineering Corp., Hawker Siddeley Dynamics (when production moved to Borehamwood), Jet Propulsion Lab at California Institute of Technology, Langley Research Center NASA (Hampton, Virginia), Manned Spacecraft Center NASA (Houston), NASA Headquarters (Washington DC) and North American Aviation Inc. That's fourteen major companies or research institutes alone, just for the vehicles...

'Yeah, I know. We would make a visit, or they would come, and Harry would adapt their advice to the requirements of the movie. And we visited many NASA and other space installations—Marshall, Langley, Grumman—taking a lot of photographs. It all just seemed to mesh together. And there was always a little tug-of-war between Harry and myself and Kubrick and Clarke developing things and over in Borehamwood Dick Frift the construction co-ordinator with his construction people, and the requirements of the special effects

*Opposite: Brochures of some of the many companies and businesses consulted during pre-production on **2001**: there were 300 files on 'product development' alone, including files from over 40 participating commercial companies.*

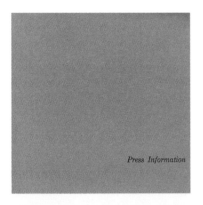

Press Information

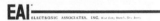

EAI ELECTRONIC ASSOCIATES, INC.

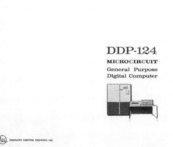

DDP-124
MICROCIRCUIT
General Purpose
Digital Computer

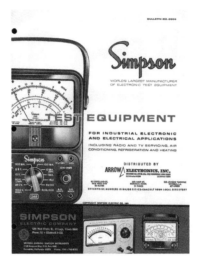

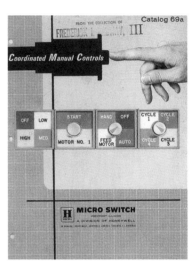

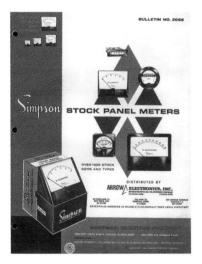

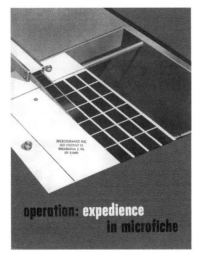

operation: expedience in microfiche

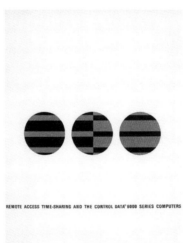

REMOTE ACCESS TIME-SHARING AND THE CONTROL DATA 6000 SERIES COMPUTERS

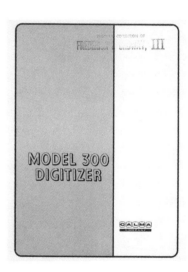

MODEL 300
DIGITIZER

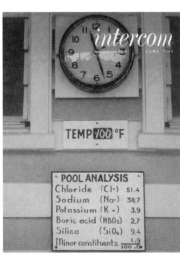

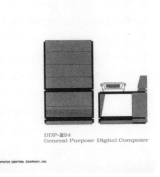

DDP-224
General Purpose Digital Computer

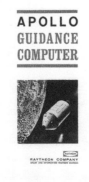

APOLLO
GUIDANCE
COMPUTER

RAYTHEON COMPANY

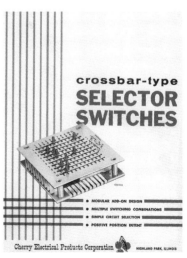

crossbar-type
SELECTOR
SWITCHES

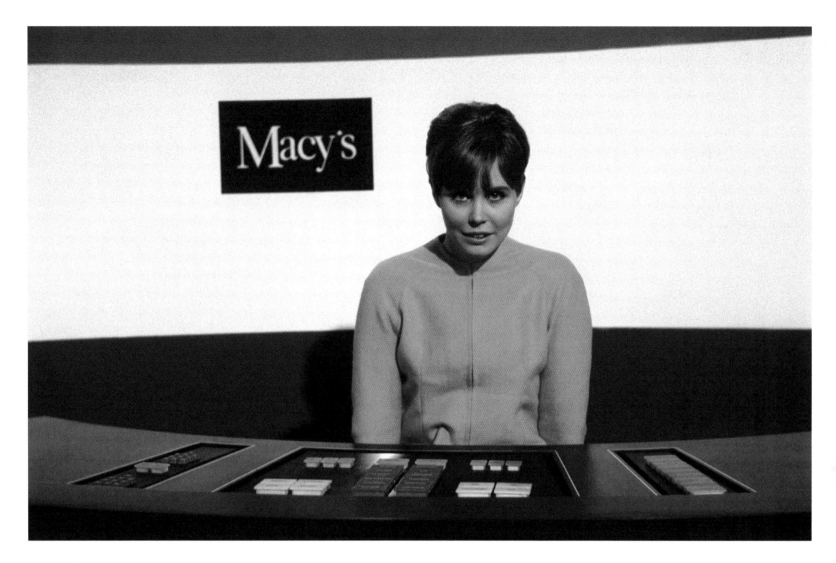

people. We all had to work back and forth. But we seemed to get things done. There were some things that Harry would do—almost exclusively—and we would build things in-house without contract help. And we also had a lot of contractors working with us over in England, helping with the physical construction of approved designs. We had the Air-Sea Rescue Division, Victoria Rubber Works of the Frankenstein Group of Manchester; M.V. Aviation of Maidenhead— they helped with the space helmets, from our designs. I even made a list of these, too. Hawker Siddeley Dynamics at Stevenage for the Space Pod interiors, Vickers-Armstrong Engineering Group for the Centrifuge... But, you see, the spacesuit and helmet design would come out of Harry—then he sent to industry to build them full size.'

In the second conversation he had with science essayist Jeremy Bernstein, for the **New Yorker** (published 12th November 1966), Stanley Kubrick said he had been 'very anxious that the spacesuits should look like the spacesuits of thirty-five years from now. After numerous consultations with Ordway and other NASA experts'— also, it should be added, with the Aerospace Medical Division, Air Force Base, Ohio; General Dynamics-Convair; and at the office

of Naval Research at the U.S. Embassy in London—he had finally settled on one of Harry Lange's designs and was examining various samples of cloth 'to find one that would look right and photograph well'. And while all *this* was going on around him, the article added, 'people were constantly dropping into the office with drawings, models, letters, cables, and various props...' to the point where Bernstein's 'head was beginning to swim'.

Then Kubrick asked if the science journalist would care for a 'little game' of chess... There was the strong emphasis on *plausibility* and *scientific verisimilitude*—very unusual, possibly unique, for a science-fiction feature film, certainly for one in the 1960s. An obsession with quality and detail. Ordway elaborates:

'Yeah, well, Kubrick told me "Fred"—one of the lessons he gave me—"Fred, let's take a look at the Hibernaculum. I don't know where I'm going to put my camera, but no matter where I put it I want it to make sense." So I had to deal with Ormond Mitchell of the New York University College of Medicine, some consultants on hibernation from California, and also the National Institute of Medical Research in Mill Hill, London—but Ormond Mitchell

Above & Opposite: Brand familiarity, to help present a plausible image of the near future: (above) there was to have been a sequence where Floyd buys a present for his daughter from Macy's online pet department over the videophone; (opposite) the Hilton at Space Station 5, with its bright red 'Djinn' chairs – originally designed in 1963.

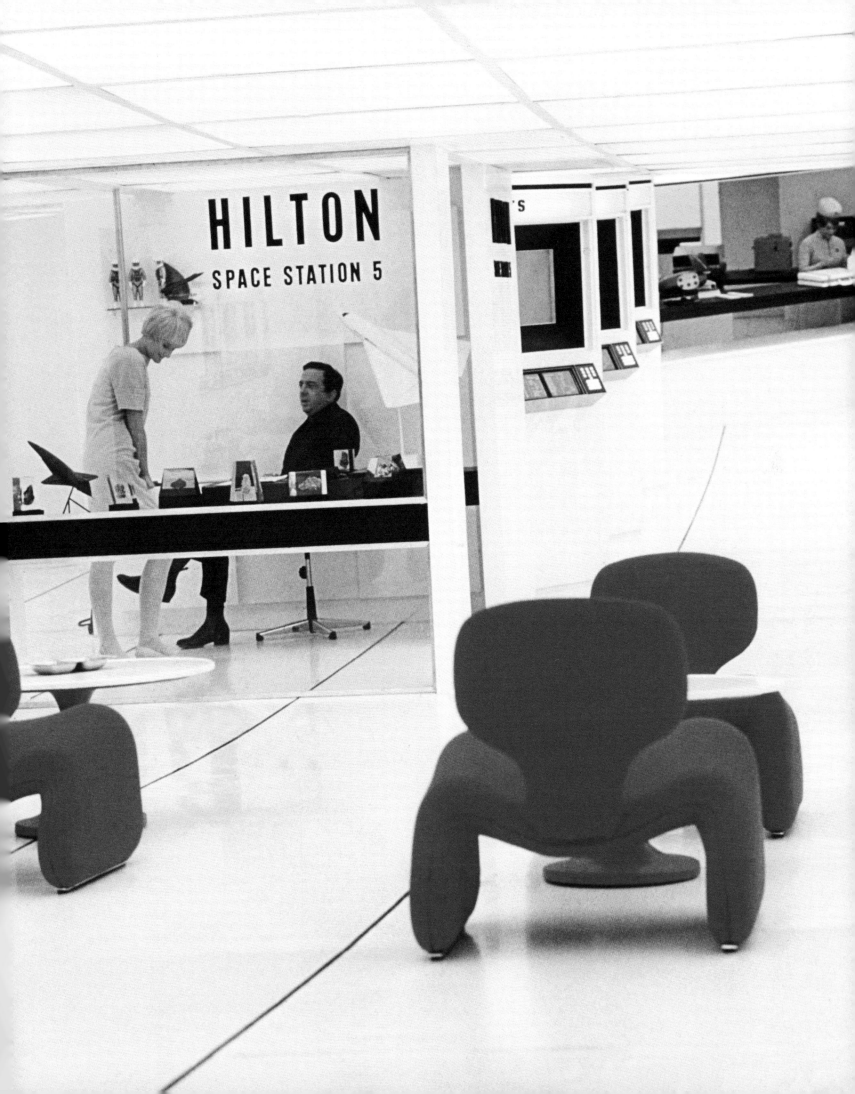

was the expert in hibernation, and he invited me over to his office and opened a fridge and all these little animals were in there, and he said that they were all hibernating off-season. "I can take any hibernator," he added, "and put him into hibernation, and I can take close species of natives of hibernation and put them into hibernation as well." And I said, "But could you put humans into hibernation?" and he said, "Well, maybe, if I had a big NASA contract and plenty of time. It's feasible." So anyway I said, "If you did put humans into hibernation, what would you be monitoring?" and he told me all the technical words for hibernation. All of these things had to make absolute sense. Because Kubrick said, "I want to know." And so we put these guys—the surveyors, the members of the survey team Whitehead, Hunter and Kaminski—into deep sleep. And most of it is not even in the movie...'

Ormond Mitchell actually published an academic article in 1972 on 'Human Hibernation and Space Travel', directly arising out of his work for **2001**. Apart from a brief explanation on a BBC 12 broadcast—and some glimpses of the closed mummy-case sleeping compartments—there is very little about the scientific background to Project Dormouse in the film. Kubrick had found the explanation too talky and too literal. Meanwhile, the team was growing fast, in the headquarters at Polaris Films in New York:

*'Well, we did all our preliminary work—Harry and I—and then the team began to join us and Tony Masters came over with John Hoesli his associate. That was in April 1965, about the time of the title change to **2001**. You've got to give Tony credit too, because as head of the art department—it all went through him—it was all put into [detailed pictorial] formats under his leadership, and he would get up a lot of things himself. Mainly interiors and passenger concepts and some props, while Harry was mainly vehicles and the space station and spacesuits. You see, Harry was working to Tony Masters, was a member of his team, but he had the ultimate design of the space elements—because he had the experience of working in that area. Harry came in as an advisor like me, but then Kubrick said—and he was right—"If Harry Lange is going to stay on this film, and we need to utilise him and his skills, we need to get him into the Union and so forth and get him a credit." Because Harry indicated that he wanted to stay in the industry and do other films, to stay in England, while I was going back to my regular career. So Harry got credit as "Production Designer" and I got credit as "Scientific Consultant".'*

Ordway was happy to be billed as the Principal Scientific Consultant; where Lange was concerned, Kubrick managed to persuade the Trades Union—not easy to do—on the grounds that by then he had served his time for two years.

Harry Lange had another consideration, where his career at NASA was concerned:

'I couldn't picture myself until the age of 65, still around just because I happened to be a permanent employee...'

Especially at a time of diminishing budgets, and later in the 1960s diminishing public interest. When he was working in Huntsville, there had been great excitement, and optimism, about the 'days of space':

'[You have to remember] everybody in America, half the world anyway, were in tears, it was so exciting. You wouldn't see a soul on the streets, every television was on. And the whole American economy came to a screeching halt when there was a launch. But it got less and less...'

Today, the involvement of the many companies and institutes would be seen as a fantastic opportunity for 'product placement' in the film itself. And they would pay large sums of money to feature their brands, products and logos. They would support the film financially—and even influence how their products were to be presented. But in 1965-6, it does not yet seem to have worked quite like that. The companies gave advice, or contributed 'future products' and in return their logo would appear, or they would agree to 'cross-plug' the film after its release. But not product placement in the modern sense, which did not begin in earnest until 1967. The logos which actually appear in the finished film include: Pan Am, Hilton Hotels, the Howard Johnson Earthlight Room, Bell Systems picture phones, American Express, IBM, Seabrook Farms and the BBC. In general, the nearer to Earth, the more prominent the logos, the more feet-on-the-ground the references. So how *did* the relationship with the companies work? Ordway explains:

'They gave us a lot of free services and expertise and data. IBM, for example, would send their guy—Neville Lockwell—I'd call and he'd be there two days later. I had good contacts with IBM. And other experts—so things were very, very accurate and up to date. And they agreed to help publicise the movie. I wouldn't necessarily have known about the money side of things.'

Sometimes, dealings with Frederick Ordway's contacts fed directly into discussions about the screenplay. After consulting with

Opposite: 'Design concepts... for thirty-five years from now': the attaché case computer developed with Honeywell; Velcro grip shoes for the Pan Am stewardess; a space-age watch from Hamilton Watch; pictorial in-flight food box from Seabrook Farms.

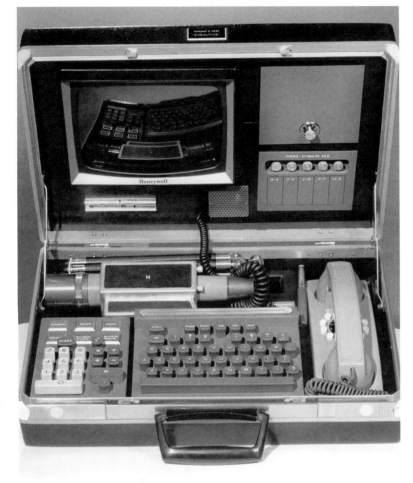

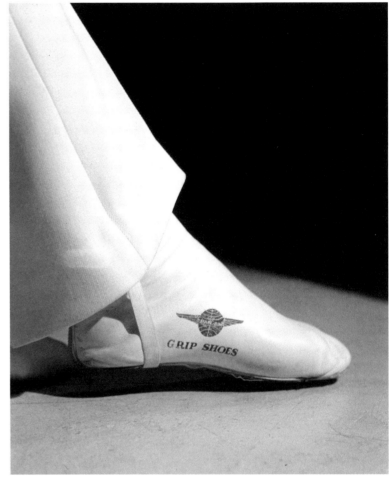

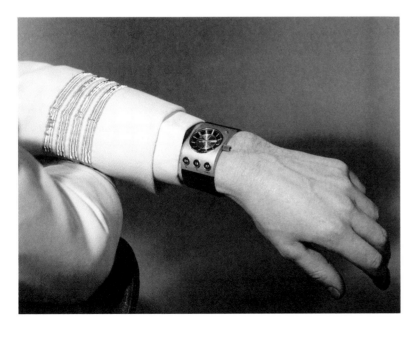

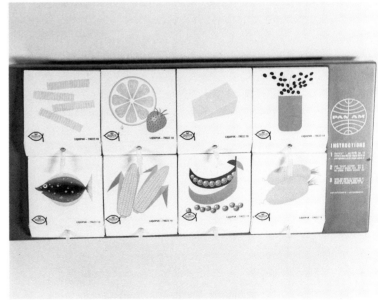

'...2001: A Space Odyssey will be a logical extension of today's rapidly developing techniques and technologies.'

the Geophysical Department of Schlumberger in Paris, for example, on 15th November 1965, Ordway suggested to Stanley Kubrick that it would be a good idea for **Discovery**, towards the end of her long journey, to do some serious research into asteroids ('new and known') using Schlumberger-type geophysical kit. Probes could be fired from the spaceship, to land on an asteroid. Or they could help with Jupiter V.

'Oh, I did a lot of that kind of advising. I was consulted by Kubrick on the screenplay and was his sounding-board as well. I gotta tell you about Schlumberger. I trained as a geophysicist at Harvard—there was no space programme yet when I was there—and my first jobs were in mining, where I met a lot of friends in Schlumberger. So when I was working on this film a few years later, I automatically had my contacts with them—and their specialists in sub-surface exploration work, applicable to the surface of the moon. And when I got to Paris, I immediately looked up my old pals at la Compagnie de Prospection Électrique Schlumberger. I brought them in to it, you see.'

Meanwhile, vice-president in charge of promotion Roger Caras was helping to liaise between Kubrick, the design team and over forty commercial companies, about new products, garments, gadgets and concepts—many yet to be launched, or at prototype/ discussion stage—which might or might not appear in the finished film. Some of these would be loaned, some specially commissioned, some the subject of 'design consultation', some entirely speculative. A significant number of the companies involved were concurrently exhibiting at the New York World's Fair in their own pavilions: they included General Electric (with its 'Carnival of Progress'), IBM, Bell Laboratories, Du Pont (for textiles), Eastman Kodak, Pepsi-Cola, Parker Pens and General Motors' Futurama featuring concept cars, one of which actually appears, briefly, in **2001** in a promotional film seen on Floyd's seatback screen aboard **Orion**. Also featured at the World's Fair was an animated space film in spherical 360° Cinerama called **To the Moon and Beyond** (1964), made by Graphic Films, to which the young Douglas Trumbull contributed visual ideas—in one of his first professional assignments. Trumbull first met special effects photography expert Con Pederson at Graphic Films; Pederson had worked at Huntsville, before joining Graphic. It was Pederson's and Trumbull's entrée into **2001**. Kubrick saw

To the Moon and Beyond at the Fair. World's Fairs were—then as now—often associated with meretricious design gimmicks such as monorails, jet packs, spotless automated kitchens, space taxis and doors that go 'whoosh' as they open. This one led to more substantial developments, at least where **2001** was concerned. The many links with companies were part of Kubrick's obsession with presenting a plausible image of the near future, down to the last everyday detail, one which would reassure the (Western) audience of the film's credentials through a kind of brand familiarity. Caras worked hard to keep all the interested parties on side. He wrote—from New York to Borehamwood—to Stanley Kubrick at the beginning of August 1965:

'I personally feel that I am doing everything humanly possible to wed an unconventional film, with an unconventional producer-director-writer, within the context of an unconventional industry, to the most conventional firms in the whole world. That ain't easy, and breakdowns are bound to occur. Believe me, you have a right to blow up at the pace these g.d. companies work. I feel like doing it, too.'

On 9th July 1965, he had written to Tony Masters at MGM Borehamwood, if anything understating the case:

'The problem of co-ordinating this now rather overwhelming list of companies is going to be a major one...'

This was in reply to Masters' request, on 29th June, for commercial advice on an assortment of props: an attaché case for Floyd, some wristwatches, pens and pencils; some shop windows and posters for the Space Stations—plus 'the medical and scientific equipment that might conceivably be used in the Centrifuge' and 'a special food box with sucking tubes as we discussed'. Also, 'some very modern and well-designed office equipment and conference room leather chairs, table etc.'

Caras replied that the magnesium attaché case—with portable computer—would probably be supplied by Honeywell, the wristwatches by Hamilton Watch, the pen by Parker Pen Company; the special straw-equipped pictorial food box and packaged food on **Aries** by Seabrook Farms—out of a kitchen unit supplied by RCA/Whirlpool—and Hewlett Packard and Bausch and Lomb had agreed 'to loan us the medical and scientific equipment'. Where the posters were concerned, 'Pan Am is in and doing our posters'. The

*Opposite: Bowman (Keir Dullea) eats a meal while watching his Newspad, aboard **Discovery**—a clear precursor of today's flatscreen tablet technology. (Below) Different versions, from Harry Lange's files, of the IBM logotype. In the finished film, IBM was only to be associated explicitly with the journey to the moon, "never with equipment failure".*

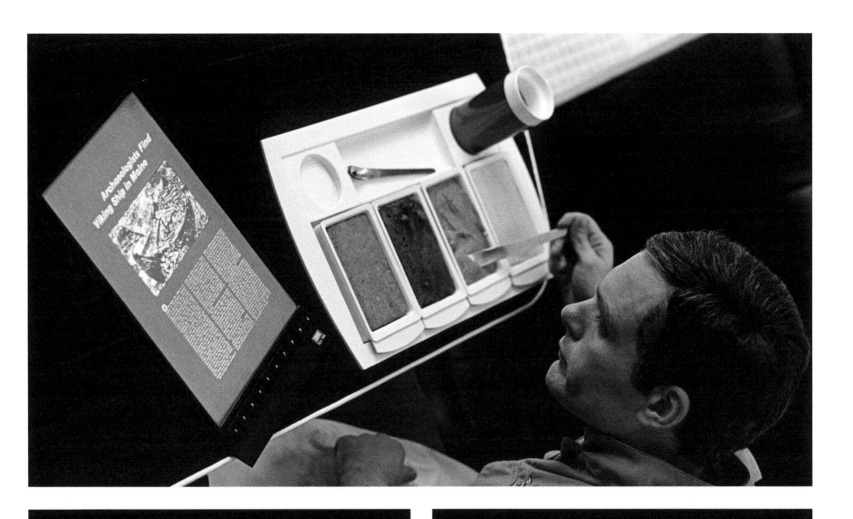

commercial connections were beginning to pay off.

No wonder Paul Sargent Clark in **Industrial Design** magazine of May 1968—which did not usually devote its columns to film design—was to conclude, when the film was released:

'*A Space Odyssey demands an unreasonably broad attention span on the part of nearly any audience, but I suspect that anyone who is interested in any aspect of design will find himself staring mesmerically at the screen long after the bulk of his blood has settled in his calves. The movie is filled with the most complexly detailed equipment ever put together for a theatrical purpose (much of it may, in fact, become part of our lives before long)...*'

The magazine had made an initial approach to Caras on 7th February 1966, because 'this project sounds as though it would be of great interest to our readers'. He had replied enthusiastically three days later, offering to supply photographs of 'the special products prepared by the design groups of a number of American and foreign industrial concerns'—when the time came:

'*These products are the design concepts of these companies for thirty-five years from now... There were over forty organisations all told who lent us assistance in the form of consultation and/or specific pieces of hardware. This hardware and this consultation were incorporated by art director Tony Masters and thirty-six members of his staff into the overall design of the film, which is truly extraordinary... The designs for our film are really quite wonderful. Very careful attention was given to the logical extension of contemporary design concepts and foreseeable breakthroughs in the future. By taking contemporary design concepts and guiding them through a logical evolution to the period thirty-five years hence, Tony Masters has been able to put together a world of design that is really breathtakingly beautiful in its utter simplicity and cleanliness. This clean beauty and uncluttered concept stands in brilliant contrast to the almost inconceivable complexity of the science and technology of the age. Clean white rooms with glowing panels instead of cumbersome lighting fixtures with color judiciously spaced to give an almost Mondrian effect, computers and electronics communications devices that stagger the imagination. The same extreme care and the same consultation with forty leading industrial and technical organisations went into the projection of the science of the future as went into the projection of the design of the future. I think that you will find 2001: A Space Odyssey offers some incredibly wonderful opportunities for design discussion...*'

Caras's initial approach to these commercial organisations, from late spring 1965 onwards, had been to put distance between Kubrick's film and any preconceptions the companies might harbour about 'science fiction'. He wrote, for example, on 3rd August 1965 to an NBC executive:

'***2001: A Space Odyssey** will be the world's first true science-fiction film. In Color and Cinerama, the film will operate without the assistance of Mickey Mouse, Buck Rogers, Russian spies, Jack Armstrong The All-American Boy [a radio and movie serial adventure hero], moths, butterflies and bumblebees destroying cities and raping Japanese women. In short, **2001: A Space Odyssey** will be a logical extension of today's rapidly developing techniques and technologies.*'

In return for 'hardware and advice', if used, the companies could expect to become part of a very extensive merchandising campaign, and maybe have their logos featured on screen. Caras wrote to the Ford Motor Company's Planning and Styling Department:

'*... we will show trade-name products in the film as they will appear thirty-six years from now. It serves the dramatic purpose of keeping the film from being too remote, the technology from being too difficult for the audience to relate to, and will provide the basis for co-operative merchandising at release time.*'

Some companies grabbed the opportunity with both hands. Caras wrote of Pan Am, for example, on 9th July 1965

'*... since Pan Am is in and is doing our posters [of future travel—featured on the Space Station walls], the Pan Am rocket, either the rocket that goes to the satellite station, or from there to the moon, will have to carry "Pan Am" in the style now used by Pan Am on their aircraft.*'

(The posters were to display new resort ideas such as 'Bahamas Underwater Hotel', 'Mount Everest Lodge' and 'Amazon Hovertel'. One of Clarke's original ideas had been to advertise 'Leopoldville—the Belgian Congo has been turned into the Las Vegas of Africa'). But Stanley Kubrick was worried about how much the company might expect in return. He wrote on 11th August:

'*Pan Am must not use the slogan "First in Space" or other obvious plugs like that.*'

The Pan Am logo appeared prominently on **Orion** and less prominently in **Aries**. Other companies agreed to help, but did not want any formal involvement in merchandising. After Fred Ordway had met the engineers at General Electric to discuss space vehicles

Opposite: 'The computer is hollow and surrounds the men who operate it': the walk-in concept of the 'IBM Athena Computer for 2001', by Eliot Noyes and Associates. Stanley Kubrick was not impressed by this. Harry Lange kept the Noyes Report in his files.

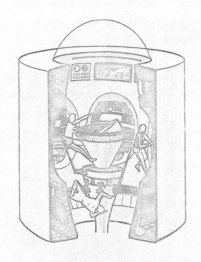

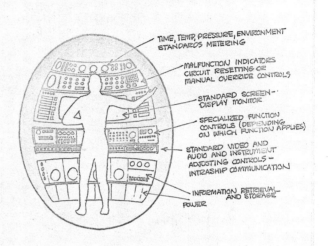

TIME, TEMP, PRESSURE, ENVIRONMENT STANDARDS METERING

MALFUNCTION INDICATORS CIRCUIT RESETTING OR MANUAL OVERRIDE CONTROLS

STANDARD SCREEN-DISPLAY MONITOR

SPECIALIZED FUNCTION CONTROLS (DEPENDING ON WHICH FUNCTION APPLIES)

STANDARD VIDEO AND AUDIO AND INSTRUMENT ADJUSTING CONTROLS – INTRASHIP COMMUNICATION

INFORMATION RETRIEVAL AND STORAGE

POWER

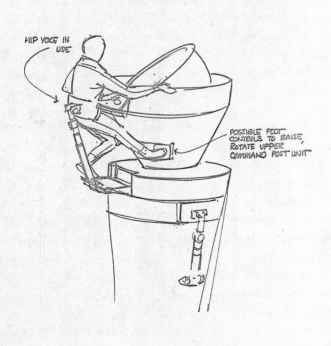

COMMAND POST

HIP YOKE IN USE

POSSIBLE FOOT CONTROLS TO RAISE, ROTATE UPPER COMMAND POST UNIT

ELIOT NOYES & ASSOCIATES – IBM MOVIE – 7-20-65

SEE FOLLOWING DWGS

IBM "ATHENA" COMPUTER FOR FILM: 2001

The overall dimension of this computer is twenty five feet high, exclusive of the observation blister (A-8) and twenty feet in diameter. The apparent large size of the device is deceiving because of the computer's base area of 314 square feet, 176 square feet of that area is work space for the Mission Commander and his crew. In other words, the computer is hollow and surrounds the men who operate it. This is a departure from the Earth and Moon based computers which are merely packages of components around which the men must move.

The Athena design offers the utmost in minimum traffic (movement of people) because it takes advantage of the little or zero gravity environment and the feasibility of "vertical" traffic movement, and because the layout of output devices is consistently circumferential. High efficiency is realized also in physically centralizing the command position to every other part of Athena.

While at his controls and the master monitor at the Command Post (A-5) the Mission Commander can see the entire interior of the computer and the on-duty crew. The Command Post rotates 360 degrees and when necessary can elevate itself hydraulically, lifting the Commander, still at his controls, into the observation blister.

Apart from the central Command Post, the interior of the computer is shaped somewhat like the inside of a very long egg, open at each end. The outboard end of the space is capped by the observation blister and its special shutter closure devices. Next to this, completely encircling the space for a depth of about five feet is a band of screen display monitors and monitoring instruments (A-1, 6, 7). The screen displays (A-6) can show closed circuit images of practically every area in the entire Discovery space ship that can be covered by miniature video cameras. They can also display an enlarged view of any meter, scope, or other control panel feature in any of the five work stations (A-9, 10, 11), as well as views of outer space required by the navigator and the commander. The display area is large enough so that engineering drawings stored in the computer's memory banks can be shown as well as the contents of all the books, movies, and other entertainment programs described in the story.

Adjoining the band of display equipment is a second "band", ten feet wide, a zone comprised of five oval areas that look as though the interior wall of the computer had been scooped out. Each "scoop" is a Work Station (A-9), and each Work Station is equipped for the particular crew member assigned to that Station. For example, the Navigation and Astronomy Officer's Work Station has several batteries of input-output devices linked directly to the navigational section of the computer's logic and memory cores. In addition to monitoring and evaluating maneuvering and course information, the Navigation

①

and matters arising, in June 1965 he suggested that Kubrick and Caras might also open negotiations with their Major Appliance Division—about such possible props as futuristic radios and televisions, kitchen equipment, coffee-makers and even toasters. In August, General Electric replied that the corporation did not wish officially to participate; however, they would be pleased to send material on their latest experimental products such as their 'show kitchen', complete with sound-wave dishwasher, fabrication of plastic dishes, microwave oven (an early version)—none of which were in fact used. But Ordway's meetings with the *engineers* had been much more fruitful. As he wrote, in the introduction to his retrospective 'Industrial Support Survey' of 4th July 1966:

*It is perhaps ironical that General Electric, who gave us such extremely valuable support in Space Station technology, lunar base design, **Discovery** instrumentation etc... will not co-operate on advertising.*

Aside from IBM, he added, from his point of view General Electric had been 'by far the most useful as compared to any other organisation, industrial or otherwise'.

The relationship with IBM had not run smoothly. On 27th July 1965, an agreement had been drawn up between Polaris and IBM which stated that in return for 'design consultation and hardware', 'Polaris will display the IBM trademark or logotype as prominently as possible on IBM-designed items on the Cinerama screen'. Together, the two companies would also explore the idea of using IBM's showroom—at release time—to present 'the world of 2001'. IBM had made a similar arrangement with Twentieth Century Fox and the producers of **Desk Set** (1957), a romantic comedy based on a Broadway play, starring Spencer Tracy as a time-and-motion specialist (or 'methods engineer') and Katharine Hepburn as the head of the research library at the 'Federal Broadcasting Network' in New York who feels threatened by the dawning age of the computer ('no machine can do our job'). IBM saw the advantages of being involved in **Desk Set** as selling the new idea of digital computers (known as 'mechanical brains') in settings beyond defence and government; calming anxieties about job security; and showing off their products—in this case their model IBM 407 with extra flashing lights and dials and 'more movement', explicitly contrasting it with typewriters, filing cabinets, papers and card indices. The IBM 407, first introduced in 1949, is there to liberate, not enslave, and is so friendly to users that it is known as 'Miss Emmy'. IBM's corporate logo was all over the credit titles, which acknowledged 'the co-operation and assistance of the International Business Machine Corporation'. The corporation not only provided the computer with its all-dancing additions, inspired by several of their computers but basically the IBM 407, they trained the actress who played the programmer to appear competent at her job. When **Desk Set** was released, their more recent model IBM 701 was placed on public display in the ground-floor lobby of IBM's headquarters at 57th

Street and Madison Avenue. The predictable punchline of the film was that Katharine Hepburn was not only converted to computers, she fell in love with the time-and-motion man. There was certainly a job of public persuasion to be done at this time. In the same year, 1957, the film **The Invisible Boy** presented a huge hangar-sized computer—complete with flashing lights and a see-through dome on top—as if it was a piece of science fantasy: 'Gentlemen, this is the *computer itself*.' And when Nigel Kneale first wrote **The Quatermass Experiment** for BBC television, computers were presented as incomprehensible pieces of the 'massive banks of apparatus' at the British Experimental Rocket Group. Kneale was not yet sure even how to *spell* the word 'computers', so in the published script there were references to 'computor-cards', 'the main computor banks', and 'the exposed computor-circuits'.

Where Stanley Kubrick's film was concerned, IBM would advise on 'the design and construction of computer panels and consoles... futuristic computer jargon and astronaut-computer interfaces... [and] on how computer-generated information would be displayed in the future'. The results would be featured on the space vehicles **Orion**, **Aries** and **Discovery**. The computer aboard **Discovery**, according to the treatment, had to be 'fantastically advanced—the brain of the ship'; it had 'a limited vocabulary of spoken words', but more usually interfaced through 'a rich-specification printer and visual display'. Its female voice 'led inevitably to its nickname—Athena, goddess of wisdom'. Eliot Noyes and Associates, IBM's assigned industrial designers, would be closely involved in visualizing this and all the computer sequences, and in designing the integrated control panels on the left arms of the astronauts' spacesuits. The 'glowing red eye' of the talking computer, the Cyclops eye, the forbidding stare, was Noyes's work, as was the concept for the 'Newspad'—precursor of today's e-readers. It has since been called 'Kubrick's Newspad': more correctly, it should be attributed to Eliot Noyes and Harry Lange, based on an idea by Arthur C. Clarke.

So Caras was optimistic about the relationship. Writing about the 'Newspad' and other devices, he commented that 'The "Buttonery" will be very crisp, very bright and very efficient—we feel this is one more good place to see the IBM name.' A crucial role for the corporation was to develop concepts for the female-voiced 'Athena' computer aboard **Discovery**—mother of the voice-activated HAL 9000—operated by Bowman (and Poole) from *inside the machine itself*. Eliot Noyes and Associates wrote a detailed report on this 'IBM Athena Computer for Film: 2001': it would be 'twenty-five feet high' and 'twenty feet in diameter'; 'the computer is hollow and surrounds the men who operate it—this is a departure from the Earth and Moon based computers which are merely packages of components around which the men must move'; the Mission Commander would sit at his Command Port, 'which rotates 360 degrees and when necessary can elevate itself hydraulically', and be able to 'see the entire interior of the computer', shaped like the inside of a very long egg, open at each end, with bands of screen display monitors and five oval work-stations; at the inbound end of the computer would be 'the logic and memory sections—most of the "guts" of the computer are micro-miniature solid state circuitry packages'; there would also be a video mounted monitor which can create 'in apparent three dimension a visualizing diagram of all the elements of any manoeuvring situation in which the Ship may be involved', 'as the Commander dictates into the recording log, the printed image of his words are instantly constructed on the screen':

'One might wonder how so many operations can be keyed on this console with so few pushbuttons and be monitored with so few indicator lights etc. However, many of the inputs to the computer are verbal…'

But Stanley Kubrick took strong exception to this design idea. He wrote to Caras on 29th July 1965:

'Dear Roger,

The IBM Athena drawings are useless and totally irrellevant [sic] to our needs and what I must presume were Fred's discussions with IBM, and most certainly irrellevant with my discussions with Fred.

I am extremely bored and depressed with all of this.

Please contact Fred, discuss this with him and assess the situation and write me a short, definite recommendation as to what your joint opinion is for further efforts with IBM.

I want detailed design concepts. But not crucial.

I want mostly equipment. I'll take the remote typewriter, or anything else they'd give.

I must have something definite soon and I do not want Fred to waste more time on further discussions with them which turn out to be a total and abysmal waste of time.

Fred should continue to work out his own concepts of the instrumentation and the computer inputs and outputs and control keying!!!

There is absolutely no time to waste. Even having to write this letter adds chips to what seems to me to be a completely lost hand.

I know this is not your fault or Fred's, and don't take this as criticism of yourselves. It is merely a total fuckup which not only fails to give what was hoped for but costs time.

ANNOYED AND DEPRESSED

BUT LOVINGLY

S.'

Caras replied on 2nd August:

'Dear Stan,

Your IBM missile exploded here this morning and I am happy to report that, although the concussion was resounding, no-one was killed by shrapnel.

Please do not feel it necessary to qualify criticism, or even an explosion, by saying it's not directed at me personally. I am well aware of that! My ego and sense of security is in better shape than that and I don't want you to feel self-conscious about blowing your top over something you feel has gone wrong. That, in part, is why I'm here.

I don't agree with you on the IBM situation but perhaps that's because I'm a little more up-to-date on what they are doing. Please allow me to qualify…

As recently as today they assured both Fred and myself that they are going to supply hardware; switches, toggles, face plates, output and input devices, mission console, etc. In their own methodical, logical way, they are breaking down these elements unit by unit and determining the cost for each. When they have all their cost figures in… they will determine how many of each they can supply within the budget they have allotted to this project and get back to you. In brief, we should know this week how much hardware will be forthcoming in the next few weeks.

I am sorry that their idea of working inside of a computer instead of around one, or across the face of one, was not pleasing to you. We thought it was a fairly good idea. Whether or not you go that route, Fred will have specific technical information about output and input devices. And you will have hardware…

Warmest personal regards,'

On 22nd September, Kubrick wrote another urgent letter to Caras, from Borehamwood to New York:

'We are badly in need of a mad computer expert who can be around and advise on dialogue and jargon to me in the computer scenes. It should be someone who has his eye on the future of computers, and not just a "stick-in-the-mud" type. Can IBM assign someone from England to serve as this part-time liaison?'

Then, on 26th October 1965—by which time 'Athena' was turning into 'HAL'—Ordway was asked to warn IBM at Armonk, New York, that in the latest version of the screenplay there would now be 'malfunctioning or unpredictable functioning' on **Discovery**'s main computer, but that it would be clearly labelled as an 'experimental research and development type'. It might be wise to consider shifting IBM's logo to **Orion** 'in the light of the changing screenplay'. By 1st February 1966, Caras was becoming concerned that the centrality of HAL to the third part of the story—as in some ways the most 'human' character aboard **Discovery**, albeit the bad guy—might jeopardise the hard-won partnership:

'As for the storyline, you heard from Fred Ordway some time ago that as the story developed there was equipment failure aboard one of the spacecraft and we took extreme caution to eliminate all IBM logos from any equipment involved in the failure. Categorically, IBM logos are only seen on equipment where there is no failure and where everything operates in a supremely professional way. The IBM logotype will never be associated in the film with failure of any kind… Seriously, we do understand that IBM has absolutely no obligation to supply anything in the way of merchandising assistance on this film until after they have seen it. Since, as I stated, the IBM logotype is only associated with successful equipment and since the film is shaping

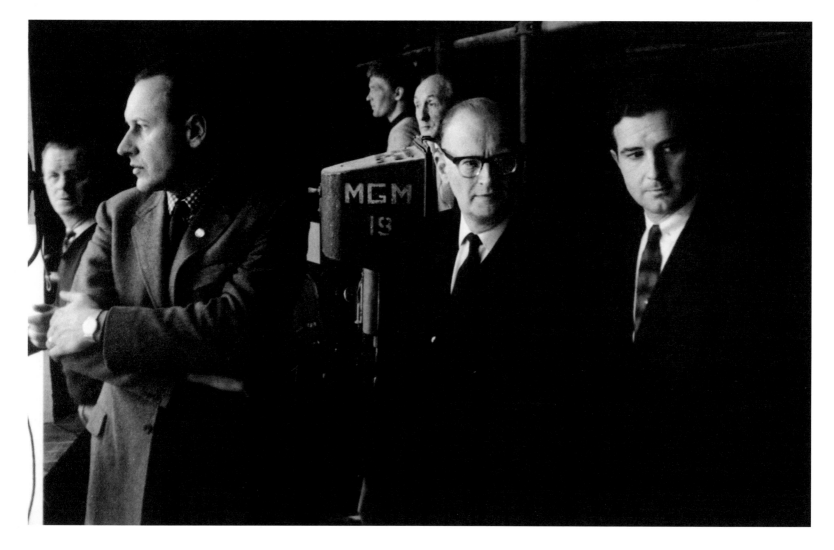

up to be a superb adventure into the future, I cannot imagine IBM walking away from us when the time comes...'

Fred Ordway confirms that IBM probably 'didn't know' how the screenplay was developing until autumn 1965, and that part of the problem was the way in which Kubrick and Clarke were working:

'I mean, when we started out I didn't have a full copy of the screenplay. I had the story treatment from Arthur which became a little bit out of date. A lot of the [resulting] detailed negotiations with the companies was by Roger Caras. That didn't come into my department. But I know that he was sometimes very frustrated...'

Harry Lange, meanwhile, had been working for some time with IBM on 'the big computer, what would a computer be capable of in the year 2001', and he too had to balance IBM's prediction about 'working inside of a computer'—a dynamic form of interaction, with the Commander at the centre of the machine—and Kubrick's more static notion of working 'across the face of one', which might be more shareable with the viewer:

'I worked with those people [IBM] for three months, at their

headquarters in New Jersey... And, oh, we got input from Honeywell, and various other companies, but IBM primarily... But actually we discovered that in the year 2001 computer science would probably have progressed even further than that [HAL], but it went to a point where if we had shown it that way we would have stepped over the edge of the plausible, you see... There was a certain amount known, but not much. I mean, we still had computers as large as this room... So the progress was unreal, but... you had to stay within the realm of possibilities, and I think it was successful.'

Microminiaturisation, mobility, distributed computation, integrated circuits and interactive design were not apparently thought by the team to be 'within the realm of possibilities'—not 'what people felt would actually exist'. So HAL became a descendant of (in cognitive science expert Donald A. Norman's words) the 'more-is-better, bigger-is-more-powerful school of technology that began in the 1940s' and went back to huge military computer systems. HAL looked like a mid-1960s mainframe. This was in fact a charitable interpretation of how it happened. But as with the propulsion

Above: An unusually informal shot of Harry Lange, Arthur C. Clarke and Frederick Ordway, caught unawares at MGM Borehamwood.
Opposite: Director and author: Stanley Kubrick and Arthur C. Clarke on a completed interior set for **2001**.

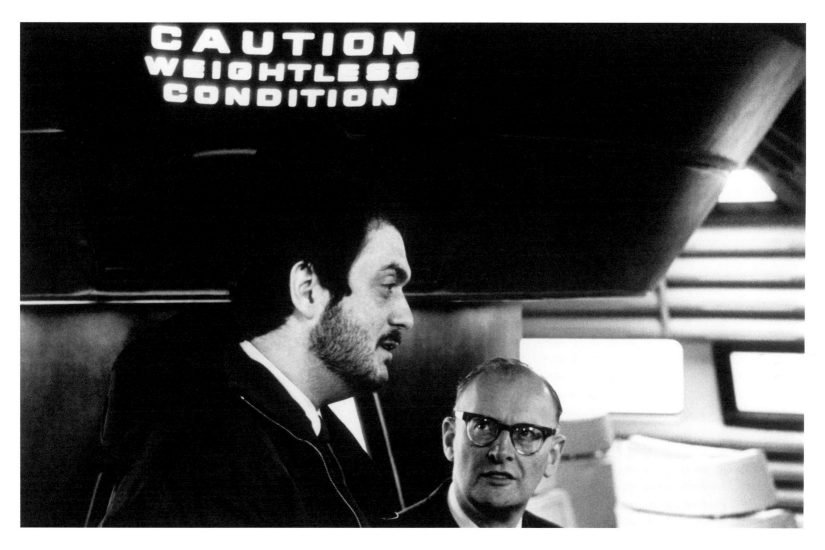

system of **Discovery**, the final design decision was inevitably about trying to balance the *look* on the screen—'would it look nice?'—with logical consistency and the latest research input. Lange continued with a favourite theme of his:

'I had seen so many computers, either down at Cape Canaveral, or in Texas, various illustrations, and there is a certain symmetry in their asymmetry, because they're purely functional, there is not one button that's not supposed to be there, nothing is arranged for beauty, it's just pure function. But there is a certain beauty in that, and that is what I was trying to establish as well, in the inside of the ships. But I've seen such incredible, horrible adaptations, in other films since then, it's incredible, you know, when people first think about it as some kind of design idea, that it certainly would not look like that, it would be totally confusing, the operator could not operate it...'

So, the computers had to *look* as though they functioned—with all that complicated 'buttonery' and the convincing-looking panels individually animated by Douglas Trumbull and colleagues, facing out towards the audience—but they also had to look 'beautiful', turning function into an aesthetic on the screen, a process that has since been called 'Project Modernism'. There was a kind of

optimism behind this process—HAL has cracked the problem of Artificial Intelligence, by January 12 1997, the date of his birth—even though it ends with the dread words 'Life Functions Terminated' and the offscreen deaths of three scientists. The equipment was to be stationary (unlike the mobile Command Post), with the astronauts or pilots doing all the movement. Eliot Noyes had suggested a more dynamic relationship between humans and machines. But as the script developed, HAL lost mobility and gained in intelligence. Even so, Bowman and Poole still took their notes about the malfunctioning AE 35 with pencil on paper attached to a clipboard...

By the beginning of July 1966, the relationship with IBM seemed to be back on track. Ordway was reporting that Hoesli and Lange were supervising 'the placement' of the corporation's logo on the central console in the **Orion** cockpit (which was similar in layout to the **Aries** equivalent, only with three screens); and Lange had been asked to arrange a medium shot to register the fact. Representatives from IBM came on set to offer advice. **Orion** it was to be—a far cry from the ambitions of the original agreement, but still a prominent logo.

At the end of August 1966, Stanley Kubrick was *still* anxious about whether IBM knew 'that one of the main themes of the story is a

'we'll have to play it by ear...'

psychotic computer': he wrote to Caras 'I don't want to get anyone in trouble and I don't want them to feel they have been swindled'. Caras replied on 13th September that, yes, he had 'explained to IBM at great length the change in the script as effects HAL' and that 'the name IBM is never associated with equipment failure .. but that is is (sic) obviously not an IBM machine'. He added, 'If IBM is not associated with equipment failure by name... they will not object to getting screen credit as long as their name is buried in a list with others'.

The fact that the letters HAL precede IBM in the alphabet was noted by some—and thought to be a hidden satirical reference to the corporation. Almost everyone involved in the film was at pains to point out that the letters—as in the novel—stood for Heuristically Programmed Algorithmic Computer. As Arthur C. Clarke was to write:

'... about once a week some character spots the fact that HAL is one letter ahead of IBM, and promptly assumes that Stanley and I were taking a crack at that estimable institution. As it happened, IBM had given us a great deal of help, so we were quite embarrassed by this, and would have changed the name had we spotted the coincidence. For coincidence it is, even if the odds are twenty-six cubed, or 17,576 to 1.'

And later, in exasperation:

'Sometimes you just can't win... For decades I too had been "trying to stamp out that story". I don't know when or how it originated, but believe me it's pure coincidence...'

Harry Lange begged to differ. He stated in interview that 'actually HAL are the letters before IBM. That's how that came about'. The letters HAL were placed just above the all-seeing eye—just as the letters IBM had been placed just above the centre screen on **Orion**. It was, he said, just a one letter shift. There has also been some debate about whether or not the song 'Daisy'—sung by HAL as his memory-units are extracted—was put in as a homage to Mrs Daisy Lange. Arthur C. Clarke said he chose it because he remembered an early 1960s recording of a computer singing 'Daisy' with the words slowed down...

The overall *look* of the space vehicles and most of the interiors in **2001**—'clinical, ultra-realistic, icily cool and sterile white'—has since been attributed by design commentators to Harry Lange. He always stressed that this was the result of function first, beauty as by-product: 'the eggshell white', for example, rather than the shiny steel of most science fiction films up to then, was there to reflect the sun and resist heat; 'all has a purpose', even 'colour and shape'. But, as he conceded, this look did involve choices about what would work best *on screen*, mixing 'with the requirements of that particular set', as well as responding to what the scientific and industrial specialists were saying and what audiences would accept.

Choices about what would *look* functional. At first the **Discovery** command module was to be given 'a metallic finish using grained silver adhesive paper'—mirroring the shiny look of **Destination Moon** and many of Chesley Bonestell's illustrations. But this was in the end superseded by an eggshell-white ceramic finish, with white padding around the walls; one of Lange's drawings shows the divisions between the ceramic panels; NASA was, as Piers Bizony points out, as a matter of fact by then using ceramic. Lange tended to sidestep questions about aesthetic choices and where they might have originated—stressing his background in NASA rather than film design—except, that is, when talking about the interior of **Space Station-5**:

'... the only thing we made look a little slicker was the space station interior; it's all white, with French furniture. That was the only time. But inside of the **Discovery** ship, there was still pretty much a World War I submarine, with pipes, and vents, and all this sort of thing—exactly what they look like today. But everything was designed not for beauty but for pure function. The only thing we used for cladding walls was a lot of padding... which in a way is very important because if your centrifugal force suddenly malfunctions, you'll be thrown all over the place... That was one of the reasons.'

Whether or not the **Discovery** resembles a 'World War I submarine'—Lange seems to have been making a point here about function and rational design rather than being literal—the interior of the lounge of **Space Station-5** was certainly stark white, relieved only by the bright-red jersey-upholstered 'Djinn' chairs designed by Olivier Mourgue in 1963, five years before **2001** was released, on which the Russian scientists sit. The 'Tulip Table' seen in the corridors was designed by Eero Saarinen, and the 'well-designed... conference room chairs' in wraparound fabric with metal legs for the curiously formal Clavius meeting room (no breakout spaces here) requested by Tony Masters came from furniture designer Geoffrey Harcourt. 'Latest' was not necessarily thought to be best. The stainless steel flatware (fork and spoon) used in the **Discovery** galley was created by the Danish designer Arne Jacobsen in 1957, not put into production until 1962. But sometimes latest *was* best. The velcro—attached to the soft grip shoes of the Pan Am stewardess (Edwina Carroll) on **Orion**—although patented in 1955, was not available for everyday garments until 1968. The 'replica hotel suite'—which became the controversial rococo Jupiter room—was originally to have been designed in partnership with Armstrong Cork, specialists in interior design materials (they proposed inflatable furniture disappearing through the floor), but was in the end largely created by Tony Masters, his most distinctive visual contribution to the film. Masters was the first to admit that he was not a specialist in space vehicles; he later acknowledged that 'Harry put the authenticity into it', and that when they were all working together as a team, they began to design within his visual idiom.

Stanley Kubrick was certainly not easy to please. In September 1965, for example, he wrote to Caras enquiring if 'anybody [was] building a camera that might be used on the Moon by an astronaut as a personal camera'. The submission from Eastman Kodak was in his view 'that silly-looking Kodak thing which at best could only be a home box-camera sort of thing'. The Nikon maquettes, made of wood, plastic and held together with yellow glue, were thought by Caras to be 'just as silly: not worthy of a ten-year-old boy... Mickey Mouse paste-ups'. Back to the drawing-board. Much thought was given to a 'game of the future' to be played by grown-ups, a successor to **Scrabble**, which the astronauts could play on **Discovery** either as a board-game or with the computer. One candidate was a game called **Universe**, being developed by Parker Brothers, involving geometric shapes and logical thinking. But Kubrick stuck to chess, his own personal obsession. Poole plays on-screen computer chess with HAL.

Sometimes, Caras was able—gently—to put even the meticulous Kubrick right on some detail or other. The director asked him, in autumn 1965, about the most appropriate American bank to validate Floyd's credit card at the Space Station. Should it be Riggs National Bank of Washington? Caras replied on 4th October: 'Why would he give a bank reference when shopping?... Could he not just put in his computerised American Express card and be billed through them? Even today, you do that in a somewhat modified form.' However, if Kubrick insisted... After which, the director duly requested a 'futuristic credit card'. American Express obliged, with a design that used fingerprint identification and CCTV. Dr Floyd would pay for his 'picture phone' call with this card, and would then purchase a bushbaby for his daughter from Macy's online pet department (a scene cut in post-production). The call's connection is made more quickly than even today's 'quick' international calls can manage.

When Caras was not fielding questions and complaints from his 'unconventional producer-director-writer', he was also letting companies know when their ideas would *not* be used. After the idea of a shopping plaza on the moon was dropped, so was a Pepsi-Cola vending machine of the future with a 'tetrahedron-shaped' bottle (an idea abandoned in October 1965); maybe this had originally been another subtle reminder of **Dr Strangelove** and its famous Coke dispenser. The General Mills 'generated protein supply' machine—creating artificial meat out of soya beans—was also dropped: Kubrick had hoped that General Mills would 'design something so that they can say that they did something and then let's take those designs and do whatever we want... this at least allows the basis for the ultimate cross-plug'. In the end, this was reduced to the briefest

of mentions of synthetic foods inside sandwiches, and how they are improving, aboard the moon bus. Detailed discussions about the zero gravity washroom aboard **Aries**, ended up with Floyd just reading the in-flight instructions. Caras also had to keep NASA—always a politically sensitive organisation—happy. On 1st July 1965, he reassured the Administration that the film would present 'NASA, and what is about to come as a result of NASA's efforts—in the best possible context'. It would help to promote space research, as Dr. von Braun hoped. Could a publicity campaign for **2001** be timed to tie in with the first Saturn-Apollo unmanned spacecraft test, scheduled for 22nd February 1966 ('we'll have to play it by ear'); or could NASA help with the voice of Ground Control, someone from Kennedy or Houston who was good at 'the almost liturgical drone that "towermen" use'?; why hadn't the large colour transparencies of Earth from Gemini been sent back to NASA—('it is *very* important that we get this straightened out'). When liaising with companies, Caras often made much of the 'two members of the staff from the George C. Marshall Space Flight Center in Huntsville, Alabama [who] spent two years on technical consultation'. They gave credibility to his claims about 'the world's first true science-fiction film': Harry Lange and Fred Ordway.

By the time they moved over to England—Lange in July, Ordway in August 1965—it seemed that much of the key design work had already been completed, give or take some changes of mind, or absorption of new research, because the models and set construction had to be, or were shortly to be, commissioned on the basis of it. A lot had happened since the meetings in May. Some of Lange's concepts and drawings were already being turned into highly-coloured pictorial formats—of hardware in action, sci-fi cover art style—by the illustrators Richard McKenna and Roy Carnon. So by July 1965, was the basic vehicle design already in an advanced stage?

*'That's right, exactly,' says Fred Ordway. 'We were in New York January, February, March, April, May, June, July. Meanwhile I was travelling like crazy on trips to the companies and universities. In New York, in June we would often be working far into the night. Stanley Kubrick, Arthur, Harry and I would typically break for dinner at Jager's German restaurant near Kubrick's penthouse. And the designs of the six main space vehicles came out of that work. They had to be designed very carefully, because we would later be dealing with full-scale interiors and reduced-scale models. And we were relying heavily on all the advice from NASA, and private companies and universities. What were the six vehicles? There was the **Orion-III** earth-to-orbit shuttle, **Space Station-5** in orbit around the earth, the **Aries-1B** earth-orbit-to-lunar surface shuttle, the **Rocket Bus** which was used to move men and materials on the*

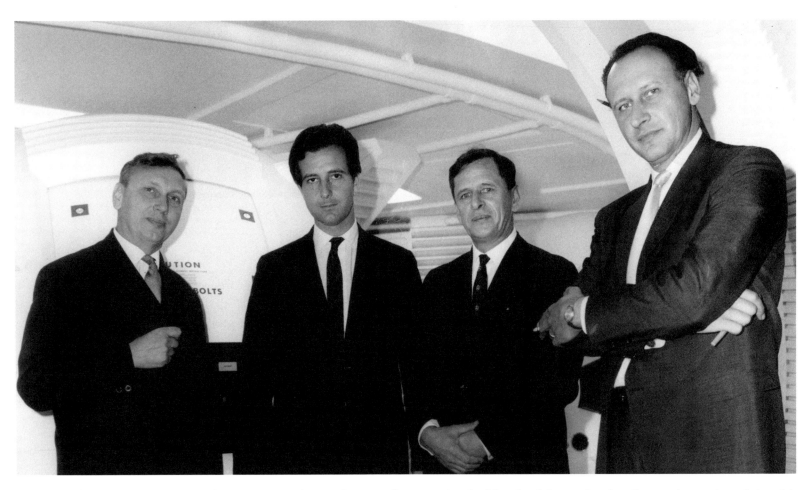

Moon, the large **Discovery** interplanetary spaceship and its small round **Space Pods** *for maintenance and local exploration. We had to know the purpose and function not just of each vehicle but of each assembly and component—right down to individual buttons and presentations on screens. And then I travelled over in August. Kubrick insisted we go by ship—he didn't want me to fly—and of course it made sense too with the twenty truckloads of material we had—all the reports, drawings and documents we were going to need. A big saloon car was waiting in Southampton on the 10th August 1965, courtesy of MGM. Harry and Daisy were already over there, and they helped us settle. And the following day, 11th August, I started work at Hawk Films Ltd.'*

The vehicles had gone through several versions and in some cases were to continue doing so until filming began in earnest. The pointed-nosed **Orion-III** space shuttle was originally to have taken off from an inclined ramp inspired by the early V1 rocket system. Once in flight, the main body of the shuttle would split off from its rocket boosters—as in Clarke's novel. In its definitive version, the **Orion**'s delta wing shape—and its passenger aircraft interior with in-flight TV viewing screen—would be strong visual reminders of its base on earth. The engine hump at the rear of the vehicle would become wider as this design developed. **Orion-III** has been called the 'closest to the here and now' of all Lange's vehicles in the film. The

massive double-wheel **Space Station-5**—rotating on its axis in orbit two hundred miles above the surface of the earth—was based on a concept by Wernher von Braun, famously illustrated over two pages in **Collier's** magazine on 22nd March 1952 by Chesley Bonestell. This illustration was to become, according to Howard E. McCurdy, 'one of the most reproduced works of twentieth-century space art'. Its use as a way-station in the film showed that Kubrick had 'one foot planted in the 1950s, his other foot in the early twenty-first century', in the words of Dan Goldin of NASA. Even in 1965-6, the latest researches suggested that the moon would be reached direct by a small lunar landing craft attached to a mother-ship. On Harry Lange's drawing board, the **Space Station** was originally a collection of units on stalks, then a single Catherine wheel, then a double wheel, then a double wheel partly under construction. The orbital hotel and office complex inside the station were intended, according to Tony Masters, to have 'the look and function of modern airports': in the production notes, the complex included reception area, medical examination room, Immigration and Customs, shops, bank, travel agency and 'a small chic restaurant and bars'. It also included an 'automatic dispenser' which produced a compressed 'space suit'—creaseless and custom-tailored—for Floyd. The spherical **Aries-1B**, complete with shock-absorbers and compressed jets, tapering towards the drive unit, like many of Lange's designs looked both

Above: A visit to the 'Pod Bay' set by the Soviet Science Attaché from the London embassy, and colleague, with Frederick Ordway (second from left) and Harry Lange (right). Opposite: Harry Lange's droll notes on the back of the photo opposite.

2 Russian Diplomats visited us at Studio. On the set of the Pod Bay the one on the left said:
"Se lettterring on Sis Wehigle would not be in Englis in 2001., but in RUSSIAN."
— pause —
Daisy was also there and she said:
No, not in russian, but in chinese "

high-tech and anthropomorphic at the same time—in this case, it resembled an amoeba. It began life as a rectangular vehicle, before going spherical. As it landed, the cockpit lights and window-slit made it seem like a face. The production notes refer to 'retro rocket effect', and exhaust flares from the rocket engine—but these proved too difficult to achieve. The **Clavius** moon base, a half-mile-wide city, was loosely based on 1965-6 speculations about where the Apollo missions might eventually lead: from small temporary lunar bases to a large colony there. Lange's design laid out the base on a strict geometrical grid pattern, like a circular version of ancient Rome, as if planned from scratch all at the same time, with a series of landing strips. The landing pad in the film is rectangular and black.

The wheel-less rocket bus, for crater-hopping, was partly based on a 1965 NASA MOLAB vehicle (Mobile Laboratory), designed in partnership with General Motors. It also harked back to the kinds of small vehicle driven very fast by Buck Rogers and Flash Gordon in 1930s Hollywood serials. According to Ordway, the rocket bus concept had distant origins in 'a project called **Project Horizon**. Harry used that as a take-off for that, because he was looking forward. The Army was preparing **Project Horizon**, to get the high ground where we would establish a nuclear rocket programme. If the Russians attacked us, we'd retaliate. It came from way back in Army Ballistic days.' In some of Lange's drawings, the bus has wheels or extendable wheels and large shock absorbers: one of his bus drawings, annotated by Kubrick, is dated 7th April 1965.

But it was the **Discovery** vehicle, designed to travel four thousand times further than the distance from the earth to the moon, which created the most problems for Harry Lange. It started life as a soup bowl or saucer or bell or inverted bell shape, sometimes with the pods attached to a rail on the exterior: Kubrick was keen to get as far away as possible from the cigar-shaped rockets, with fins on their backs, featured in such films as **Destination Moon** and **When Worlds Collide**; he knew that a single-stage V2 in the real world had a maximum vertical range of a hundred miles. **Destination Moon** had tried to sidestep this little problem by adding 'atomic power' to the rocket. Kubrick also knew, from his viewing of earlier science-fiction films, that rocket design in the movies tended to be strongly influenced by wider cultural fashions and vice versa: from submarines in the early days, to tubby art deco fish-ships in **Flash Gordon**, to the V2 just after the Second World War—with its fins transposed to 1950s cars. He was particularly exercised by how the vehicle might be propelled: what would be a viable power source for a mission to Jupiter and beyond?

Arthur C. Clarke was to recall, in 1972:

*'Like everything else in **2001**, the good ship **Discovery** passed through many transformations before it reached its final shape. Obviously, it could not be a conventional, chemically propelled vehicle, and there was little doubt that it would have to be nuclear-powered for the mission we envisaged. But how should the power be applied...?*

There were several alternatives—electric thrusters using charged particles (the ion drive); jets of extremely hot gas (plasma) controlled by magnetic fields; or streams of hydrogen expanding through nozzles after they had been heated in a nuclear reactor. All these ideas have been tested on the ground, or in actual spaceflight; all are known to work.'

On 16th September 1965, shortly after the move to MGM Borehamwood, Stanley Kubrick was still writing to Fred Ordway about these basics:

'Dear Fred,

*Could you please work out a brief, concise explanation of the propulsion system and general operating features of **Discovery**? This will be used for Bowman explaining to a Television Interviewer something about the ship. I am also still awaiting your rough breakdown of acceleration; distance travelled; velocity, and whatever perimeters might be interesting for the basic phases of the mission:- First day, first week, middle of the mission, deceleration etc.'*

Then on 26th October, Clarke had his discussion with Stanley Kubrick about the idea that **Discovery** should be nuclear-pulse-driven—the discussion which 'rather upset' the design staff. It meant that the rear end of **Discovery**, parts of its spine and its fuel containers would have to be completely redesigned, 'to the great alarm... of the Art Department'. The report on Project Orion had, apparently, been sent to Kubrick by 'scientists indignant about the demise of [their research] project'. Ordway adds: 'Yes, that was one concept, that's true—a serious idea at the time put out by [physicist] Freeman Dyson.' The basic idea was that the ship would carry a lot of nuclear bombs and throw them out one at a time 'putt-putting away from Earth'. So Harry Lange produced several design studies which had to include heavy-duty shock-absorbers and heat panels to protect the main ship from the nuclear explosion. Then, as Clarke observed:

*'... recalling the finale of **Dr Strangelove**—it might seem to a good many people that [Kubrick] had started to live up to his own title and had really learned to love the Bomb. So he dropped Orion, and the only trace of it that survives in both movie and novel is the name.'*

Kubrick decided to stay with 'Cavradyne' gaseous-core nuclear reactor engines at the rear of **Discovery**—three huge hexagonal propulsion units, each with two exhaust nozzles, with hundreds of feet of tankage separating them from the spherical command centre. Lange continued to feature large cooling panels drawn from various angles until these, too, were ditched because they were thought to look too much like wings. So the dispersal of excess heat, of which Clarke had made much in the novel, ceased to feature in the vehicle's design.

As Clarke remembered:

*'The final decision was made on the basis of aesthetics rather than technology; we wanted **Discovery** to look strange yet plausible,*

*futuristic but not fantastic. Eventually we settled on the plasma drives, though I must confess that there was a little cheating. Any nuclear-powered vehicle must have large radiating surfaces to get rid of the excess heat generated by the reactors—but this would make **Discovery** look somewhat odd. Our audiences already had enough to puzzle about; we didn't want them to spend half the picture wondering why spaceships should have wings. So the radiators came off.'*

Harry Lange added:

'I've seen pulse engines for real, and there is a certain practical design of these things which is absolutely beautiful. But you cannot just pick out of the sky and put down on paper... you try to mix it with the requirements of that particular set, and that's how it goes.'

As to the overall shape of the fuselage of the 510-foot-long **Discovery**, it began as a soup bowl and morphed into a 'dragonfly' with heat shields (again matching Clarke's description); interestingly, H.G. Wells had referred to the fearsome German flying machines in **War in the Air** (1908) as 'dragonflies', at the dawn of air travel. The accommodation—or life-support—blocks were at first separated, then integrated. Then Lange settled on a long, thin skeleton-like structure with nuclear tail, spherical head (for navigation and recreation) and hundreds of feet of tanks and storage compartments in between. He spent a lot of design time on the AE 35 communication dishes. Those hundreds of feet also protected the crew from the nuclear propulsion which moved their ship towards Jupiter. **Discovery** has since been likened to 'a dinosaur skeleton' and 'an awkward structure resembling a fish skeleton'. Partly, the concept was based on research. Ordway recalls:

*'We had previously been working on a joint Marshall Space Flight Center-General Electric payloads requirements study for the planned Saturn 5-N (for Nuclear) type vehicles designed for Mars missions. Those studies called for the incorporation of a nuclear third-stage designated S-NB... Studies in 1964-5 showed that by clustering nuclear stages of modules in orbit, it would be possible to achieve manned orbiting, and possibly landing, flights within the next fifteen years... In developing our design concept for **Discovery**, we used many available published reports and gradually evolved the vehicle which appears in the film.'*

Partly, again, the concept was also based on what the public might be expected to accept. And partly on Lange's combination of designs which *looked* authentic and at the same time resembled mechanical creatures. His small, white, round one-man space pods for inspection and repair work may have looked 'technical'— with their grooved radiators, remote control cameras, gas jets and handholds—and they too went through various phases including square and rectangular versions with see-through spaces on their prows, one seat or two seats, but finally with their robotic

Opposite: Memoranda from Stanley Kubrick to Harry Lange about the model-making schedule, and the question of overtime.

MEMORANDUM

TO Harry Lange   DATE June 12

Please give me your
projected schedule for
detailing the remaining
models — after checking
Terry tinsmith on date
he expects Astrodome to
be ready.

Thanks.

No 201510   FROM Stanley

MEMORANDUM

TO Harry Lange   DATE June 13

In view of problem of chance of
running out of work,
please make certain
no overtime is worked
during this period.

No 201531   FROM S.K

19

Harry Lange June 15

Please give me a
revised model
completion schedule — and
Confirm no overtime
is being worked now —

Thanks

S.K

044350   REF. LIN/654/3   PRINTED IN ENGLAND

31st July, 1967.

To: Harry Lange

I notice in your last
schedule you expect to
receive the small Landing
Pad from Wally on July
31st, and that you will
complete the Large Pad
by July 28th. How
accurate is this at this
time?

Thanks.

Stanley

manipulator grab-arms with claws and round shells they came strongly to resemble crabs; crabs which came to life within the crevices of the mother-ship. The arms were relocated during the later design process, and headlights were added for dramatic effect. To start with, they had stubby fingers with spikes, then claws. The production notes specified that these extendable arms would have to be 'moveable in their 2-directional joints by means of a small motor'. The interiors of the pods were womblike, or maybe like some of the wackier designer-chairs of the period. Space probes were also designed, for the final sequences, but never used.

Even when the technical specifications had been agreed—and the final design signed off—Stanley Kubrick could sometimes have second, or fourth, or eighth thoughts. On 10th November 1965, Clarke noted in his log, he was taken by Kubrick to view the set of the **Orion** flight deck, on the stage at Borehamwood—with dials and knobs and displays painstakingly dressed by Lange and Ordway:

'Accompanied Stan and the design staff into the Earth-orbit ship and happened to remark that the cockpit looked like a Chinese restaurant. Stan said that killed it instantly for him and called for revisions. Must keep away from the Art Department for a few days.'

So, until quite late in the day, Harry Lange was still adapting his space vehicles and spacesuits, and Frederick Ordway was still liaising with all those industries and organisations—while Arthur C. Clarke had not yet finished the last third of his novelised story, and Stanley Kubrick was still developing the screenplay based on it. Ordway continues:

'That's the other strange part of this whole thing: and of the arrangement we'd made... Think of this: here we've got a movie to be made by a world-famous director and a world-famous science-fiction author and we are starting things while the screenplay is being written. And the screenplay was being written while the novel was being written. And so there was always a lot of give and take between Stanley and Arthur—as the novel was being written up, on the basis of which the screenplay would be co-written, and then Arthur's book was not to come out until after the film was released, which is quite the opposite of the usual way. As you know, usually you write the book, it comes out, and the film is based on the book.'

Even at the time of Ordway's move from New York to Borehamwood, the novel, and the screenplay—especially the HAL sequences and the Stargate section—had not settled. How did he manage to liaise, and produce definitive designs, when things were still in such a state of flux?

'I know. That's what we were working with. It was very, very difficult. That's why it took as long as it did. And why we worked very long hours. Even the black monolith or whatever you call it, we spent fifty thousand dollars and Kubrick said, "No. I don't like it." It was difficult. Here we were working, and of course I knew MGM was fussing about the budget going up and up, already at the time of the move, but it all somehow happened. I did all I could. He was

the boss. And I know that there was a lot of back and forth between Arthur and Kubrick on the screenplay, and there were elements and sidelines—can we do this and can we do that?—changing subplots— the ending. They all had technical consequences. And of course the special effects people got into this quite a bit too. And Dick Frift of construction. You can't just keep changing around when you've booked a studio and you have a contract out for construction. You can't just change things around all the time.'

In August 1965—the same month as Frederick Ordway—Arthur C. Clarke had arrived at MGM Borehamwood from his home in Ceylon. He was immediately struck by the sheer *scale* of the operation:

'His [Stanley Kubrick's] empire had now expanded vastly, the art department was in full swing, and impressive sets were being constructed. My time was now divided between the apparently never-ending chore of developing ideas with Stanley, polishing the novel, and almost daily consultations at the studio.'

Ordway, meanwhile, was—from 11th August onwards—coping with the 'possible mismatches between what Kubrick had in mind for the picture, what Clarke was wishing, and equipment and vehicular realities emerging from Tony Masters, Harry Lange and other designers in the Art Department and construction supervisor Dick Frift and his team.' There were, he recalls, 'innumerable sessions' at the studio about 'the changing subplots of Clarke's evolving screenplay' and their practical consequences:

'Could our vehicular designs and stage geometry accommodate them without major revisions to what had been accomplished in New York and what was emerging from the drafting boards in Britain?'

Where interior and exterior sets were concerned, the design concepts created in New York were already being translated into 'hard engineering drawings' for the construction crew; and the models were being made. Plus there were the 'various hardware contractors in and around London, Birmingham, Manchester and elsewhere'. So changes to the screenplay now had immediate repercussions. Part of Ordway's role was also to 'co-ordinate the physical construction of approved designs' and make them look as plausible as could be. He and Harry Lange supervised the placing of information plaques, screens and switches, as the production notes had anticipated: *'We had to set up all the instrumentation we'd brought in—to position things all around the set. It was very exciting.'* Some special effects filming had begun, with Kubrick directing from New York—some of the 'Star Gate special effects', according to Clarke, were in a screenable state by 4th February 1966—but most of it began in earnest after much of the live action had been completed in August 1966.

On 5th September 1965, over dinner at the fashionable White Elephant Club in Curzon Street, Mayfair, Stanley Kubrick suddenly turned to Frederick Ordway and asked him how he would react to the radical idea of 'substituting Saturn for Jupiter on the target of the spaceship **Discovery**'. Ordway replied that it might be 'a bit late' to make such a change to the screenplay.

'He persisted, pointing out the beauty of the Saturnian ring system and the spectacular visual effect of the **Discovery**'s travelling near or even through it. Would I do some investigation and prepare a memo outlining that latest knowledge of Saturn, its rings, and its moons, he asked? And would I focus on anything that seemed out of the ordinary...?'

Clarke was to recall of this spectacular change of direction:

'We... wavered uncertainly between Jupiter and Saturn as **Discovery**'s target planet. In the novel, we greedily chose both, using the "slingshot effect" of Jupiter's gravitational field to boost the spaceship on to Saturn... Stanley and his special effects team spent a great deal of time working on Saturn before it was decided to stick to Jupiter... [The] more accurately we reproduced this extraordinary world, the less believable it seemed.'

He was 'rather sorry', he said, that the Saturn idea had to be abandoned in the film.

What actually happened was that Ordway prepared a detailed memo, 'Kubrick was delighted', and everyone *seemed* happy. But, as Ordway continues:

'All except Wally Veevers, Doug Trumbull and others in the Special Effects Department. Despite their wizardry, they felt uncomfortable with the thought of having to accommodate the **Discovery**'s moving within the Saturnian ring system. On top of all their problems, they were not in the mood to tackle a new one that might prove intractable. They just dug their heels in—said they couldn't handle it, that it would be just too much. You've got to remember that time was going by. And we knew that MGM was stressing. And Special Effects won the day...'

Three weeks later, Dr George Mueller, director of NASA's Office of Manned Space Flight, and 'Deke' Slayton, astronaut, were given a conducted tour of the sets, including a look at the models, and according to Clarke 'George made several useful suggestions and asked wistfully if he could have the model of **Discovery** for his office when we had finished with it'. Apart from anything else, his office at NASA rather resembled Ordway's and Lange's on the lot, as Ordway recalls:

'When Mueller looked at our office and saw the amount of documentation Lange and I had brought over with us from the States, he dubbed our office complex "NASA East"!'

Much later, there would be a visit from the Soviet science attaché at the London Embassy, Boris Polikarpov and colleague, who apparently took a close look at the technical instructions displayed in **Discovery**'s cockpit, and observed 'that they should all be in Russian!' (Daisy Lange added later that maybe they should be in Chinese.) Frederick Ordway had been liaising with Polikarpov for some time:

'You see, we needed their lunar photographs, which we didn't have. They were ahead of us on that... I had to check with the local FBI officer there, because I was an Air Force Reserve officer and stayed in the Air Force Reserve for a big chunk of my life. Just out of courtesy, I wanted to make sure. And the people I dealt with at the Embassy, I checked with them and they actually put me in touch with my counterparts over there. We'd have lunch sometimes. They never once asked me an inappropriate question.'

On the issue of 'national security', it has been claimed that some of Harry Lange's drawings for the film had to be submitted for security clearance by NASA because they were based on classified information and were so very accurate. This was still a very sensitive issue in the Cold War:

'Well, that was the situation. Because he was on leave from NASA, so to speak, like I was. I mean, he was fully expected to return as I did. But that was always a little issue. I don't know how they finally resolved that. Let me go back a little bit. The vessels that we were dealing with—the **Redstone**, the **Juno 1**—the first American satellite was on a ballistic missile. So that was classified, the first stage; other stages with the instrumentation—probably not. And then there were the **Jupiter** vessels. There was this big thing going on between the Air Force and the Army. You know what happened to that **Jupiter** vessel? This is something that people don't want to talk about, even now. It was all secret. Those **Jupiters** were placed on the underbelly of the Soviet Union... So we started the missile crisis. And Russia responded by putting their missiles in our underbelly, with their allies Cuba... I didn't have to deal with the issue of classified or not-classified, but Harry might well have because of his designs. Everything I got from NASA I got with their permission and their full support.'

On 4th October, Kubrick at last prepared to issue a press release: 'ORDWAY AND LANGE JOIN STANLEY KUBRICK IN LONDON'. He had been working closely with the two men for nearly ten months but, with filming set to begin in November, this seemed the strategic moment. The draft release was amended by Ordway:

'Frederick I. Ordway, III and Harry H-K Lange, formerly with the Army Ballistic Missile Agency and NASA's George C. Marshall Space Flight Center and now with the General Astronautics Research Corp. of Huntsville, Alabama, have arrived in London to provide consulting and design services for the Stanley Kubrick/Metro-Goldwyn-Mayer/Cinerama space exploration film **2001: A Space Odyssey**...

To ensure the scientific and technical accuracy of the motion picture, Kubrick has worked in close co-operation with many elements of NASA and with leading American and British industrial, research and academic organizations from the film's inception. Ordway is responsible for much of the required liaison with these diverse organizations and for ensuring plausibility in the extensive space sequences which require many of the world's foremost special effects experts. Lange is a member of a design team responsible for both the interiors and exteriors of the space vehicles appearing throughout the film as well as a wide variety of space-age accessories. Experts

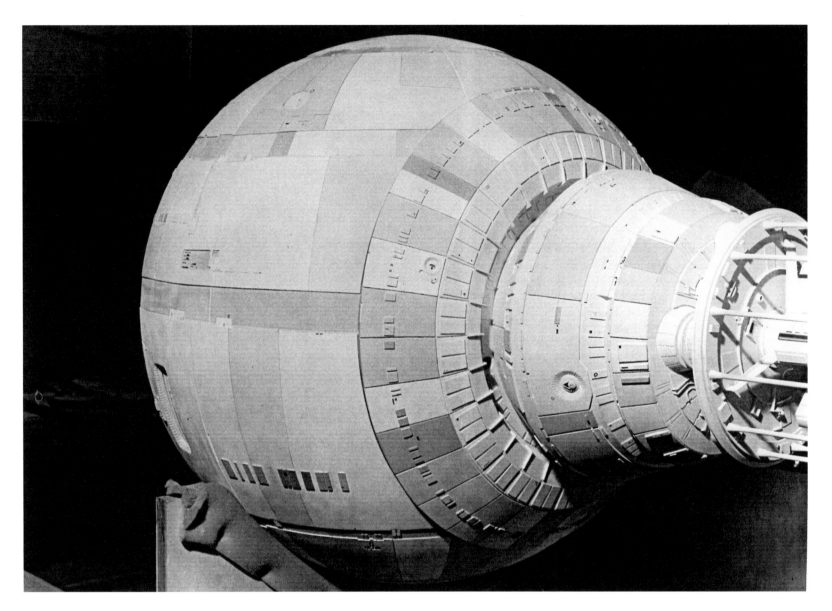

and technicians from several nations and representing a broad base in the disciplines involved round out the team.

2001 features dramatic scenes on Earth at the beginning of the 21st century; in a large space station; on Earth-orbit and orbit-lunar shuttles; on the Moon, and in an interplanetary spaceship bound for the outer Solar System. It is being made by Hawk Films Ltd. at M-G-M's British Studios, Borehamwood, Herts., England. Release in Cinerama will be... at the end of 1966 or early 1967.'

So with a few weeks to go before shooting, Ordway still thought that there were to be scenes set 'on Earth'—presumably at the World Space Center in New York, described in the production notes, where the secret Jupiter Mission Project was to be explained. And it was still thought that the film might be ready for Christmas 1966 release. It was in fact released in April 1968.

Ordway remained 'the front man' for conducted tours and public relations events right through to summer 1966. 'Kubrick would not

come to any of those events. He was photographed all the time by the stills guy but I never heard him utter a sound on camera.' When a documentary crew, directed by Thomas Craven, visited the set in April 1966—to film the Centrifuge in action, 38 feet in diameter, the largest the studio could accommodate, 'a colossus' built at vast expense as the documentary pointed out—Kubrick was shown looking at a black-and-white TV monitor, and directing the Centrifuge sequences, but never speaking. Instead, Ordway and Lange were filmed arriving at the MGM studio, discussing 'the scientific integrity of the film' and its 'base in reality', and in the case of Harry Lange explaining how the blue 'memory package' on the astronaut's space helmet worked, 'connected with a computer console on the main ship' and how the arm unit was activated—an early example of intelligent fabrics. Ordway, however, did most of the talking.

The start of principal photography was postponed a couple of

*Above & Opposite: Detailed large-scale models of the spherical command module – for navigation and recreation – of the **Discovery** interplanetary spaceship, with different paint finishes.*

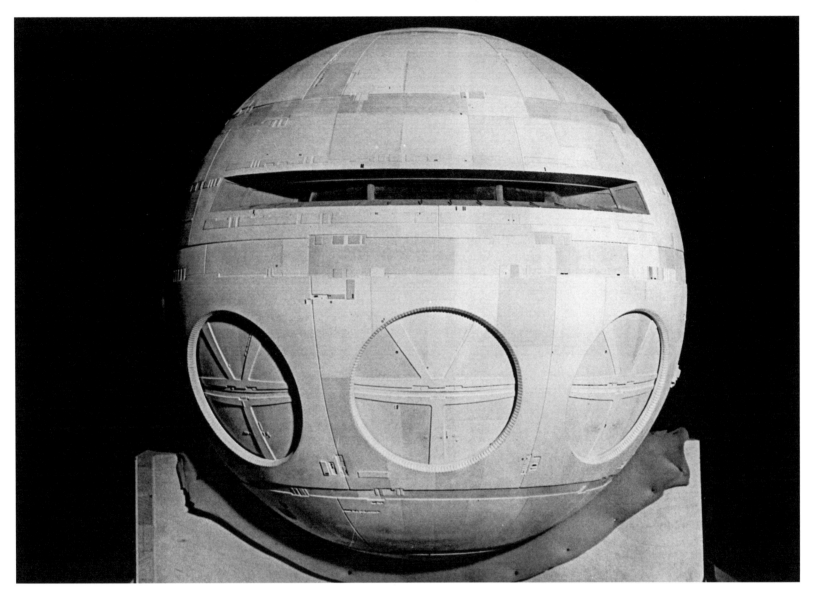

times. First it was to be November, then early December, then late December. Frederick Ordway recalls:

'I know that on the last possible day, Kubrick said "We've got to do it." I've always remembered that. Of course, I didn't get inside a lot of the things between Kubrick and MGM, but we were certainly aware of the issues.'

Clarke also remembered that by December 1965 'we were really under the gun... Stanley was up against an unbreakable deadline'.

On 16th December, after lunching with Stanley Kubrick and Arthur C. Clarke at the studio, Ordway wrote in his daily log that Kubrick

'... probably due to intense pressures of work, is becoming less friendly to those around him, adding to the displeasure of his associates. One result: a top member of the crew abruptly resigned. Earlier, I had observed that "... we are continually facing difficulties in terms of decision-making at the Kubrick level..." What U.S. industry comes up with (e.g. design suggestions for equipment and for its use) does not always please Stanley, often placing us in a

difficult position. And, many design aspects of the vehicles in the film change regularly so that it becomes impossible at times to finalise anything. Moreover, we are faced with the fact that the screenplay has a definite tendency to change rather rapidly, but even as it is, we are moving forward. The film experts here say this is a highly unorthodox and difficult film, made more so than necessary.'

Reminded of this log entry, Ordway says:

'I shouldn't have written that but I did. It was true and there were some resignations. A lot of pressure. Wally Gentleman left... there were things beyond my ken. Some other people just left and said "to hell with this" or something—and it was a tension to get that first filming done. These are my memories of it... Right up to the day we started, Arthur kept looking at his calendar. He was a Brit out in Sri Lanka and he was only allowed to be back in his country for so many days, for tax reasons. "I've got to be out of here." I was in that conversation, "just one more day, Arthur." "But what if there's a storm in the channel?" That was a big problem with a lot of movie people, by the way...'

I can remember standing there with a couple of bombs on my desk, trying to make them look "technical"

How did Stanley Kubrick cope with all the pressures? Was he the sort of personality who could handle it?

'Well, I kept remembering something that struck me when I first met him. One day we were at the Polaris Production offices and he said, "Fred—you see that man on that bench over there across the street, Central Park way? He's been sitting there for a long time. Do you have any idea what he's doing?" "I don't think he's doing anything." He thought he must be some reporter, who would capture a picture of him coming out. He was a very secretive man. We used to go to regular restaurants together—Harry and Arthur and Roger Caras— and he'd always ask for a table where no-one would recognise him...'

Arthur C. Clarke, too, on 19th April 1965 noted in his log:

'Some psychotic who insists that Stanley must hire him has been sitting on a park-bench outside the office for a couple of weeks, and occasionally comes to the building. In self-defense, Stan has secreted a large hunting-knife in his briefcase.'

Maybe it was the same man, sitting in the park. Ken Adam recalled that Kubrick was worried that someone could take a pot-shot at him from across the street, when he was standing on his penthouse balcony...

No-one had a holiday that Christmas of 1965. On 20th December, Ordway had a meeting with IBM representatives about the computers aboard **Orion** and **Aries**. On Christmas Eve he 'worked late with Kubrick, Masters, Lange and others in the Art Department offices'. And on 29th December, filming at last began on the enormous **Tycho Magnetic Anomaly** set at Shepperton studios, 'a 150 x 50 x 20 foot hole, with equipment scattered around it'. Kubrick *had* to begin then, because the set was scheduled to be torn down by the first week of the New Year. Frederick Ordway and Harry Lange were there, and on the 30th *and* the 31st, when the six space-suited scientists were filmed walking down to the monolith buried 40 feet below the lunar surface.

'Tycho is 43 degrees south latitude, ten degrees west longitude. It was a splendid view.'

On the 31st, Roger Caras wrote to Walter Wiesman of the Marshall Space Flight Center, back home in Huntsville, who had just sent over some research materials:

'It's a small world! I am sitting here with your kind note and bundle of goodies from NASA before me here in London and across the room, on my couch, drinking my gin, and reading my copy of **Le Figaro***, is the mad Frederick Ordway III. On the other side of this MGM lot on this rainy foggy New Year's Eve is Harry Lange. It all comes full circle! The three of us are here together in London helping Stanley Kubrick and Arthur C. Clarke carry motion picture audiences ahead 36 years, deep into the space age in the Stanley Kubrick Cinerama production for MGM,* **2001: A SPACE ODYSSEY***. Fred has just reminded me that in a matter of 6½ hours it will be just 35 years to the year 2001. If you keep on living your clean life you might make it!*

It was good to hear from you, Walter, and thoughtful of you to send me the material on NASA... Fred, a grin frozen to his face from his tremendous injection of gin, joins me in wishing you a very merry Christmas...'

The gin reference, Ordway hastens to add, was poetic licence. Live action photography at Borehamwood commenced on 8th January 1966. By the end of the month, the Space Station interior scenes had been completed. The scenes involving Keir Dullea and Gary Lockwood were filmed between February and July 1966. Special effects and model filming took place between August and early 1967. Ordway

'... divided my time [until summer 1966] between the active stage set and preparing for the follow-on shooting sequence. Sometimes filming would be fairly straightforward; at other times, as on the complex Centrifuge set, we would run into exasperating difficulties and delays... Of the 10.5 million dollars budget, an estimate 6.5 million was spent on artefacts and special effects photography: Kubrick wanted to make certain that every special effects shot would be completely convincing.'

So, out with the primitive optical effects of the Chesley Bonestell era—at least for most of the spaceships—and in with a large model of the Discovery, supported by a steel armature, and the camera moving beneath or beside it. Ordway also offered advice to the actors: Gary Lockwood was to remember 'long dull sessions with NASA advisors to understand human reactions in space', when it was much more productive to work out the conception of the character 'personally'. He also remembered that 'what was really impressive [about Stanley Kubrick] was that he knew when to make a change even though it could change the set plans and cost a

Opposite: Table-model of the moon base inside Clavius crater with 'the look of a circular city laid out on a grid pattern'.

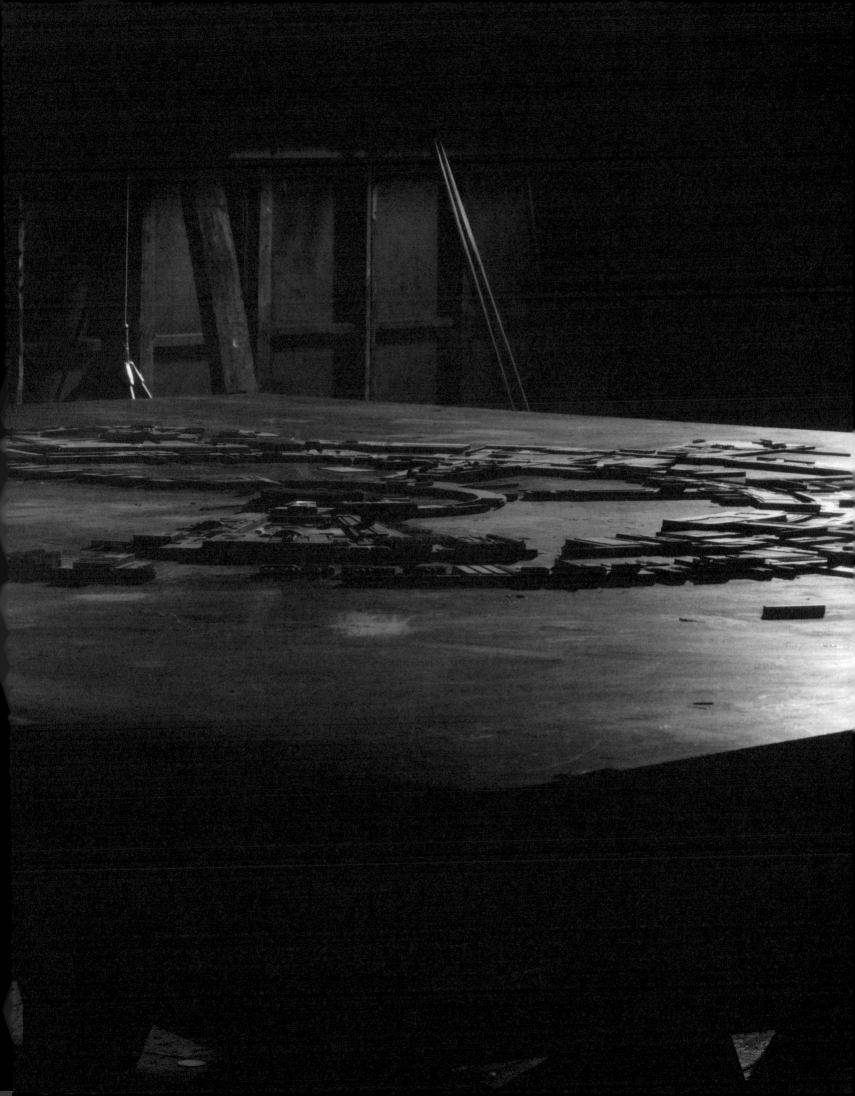

great deal of money'. Impressive to him, less impressive to the design departments.

The model-making shop had been hard at work, interpreting Harry Lange's drawings, and artwork derived from them, since summer 1965. David Watkins joined the team in early summer 1966. He is today an artist in jewellery with an international reputation, ex-Professor of the subject at the Royal College of Art. In summer 1966, he had recently graduated as a sculptor from the University of Reading and was teaching part-time in various art schools in addition to developing his practice. At the beginning of the summer vacation, he replied to a small ad in the London **Evening Standard**: 'There were two ads that day I could possibly apply for,' he recalls. 'The other one was for a Bird's Eye salesman.' The ad said:

Major Motion Picture Company requires skilled model makers for fine detailing and finishings. Must have samples of work...

In the two-stage modelling process—machining to industrial standards, or hand-crafting, the basic shapes in hardwood, plywood, fibreglass or custom-moulded plastics; then adding intricate surface details in acrylic and plastic—Watkins was offered the post of model-maker in the second stage, on an open-ended contract:

*'I was interviewed by Doug Trumbull. I seemed to be the only one taken on because they had an established little unit of model-makers in a shed somewhere near Wally Veevers' office at the front of the main lot—and there were about five or six of us at that stage. By the time I arrived, they were well into the Pan Am **Orion**, the **Aries** moon-landing vehicle and the little bus that travelled across the lunar surface. There was a sculptor called Rodney who had come from **Thunderbirds**—just a bit older than me—and a mechanical genius whose name I can't remember but who did all the mechanics for the **Aries 1-B** vehicle, the hydraulic landing-legs and all that kind of thing, achieved by solenoids and geared racks. He was very smart. But running the whole outfit at the beginning of my time was Brian Johncock, who later changed his name to Brian Johnson and who had come out of **Thunderbirds** as well [where he worked 1965-6], in charge of the model shop there. He was about twenty-five years old. Later, he worked on **Alien**. On **2001**, he didn't get a credit. He ran that little shop—Harry Lange was not much around at the beginning—and we were also overseen by Doug Trumbull. I worked as a model-maker on the film for seventeen months, until December 1967/January 1968.'*

He was one of the very few to stay the course, his perfectionism much in demand. There was a high attrition rate among staff. Ronnie Bear, manager for Hawk Films, was to call him 'a star member of this particular section because of his specialised knowledge in miniature work'. Another **Thunderbirds** import was Roger Dicken, who worked on making the surface of the moon look convincing. By the time Watkins arrived, the 'established little unit' was about to change its size and shape:

'It had almost come to the end of its days. What I guess happened was that suddenly, having got those first few models finished, there was a hurry on—which more or less coincided with Harry Lange being more in evidence. That original unit of model-makers and finishers was disbanded and a couple of us stayed on, we were moved to another workshop—a properly established shop near the carpenters' and set-builders' workshop further away on the lot. And Harry had a little office there.'

The first model that came into the newly-formed workshop was the 54-foot long **Discovery** in milled hardwood—representing the gigantic spacecraft on a scale of about one in ten—which is still said to be the largest model ever to be made for a film. There was a smaller 15-foot version as well, for long shots. Both would seem—unlike in previous science-fiction films—to be moving *very slowly*: there was no need for speed in the outer reaches of space. Up to then, rockets had whizzed around at full throttle. One version of the (detached) spherical command module was a fibreglass ball six feet in diameter, accompanied by a very slightly larger sphere which provided plastic panels to be stuck onto the module itself. Kubrick was not keen on using plaster—which could show blemishes too easily. Watkins also worked at that time on the orbiting nuclear bombs, based on designs by Lange, which would feature in the first space sequence set in 2001:

'I can remember standing there with a couple of bombs on my desk, trying to make them look "technical". Although it sounds grand, the workshop was not very big—about thirty foot by twenty foot. And it was on the front of a building, with big barn doors which made it bloody cold in the winter. It had some workbenches laid out around three sides and in the middle a passageway which was taken up with parts of the huge Jupiter Mission model for quite a long time. Harry had a little office directly opening off the workshop.'

Was he present for a lot of the time?

'He was certainly in evidence. He'd come in some time during the morning and sit in his office and do sketches of work that still had to be made. But as time went by—when we were getting towards the end, and the crew was reducing—he came in less often. He had become interested in horse-riding, especially dressage. He used to go riding in the morning and arrived at the workshop late—sometimes in his riding boots, with a riding crop unless I'm imagining it. And he'd walk around and say, in his accent, "Yes, yes, very nice," go into his office and do a bit of sketching... then he'd disappear again. When we were in that building, very soon after we moved in, the management decided that they needed many more people to push through these models: I always thought it was counterproductive, but they introduced a nightshift so there were one crew during the day and another during the night, and we didn't communicate

---

Opposite: Filming the one-man space pod, with its crab-like manipulator grab-arms, as if in outer space—suspended from the roof of one of the stages at Borehamwood.

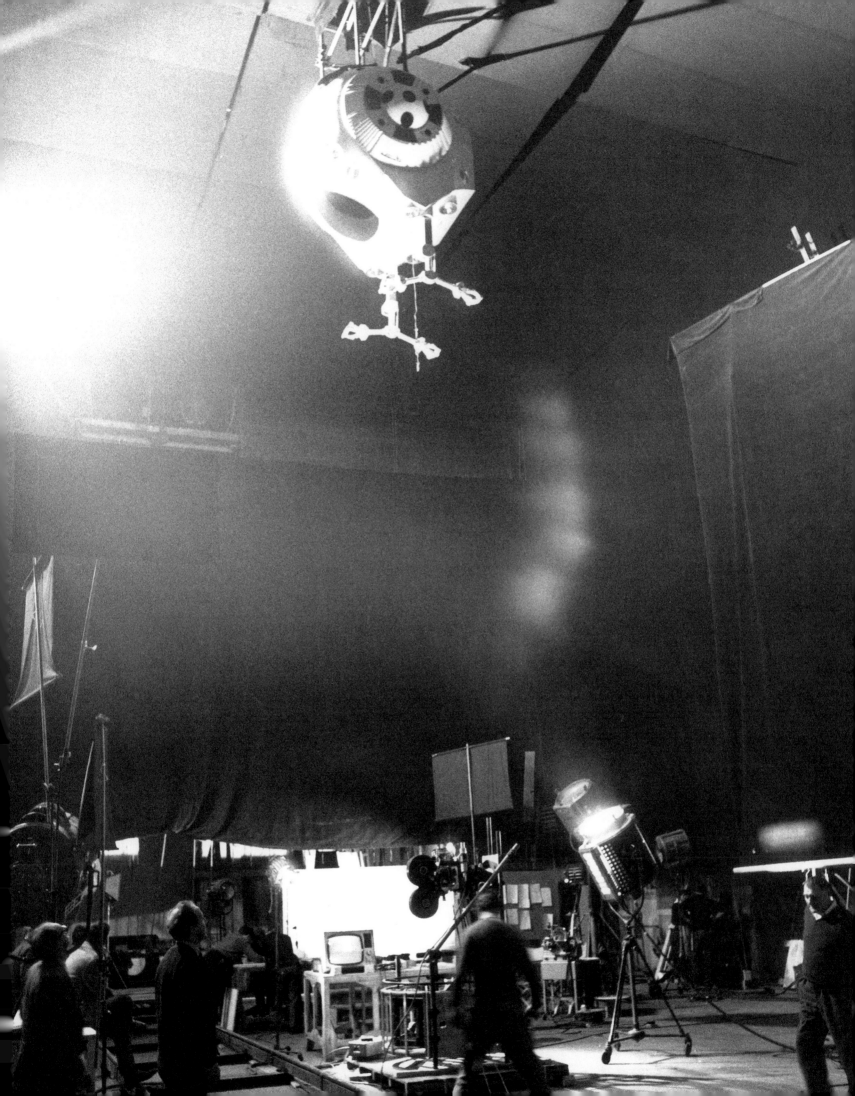

He didn't encourage people to come and see 'how it was done'

very much with each other. So I don't know what on earth was going on at night but not very much is my guess. That continued for quite some time, until it became evident that it wasn't producing any faster results.'

At the peak of pre-production, 103 model-makers were employed on the MGM lot. But did David's team of model-makers work from technical drawings, derived from Harry Lange's designs?

'No, we had a huge amount of freedom. What happened was that Harry produced these rather Bauhausy-looking sketches of the space vehicles. I don't think he did any technical drawings. I never saw any from Harry. I had recently been teaching the Bauhaus "basic course"—geometry, shapes, colours, textures—and when I saw Harry working on his sketches I saw that sort of aesthetic in action. Which was interesting. And he was very, very quick. I suspect that what happened was that his sketches went off to the set or carpentry workshops—the MGM model-makers, who made the bare essentials—and they did their own shop drawings, scale drawings. Then they would produce these great blocky things to Harry's sketches, constructed out of wood or sometimes fibreglass with some plaques of perspex on them to indicate the kinds of panels he favoured, and they were all spray-painted [anti-flash] white and delivered to us to begin dressing them. So they came in as very simple, very well-made constructions, and our job was to make them look as if they were "technical"—putting pipework and connections and all sorts of things like that onto them. And we basically made it up as we went along. At the beginning—though it came to an end with the move from one shop to another—we used to go and see the rushes in the morning and occasionally Stanley would throw up some bits of other science-fiction films he admired, just to keep the juices flowing. To inspire us. Other science fiction films. The only one I can recall was **Fantastic Voyage**, the one for which Isaac Asimov wrote the novel. It involved people in a miniaturised submarine travelling around the bloodstream of someone's body. Stanley was interested in that one. It had recently been released [another must have been **Destination Moon**]. It was a pity he stopped us going to the rushes—because he took the view that it was wasting precious time. It was extraordinary to sit in and listen to the discussions between Stanley and Wally Veevers and Con Pederson and Doug Trumbull—and the cinematographers. And to hear about all the problems they were having with film stock, and post-production pressures. It was all absolutely fascinating and I learned so much technically—or half-learned so much—that it was unbelievable. But to some extent the style of the dressing had

been already set, in that earlier small unit—set by the moon-landing vehicle and the hovering rocket bus—and we carried on in the same vein. Sometimes, there were bits of fancy—"how do you think this might look?"—and we did make things up as we went along. With bits of copper wire, bits of plastic, bits of perspex, plastic card, tubing, bits from small model kits...'

This last seems to have been central to the model-making process: a constant supply of model kits by Airfix, Revell and Renwal, cannibalised and cut up to create convincing surface details on the spacecraft, and on the moon base:

'Yes, that certainly was one of the key factors in our work. From the first, when Brian Johncock was still there, he used to go out and scour all the model shops for interesting kits that would provide bits that could be disguised and look "futuristic"; and he would come back with armfuls of boxes, as well as dental tools and wires and all that kind of thing. Obviously he had the experience at **Thunderbirds** of what worked and what worked quickly. And we had shelves of these things to pull. Our favourite was a Polaris submarine, because there were more little parts on that for us to use than in any of the others. We used to butcher these things and file all the little parts up, and there were some favourite recurring parts that always came in useful: nozzles, fuel tanks, those kinds of thing.'

In the carpentry workshop, there were skilled wood-millers and joiners, wood- and metal-lathe operators. When the staff numbers expanded, with the move to the new workshop, did any extra model-making skills arrive with them?

'Well, among the people who came in on the second development— when they suddenly in a rush employed about ten or twelve extra people—there were some real model-makers in the sense of railway model enthusiasts, and they were used to building not only locomotives but carriages and trucks—from scratch—and they were full of knowledge about how to handle these materials in the miniature. Frankly, the serious issues came down to "how well do you get them to stick?" and "will they stand painting?" or "how much care do you have to take over finishing edges?" and so on. The level of detail and craftsmanship in putting those models together was quite extraordinary. And that took a great deal more time than the production team ever envisaged—which is why they tried this manoeuvre of throwing more people at it, and the nightshift.'

So the wooden or fibreglass models arrived and the second-stage modellers dressed them. Was Harry Lange ever involved at the model-dressing stage?

Opposite: Stanley Kubrick looking at the set through the view-finder of his camera: note that he is wearing two wristwatches...

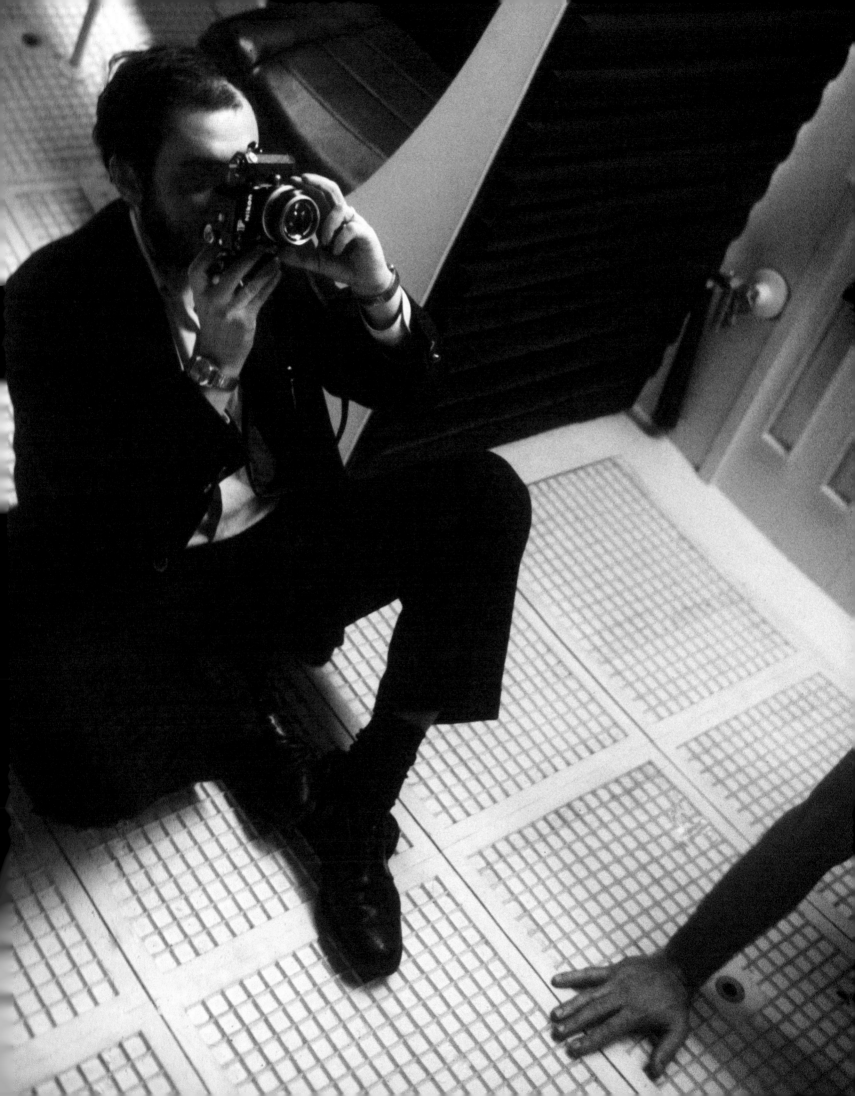

'He came in and had a look at things, but I don't think he had a huge amount to say about what we were doing. He seemed perfectly satisfied that all was proceeding well. Harry was that kind of presence, really—very affable, very correct, smart, well-turned-out in his riding boots, very Germanic, he looked the part—but I think he related to Stanley and the production team. There was nothing coming back to us that I was aware of. We just got on with it and if Stanley liked what we were doing, he liked it, and if he didn't, well, we would get a little feedback—but it was very basic, like "that's a bit too grey"...'

Stanley Kubrick was famous for using designs to help him discover what he *didn't* like. He needed to *see* things. Were there any major changes of direction, during Watkins' time in the workshop?

'I wasn't aware of that, though we were sometimes a bit disappointed to see what then happened to the models. We'd made them totally in the round, finished in every respect, very detailed and photographable from any angle, and then some of them Stanley just took away, photographed them and used them as travelling mattes. So we'd stand there, scratching our heads and muttering "Why on earth didn't he say in the first place that he just wanted to photograph them from one side... it would have involved half the work." You see, he wanted all options from us. But even that moon vehicle—the little rocket bus—that was a lovely little model but it was only ever used as a flat travelling matte and actually it was one of the poorer pieces of realisation in the film; it didn't look right. But that's what he did. He did it with the nuclear bombs too, which were lovingly made in the round, to be photographed from whatever angle... made so that they could do whatever they liked with them.'

Apart from the bombs, and **Discovery**, were there any other models that David Watkins could recall working on?

'There were two other major things. One was the Moon base inside Clavius crater. That model was made in March 1967. I can remember having the Beatles' **Penny Lane/Strawberry Fields** as our constant background. The record had just been released, so that's how I can remember the date. They'd filmed the actors and then the model went in much later, during post-production. By that time, the crew for model-making was quite reduced, and a young woman was brought in to work with us as a specialist just on the Clavius base. And we worked on that lying down almost on the floor, on maybe a twelve-foot square base—it was meant to be half a mile wide—with all the basic layout already there from Harry's drawing—just as blocks of perspex. And we had to dress that up to look as if it was a functioning base of some kind, with power-lines and generators and the look of a circular city laid out on a grid pattern. All kinds of stuff...'

Did people visit the workshop, on conducted tours of 'behind the scenes'?

'Fred Ordway certainly visited. Very dapper and wearing black gloves. We all thought he must be a CIA man! But Stanley was very secretive. He didn't encourage people to come and see "how it was done". In fact at one stage we were told very clearly that we shouldn't let anyone come in. There was this veil of secrecy, which may well have been in the later stages when he was either in dispute with MGM over time and cost, or with the American government, or NASA, about the ownership of the models... Some things filtered through to us, like MGM being increasingly worried about the money he was spending. Or the fact that NASA was putting something in, because it was part of their drive to sell the space race. And all that must have been coming to a head when we got the instructions about secrecy. And Stanley started locking things up somewhere out on the backlot when he'd finished filming them, to make sure they didn't fall into the wrong hands.'

What was the other 'major thing' Watkins worked on?

'It was in fact the very last thing we worked on—just the two of us—the Space Station itself, the two rotating wheels in space. That really was the end of it. **Space Station-5** was quite a big object—about eight foot in diameter, meant to be a thousand foot in diameter. And we had it on a rig where there was a bearing we could turn it round on. It came to us with this very large metal hub, which it had to have because that was where were was a control room, and you get to see it in the film—and a flight deck for the **Orion** to fly into. It was constructed essentially of metal because it had these heavy tubular spokes going out to the outside circumference. Harry must have sketched that in some detail so it would look as if it was still under construction, still incomplete. In other words, there was a metal framework, scaffolding still exposed and some areas, most areas, which were quite built up, quite blocky. We did a huge amount of work on that because it was a very simple model when it arrived. It had to look very "busy"—apart from the incomplete bit, which was made of pieces of copper welded on—"busy" was the technical word! Even though it bore out my suspicion about bringing in all these people, and nightshifts, because we two guys cracked on through that and did a tremendous amount of work in a relatively short time. It might only have been three weeks.'

Space engineers have sometimes said since then that the 'incomplete' section of the rotating wheel, with component parts being sent from Earth, would present a major problem. You don't send up a wheel, in segments, that is not fully finished—if you do, you may create unnecessary difficulties for yourself, say the engineers.

'It was unlike Stanley Kubrick to make that kind of mistake, actually.'

Opposite: Memorandum from Frederick Ordway, with annotations by Harry Lange, about the proposed exhibition of artefacts from **2001** to be shown at the National Aerospace Museum in Washington DC. It never happened.

LANGE

November 22, 1966.

"2001" SETS, MODELS, etc. FOR WASHINGTON EXHIBIT

1. At the same time that the acrylic block is prepared for transfer to Washington via Baltimore, it is desired that the rest of the "2001" set, model, prop and illustrative materials be shipped.
In accordance with our conversations, it is estimated that this will take place during April 1967.

2. Appended to this memorandum is a list of the items we feel can most effectively be exhibited at the International Space Museum and Gallery. Approximate dimensions are noted on the right.

3. In the case of illustrations, some time next spring we would like to make a final selection so that plans for framing and exhibiting can be finalised.

4. Dick Frift advises me that a shipping firm nearby would be admirably suited to handle crating and transfer.

Mr. Fleet
Ballous, Wed.
June 7 '67
Els 1661

Mr. Heywood
Tues 13 Jun
11:AM
Insurance

List from
Cleary Jun 12

Quotation from
Mr. Fleet on
all models
we Monday
June 12 '67
15:00

TO :   Victor Lyndon
FROM : Fred I. Ordway.
c.c.   Roger A. Caras.
        Dr. Carsbie C. Adams.

'Why have Buck Rogers for six million dollars, when you can have Kubrick for seven…?'

Plus real space stations—such as MIR—look more like junkyards or used-car lots in space than sleek revolving wheels with orbital hotel, shops and office complex, looking like some ad agency of the future…

Did the experience of working on **2001** have an influence on David Watkins' future career?

'When I saw the finished film, I thought "this is the beginning: there is going to be a whole wonderful world of science-fiction films and I'm going to have some fun"—but of course it all died and it didn't happen then. I can remember when Fred Ordway and Co. came in, he left us with all these books about their predictions—thinking about other planets and what kinds of vehicles you would need to get there. He left them with us for a few days—I can't remember why. And I was thinking "this could be a career" and started drawing all kinds of weird creatures. Maybe there would be a market for this kind of thing. And some of the things I was drawing would not have been out of place in the bar at the end of the universe. But anyway that was not to be. I applied to work with Wally Veevers at Pinewood, had a couple of interviews with the film industry and I did go on to work for Gerry Anderson's unit on a live-action film, but the quality was extremely low so I got out.'

The jewellery David Watkins designed and made, from 1971 onwards as a studio jeweller—with its geometric patterns of space-age imagery, 2001-type materials, and extreme precision—also owed much to his experience model-making for Stanley Kubrick. Douglas Trumbull has written in **American Cinematographer** (June 1968) of that experience, in more general terms:

*'The models in **2001** are probably the most precisely detailed ever constructed for a film. As soon as the overall design was completed on each model, the construction was begun to produce the basic form of the spacecraft, and this process often took several months. Then the arduous task of detailing and painting the model would begin. Massive crews of model detailers worked around the clock for several months to produce the finished result.'*

Watkins was one of the most important of them, 'a star member'.

When no more models were required, and the **Space Station** was finished, there was talk of shipping the results of their labours over to the States for an exhibition about the making of **2001**. Harry Lange prepared an inventory of exhibits for the purpose. David Watkins recalls:

'I remember that at the end Harry Lange was supposed to take a small crew over to Washington to install the models in the Smithsonian.

And two of us—the last remaining model-dressers—were supposed to go with him, and this was the great white hope. We were quite excited, but it all fell through because of some disagreement between Stanley and the others.'

Frederick Ordway confirms this:

'After the film was made, Kubrick was very anxious to preserve the artefacts, so I told him that a good friend of mine at the National Aerospace Museum—Frederick Durant—could put up some money to bring these things over, and Kubrick had me work with Dick Frift packing the models to send over to Washington. I'd gone back over to England. We rented a warehouse to stack them and so forth. And there was Kubrick just like a mother hen making sure it was all okay… And I flew back to the United States, I had to get back to my work. When I got there, after a week or so, I received a message from Kubrick: "I've decided not to send the artefacts—it will destroy the reality of the film. If they are on exhibition, people will say 'we know this film isn't real'." I've kept the message. And that's another whole story—where are these artefacts? Anyway, he didn't send them. And then we heard that he had given them to a local school in Borehamwood. Then there were rumours about collectors… A big model was discovered in a junkyard or field somewhere around Borehamwood. And I know there's a guy who has Bowman's helmet… The bad point was when he cancelled the exhibition, and we'd gone to considerable expense… But Kubrick did finally pay the cost of that decision, after being persuaded by Victor Lyndon, who had left the film by then.'

The artefacts which did survive Kubrick's decision—and the closure of Borehamwood a couple of years later—included the face plate of HAL, a model of the **Aries-1B** Space Shuttle and Bowman's red helmet: the Space Station was indeed spotted lying among some rubbish, but too late.

After watching a preview of **2001**, Frederick Ordway prepared a detailed memo to Stanley Kubrick in which he offered advice about how the science in the film could have been clarified if only some of the 'splendid work of narration' had been kept in. The scenes aboard **Aries-1B** were 'good as far as they went, but their effectiveness was lost by the deletion of narration at the beginning (only a few lines were necessary)'. The same went for the landing of **Aries** and the explanation of the **TMA-1** artefact's 'burst of electromagnetic energy':

'With these missing, but available, pieces, the great symphony becomes coherent. In an age of super-science, of incredible

*information-processing and display devices, of computer-assisted thinking and delicately-timed responses, nothing less than total understanding can be tolerated. We are now on the **Discovery** midway between Earth and Jupiter. And the audience must know why. Fuzzy thinking, incomplete explanations, lost coupling scenes, missing bits of information have no place in **2001**.'*

Where 'the **Discovery** portion of the film' was concerned, there was, he reckoned, 'too much exercising around the centrifuge for Poole, and the pod EVA sequences could be shortened':

'Indispensable dialogue regarding the three hibernating astronauts was lacking ... particularly where Bowman and Poole first become aware that "there is something about the mission the sleeping beauties know and that we don't know..." Those few words are probably the most critical to the logic structure of the entire film, and lead to a valid reason why HAL breaks down. Yet they were inexplicably cut out.'

In general,

'because of the unfortunate cutting of key preceding material, much is lost to even the most perceptive members of the audience. It's like a marvellously complicated and beautiful puzzle that has taken years to prepare. Yet, when one sits down to put it together, one finds that many of the pieces are missing. There is nothing striking, intellectually or visually, about gaping empty spaces where gaping empty spaces don't belong.'

Did Ordway actually send this memo?

'Yes. The film was confusing to people. I would have liked some guidance about where we are. That was my feeling anyway. There were visual connections but no intellectual connections. And Arthur had written the text. It was available, you see.'

And did Stanley Kubrick respond to it?

'I don't think he did. I don't remember any response after that. We did have a little period when we had bad relations... '

Kubrick's standard response to such criticisms was to evade them by saying to journalists that the film should be treated as a purely visual experience. The message was the medium.

*'I don't like to talk about **2001** much because it's essentially a nonverbal experience. Less than half the film has dialogue. It attempts to communicate more to the subconscious and to the feelings than it does to the intellect. I think clearly that there's a basic problem with people who are not paying attention with their eyes. They're listening. And they don't get much from listening to this film. Those who don't believe their eyes won't be able to appreciate this film.'*

*'How much would we appreciate **La Gioconda** today if Leonardo had written at the bottom of the canvas: "This lady is smiling slightly because she has rotten teeth"—or "because she's hiding a secret from her lover"? It would shut off the viewer's appreciation and shackle him to a "reality" other than his own. I don't want that to happen to **2001**.'*

So all that science had been a strategy after all, to make a 'nonverbal experience' seem more credible to audiences, to make them suspend their disbelief. Ordway thought that **2001** was an astonishing film, a marvellous experience, but that more explanation would have improved it. So much trouble had been taken over the scientific background, after all. But the final cut of **2001** left it up to the viewers to fill the gaps. There was no narration and very little explanation. Viewers were expected to concentrate on the visuals, notice the few clues there were about the plot, and let the concert—Richard Strauss, Johann Strauss, Aram Khachaturian, György Ligeti and heavy-breathing in the pod sequences—do the rest. **2001** worked on a sensory, almost subliminal level, right up to the glorious, transcendent, unexplained ending. The research, the consultations, the advice from NASA—all were intended to make viewers 'believe their eyes'. Fred Ordway had not fully appreciated this, during the long period of preparation. He had hoped that the audience might be encouraged to understand the *science*, as well.

As a result of the experience of working on the film, Harry Lange decided to stay in Britain, and continue as a designer for films—often specialising in space hardware. 'He decided he was ready to do that,' even though he continued modestly to call himself 'a craftsman' or maybe 'technological artist'. He contributed to the sets and/or hardware in, among others, **Kelly's Heroes** (1970), **The Empire Strikes Back** (1980), **The Dark Crystal** (1982), **Return of the Jedi** (1983), **Monty Python's Meaning of Life** (1983)—and **Moonraker** (1979, as 'art-director—space'), working to Ken Adam who was overall production designer. When James Bond arrives at a pheasant shoot in **Moonraker**, a trumpet plays the opening three notes of **Also Sprach Zarathustra** from **2001**—a smart in-joke. Harry Lange died in May 2008, at the age of 77. Frederick Ordway, on the other hand, after working on **2001**, returned to his full-time job at NASA. The film world was not for him. He died in July 2014, at the age of 87.

'I've got to tell you what happened some time after that. I get a call from Ridley Scott one day, when I'm back in Washington. He said "My name is Ridley Scott and I'd like to invite you to lunch" and I said "Well, I'd be delighted." And he proposed to me to become the technical advisor on Alien. And I replied "2001 was a single event in my career. I have my normal professional career and I'm settled back in Washington doing my work. So, no thank you. It was an honour to do 2001, I lecture on it, I'm very fond of the film, but I must go back to my professional career." You see, I really respected Stanley Kubrick—we'd have debates here and there and arguments, but I have nothing but warm memories of the whole thing. But in the end it was a single event in my life...'

Robert O'Brien, the amazingly patient head of MGM, summarised the **2001** saga in a famous **Variety** interview: "Why have Buck Rogers for six million dollars, when you can have Stanley Kubrick for seven million dollars?". In point of fact, the film cost 10.5 million dollars. Dr Wernher von Braun was reported to be pleased with the result.

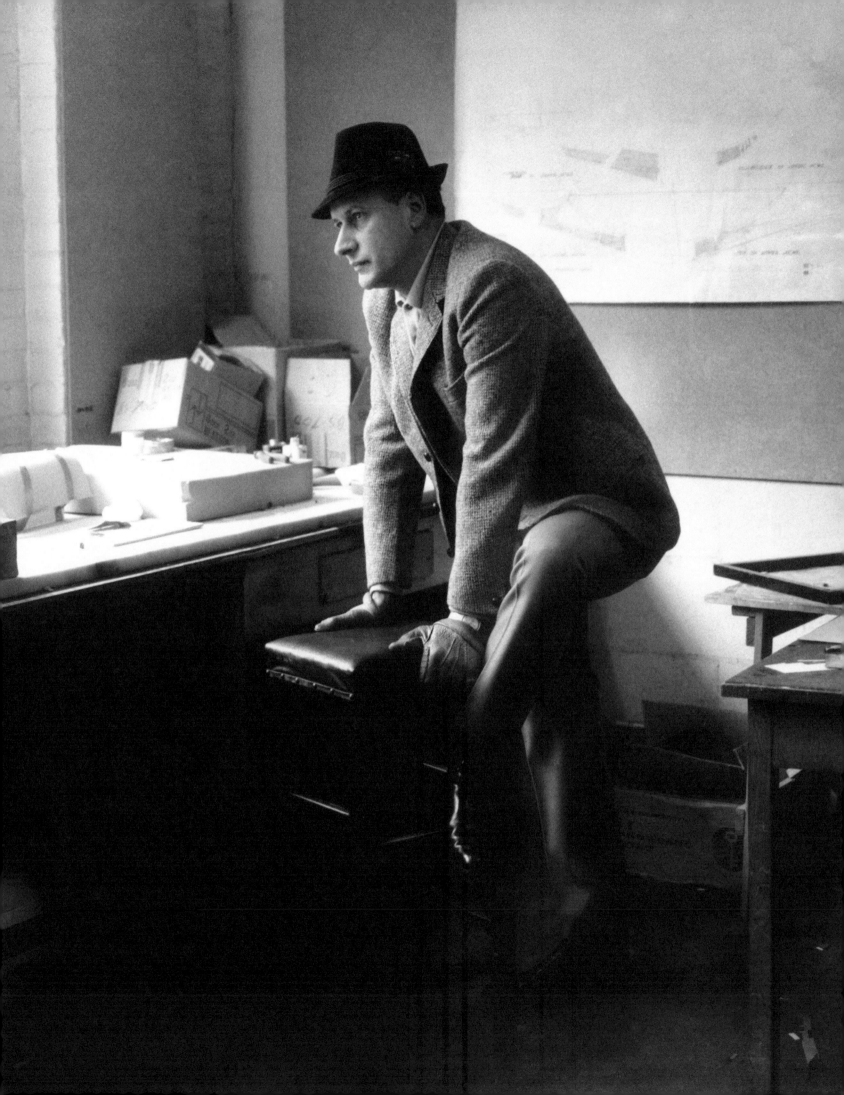

THE HARRY LANGE ARCHIVE

*Thumbnail sketches, drawings, blueprints and photographs
from the designer's personal collection.*

HARRY LANGE'S EARLY WORKS
A selection

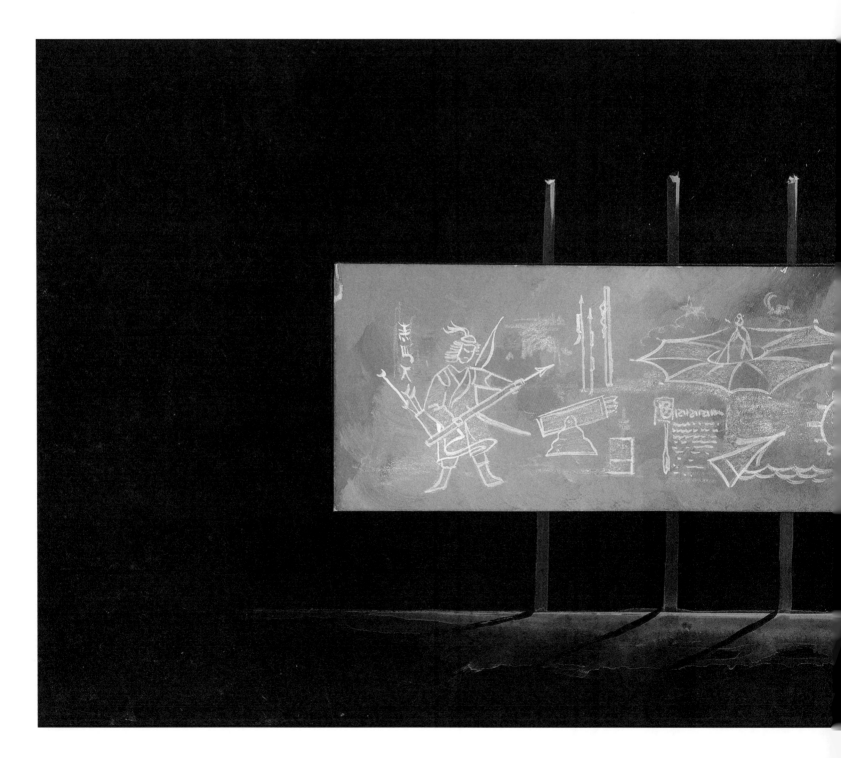

A Harry Lange painted mural board, showing the history of rocketry.

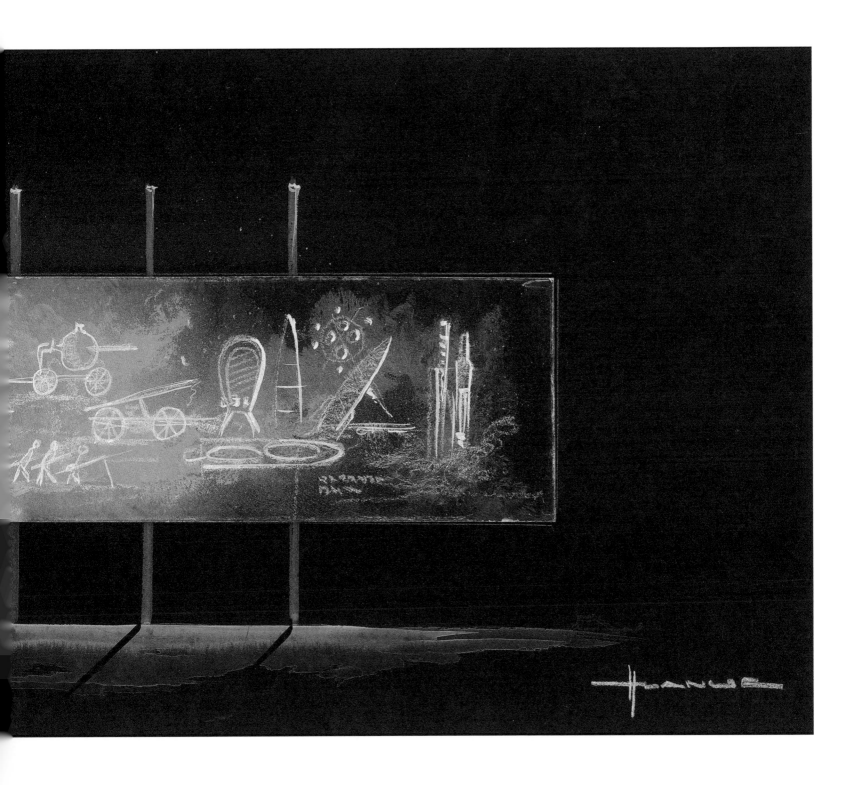

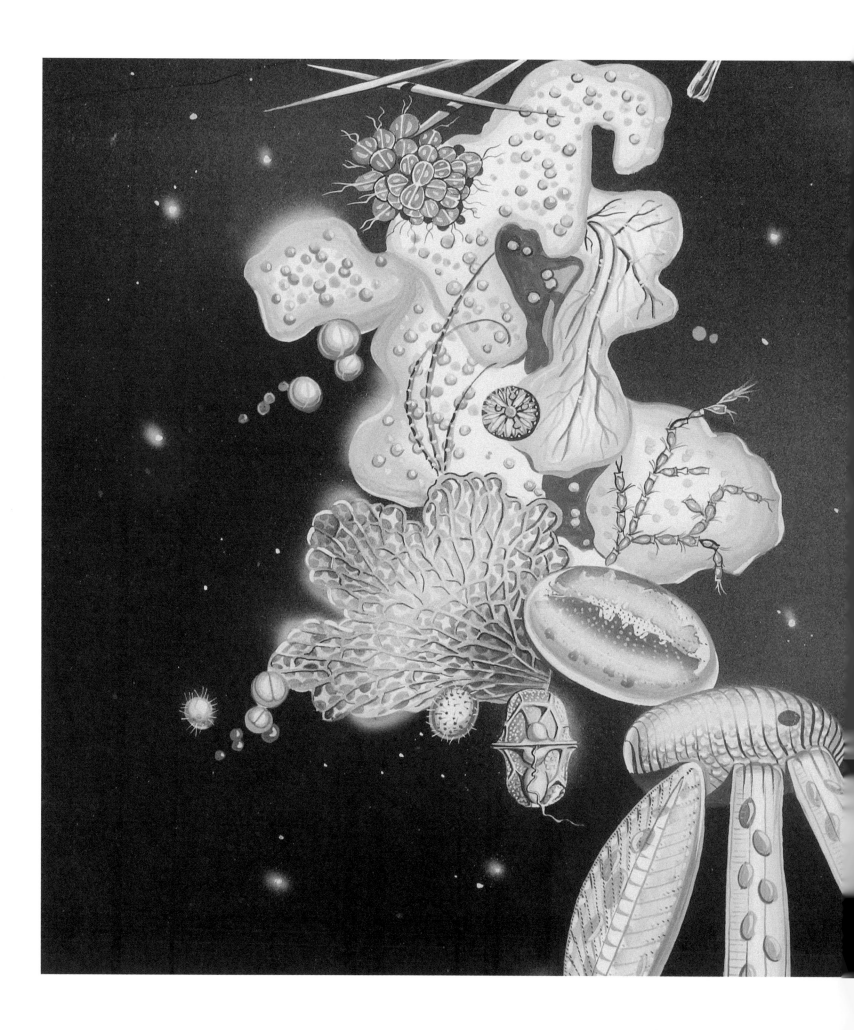

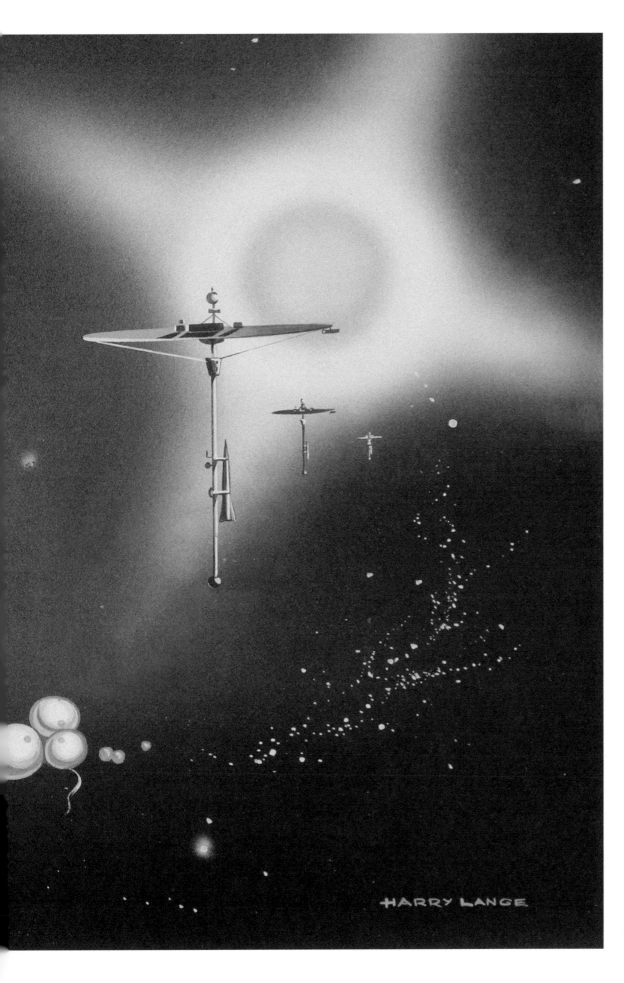

HARRY LANGE

Vegetation, and Ion spaceship design (by Ernst Stuhlinger), floating in the vastness of space like a space age crucifixion.

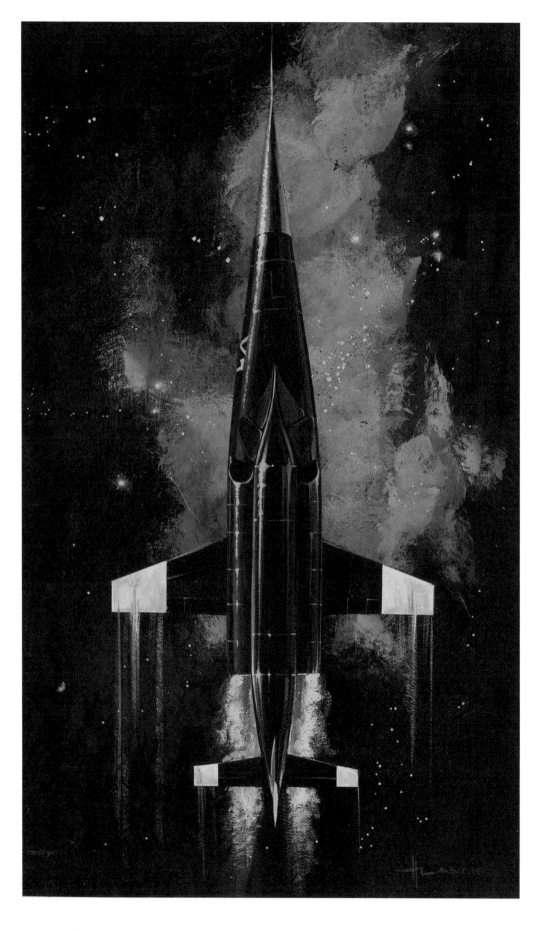

Above: Single-stage rocket-plane concept. Opposite: Astronaut at the controls, with an array of switches and 'buttonry'—a mix of traditional and modern.

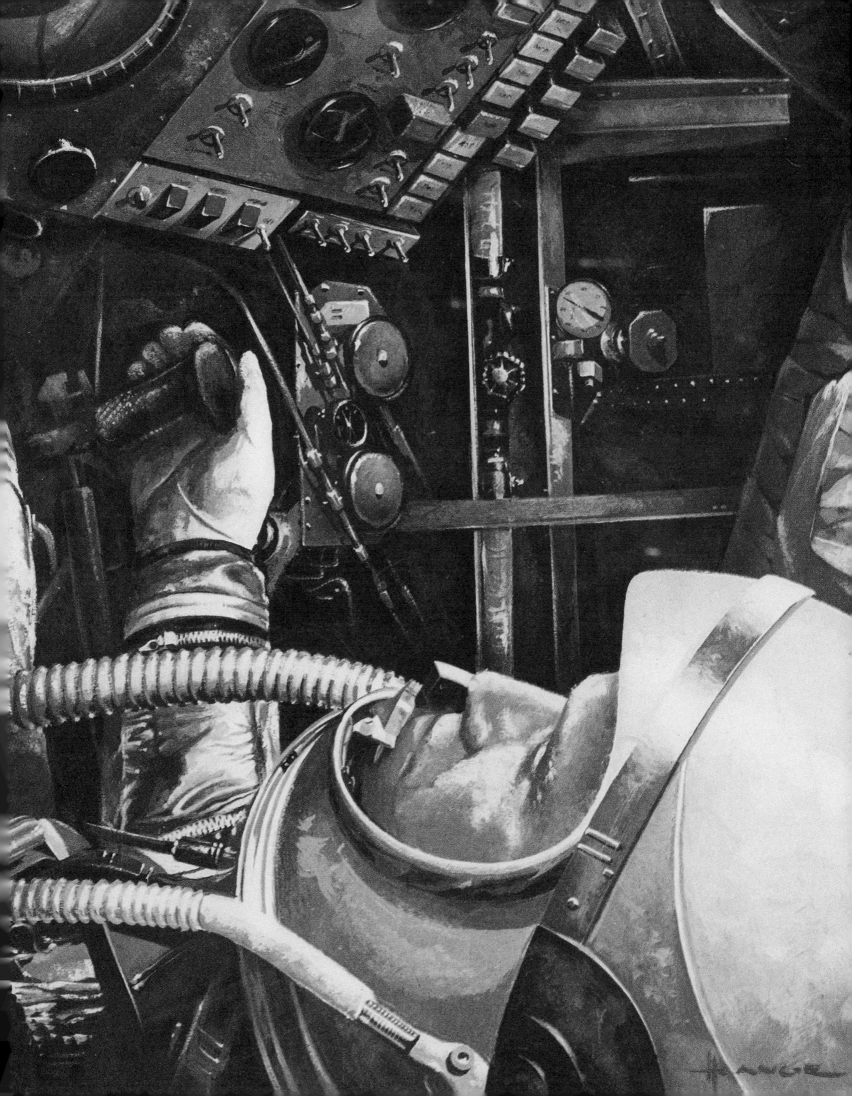

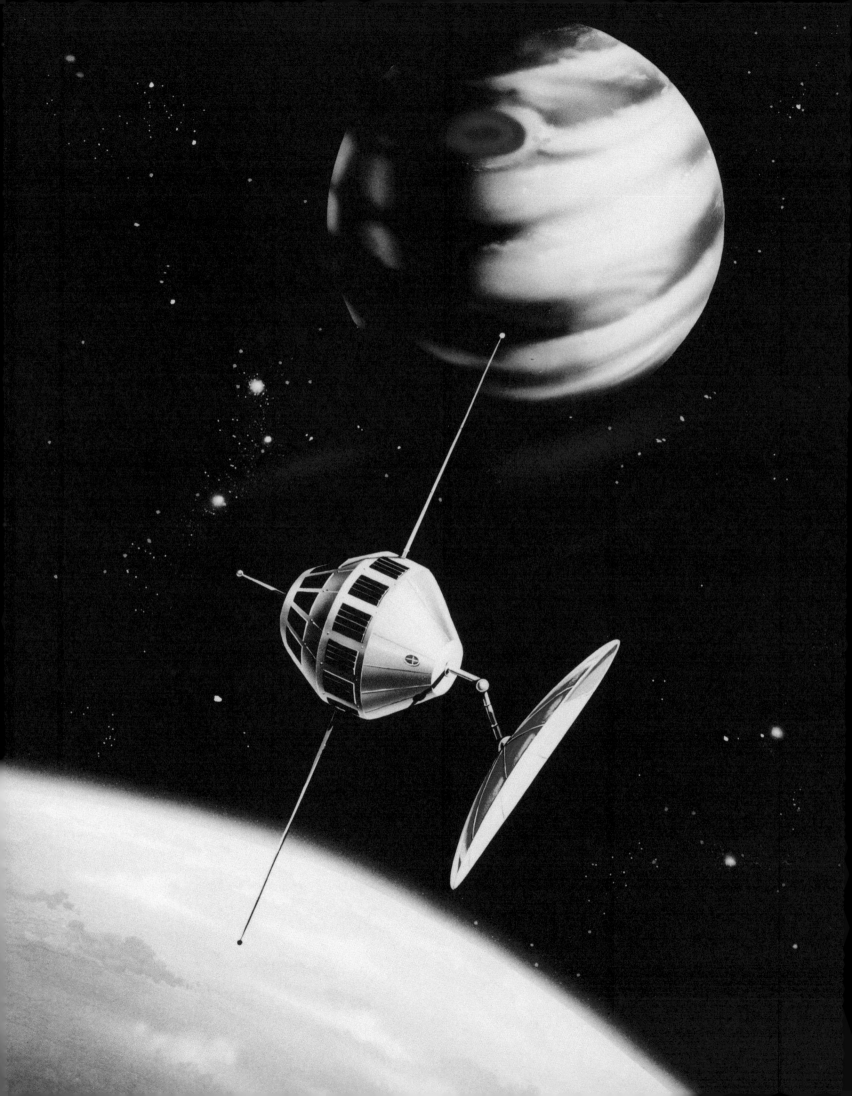

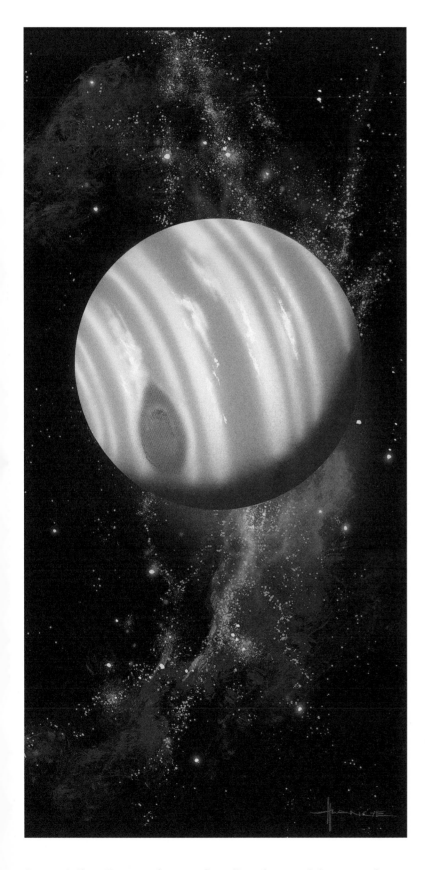

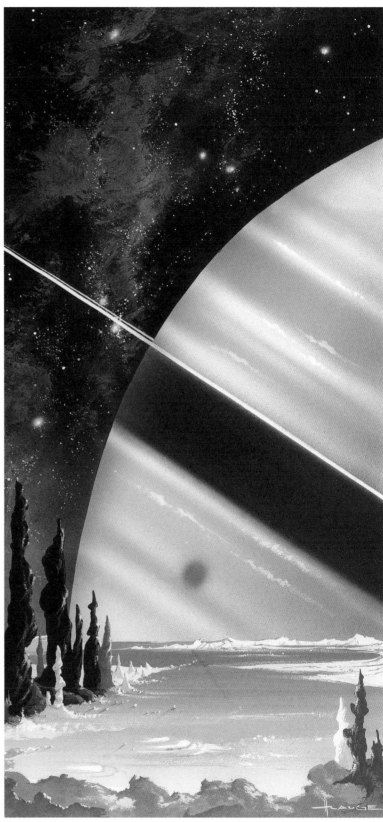

Opposite & Above: Paintings of space-craft, satellites, planets and planetary surfaces were among Harry Lange's specialities at NASA—for promotional purposes.

1   2   3   4   5   6   7

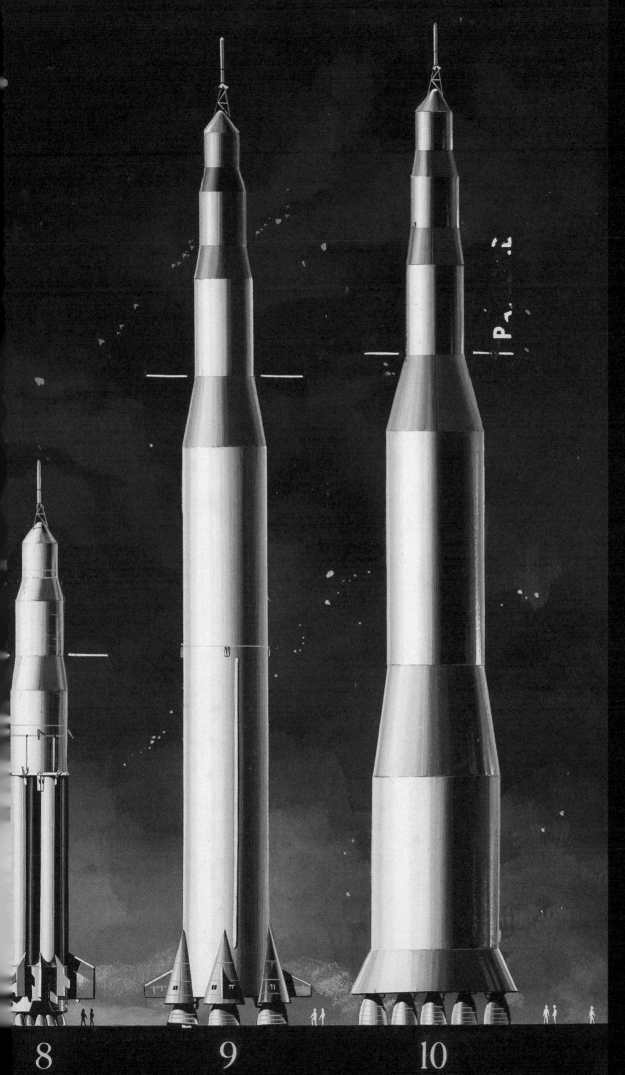

Rockets of increasing scale—with pairs of human beings for comparison—resembling the models on Dr. Wernher von Braun's desk and on the wall of his Huntsville office.

8 9 10

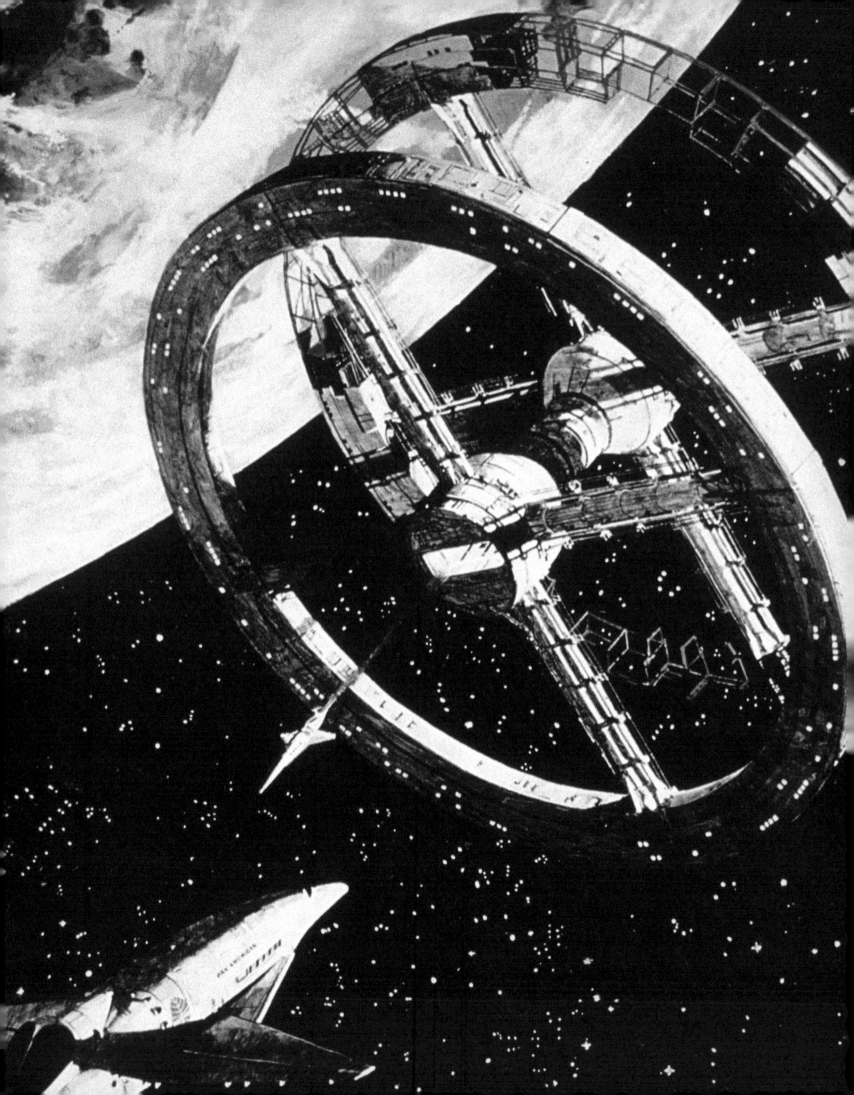

ODYSSEY I
INTO SPACE

From Earth to Space Station-5, altitude 200 miles, on the 175 foot long Orion-III earth-to-orbit commercial passenger space plane.

ARRIVAL
Space hardware

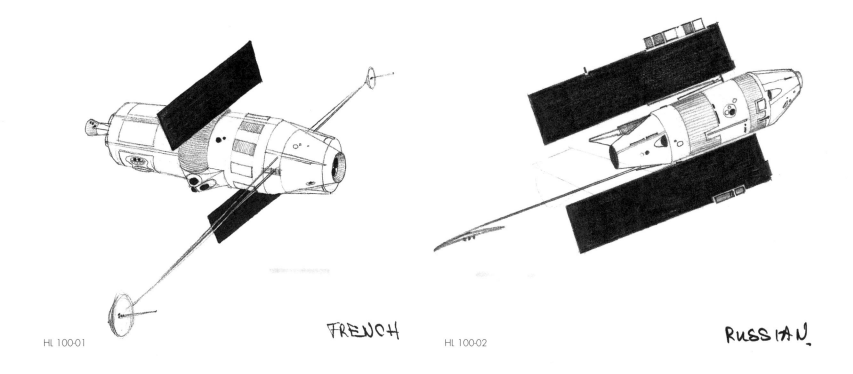

HL 100-01   FRENCH   HL 100-02   RUSSIAN.

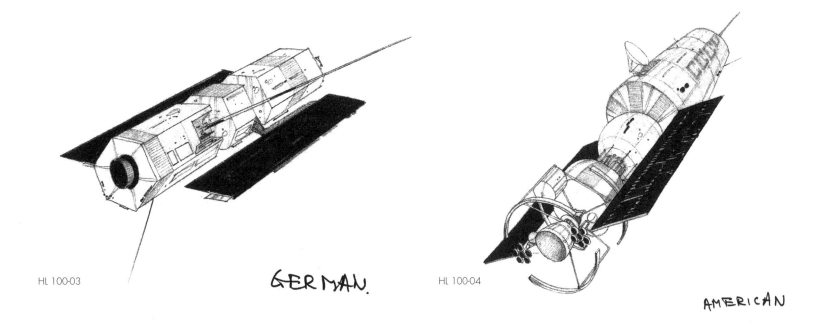

HL 100-03   GERMAN.   HL 100-04   AMERICAN

HL 100-01 *Probe 3 (French).* **HL 100-02** *Probe 4 (Russian).* **HL 100-03** *Probe 5 (German).* **HL 100-04** *Probe 1 (CCCP) with annotation 'American'.* **HL 100-05** *Satellite with nuclear propulsion system and heat radiation panels.* **HL 100-06** *Satellite with four solar panels.* **HL 100-07** *Corrugated solar panel wings.*

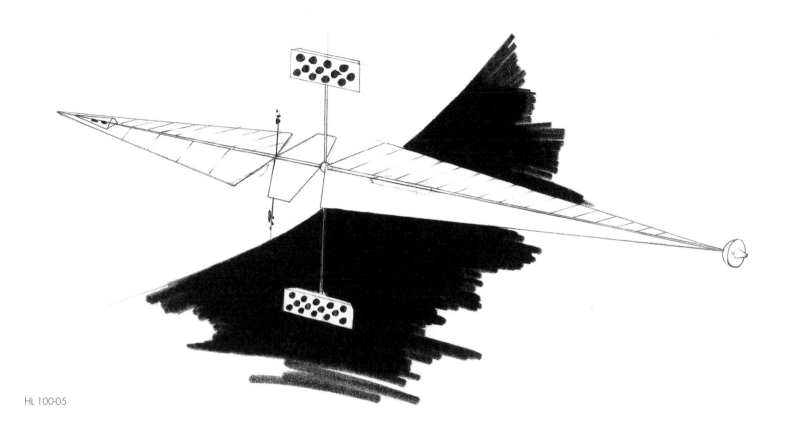

HL 100-05

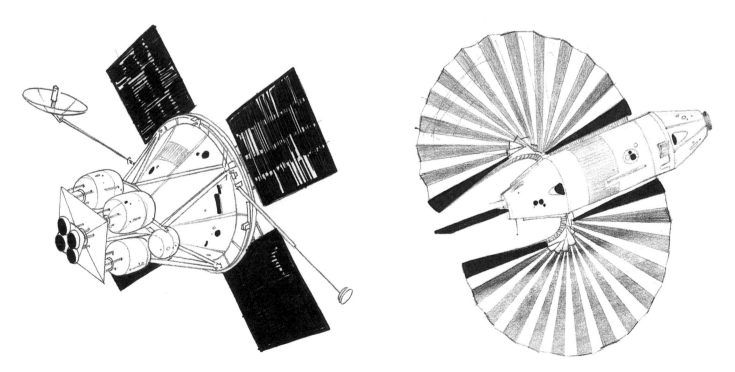

HL 100-06   HL 100-07

ARRIVAL

Orbiting spacecraft (originally nuclear weapon platforms)

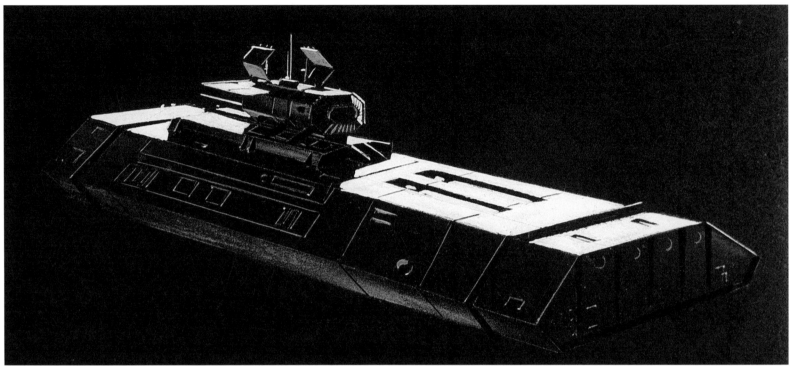

HL 102-01

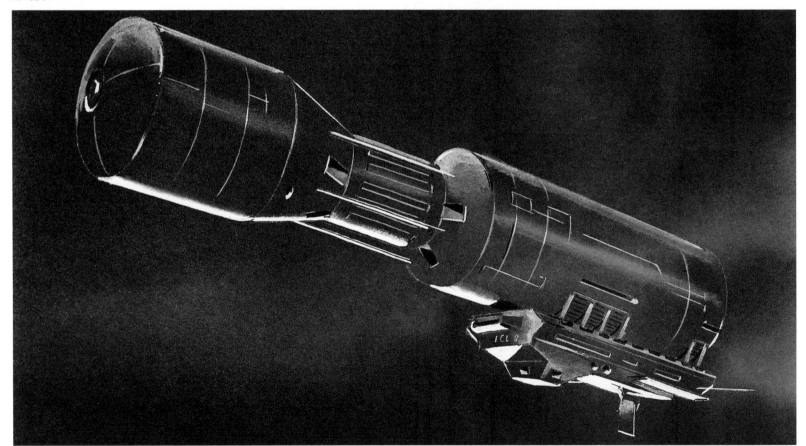

HL 102-02

These designs were evidently intended to look aggressive—like aircraft carriers and cannons: they started life as nuclear weapon platforms.

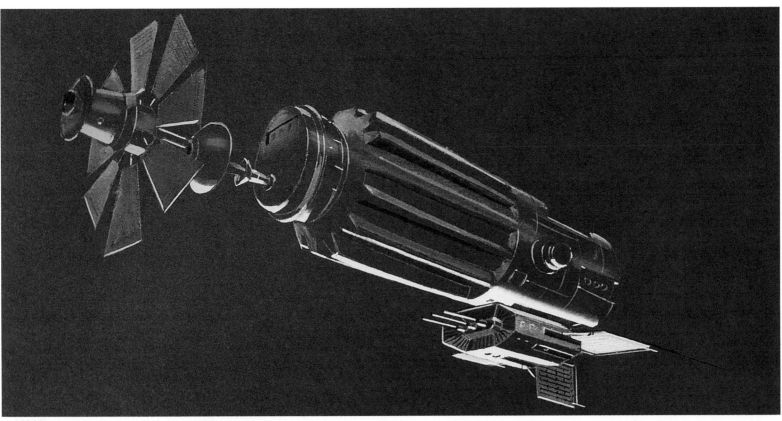

HL 102-03

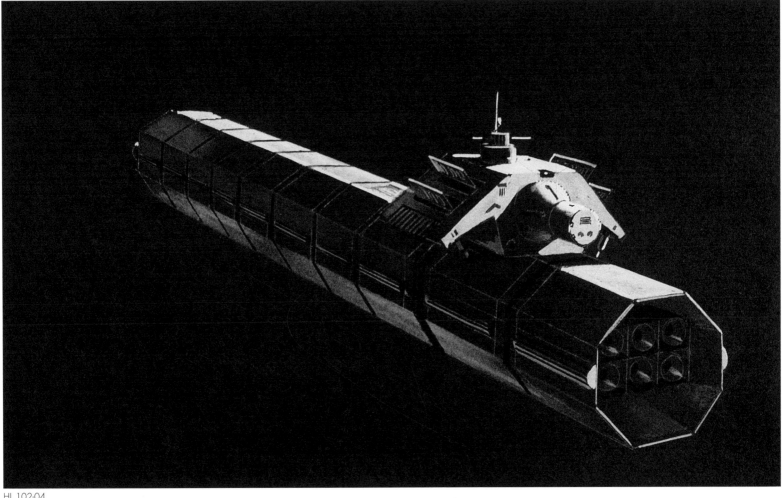

HL 102-04

ORION-III SPACE PLANE
Early design concepts

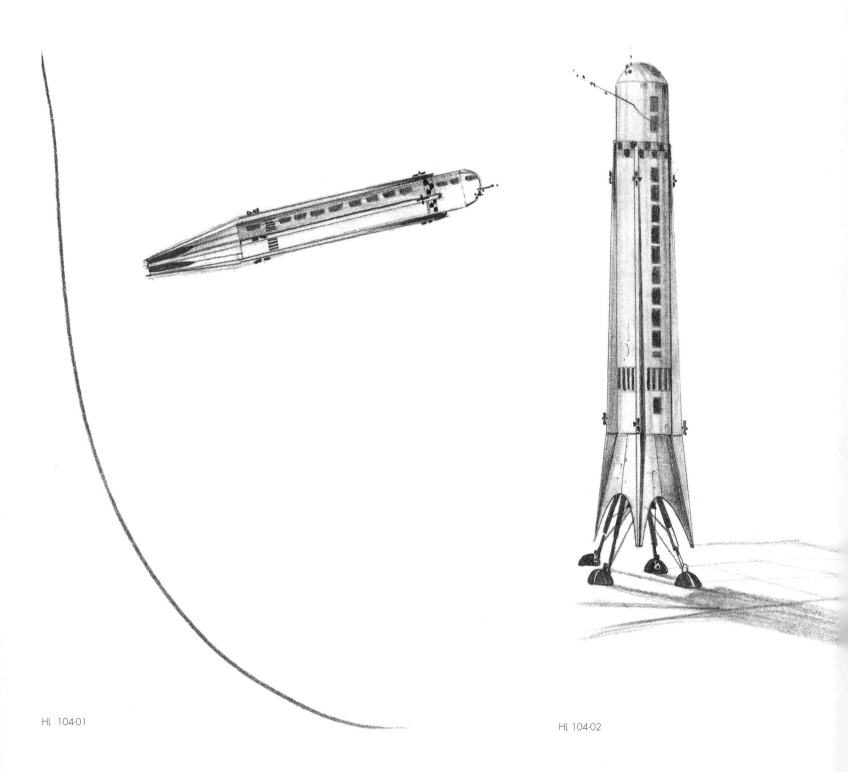

HL 104-01

HL 104-02

HL 104-01 *Early concept for space plane (side elevation).* **HL 104-02** *Space plane with hydraulic undercarriage (side elevation).* **HL104-03** *Early concept for Orion-III with carrier plane.*

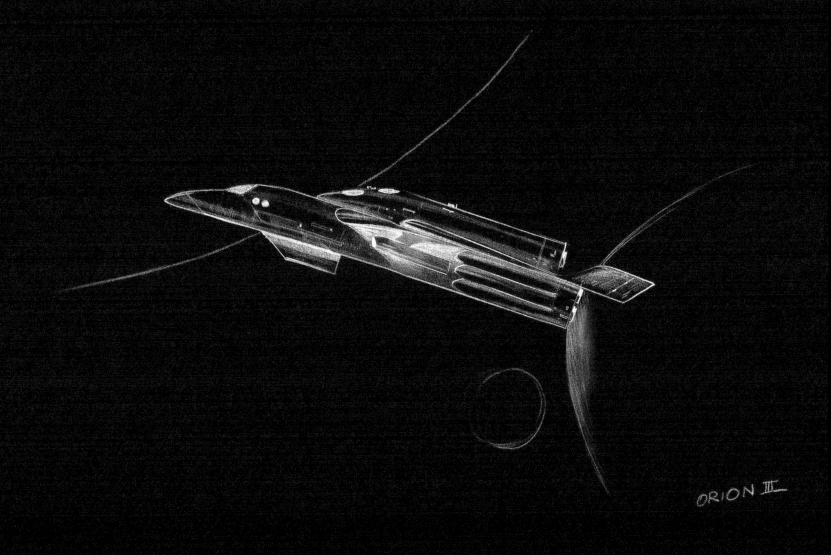

ORION Ⅱ

ORION-III SPACE PLANE

Early concepts, including launch

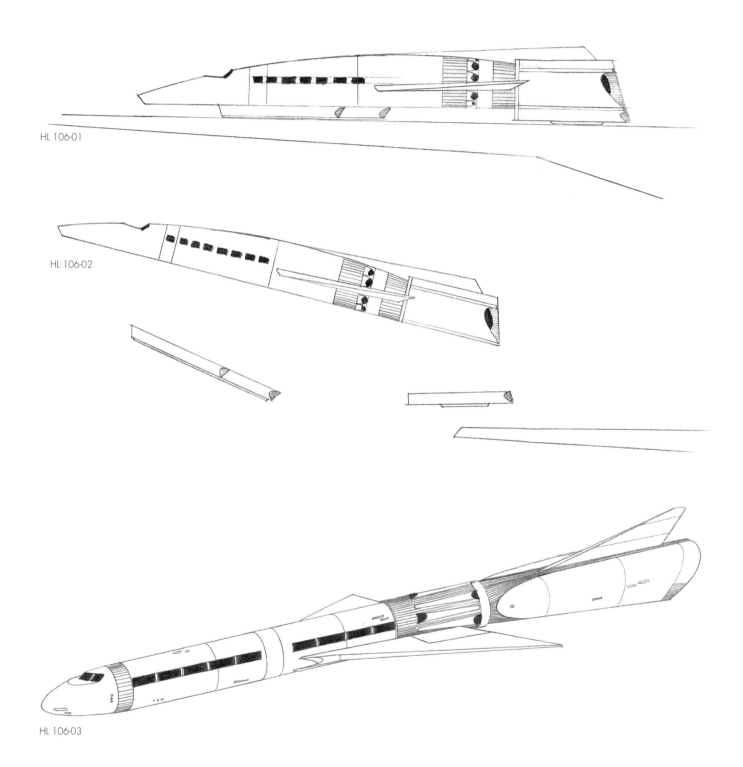

HL 106-01

HL 106-02

HL 106-03

HL 106-01 *Perspective view with pencil annotation.* **HL 106-02** *Space plane concept in launch mode.* **HL 106-03** *Early concept for space plane.* **HL 106-04** *Early concept for space plane (plan view).* **HL 106-05** *Early concept for space plane.* **HL 106-06** *Early concept for space plane.* **HL 106-07** *Early concept for space plane (plan view).*

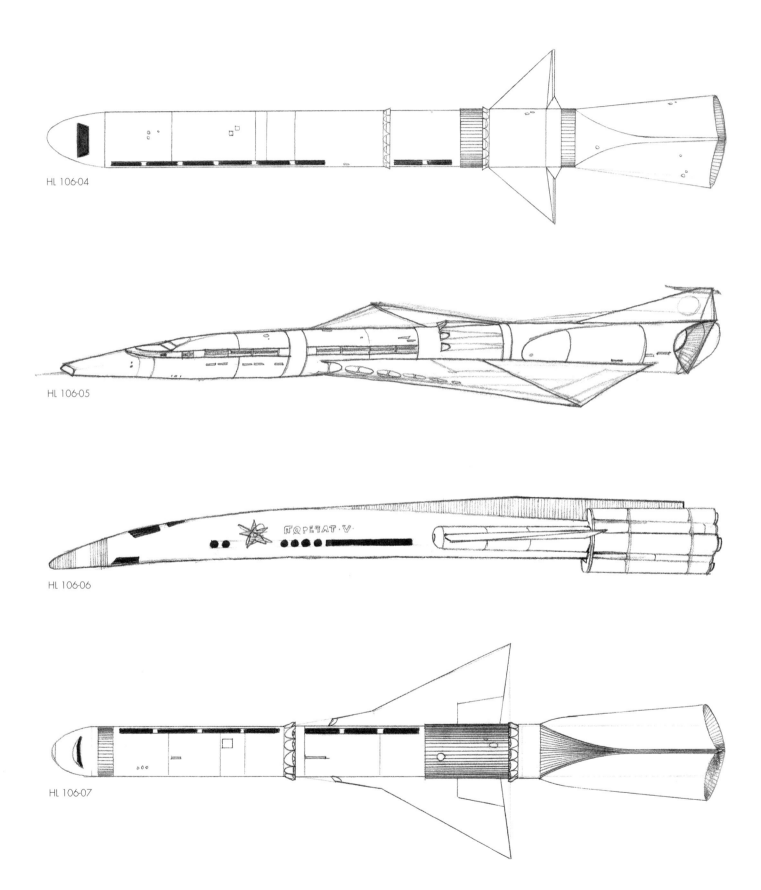

HL 106-04

HL 106-05

HL 106-06

HL 106-07

ORION-III SPACE PLANE

Early concepts with delta wings, and with detachable rocket booster

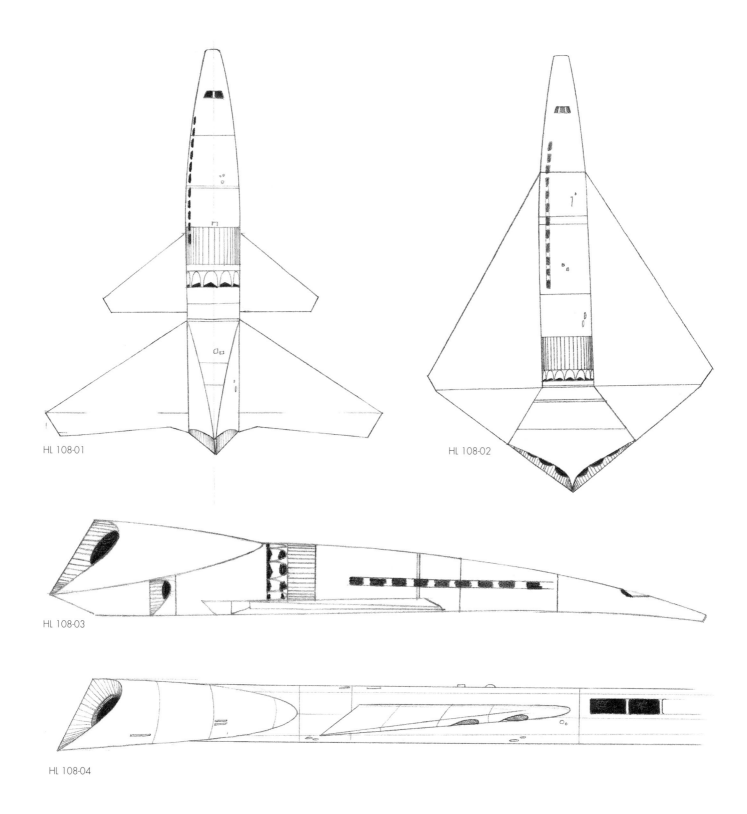

HL 108-01

HL 108-02

HL 108-03

HL 108-04

HL 108-01 *Early concept for space plane with delta wing configuration.* **HL 108-02** *Space plane with double fixed wings (exterior plan view).* **HL 108-03** *Space plane concept (exterior side elevation).* **HL 108-04** *Space plane concept with fixed wing and rocket booster (exterior side elevation).* **HL 108-05** *Space plane concept with fixed wing detachable rocket booster (exterior plan view).*

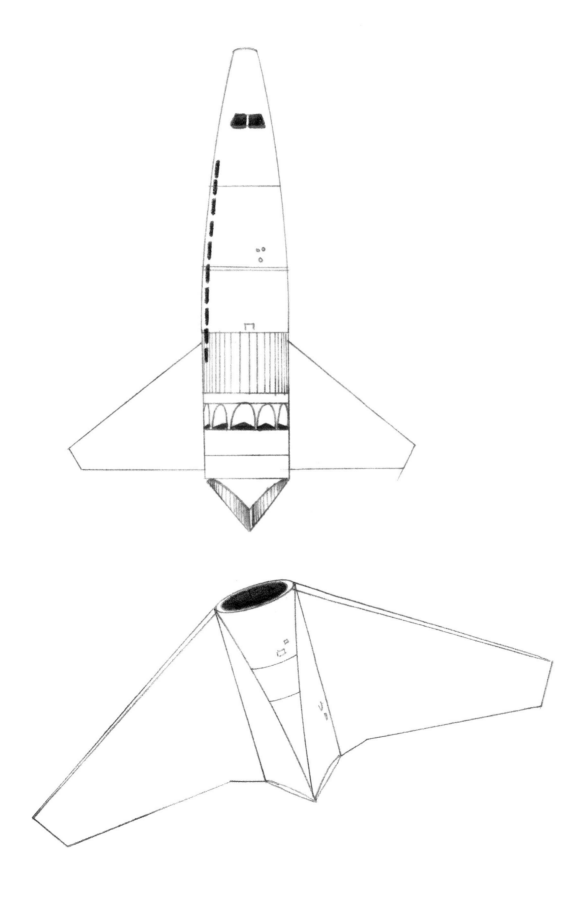

ORION-III SPACE PLANE

Early concepts with rocket boosters

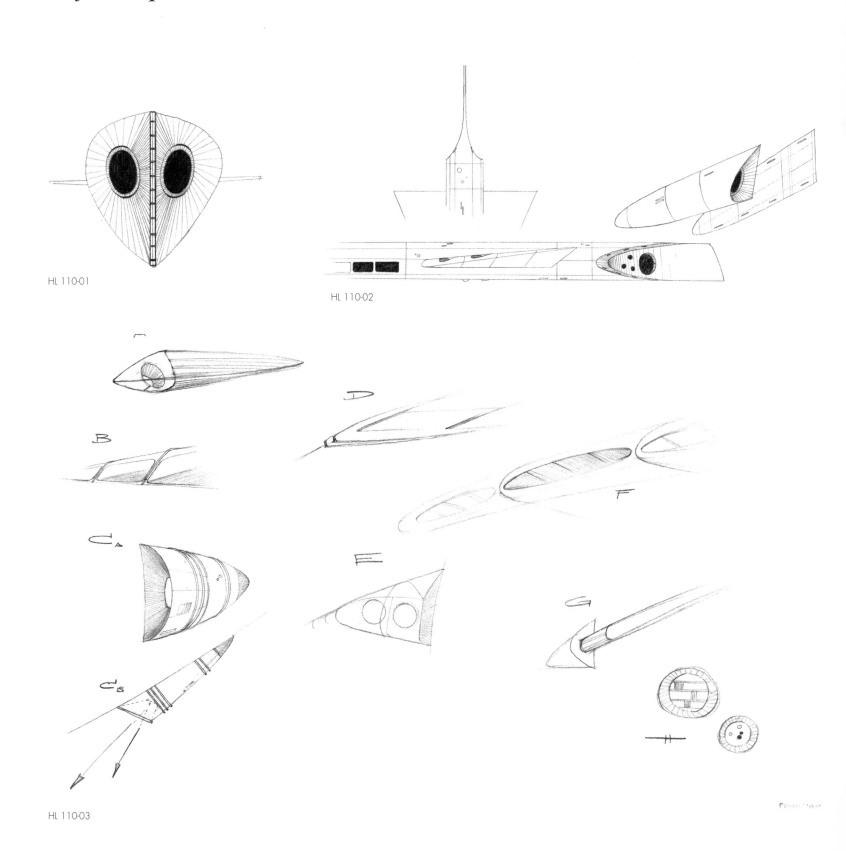

HL 110-01

HL 110-02

HL 110-03

HL 110-01 *Rear view of space plane showing propulsion system.* **HL 110-02** *Early concept for space plane with detailed study of detachable rocket boosters.* **HL 110-03** *Orion rocket booster detail, 9 views.* **HL 110-04** *Space plane with detachable rocket boosters (exterior plan view).* **HL 110-05** *Space plane concept (exterior plan view).* **HL 110-06** *Concept for space plane with detachable winged rocket booster (exterior plan view).*

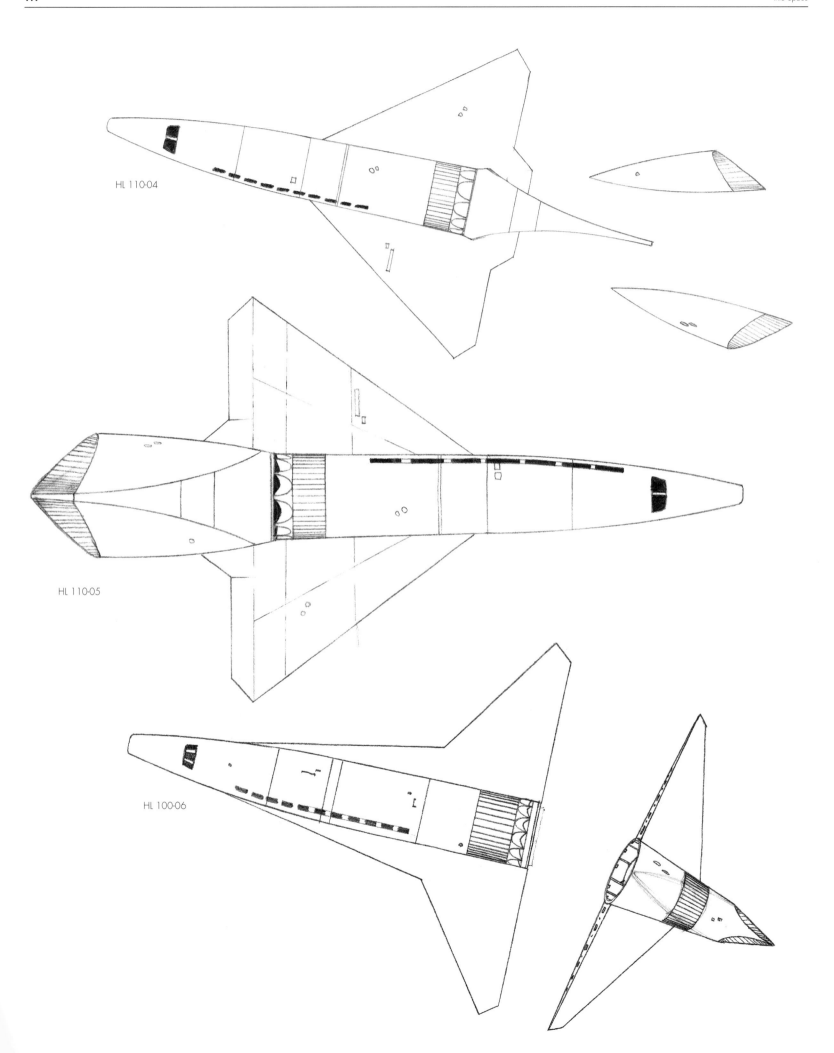

HL 110-04

HL 110-05

HL 100-06

ORION-III SPACE PLANE
Towards the final design

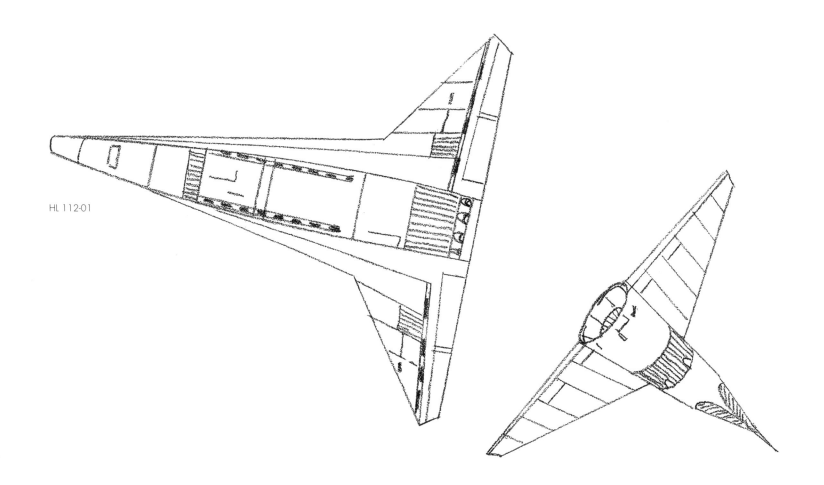

HL 112-01

HL 112-01 *More developed space plane design, still with detachable rocket booster.* **HL 112-02** *Angled space plane design, with attached propulsion system.*

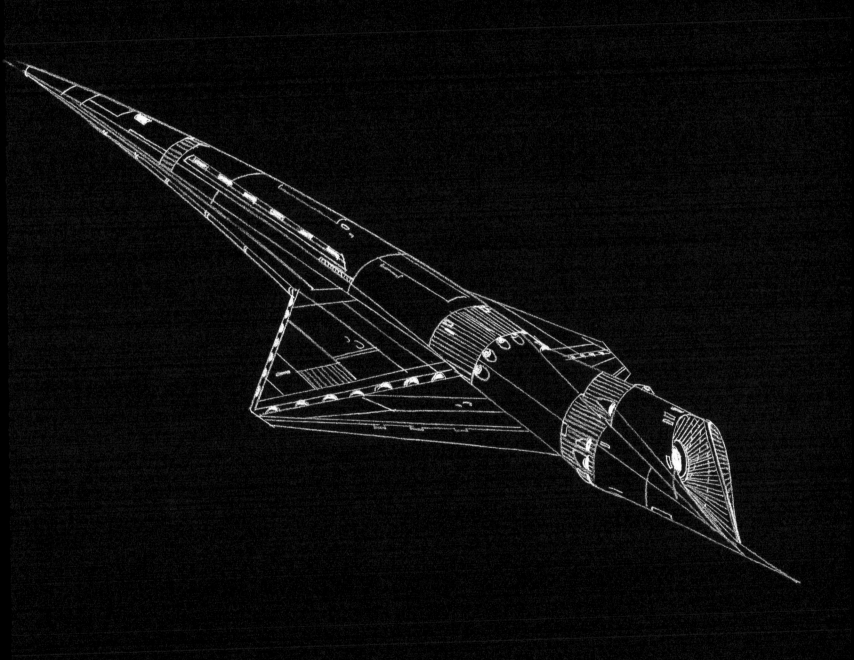

HL 112-02

ORION-III SPACE PLANE
Developed concepts

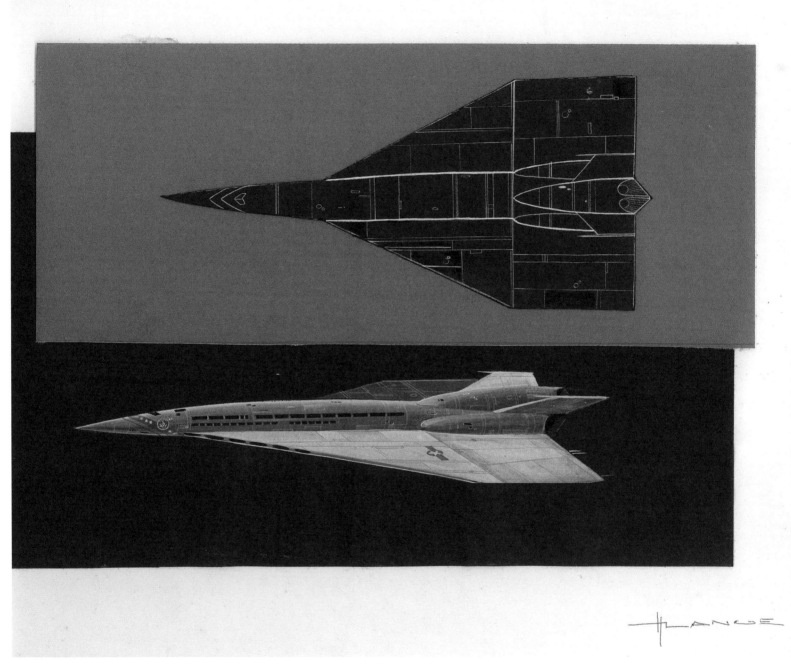

HL 114-01

Two double mounted perspective views, and plan views of the Orion space plane (acrylic on black paper).

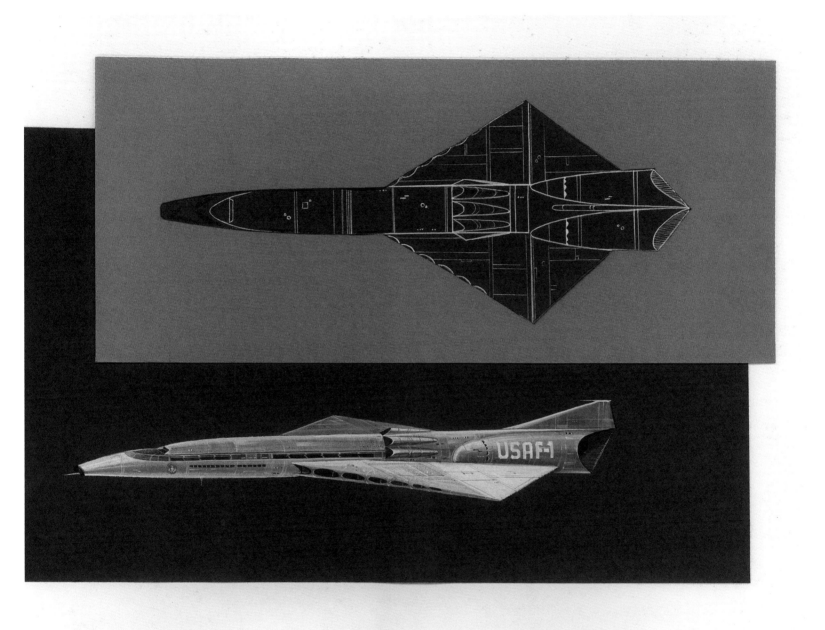

HL 114-02

ORION-III SPACE PLANE
Seating concepts

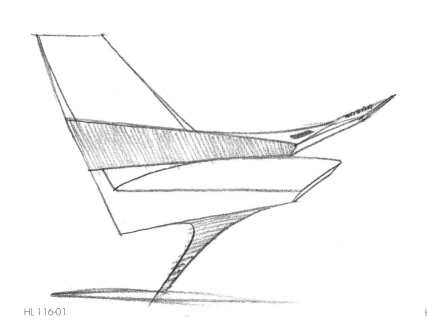

HL 116-01

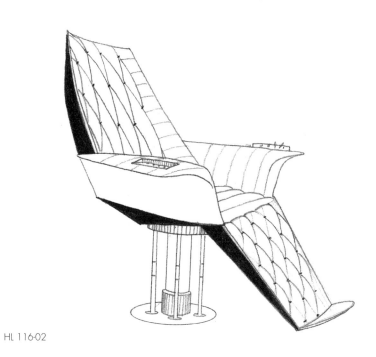

HL 116-02

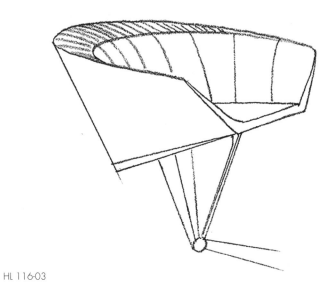

HL 116-03

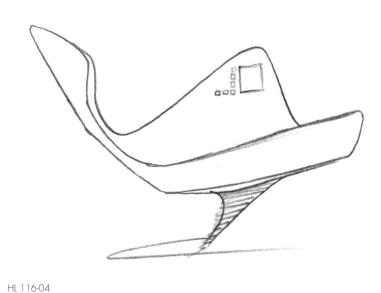

HL 116-04

'Thumbnails' and more developed drawings of seats, most with integral arm rest consoles, and some with adjustable bases.

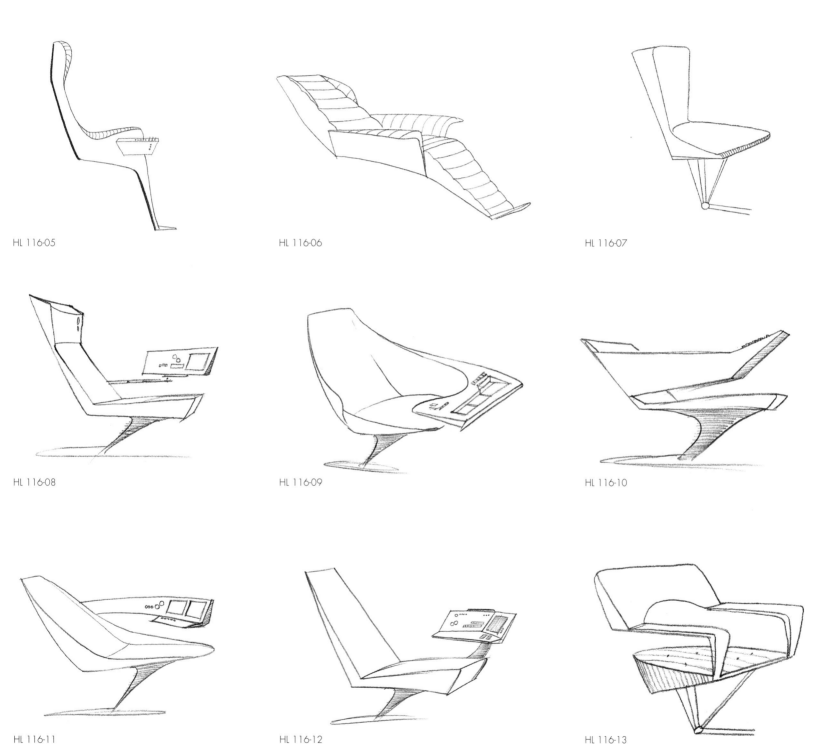

HL 116-05

HL 116-06

HL 116-07

HL 116-08

HL 116-09

HL 116-10

HL 116-11

HL 116-12

HL 116-13

ORION-III SPACE PLANE

Cockpit interior concepts

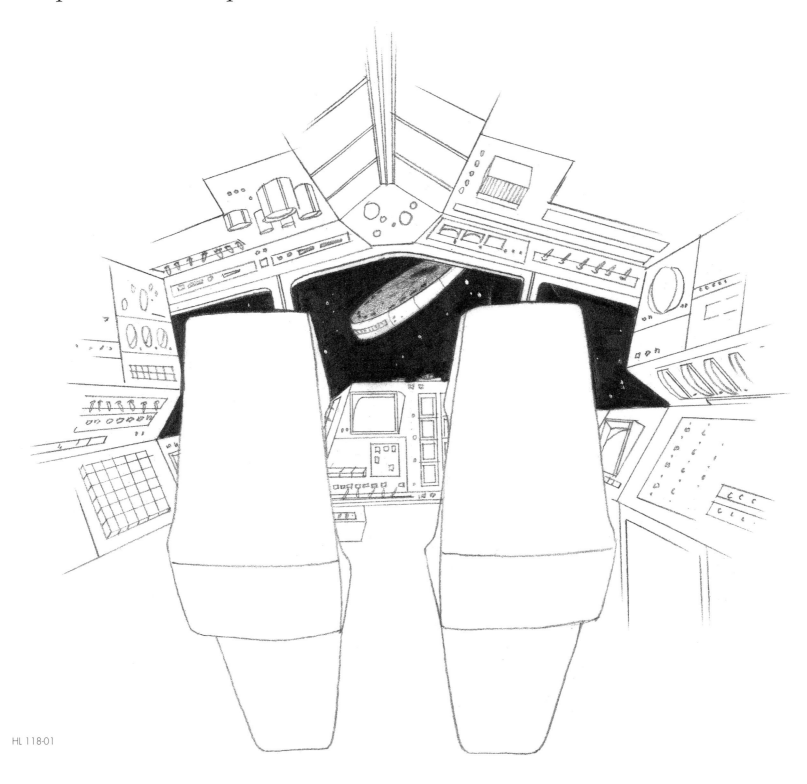

HL 118-01

HL 118-01 *Space plane cockpit interior with space station in distance.* **HL 118-02** *Space plane cockpit interior.* **HL 118-03** *Space plane cockpit interior, alternative view, with navigation instrumentation.*

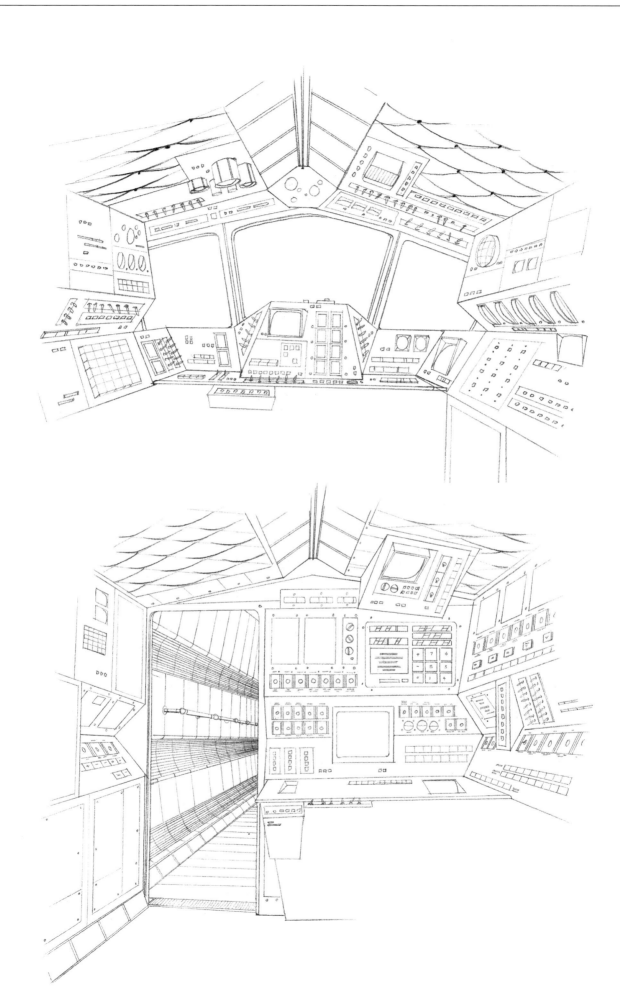

HL 118-02

HL 118-03

SPACE STATION-5

Early concepts

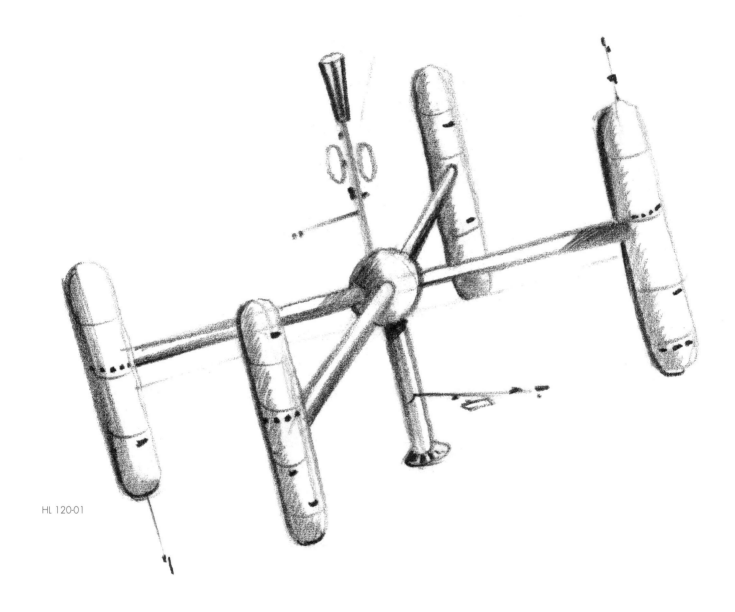

HL 120-01

HL 120-01 *Early concept for Space Station with four elongated accommodation blocks.* **HL 120-02** *Early concept for Space Station with space plane arriving.*

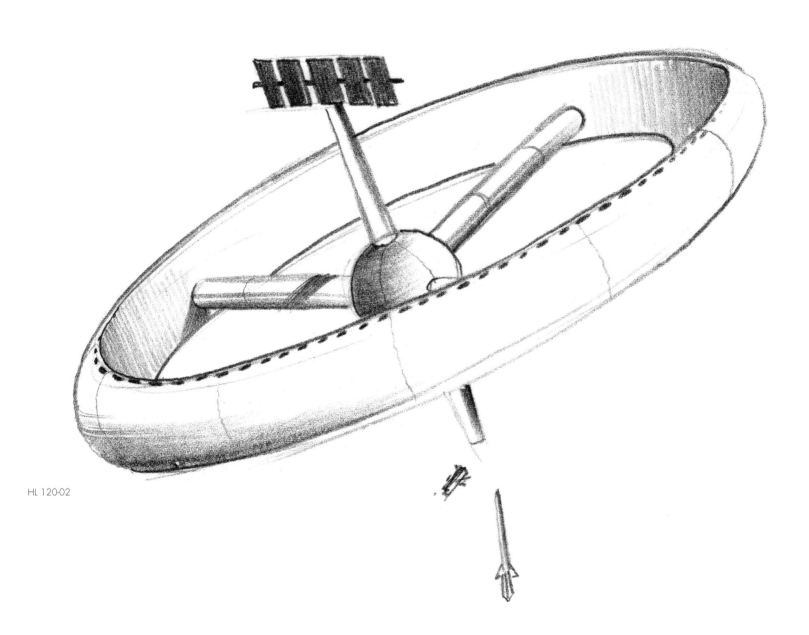

HL 120-02

SPACE STATION-5

Early concepts

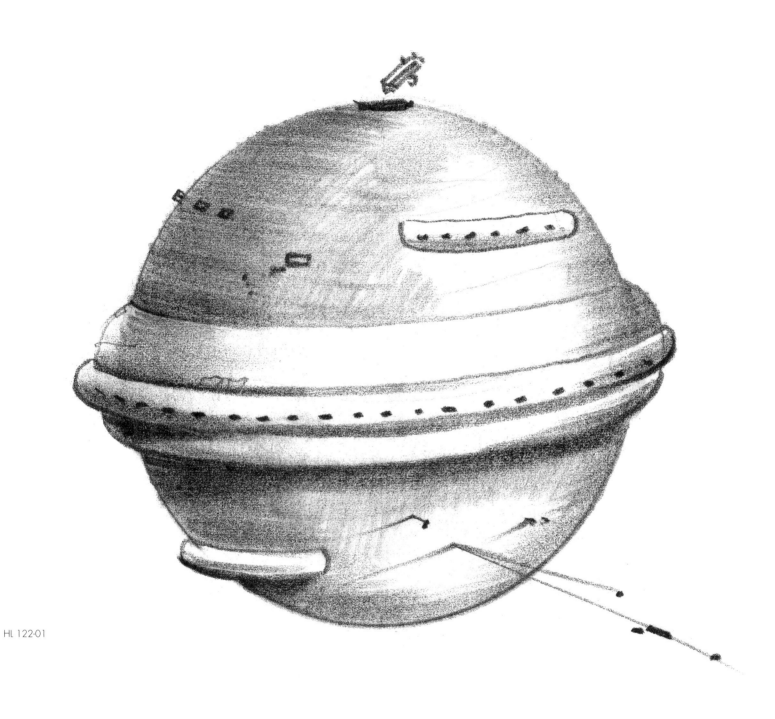

HL 122-01

HL 122-01 *Early concept for spherical Space Station with central accommodation block.* **HL 122-02** *Early concept for conical Space Station with space plane.*

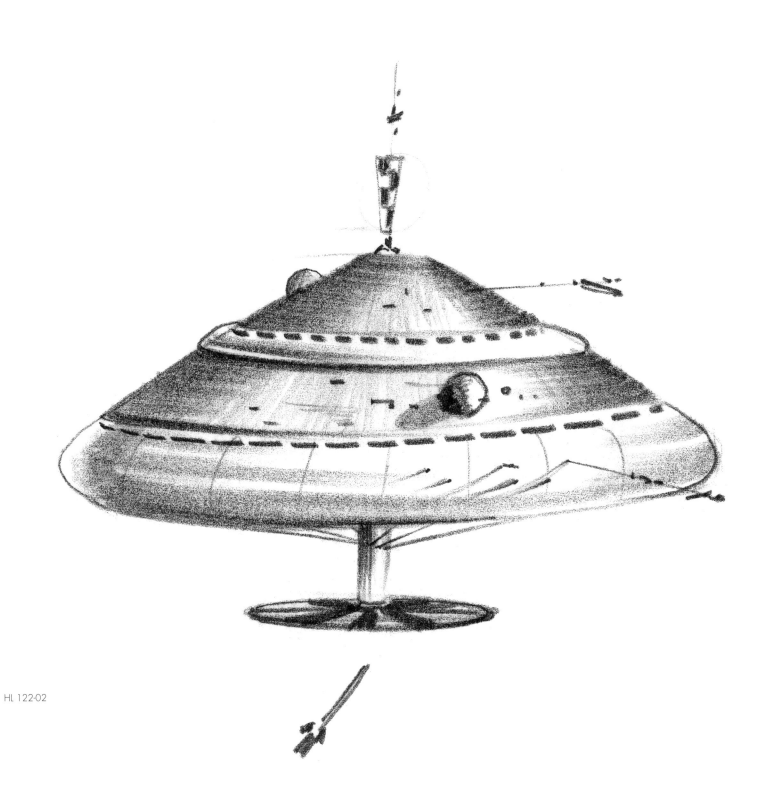

HL 122-02

SPACE STATION-5

Early concepts

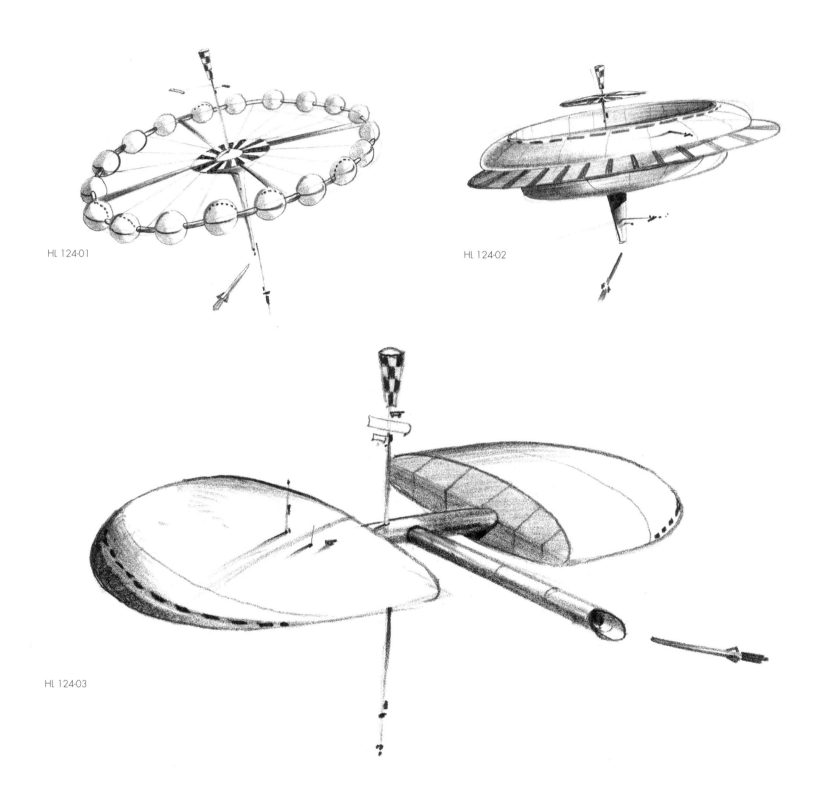

HL 124-01

HL 124-02

HL 124-03

HL 124-01 *Early concept for Space Station with string of spherical accommodation blocks.* **HL 124-02** *Early concept for Space Station with arriving space plane.* **HL 124-03** *Early concept for Space Station with double accommodation blocks and space plane docking bay.* **HL 124-04** *Early concept for multi-element Space Station.* **HL 124-05** *Early concept for Space Station with six rectangular accommodation blocks.* **HL 124-06** *Early concept for Space Station with six accommodation blocks connected to central column with extended arms.*

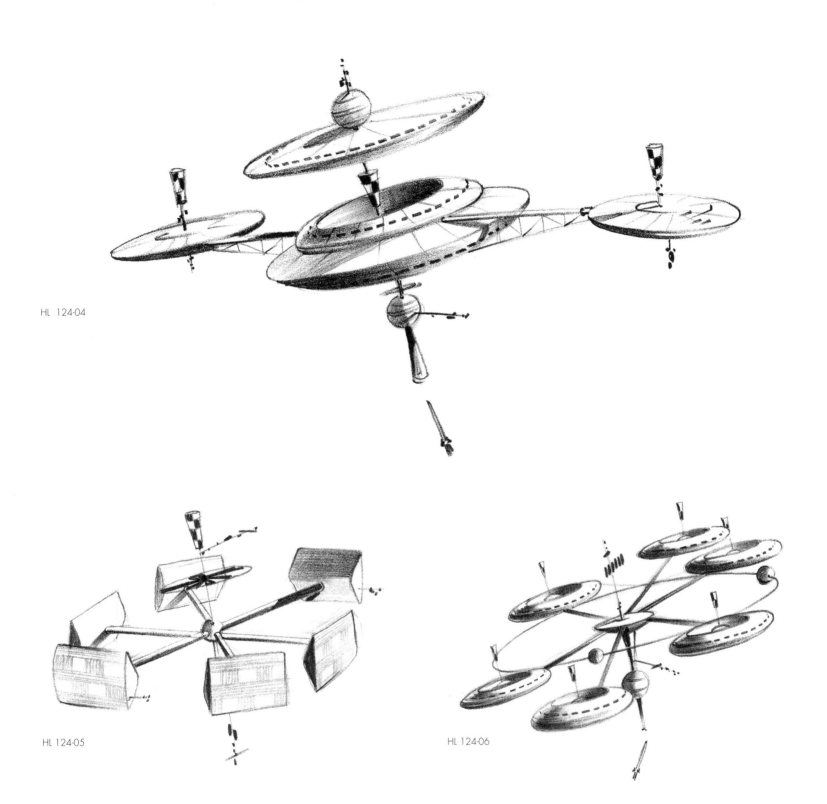

HL 124-04

HL 124-05

HL 124-06

SPACE STATION-5

Early concepts

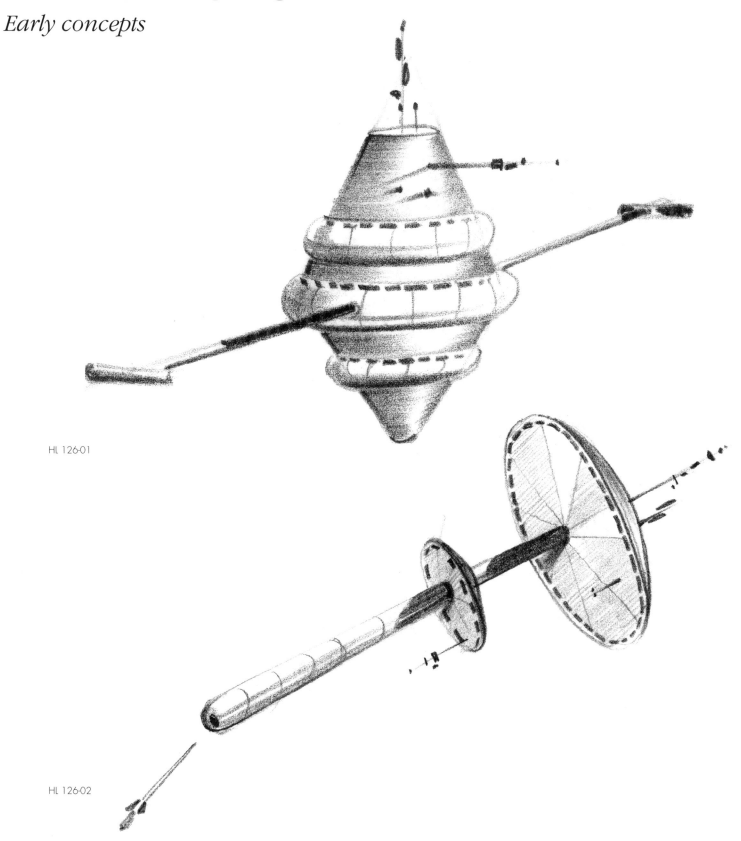

HL 126-01

HL 126-02

HL 126-01 *Early concept for Space station with three central accommodation blocks.* **HL 126-02** *Early concept for Space Station with double accommodation block construction and space plane.* **HL 126-03** *Early concept for Space Station with single fixed accommodation block construction.* **HL 126-04** *Early concept for Space Station with circular accommodation block construction.* **HL 126-05** *Space Station with radiating accommodation block.* **HL 126-06** *Early concept for Space Station with wedge shaped accommodation block.*

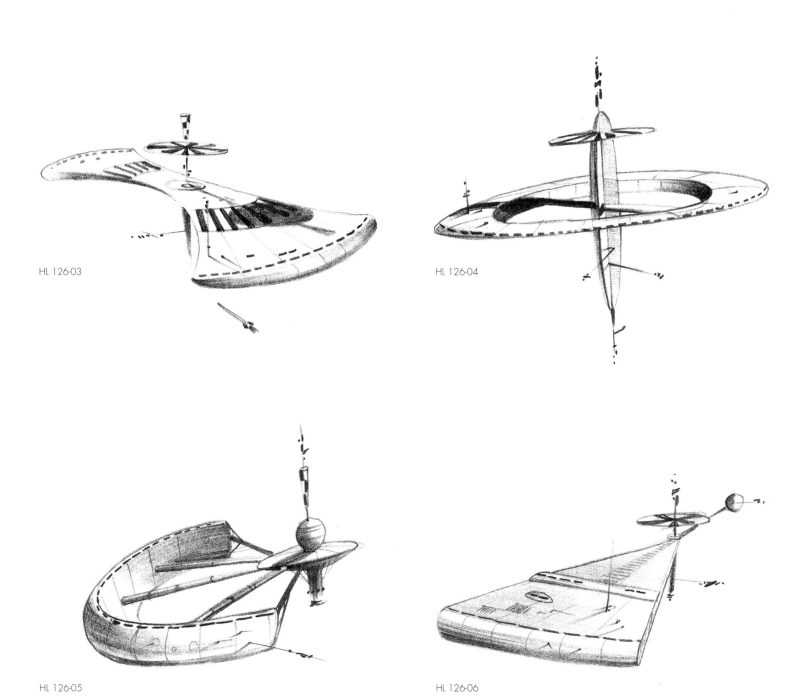

HL 126-03

HL 126-04

HL 126-05

HL 126-06

SPACE STATION-5

Early concepts

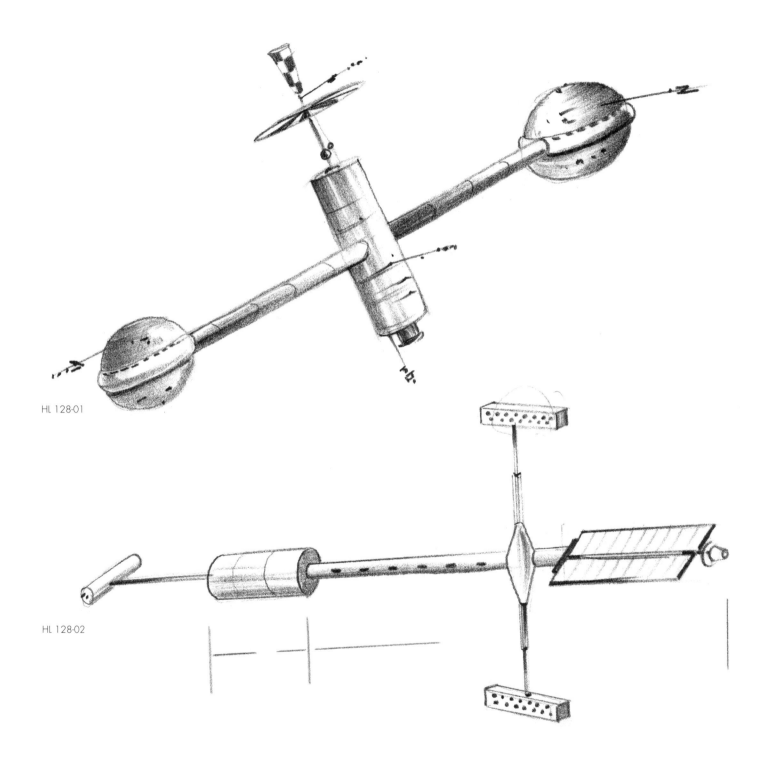

HL 128-01

HL 128-02

HL 128-01 *Early concept for Space Station with two circular accommodation blocks.* **HL 128-02** *Space Station with two rotating accommodation blocks and heat radiation panels.* **HL 128-03** *Spherical Space Station with striped central accommodation block.*

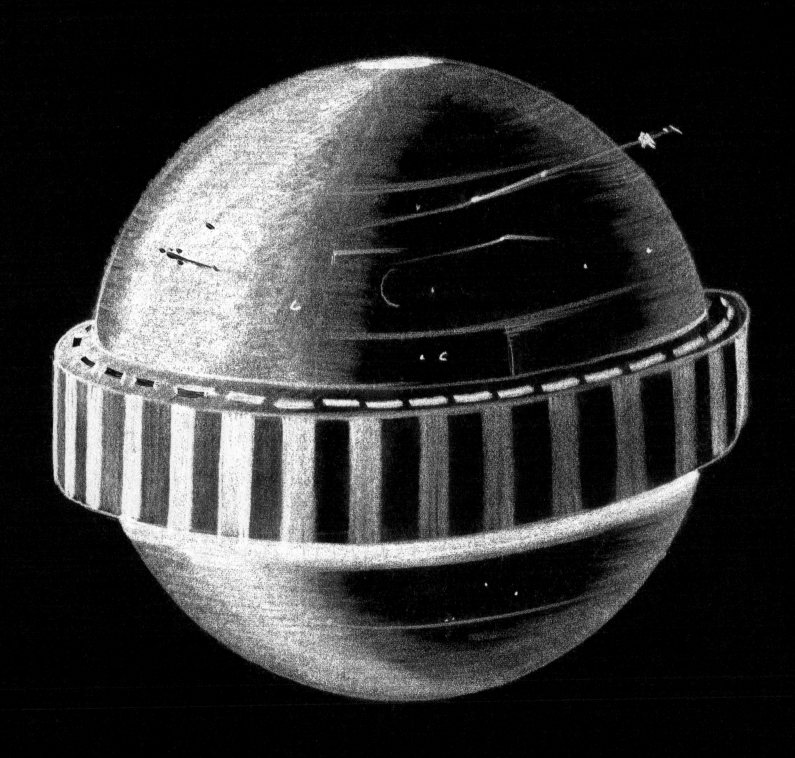

SPACE STATION-5

Early circular concepts

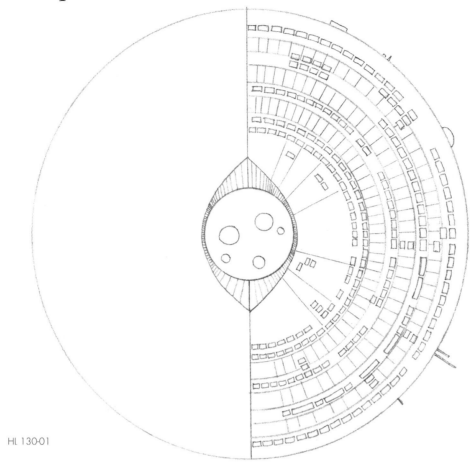

HL 130-01

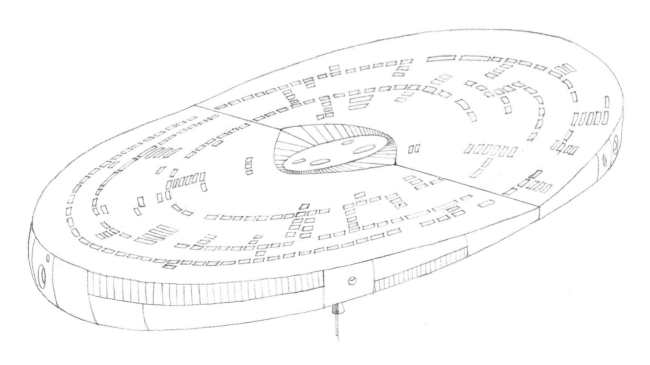

HL 130-02

Three views of circular Space Station, with central space plane docking bay.

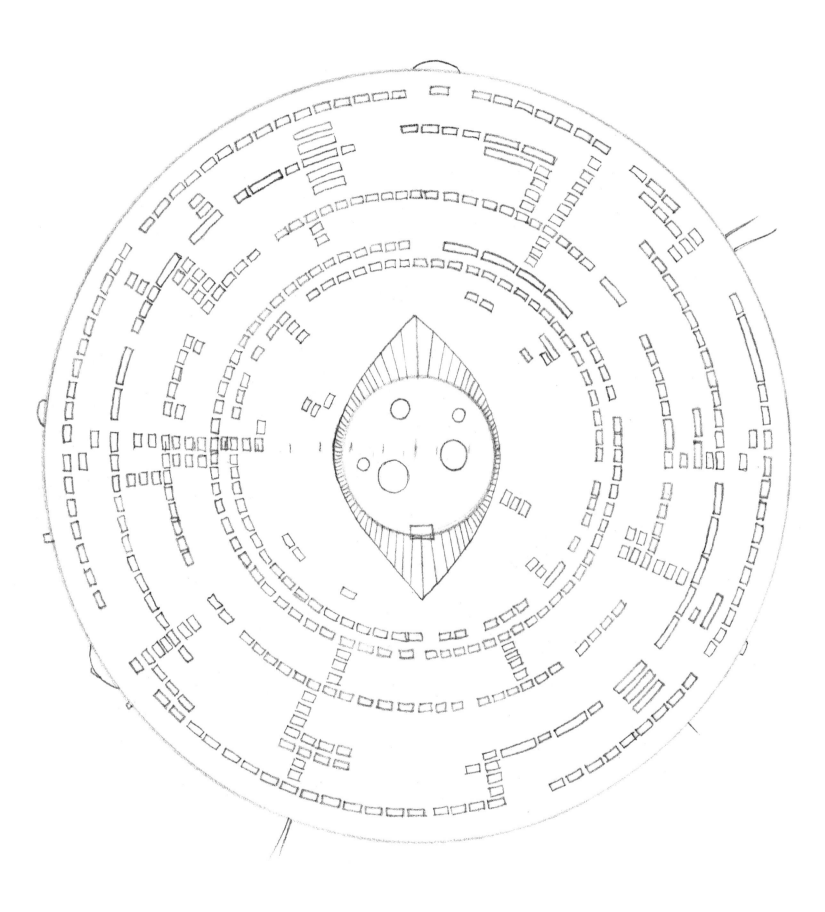

SPACE STATION-5

Early concepts, with docking bays

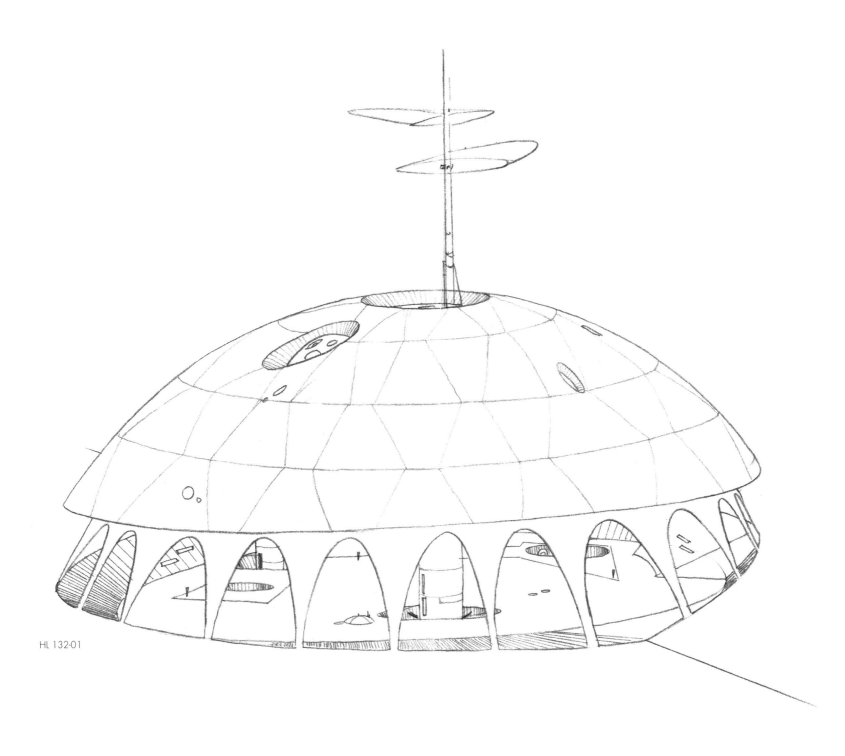

HL 132-01

HL 132-01 *Docking bay detail for space plane on Space Station, with exterior finish.* **HL 132-02** *Enclosed circular Space Station with antenna.* **HL 132-03** *Space Station central docking bay (exterior view).* **HL 132-04** *Space Station docking bays for space planes.*

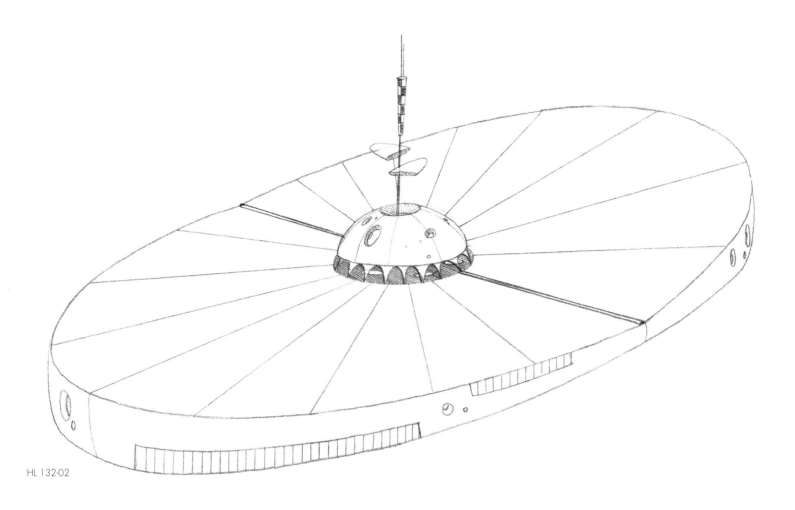

HL 132-02

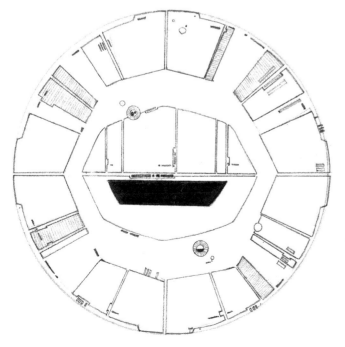

HL 132-03

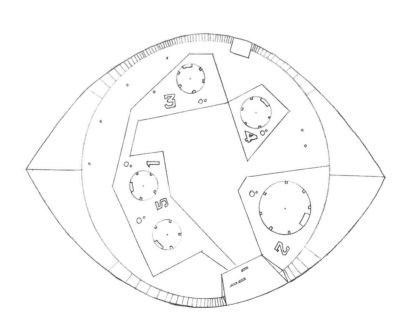

HL 132-04

SPACE STATION-5

Early circular concepts

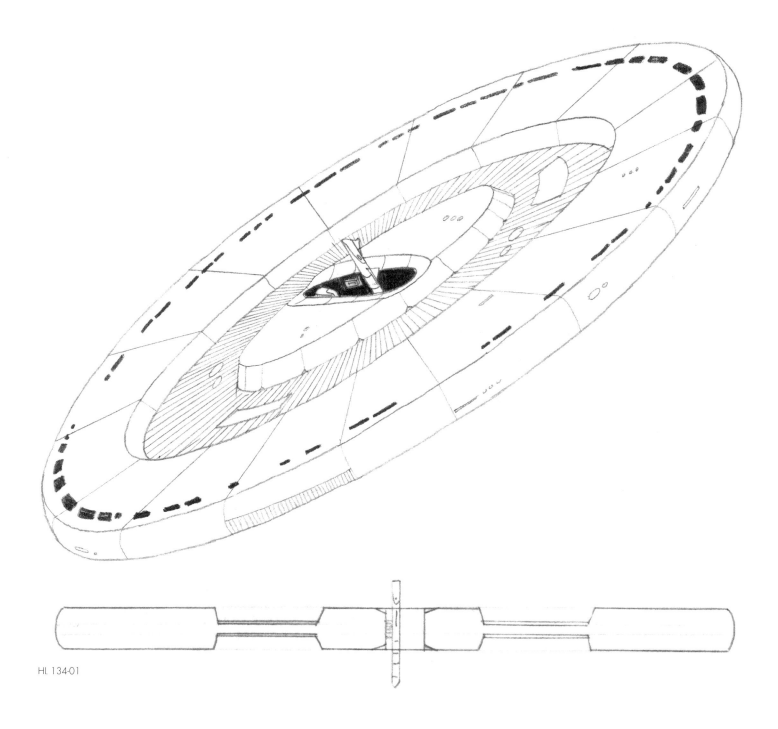

HL 134-01

HL 134-01 *Circular Space Station with central docking bay for space plane (including cross section).* **HL 134-02** *Docking bay cross section concept with assorted space craft—crossover with space pods: a composite drawing.*

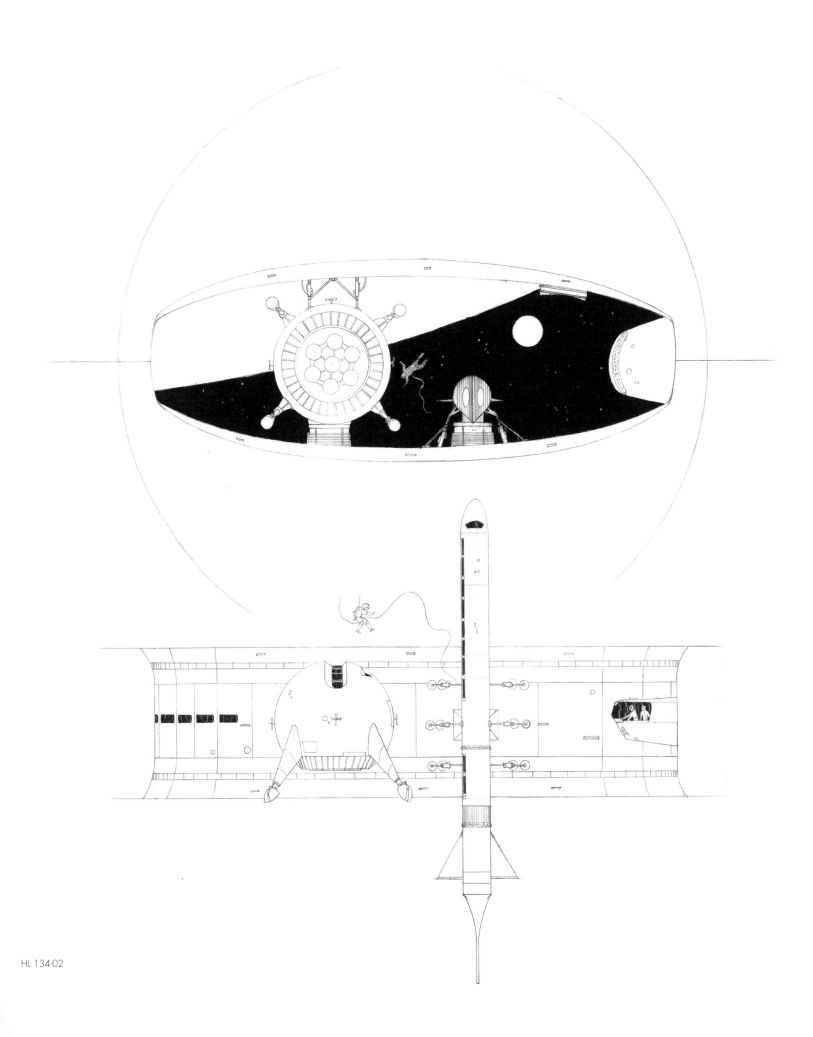

SPACE STATION-5

Docking bay details

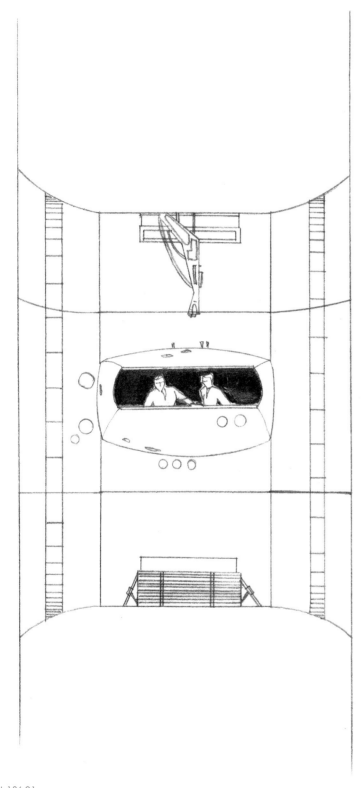

HL 136-01

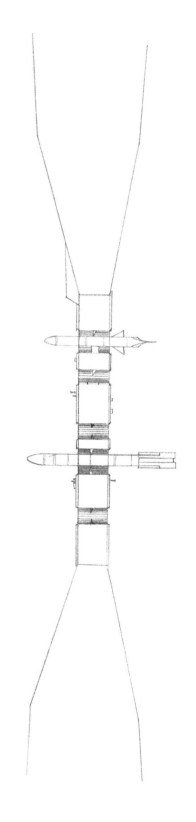

HL 136-02

HL 136-01 *Interior docking for space plane.* **HL 136-02** *Cross section of space plane docking bay in Space Station.* **HL 136-03** *Space planes in Space Station docking bay.*
HL 136-04 *Space plane docking bay, looking upwards.*

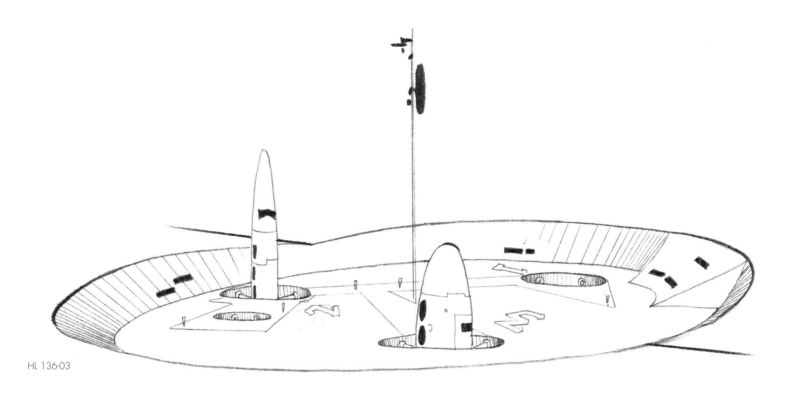

HL 136-03

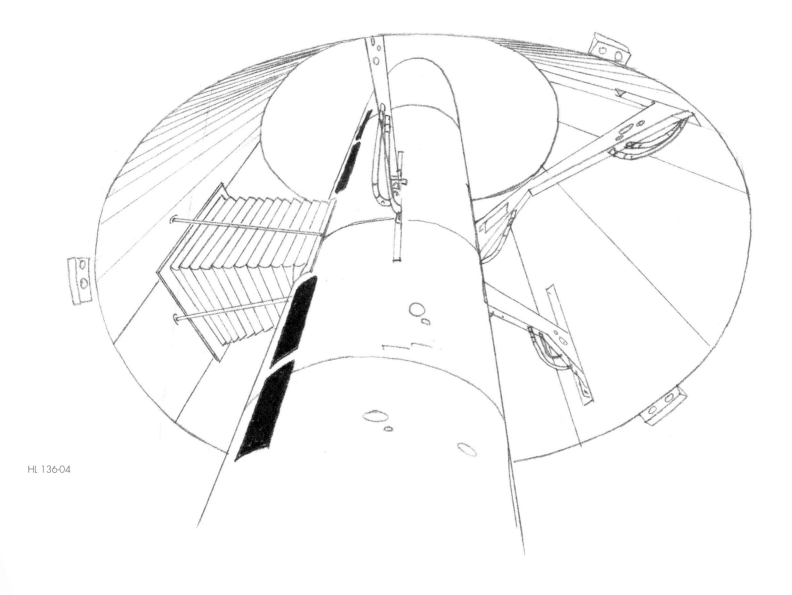

HL 136-04

SPACE STATION-5

Early Catherine wheel concepts

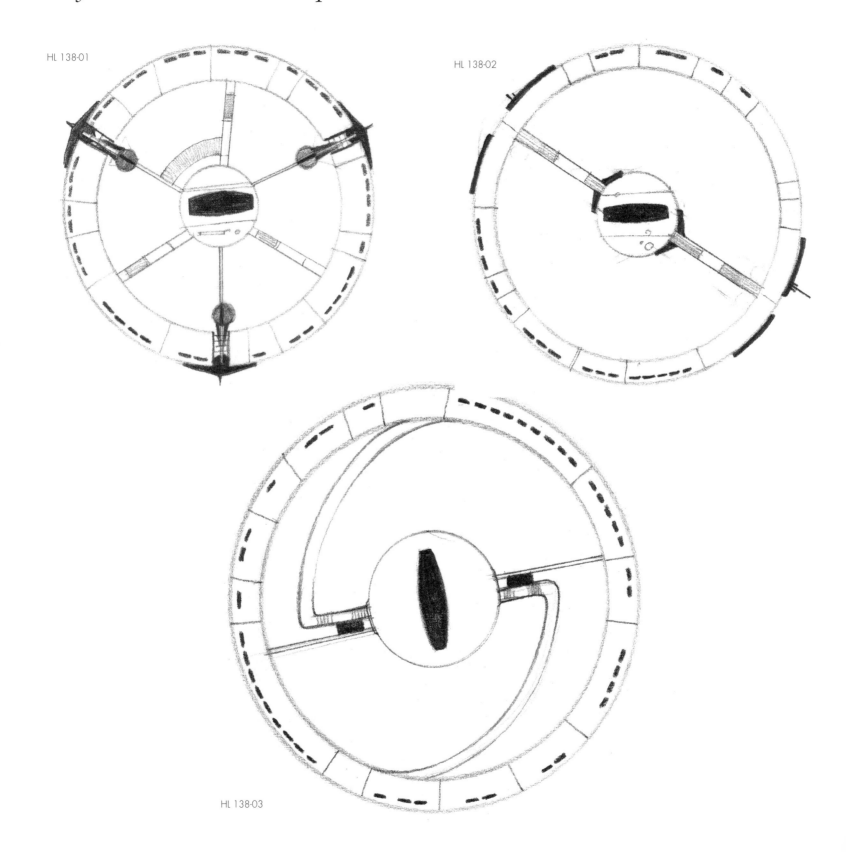

HL 138-01

HL 138-02

HL 138-03

HL 138-01 *Catherine wheel design with three broad accommodation blocks and central docking bay (exterior view).* **HL 138-02** *Catherine wheel design with central docking bay and two connecting columns.* **HL 138-03** *Catherine wheel design (from above).* **HL 138-04** *Catherine wheel design with four broad accommodation blocks and central docking bay (exterior view).* **HL 138-05** *Catherine wheel design with four broad accommodation blocks (perspective view of the one above).*

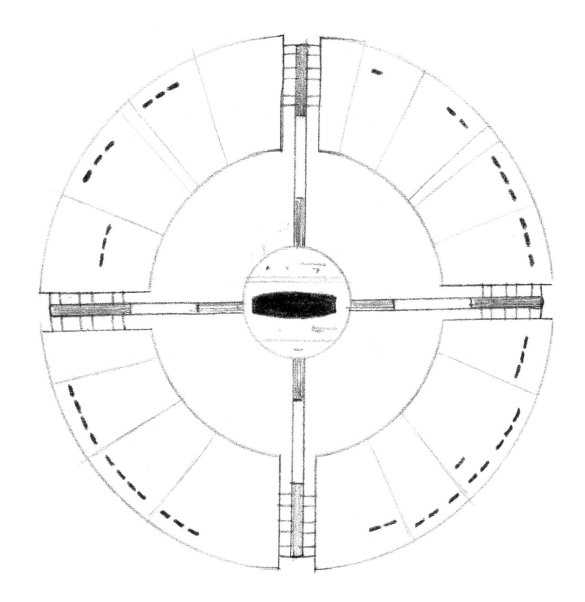

HL 138-04

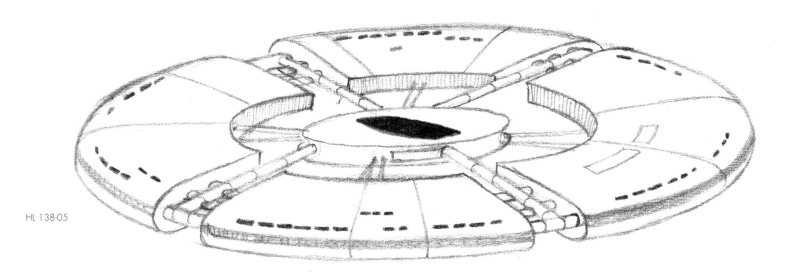

HL 138-05

SPACE STATION-5

Details of window apertures, and of interior

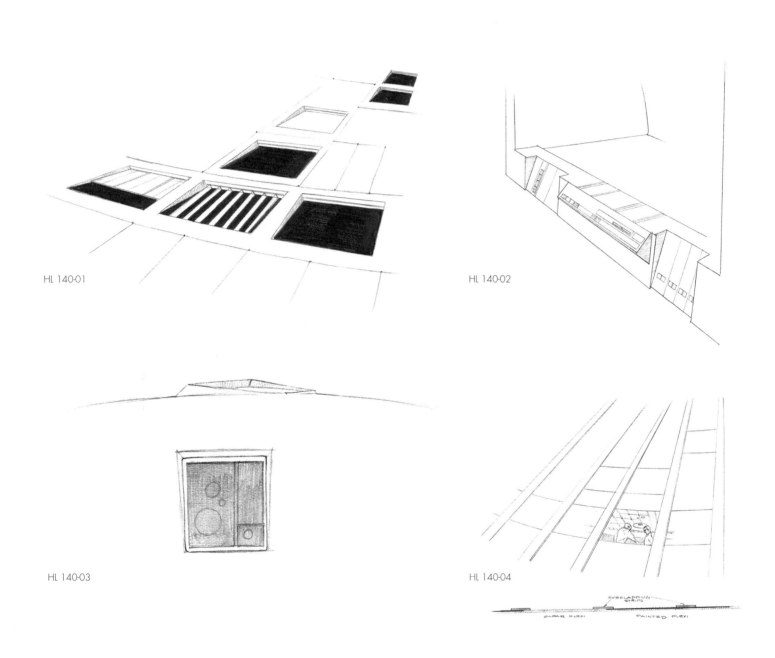

HL 140-01

HL 140-02

HL 140-03

HL 140-04

HL 140-01 *Space Station exterior window apertures with adjustable shades.* **HL 140-02** *Space Station interior window, with console.* **HL 140-03** *Exterior window aperture (front and side view).* **HL 140-04** *Perspective window view of Space Station with construction detail.* **HL 140-05** *Two designs of Space Station interior with three window apertures, entrances and vegetation.*

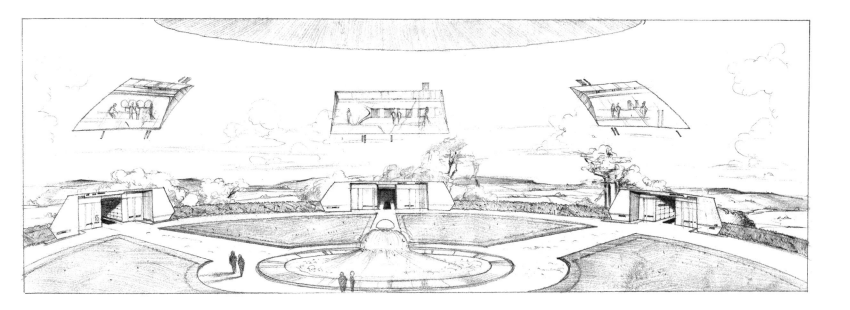

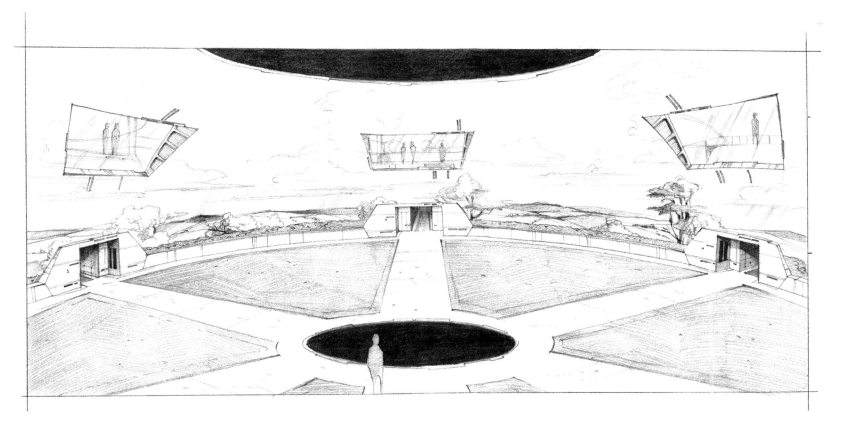

HL 140-05

SPACE STATION-5

Context drawing

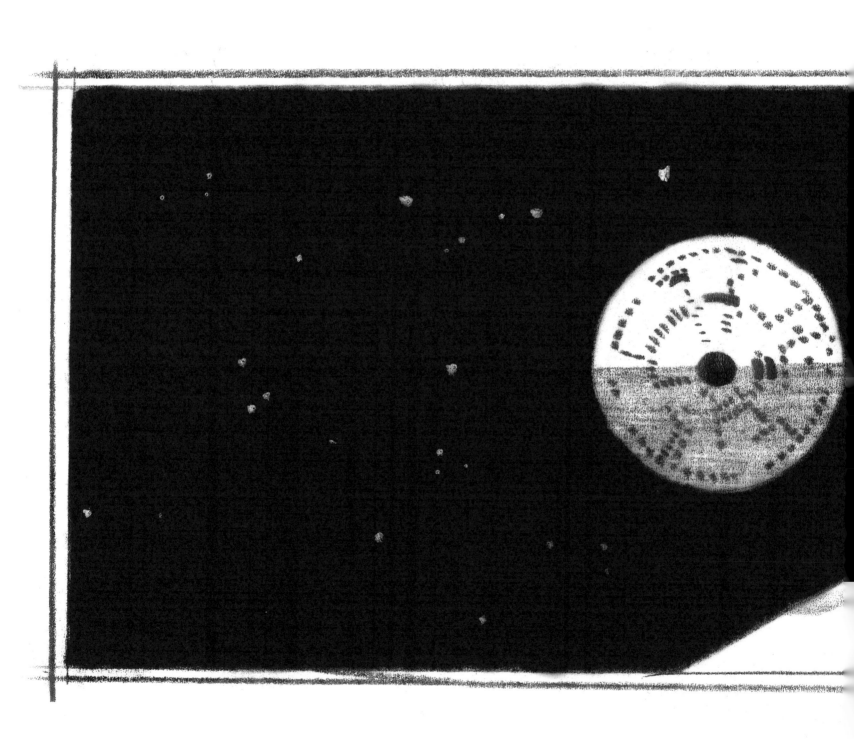

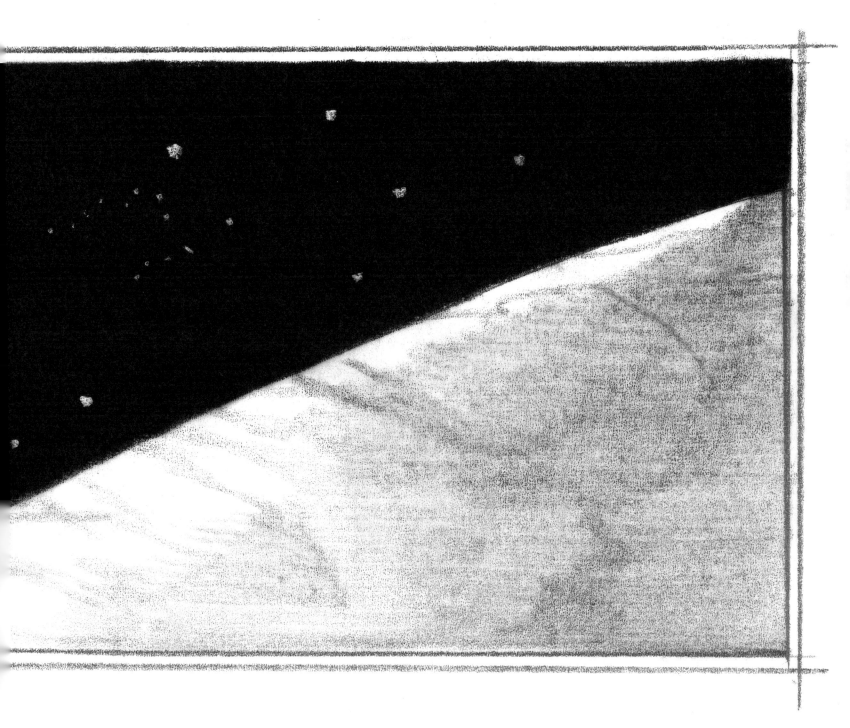

SPACE STATION-5

Towards the final design

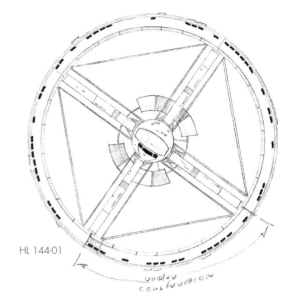

HL 144-01

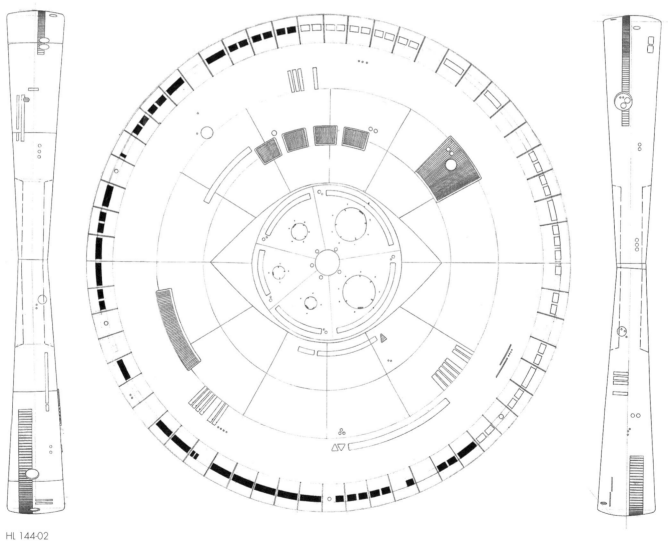

HL 144-02

HL 144-01 *Circular Catherine wheel design with annotation under one section 'under construction'.* **HL 144-02** *Space Station plan view and 2 side elevations.*
HL 144-03 *Developed design of double Catherine wheel Space Station with inscriptions 'USAA' and '137-5'.*

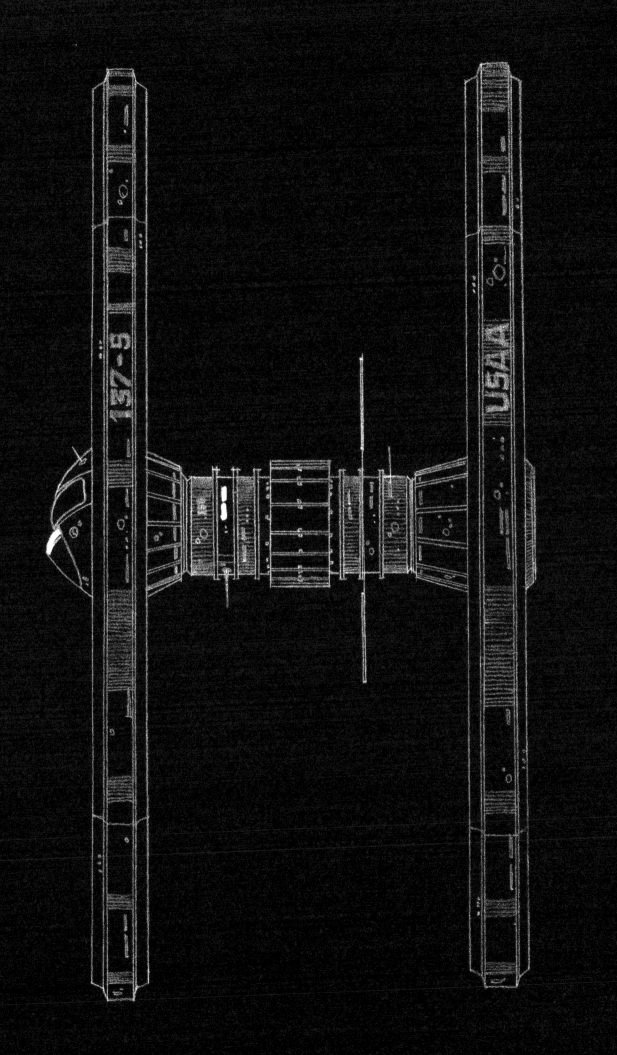

HL 144-03

SPACE STATION-5

Final design blueprint

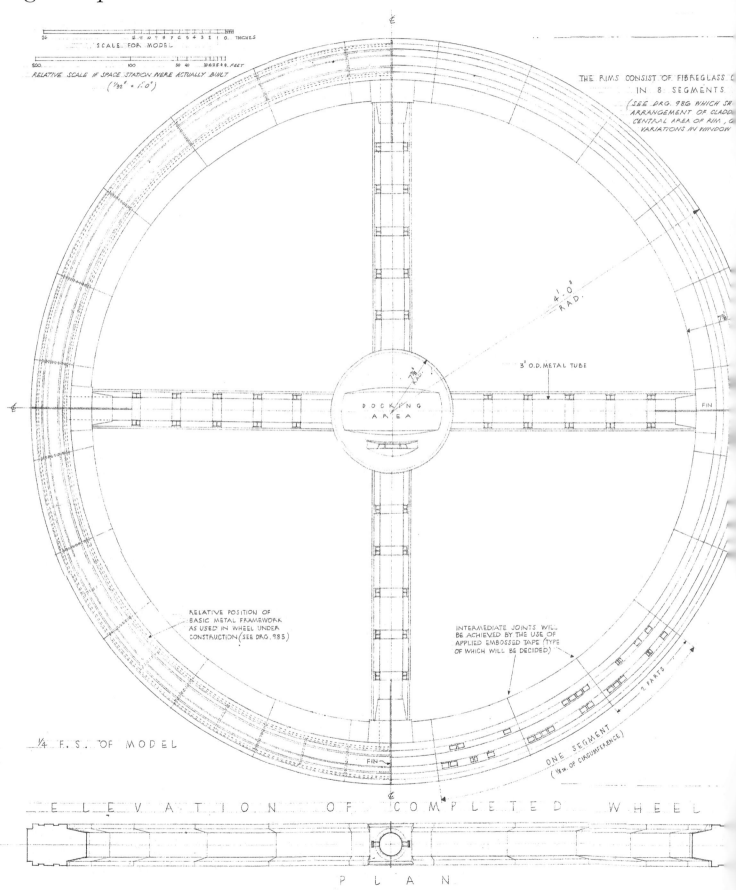

Detailed insructions for model of Space Station-5.

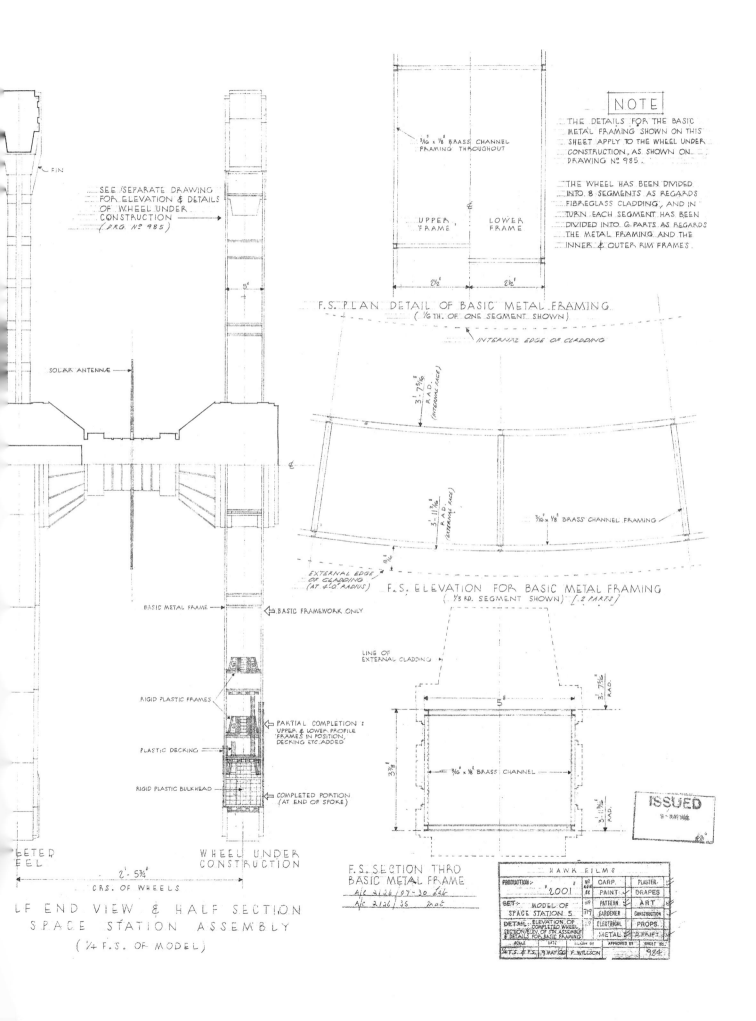

SEE SEPARATE DRAWING
FOR ELEVATION & DETAILS
OF WHEEL UNDER
CONSTRUCTION
(DRG. Nº 985)

FIN

SOLAR ANTENNÆ

BASIC METAL FRAME ← →← BASIC FRAMEWORK ONLY

RIGID PLASTIC FRAMES

← PARTIAL COMPLETION :
UPPER & LOWER PROFILE
FRAMES IN POSITION,
DECKING ETC. ADDED

PLASTIC DECKING

RIGID PLASTIC BULKHEAD

← COMPLETED PORTION
(AT END OF SPOKE)

PLETED
EEL

WHEEL UNDER
CONSTRUCTION

2'- 5¾"
CRS. OF WHEELS

LF END VIEW & HALF SECTION
SPACE STATION ASSEMBLY
(¼ F.S. OF MODEL)

³⁄₁₆" × ⅛" BRASS CHANNEL
FRAMING THROUGHOUT

NOTE

THE DETAILS FOR THE BASIC
METAL FRAMING SHOWN ON THIS
SHEET APPLY TO THE WHEEL UNDER
CONSTRUCTION, AS SHOWN ON
DRAWING Nº 985.

THE WHEEL HAS BEEN DIVIDED
INTO 8 SEGMENTS AS REGARDS
FIBREGLASS CLADDING, AND IN
TURN EACH SEGMENT HAS BEEN
DIVIDED INTO 6 PARTS AS REGARDS
THE METAL FRAMING AND THE
INNER & OUTER RIM FRAMES.

UPPER
FRAME

LOWER
FRAME

2½"   2½"

F.S. PLAN DETAIL OF BASIC METAL FRAMING
(⅙ TH. OF ONE SEGMENT SHOWN)

INTERNAL EDGE OF CLADDING

3'- 7⁵⁄₁₆" RAD. (INTERNAL FACE)

3'- 11³⁄₁₆" RAD. (EXTERNAL FACE)

³⁄₁₆" × ⅛" BRASS CHANNEL FRAMING

EXTERNAL EDGE
OF CLADDING
(AT 4'·0" RADIUS)

F.S. ELEVATION FOR BASIC METAL FRAMING
(⅓ RD. SEGMENT SHOWN) [2 PARTS]

LINE OF
EXTERNAL CLADDING

3'- 7⁵⁄₁₆" RAD.

5"

3⅞"

³⁄₁₆" × ⅛" BRASS CHANNEL

3'- 11³⁄₁₆" RAD.

ISSUED

F.S. SECTION THRO
BASIC METAL FRAME
A/c 2126/97-30 Lab
A/c 2126/35 mat

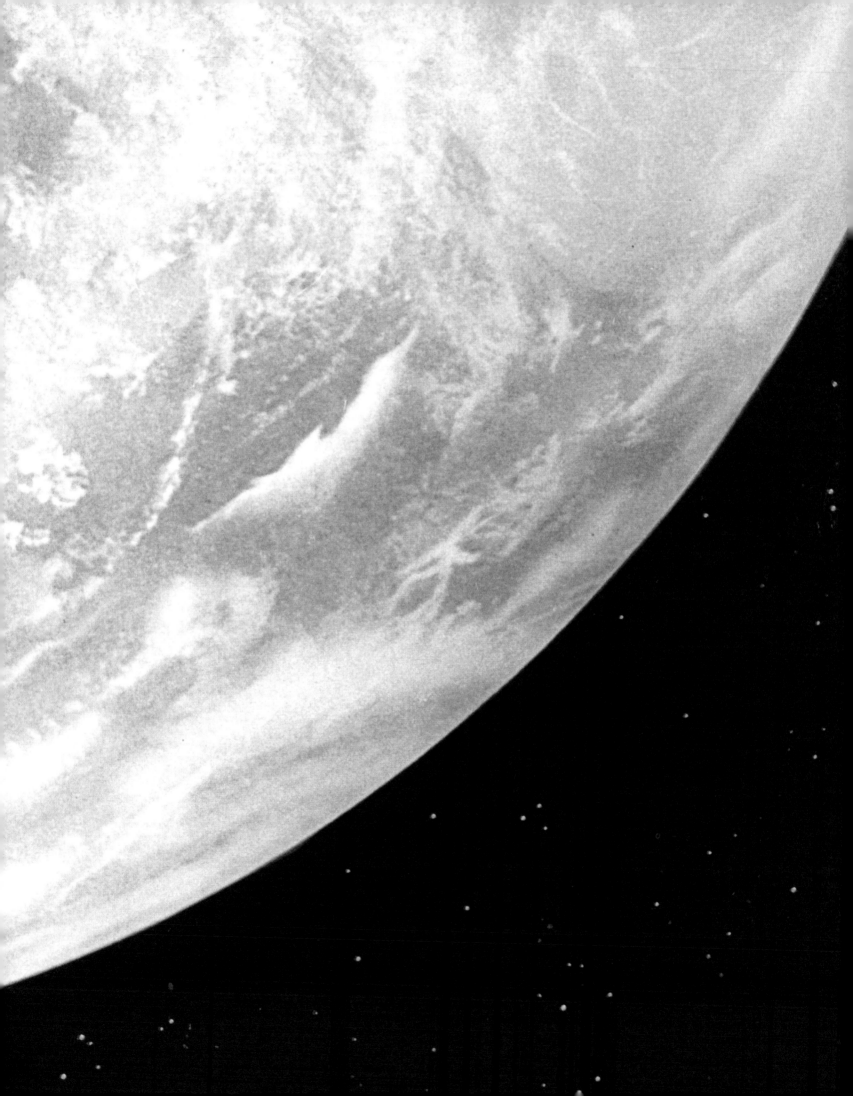

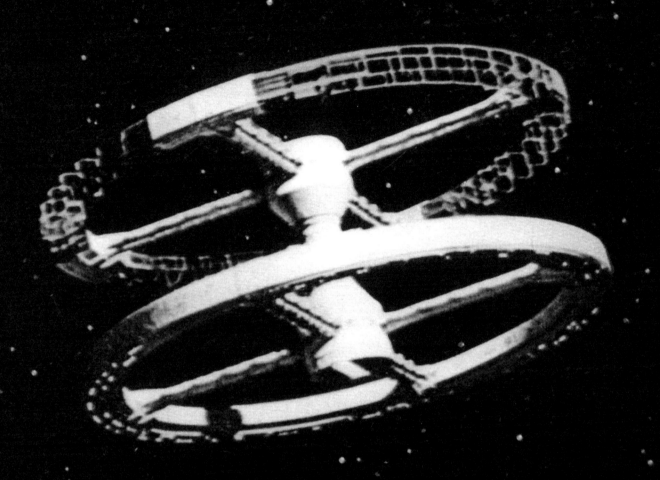
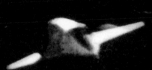

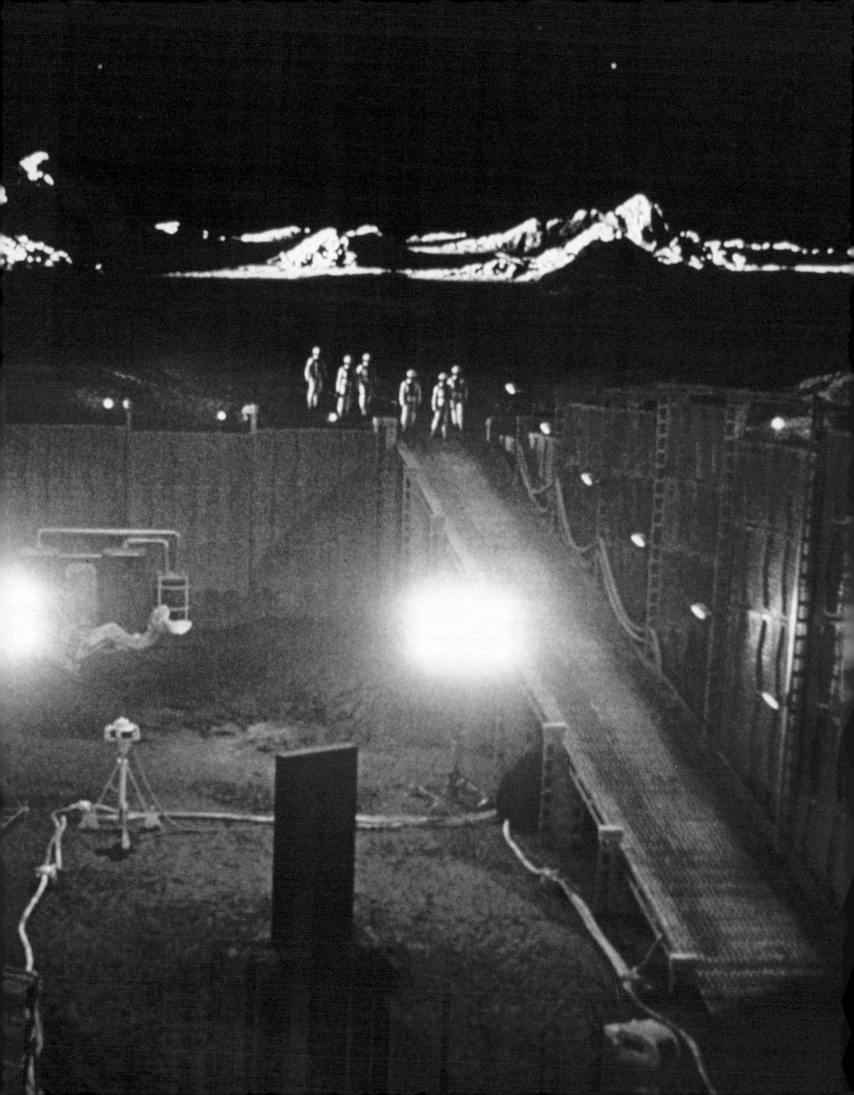

ODYSSEY II
TO THE MOON

From Space Station-5 to the Moonbase in Clavius crater on the southern highlands of the Moon, on the 42 foot diameter Aries-1B earth-orbit-to-lunar-surface shuttle.

ARIES-1B LUNAR LANDING SHUTTLE

Early concepts

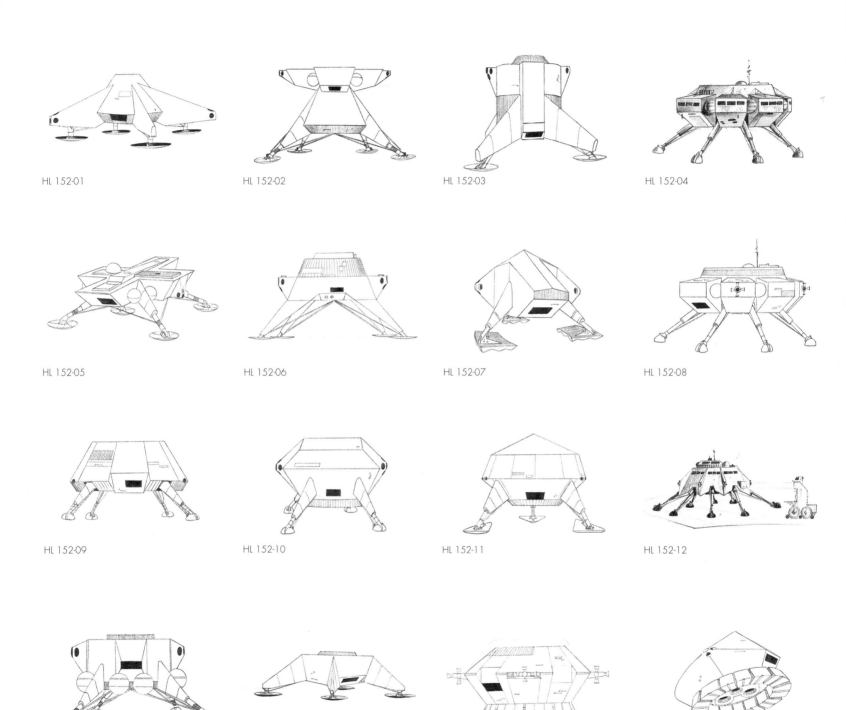

HL 152-01

HL 152-02

HL 152-03

HL 152-04

HL 152-05

HL 152-06

HL 152-07

HL 152-08

HL 152-09

HL 152-10

HL 152-11

HL 152-12

HL 152-13

HL 152-14

HL 152-15

HL 152-16

ABOVE *Early concepts for Aries (exterior views).* **OPPOSITE** *Early concepts for Aries—with views from below.*

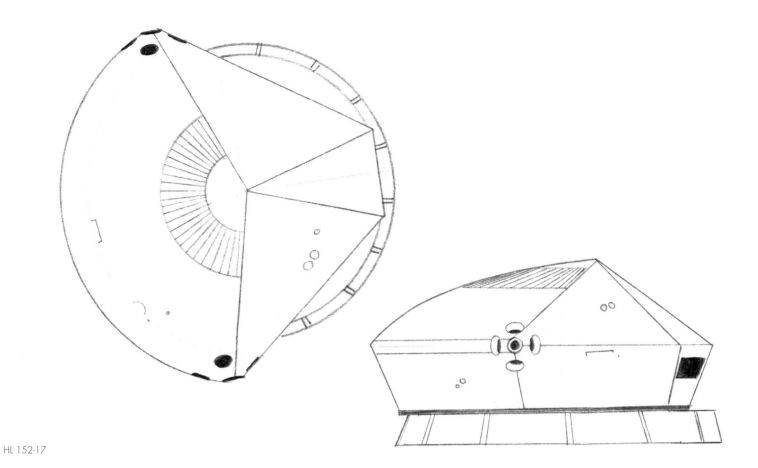

HL 152-17

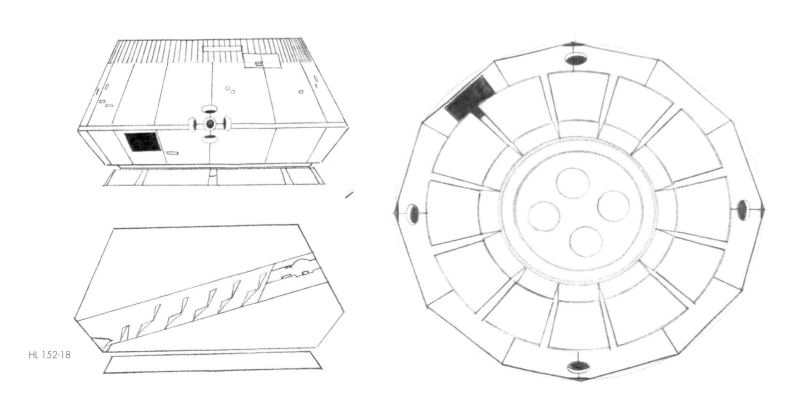

HL 152-18

ARIES-1B LUNAR LANDING SHUTTLE
Towards the final design

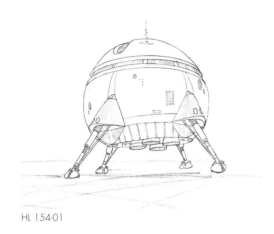

HL 154-01

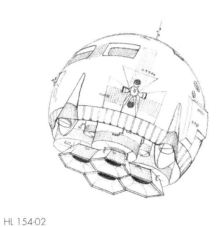

HL 154-02

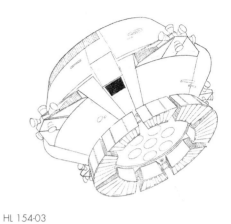

HL 154-03

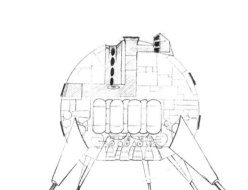

HL 154-04

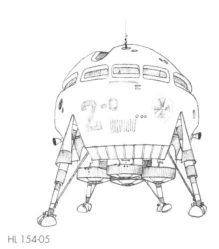

HL 154-05

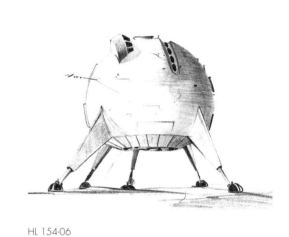

HL 154-06

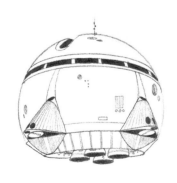

HL 154-07

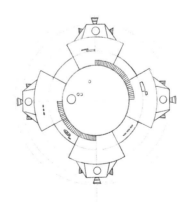

HL 154-08

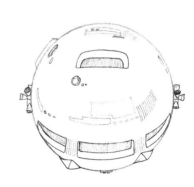

HL 154-09

ABOVE *Nine concepts for Aries, 'with varied detailing', some with retracted undercarriage.* **OPPOSITE** *For comparison—3ft diameter model of Aries lunar landing shuttle, complete with 'motorised' hydraulic landing legs (retracted) and compressed air-jets, with steel tube—top left—holding it up.*

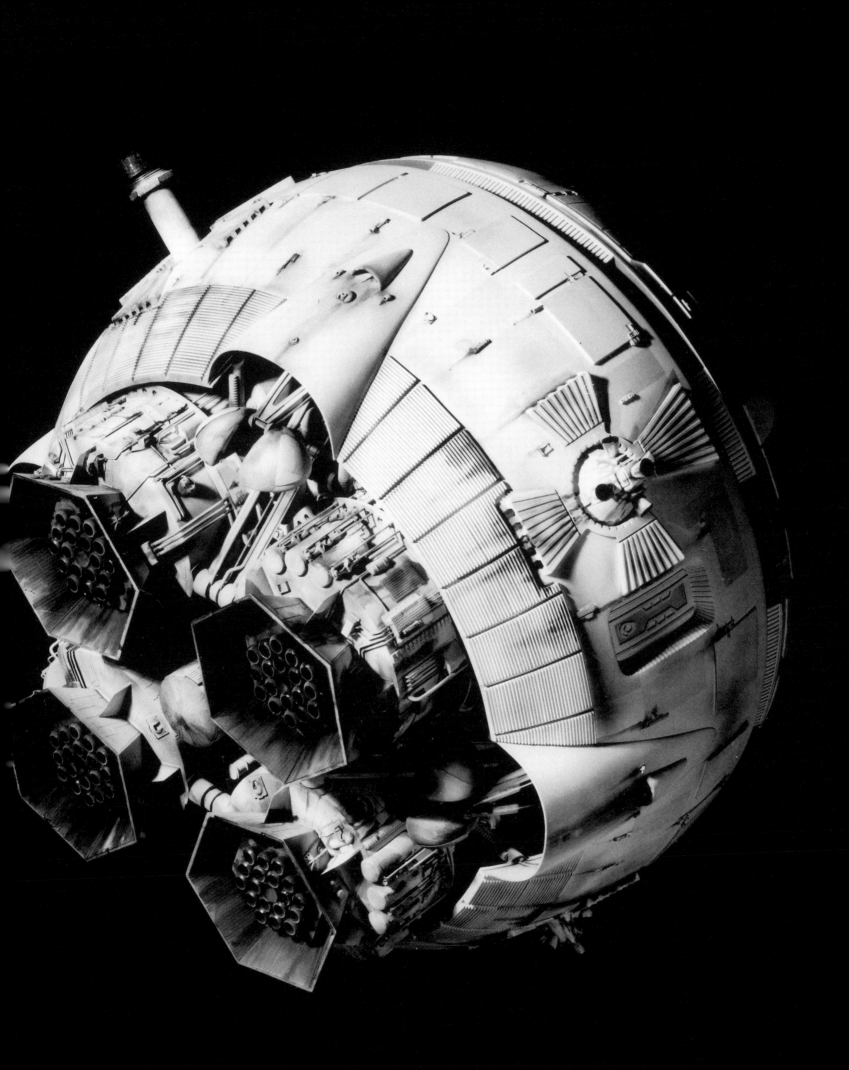

ARIES-1B LUNAR LANDING SHUTTLE

Towards the final design of landing mechanism

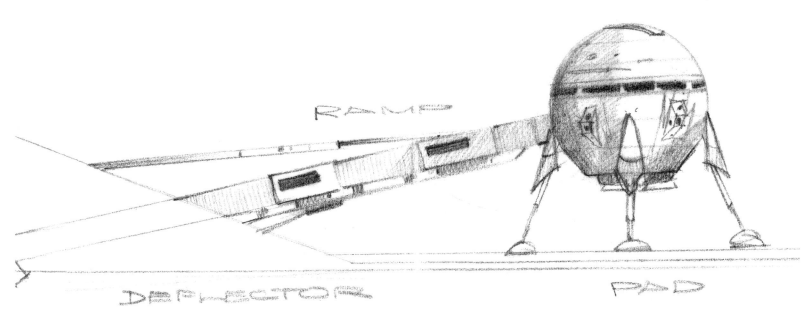

HL 156-01

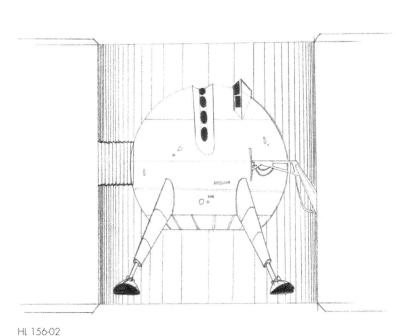

HL 156-02

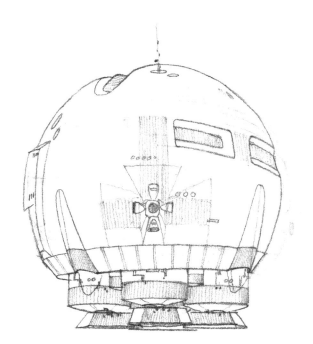

HL 156-03

HL 156-01 *Aries on moon base landing pad with ramp.* **HL 156-02** *Aries in docking bay.* **HL 156-03** *Aries with retracted shock absorbers, and jets.* **HL 156-04** *Aries with extended landing legs.*

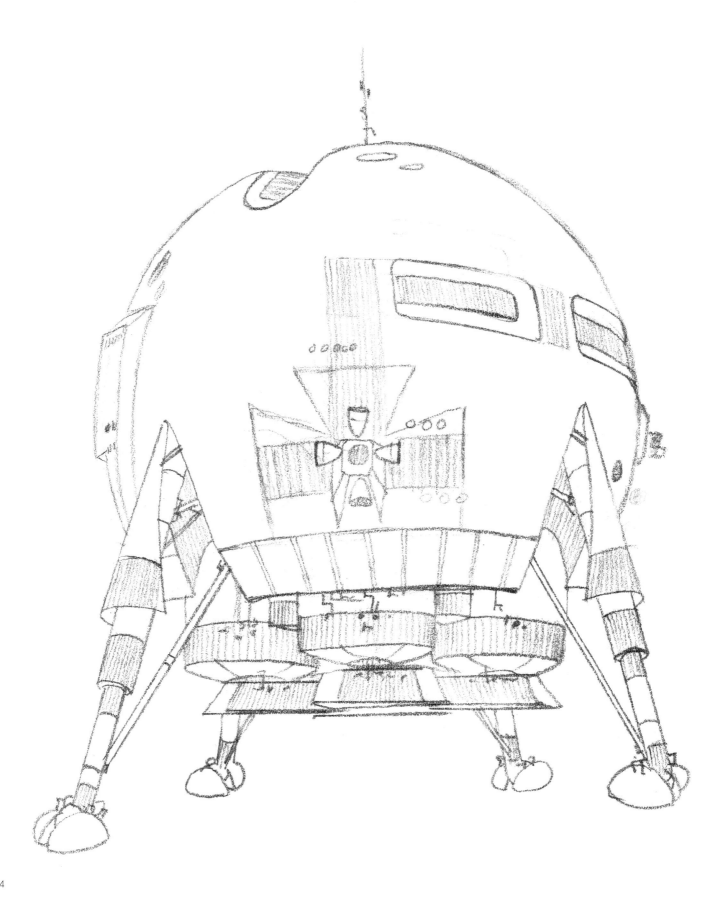

ARIES-1B LUNAR LANDING SHUTTLE

Interior and underside

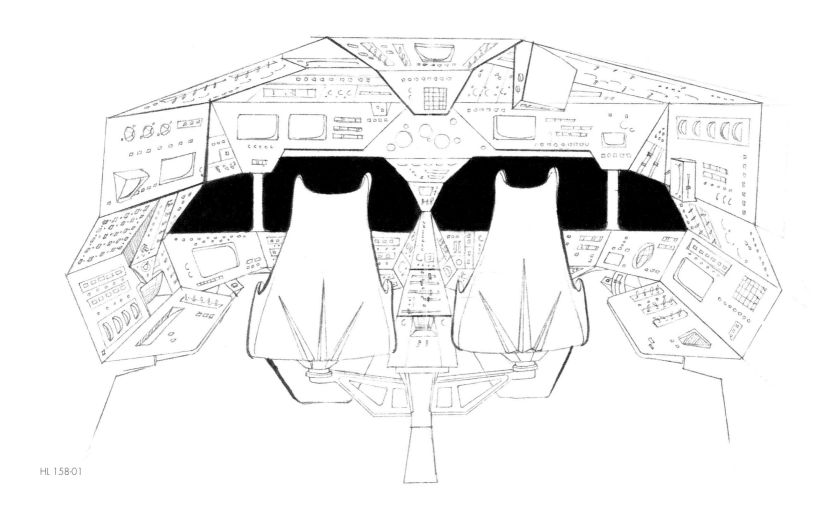

HL 158-01

HL 158-01 *Aries cockpit view, similar to that in Orion-III. The production notes specified that in the adjoining passenger compartment, there would be seats like 'small, compact armchairs which can swivel'.* **HL 158-02** *Detailed treatment of Aries underside (from below), showing engines and landing mechanism.*

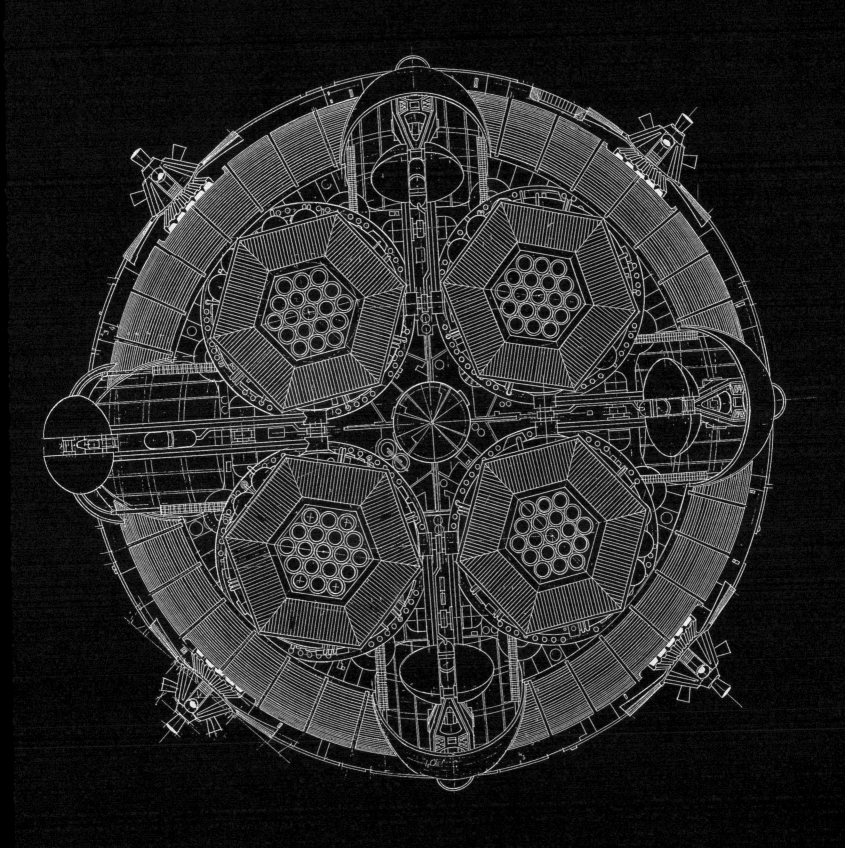

HL 158-02

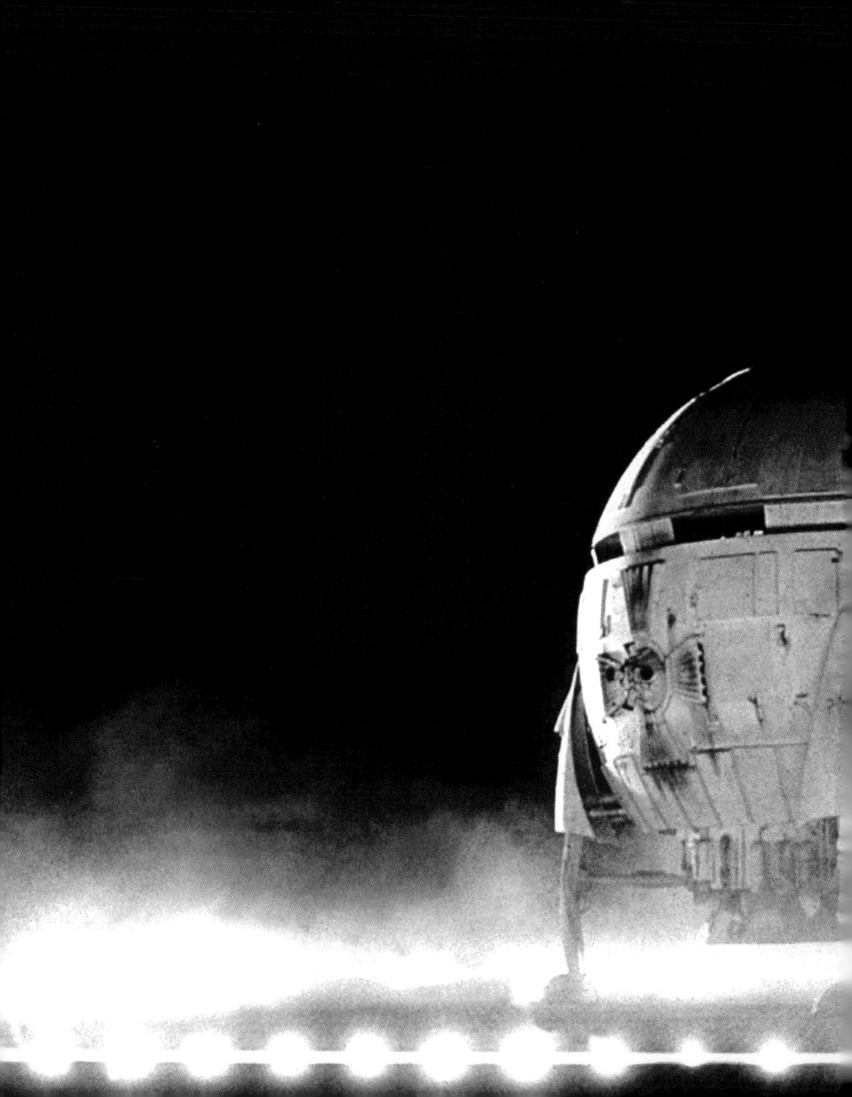

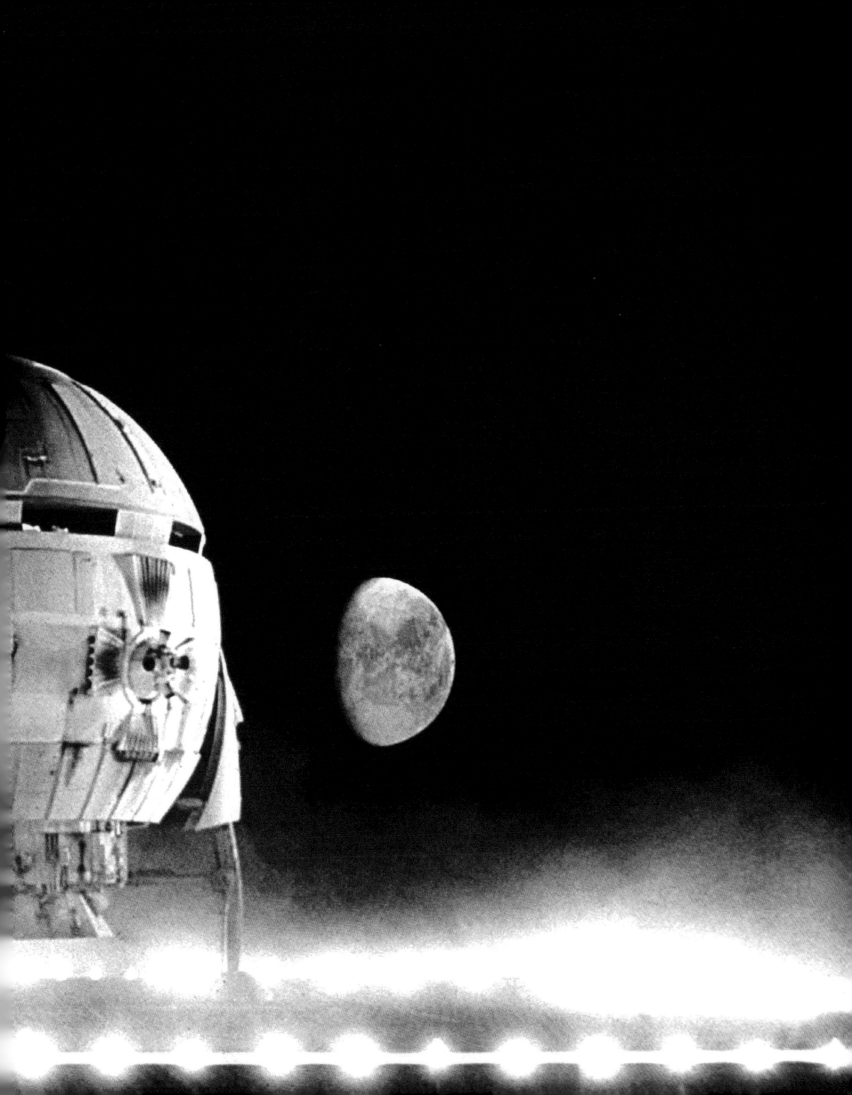

CLAVIUS MOON BASE
Landing pads

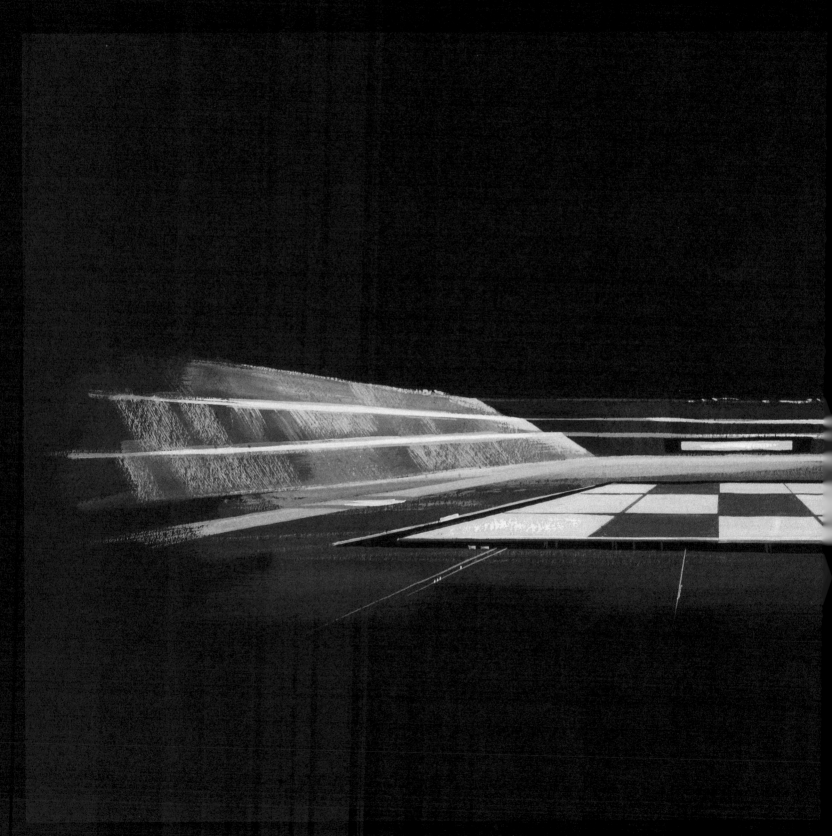

HL 162-01 *Moon base landing pad (acrylic on black paper).* **OPPOSITE: HL 162-02** *Four Moon base landing pads.*

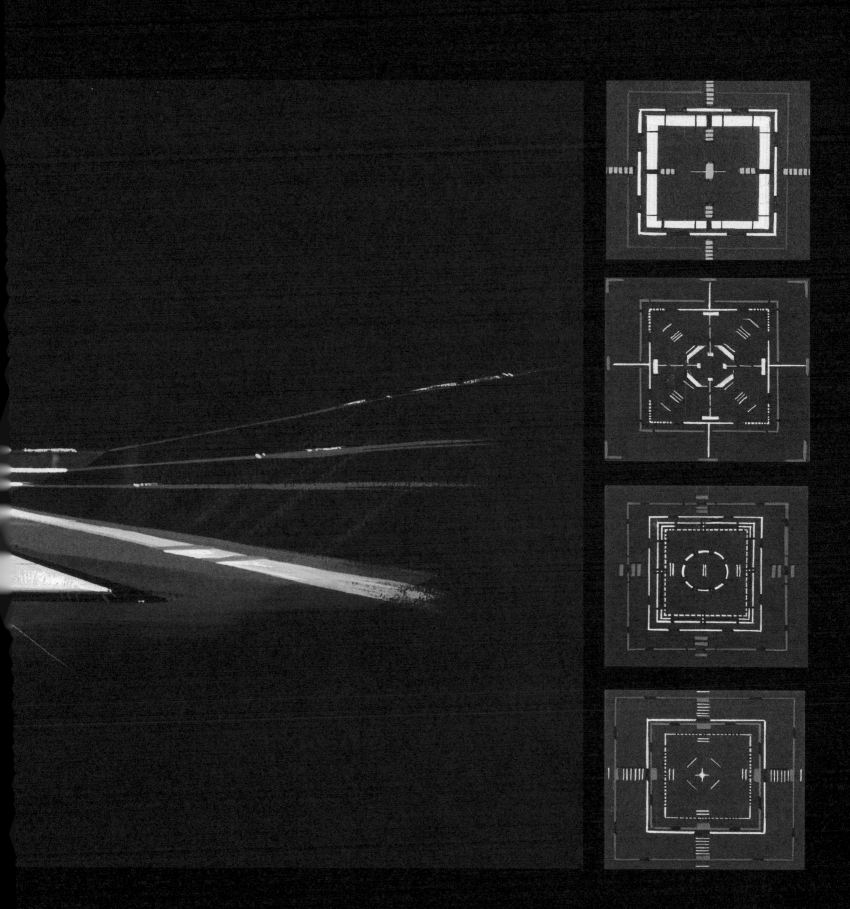

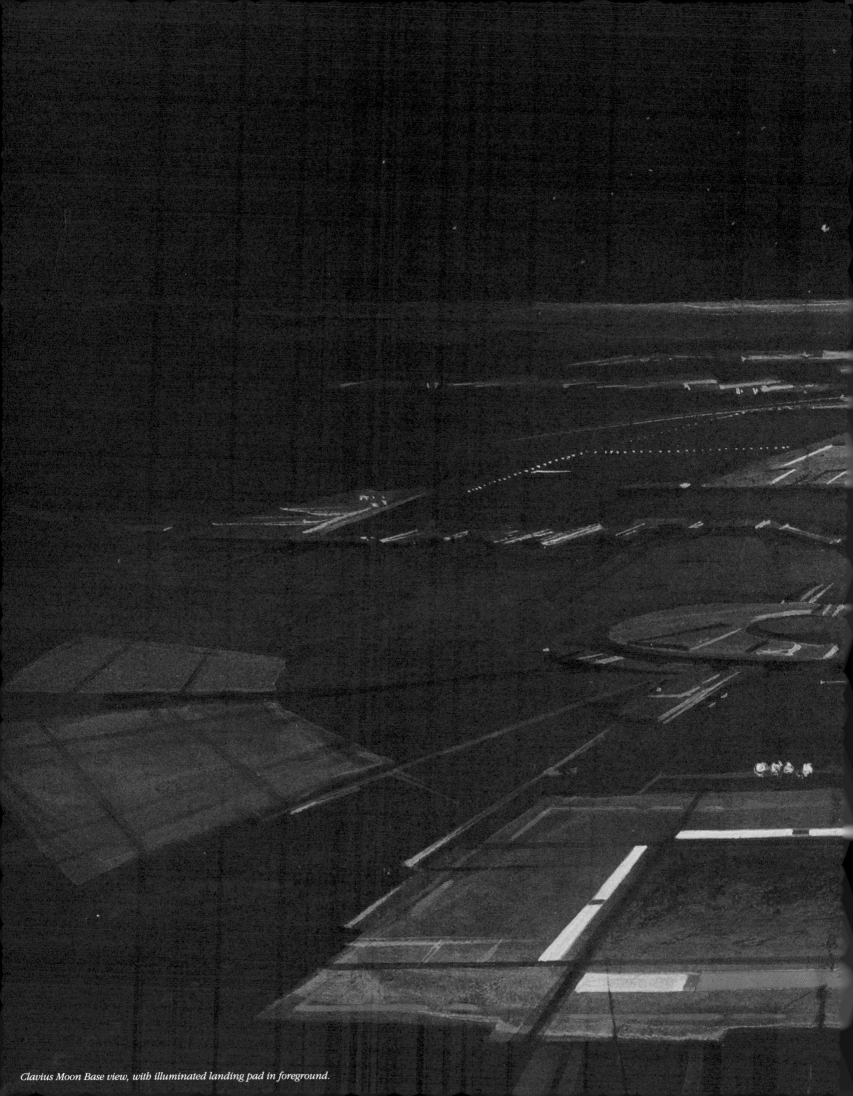

Clavius Moon Base view, with illuminated landing pad in foreground.

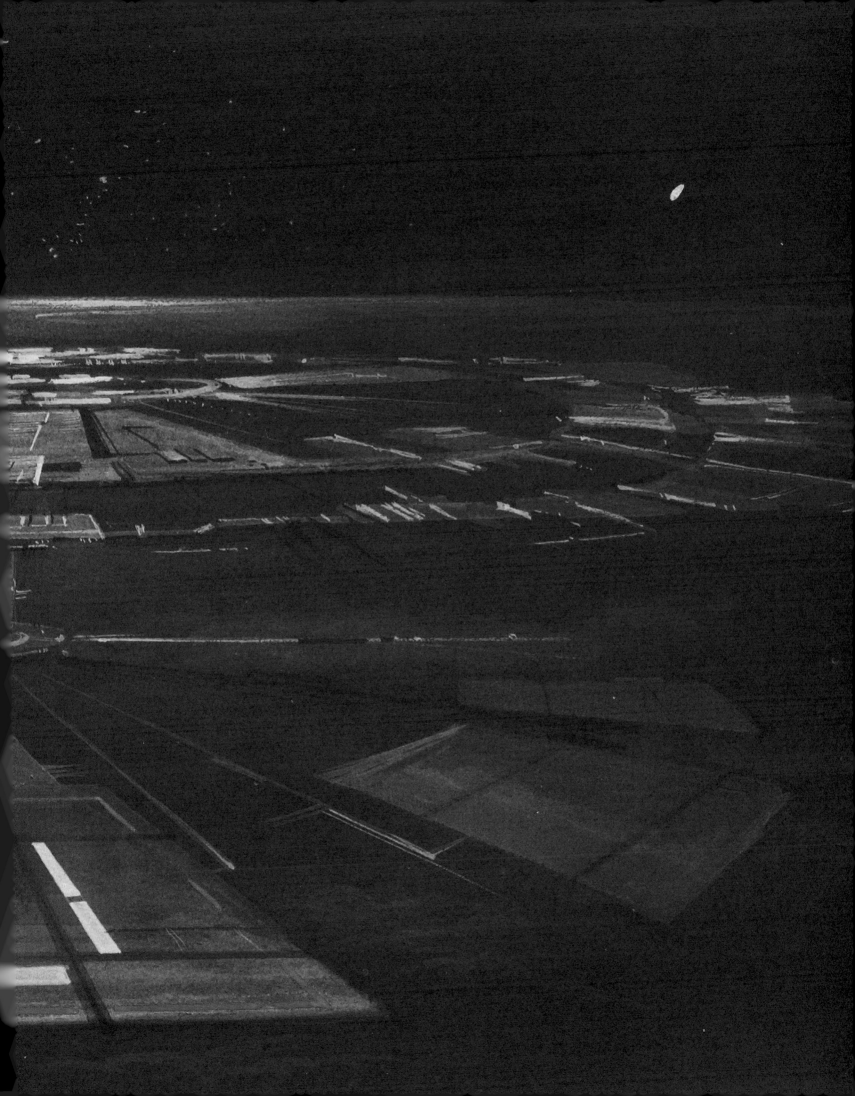

CLAVIUS MOON BASE
Landing pads

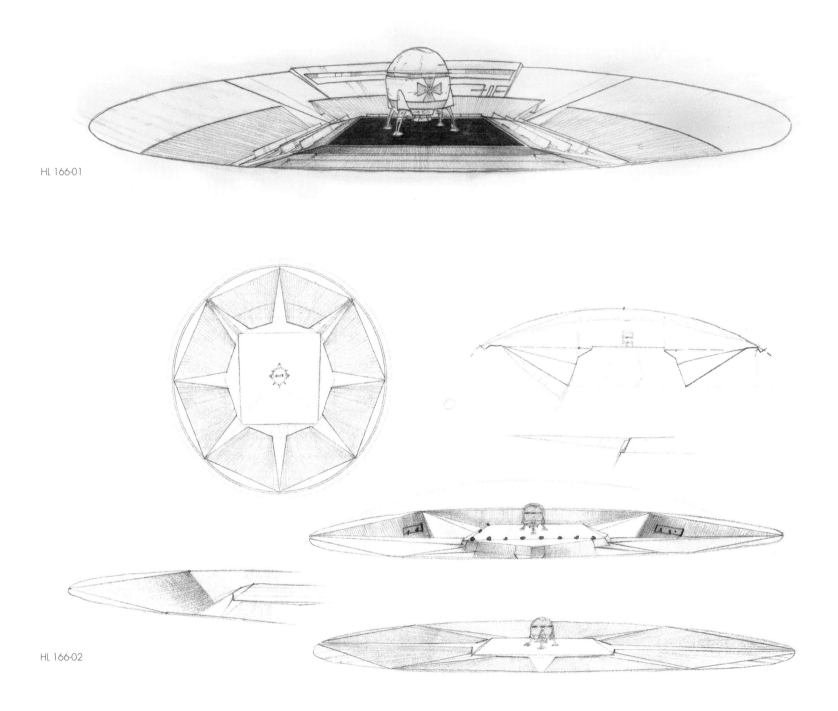

HL 166-01

HL 166-02

HL 166-01 *Moon Base landing pad with Aries space craft.* **HL 166-02** *Plan view with landing pads and surrounding accommodation blocks.* **HL 166-03** *Aries descending from Moon Base landing pad.* **HL 166-04** *Moon Base landing pad concept.*

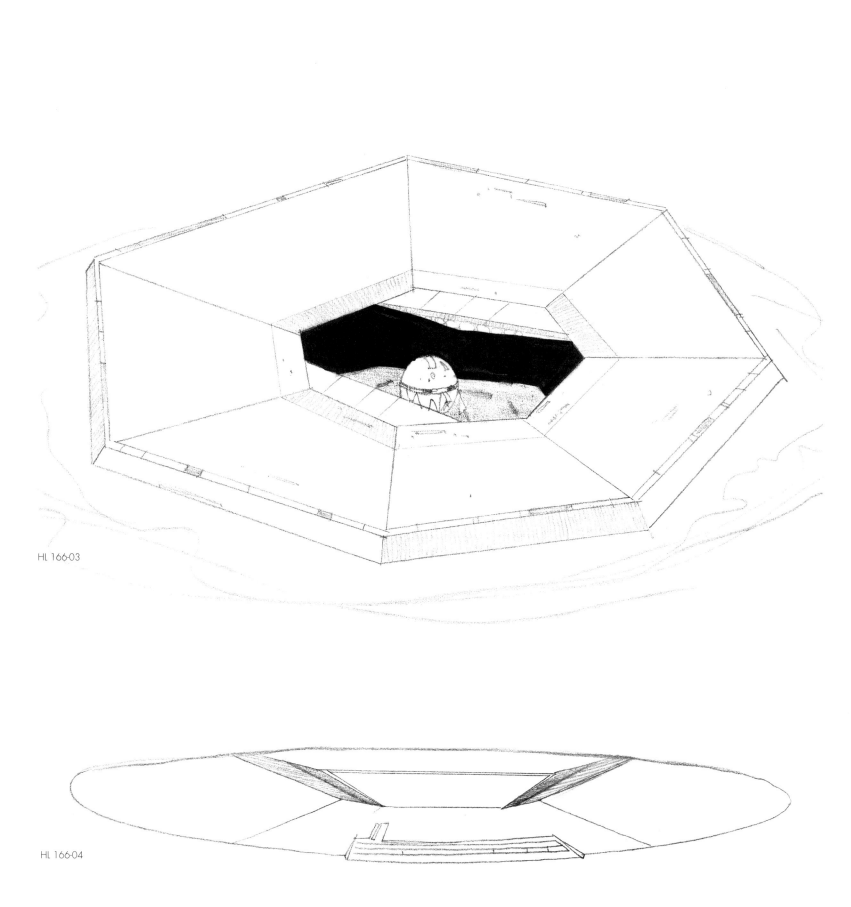

HL 166-03

HL 166-04

CLAVIUS MOON BASE

Landing pad and platform details

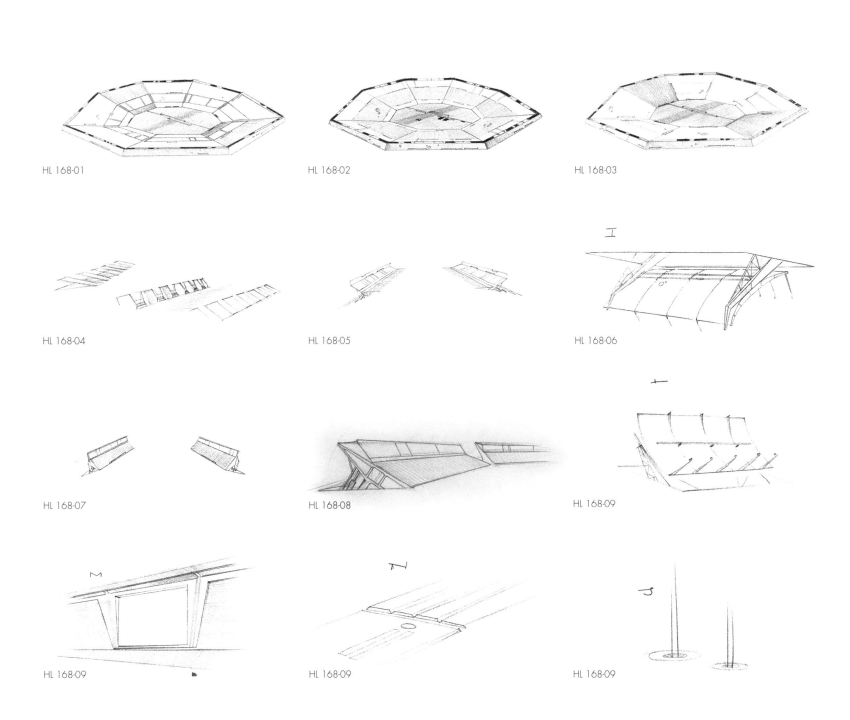

HL 168-01

HL 168-02

HL 168-03

HL 168-04

HL 168-05

HL 168-06

HL 168-07

HL 168-08

HL 168-09

HL 168-09

HL 168-09

HL 168-09

HL 168-01 *Moon Base landing pad with hydraulic platform.* **HL 168-02** *Moon Base landing pad with hydraulic platform.* **HL 168-03** *Moon Base landing pad with hydraulic platform.* **HL 168-04** *Hydraulic landing lights.* **HL 168-05** *Hydraulic landing lights.* **HL 168-06** *Hydraulic landing lights.* **HL 168-07** *Hydraulic landing lights.* **HL 168-08** *Hydraulic landing lights.* **HL 168-09** *Moon Base landing pad design details—4 drawings.* **HL 168-10** *Moon Base landing pad with coloured lighting configuration and hydraulic platform section.*

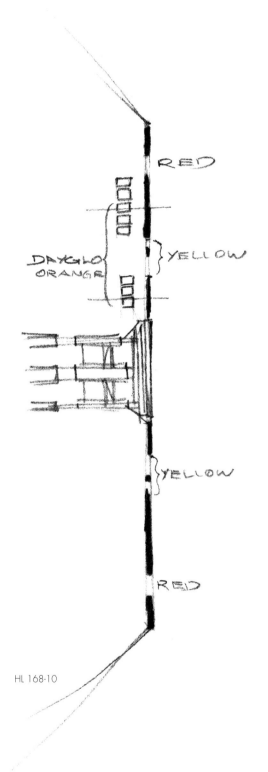

RED

YELLOW

DAYGLO
ORANGE

YELLOW

RED

HL 168-10

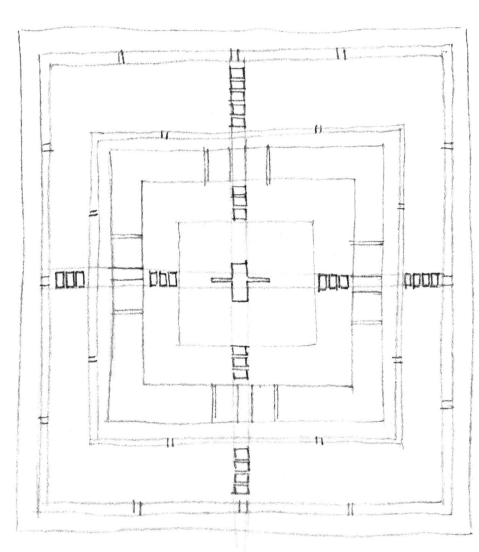

HL 168-10

CLAVIUS MOON BASE

Landing platforms

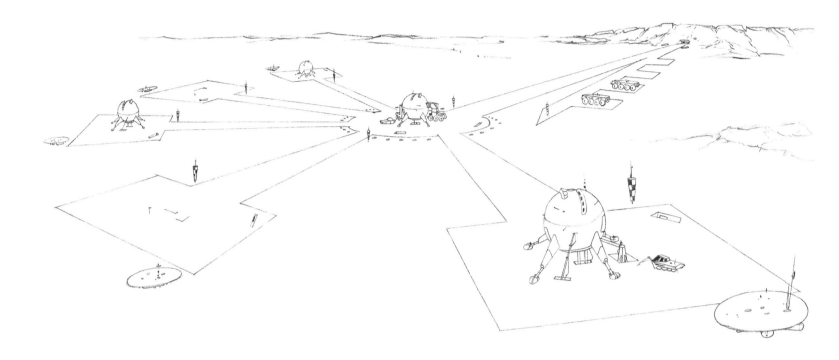

HL 170-01

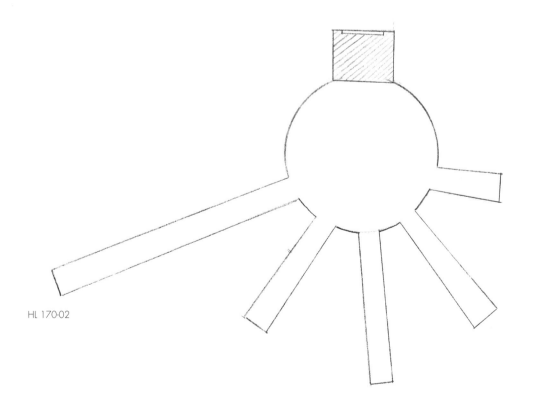

HL 170-02

HL 170-01 *Clavius Moon Base showing landing pads with 4 Aries lunar craft.* **HL 170-02** *Moon Base landing strip.* **HL 170-03 & HL 170-04** *Two detailed drawings of the Moon Base landing area, with the spherical Aries descending on a hydraulic platform: the black areas later to become views of the moon base crew at work.*

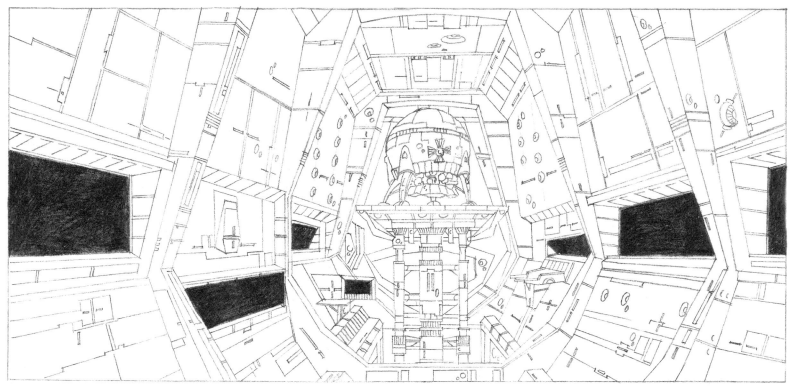

HL 170-03

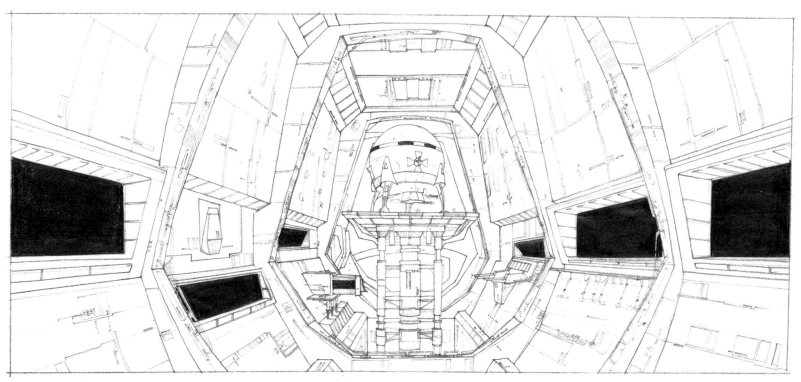

HL 170-04

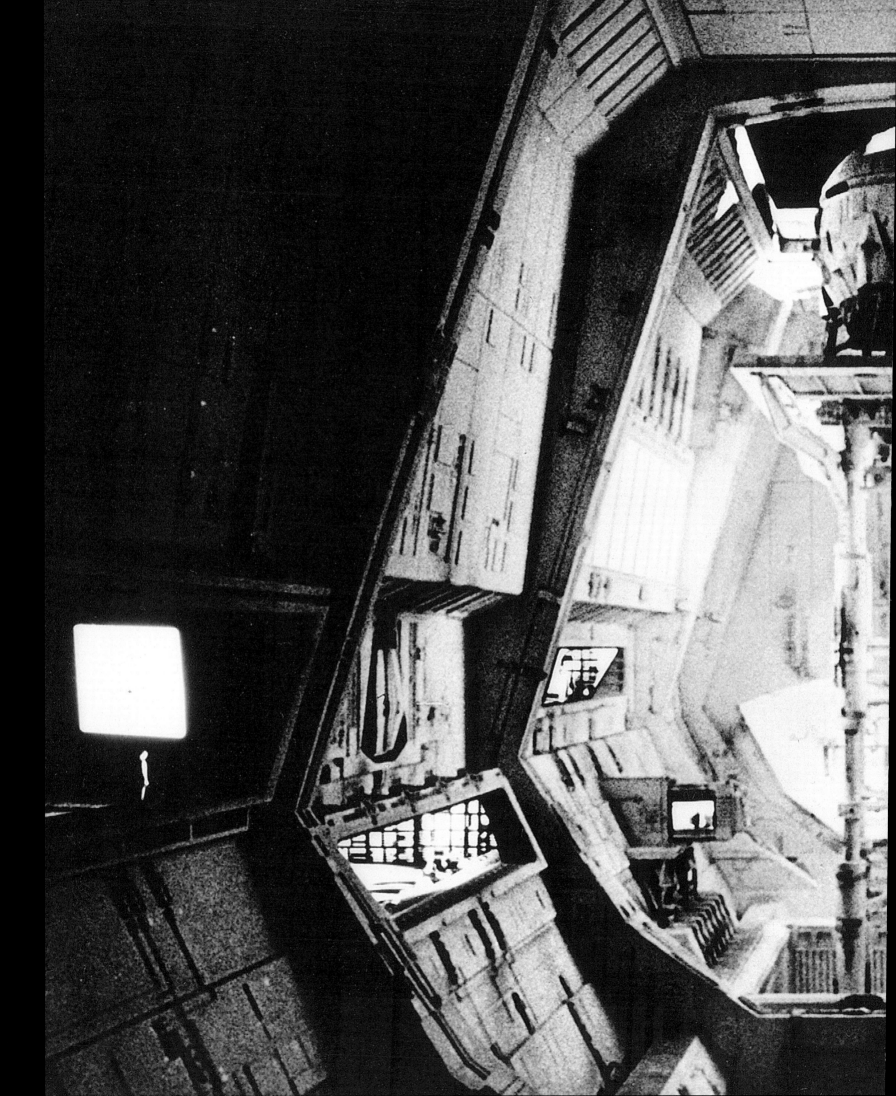

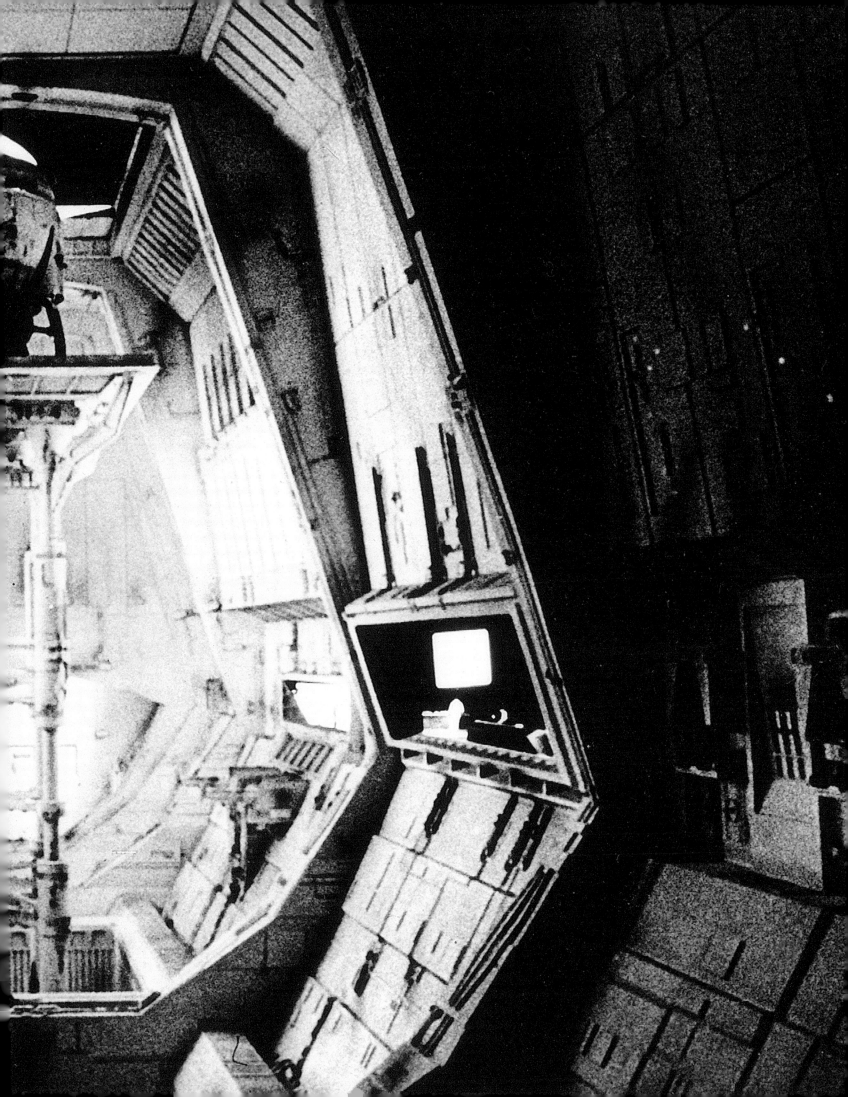

CLAVIUS MOON BASE
Ground plans

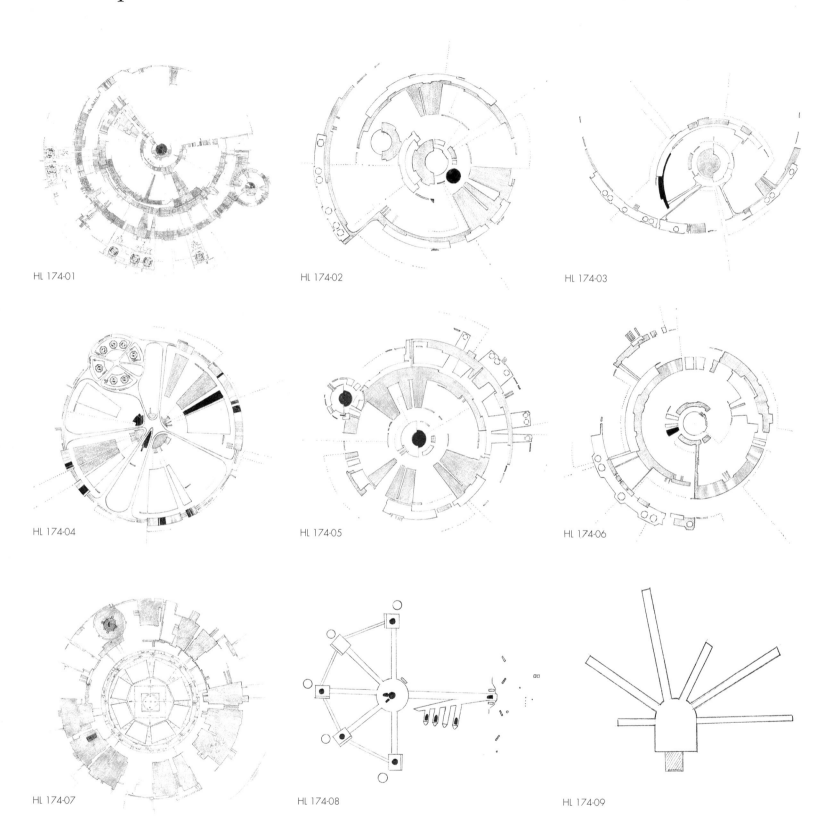

HL 174-01

HL 174-02

HL 174-03

HL 174-04

HL 174-05

HL 174-06

HL 174-07

HL 174-08

HL 174-09

Various ground plans of Clavius Moon Base, some showing landing pads. **OPPOSITE** *Blueprint of landing pad model, with dimensions.*

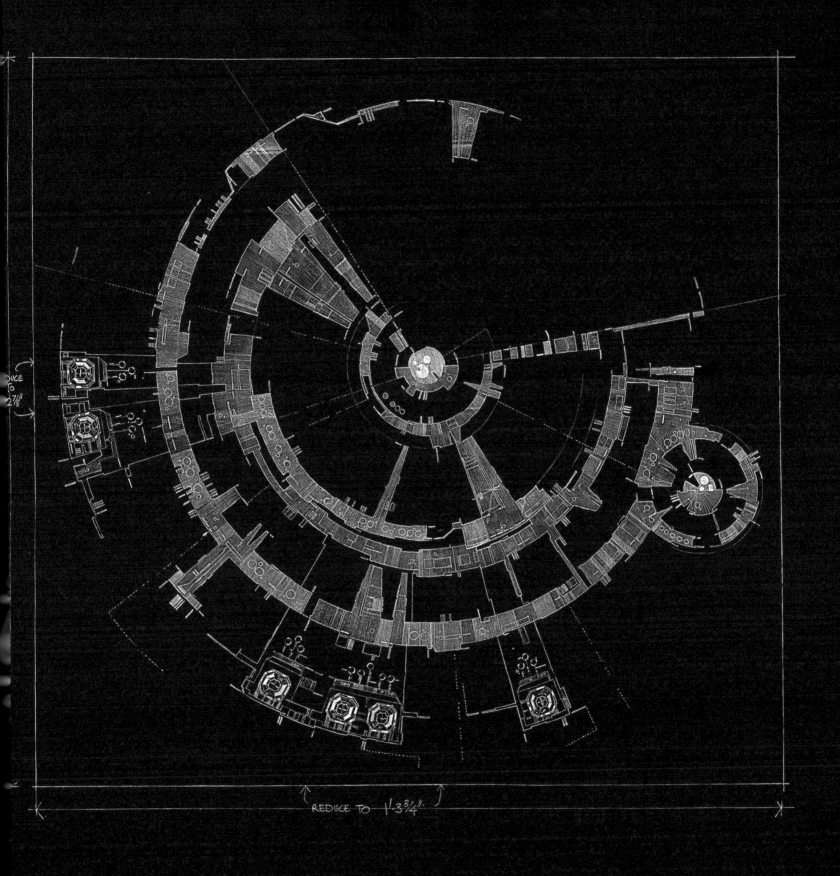

DUCE
O
2⅞"

HL 174-10

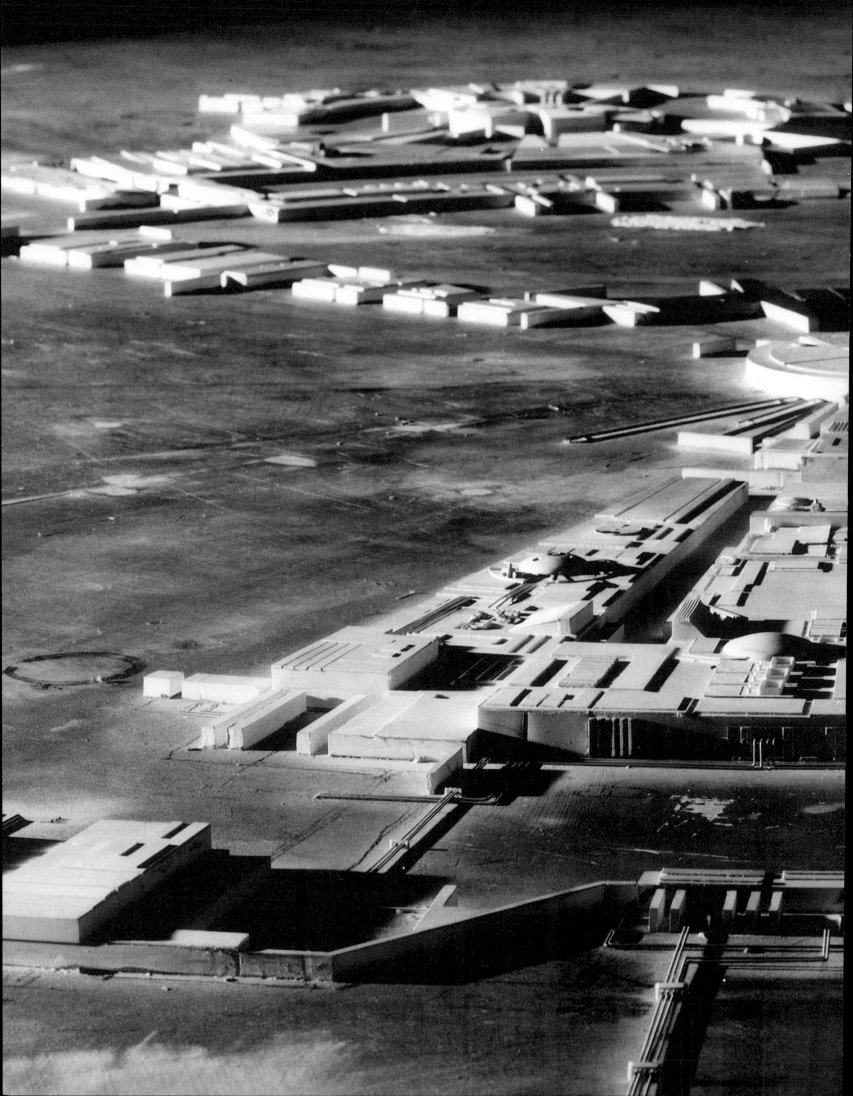

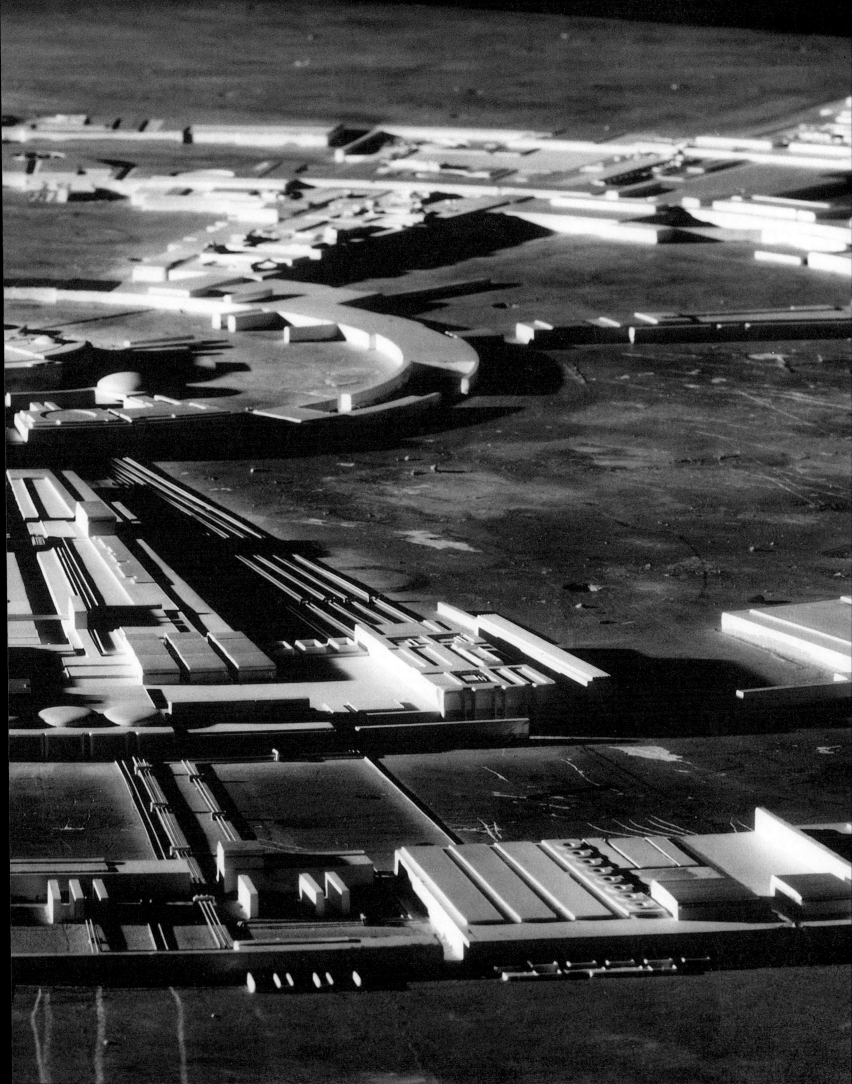

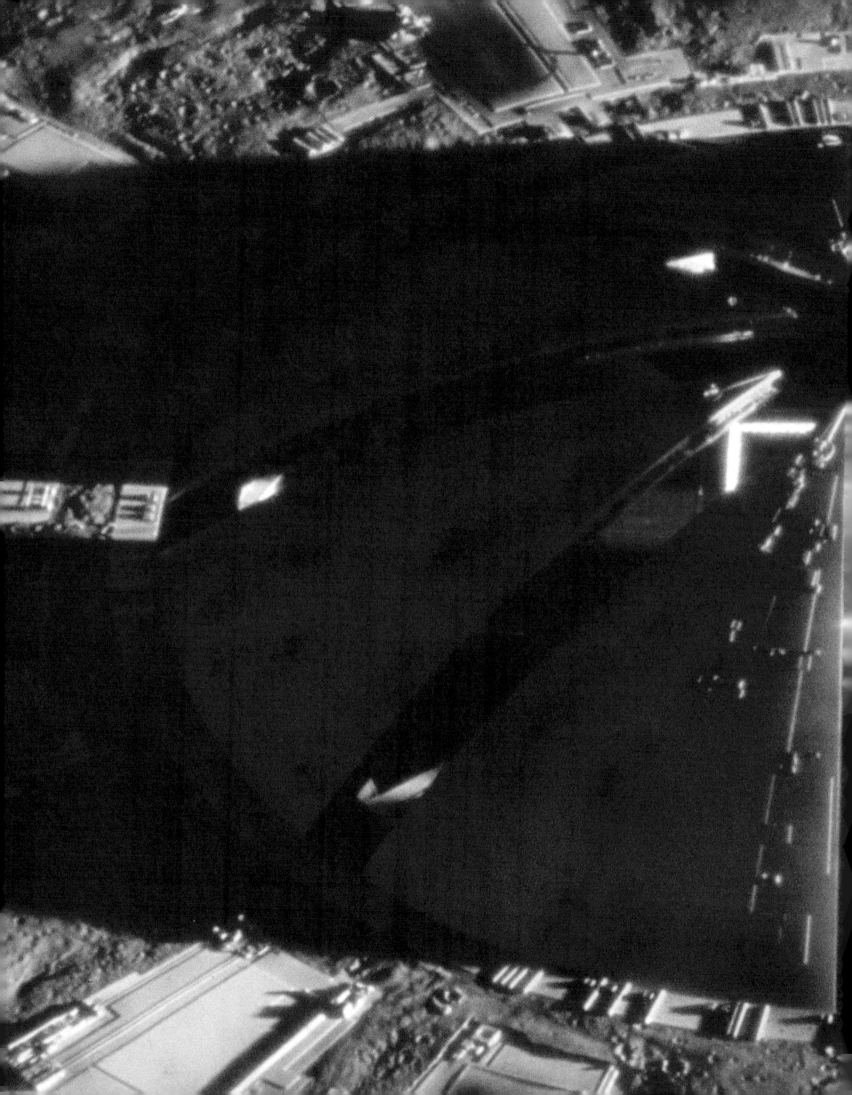

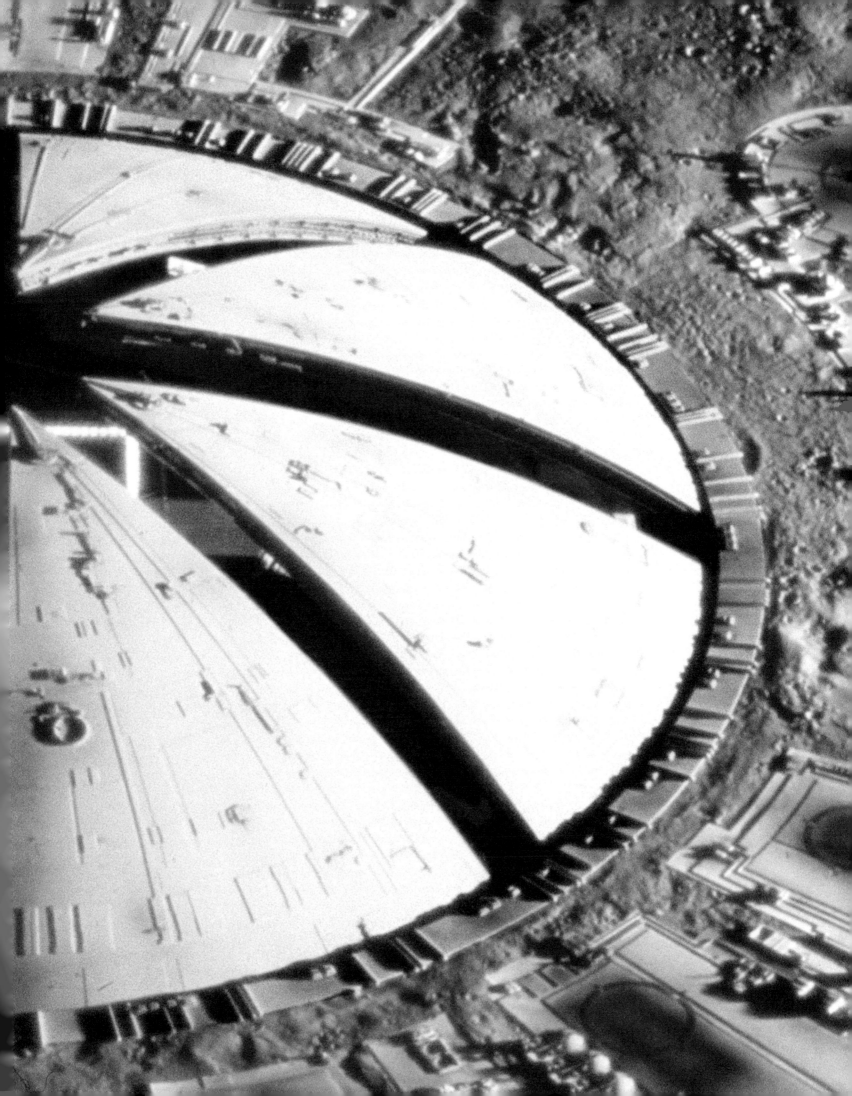

LUNAR DOCKING VEHICLES
Early concepts

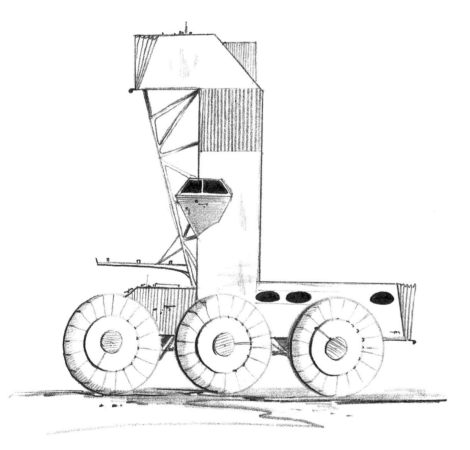

HL 180-01

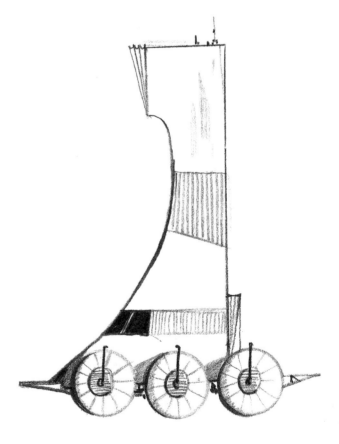

HL 180-02

Three versions of the 'Aries lunar mobile docking vehicle'.

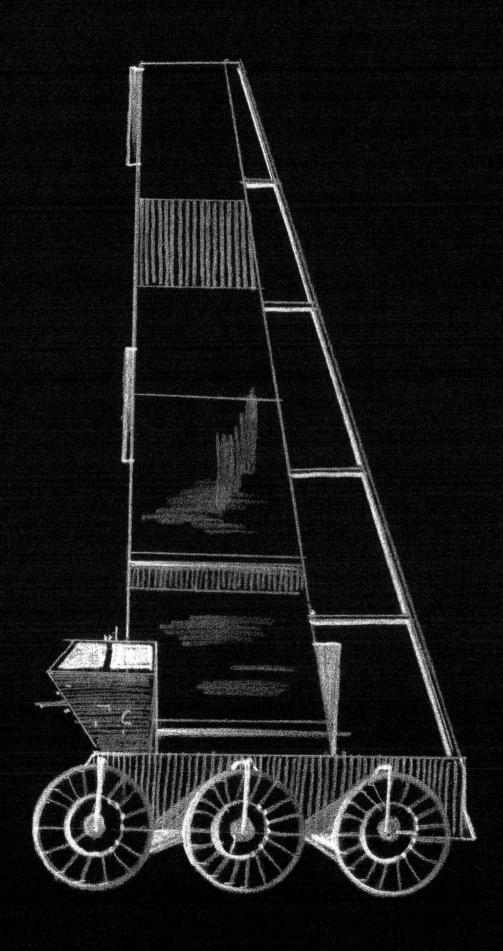

HL 180-03

CLAVIUS MOON BASE

Logo

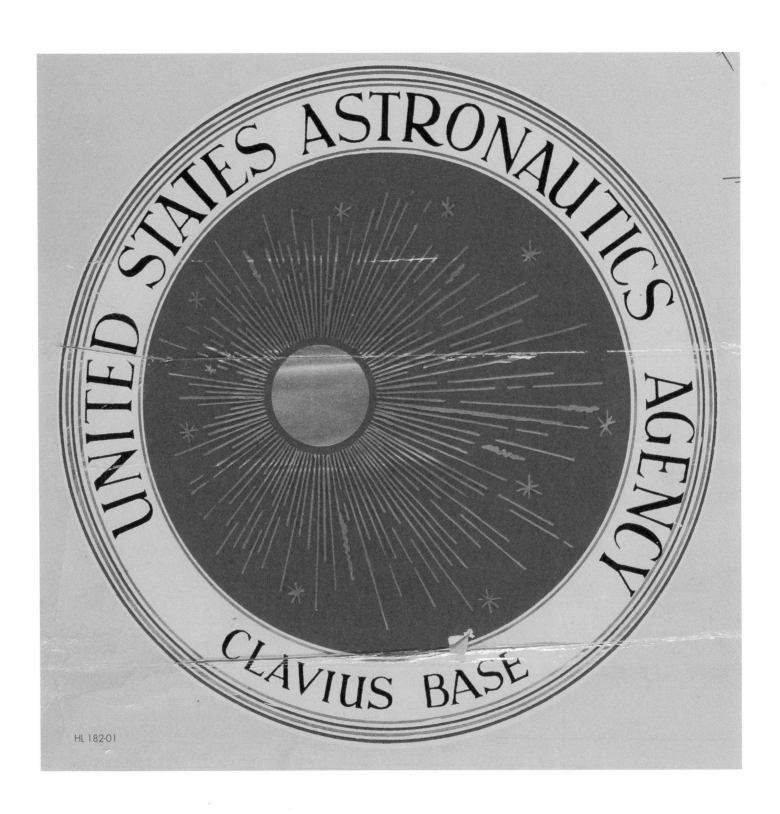

HL 182-01

HL 182-01 *Clavius Moon Base logo used for helmets and branding.* **OPPOSITE** *Dr. Heywood Floyd (William Sylvester): corporate man with corporate logo.*

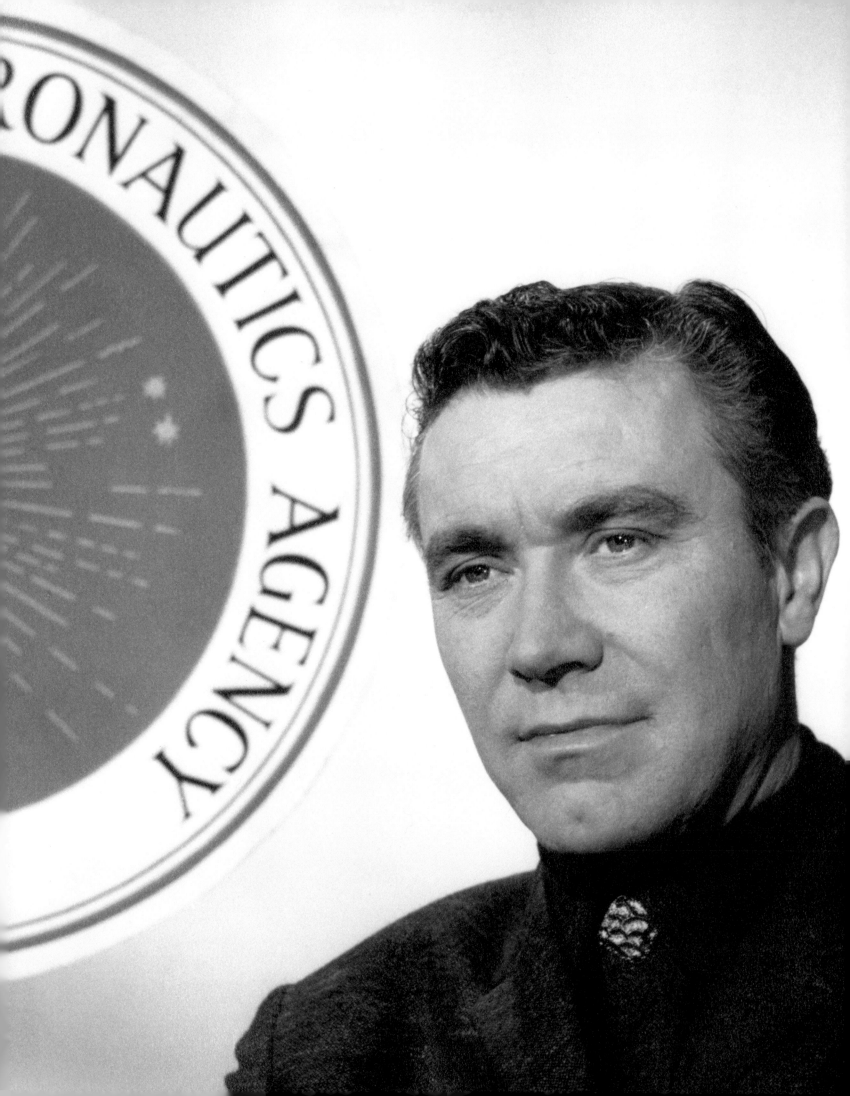

TYCHO CAVE SITE

Concepts for entrance to TMA-1 cave site

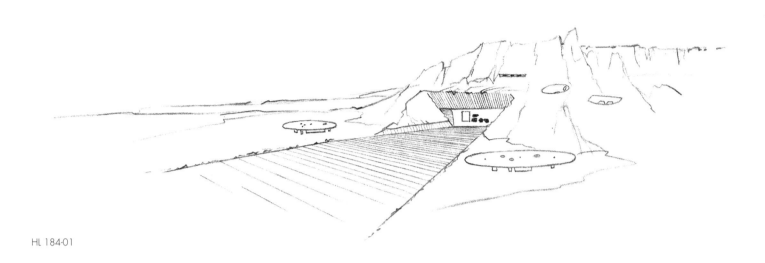

HL 184-01

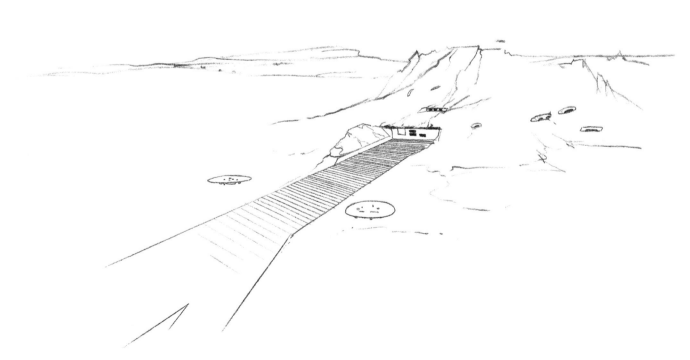

HL 184-02

HL 184-01 *TMA-1 research site with landing strip.* **HL 184-02** *TMA-1 research site with landing strip.* **HL 184-03** *Lunar observation post.* **HL 184-04** *Entrance to TMA-1 research site.*

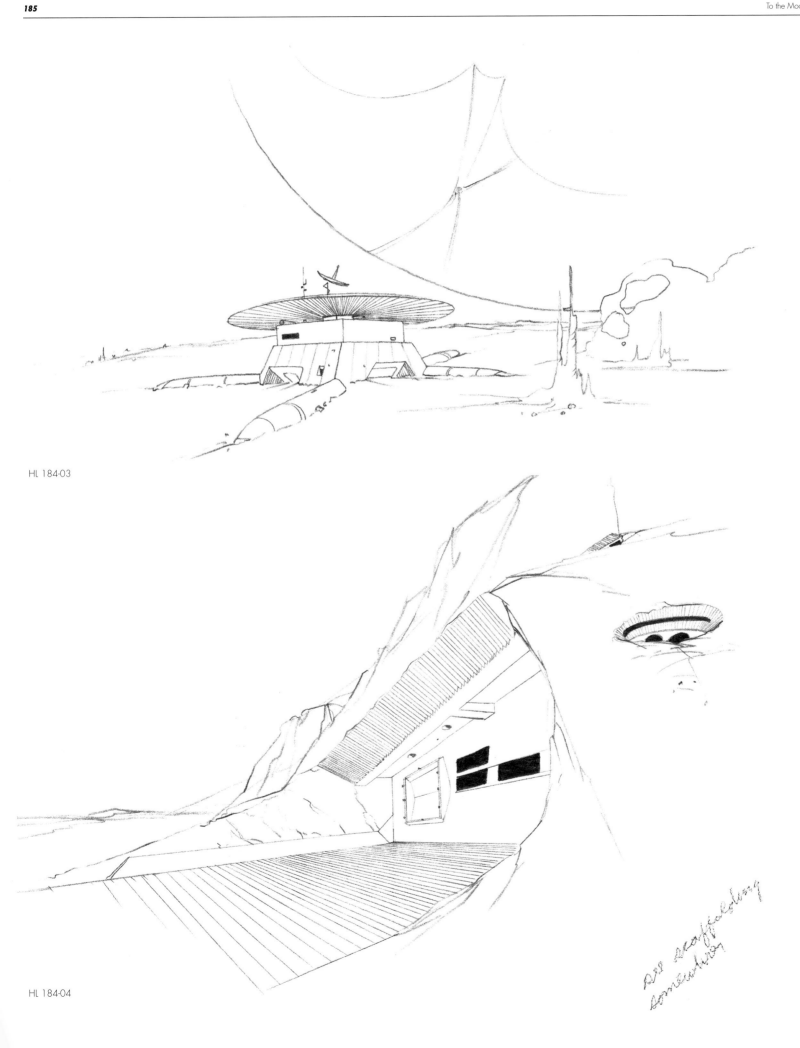

HL 184-03

HL 184-04

TYCHO RESEARCH SITE
Surrounding moonscape

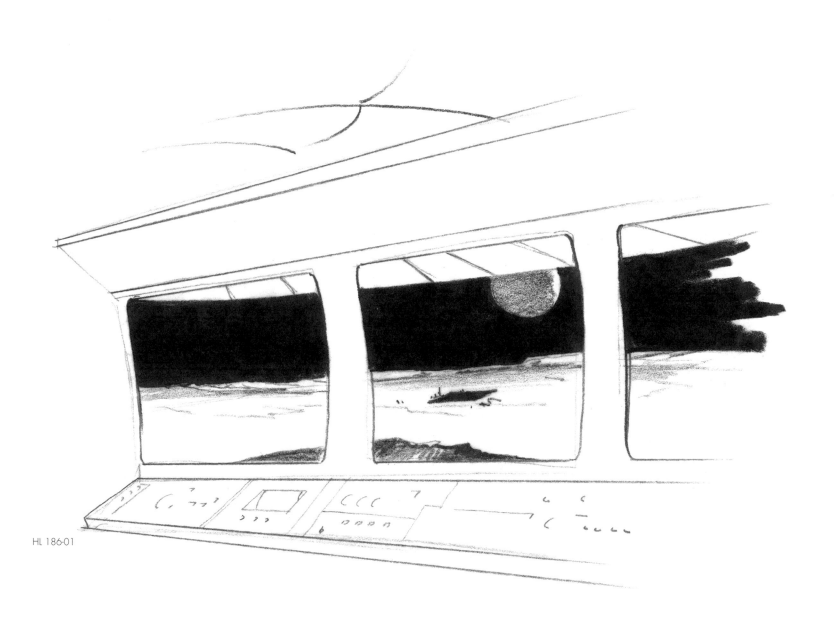

HL 186-01

HL 186-01 *Lunar trench viewed from interior of TMA-1 research site.* **HL 186-02** *Lunar landscape with TMA-1 research site.* **HL 186-03** *Lunar landscape with TMA-1 research site, moon bus and excavated trench in distance.* **HL 186-04** *Research site with moon bus on left and excavated trench in distance. The original treatment of* **Journey Beyond the Stars** *specified that the TMA-1 site would feature pressure domes 20 feet across. It was then known as 'the cave site'.*

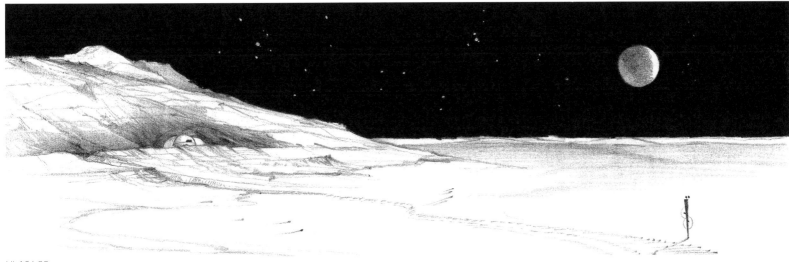

HL 186-02

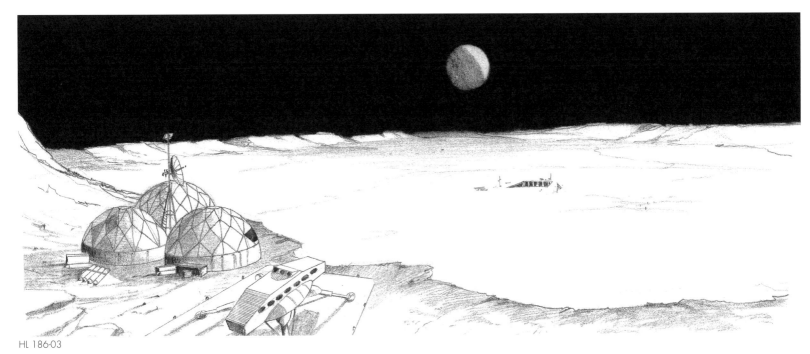

HL 186-03

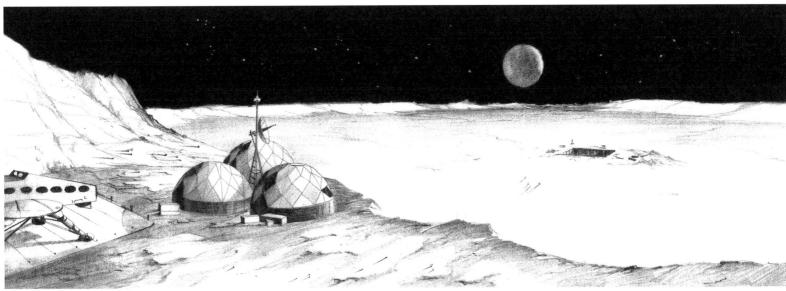

HL 186-04

LUNAR VEHICLES
Early caterpillar concepts

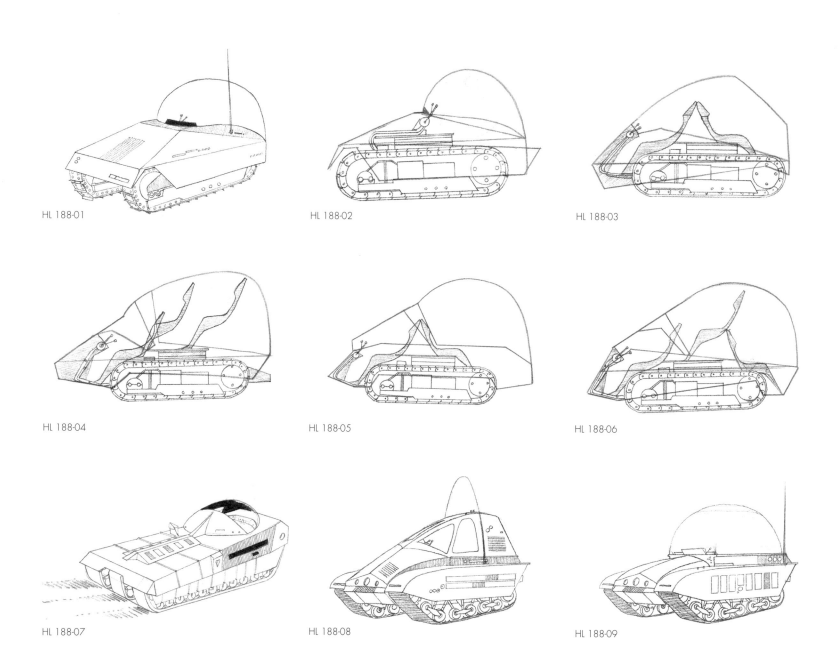

HL 188-01

HL 188-02

HL 188-03

HL 188-04

HL 188-05

HL 188-06

HL 188-07

HL 188-08

HL 188-09

HL 188-01 *Lunar vehicle perspective view exterior.* **HL 188-02** *Lunar vehicle section with exterior overlay.* **HL 188-03** *Lunar vehicle section with exterior overlay.* **HL 188-04** *Lunar vehicle section with exterior overlay.* **HL 188-05** *Lunar vehicle section with exterior overlay.* **HL 188-06** *Lunar vehicle section with exterior overlay.* **HL 188-07** *Lunar vehicle perspective view exterior.* **HL 188-08** *Lunar vehicle perspective view exterior.* **HL 188-09** *Lunar vehicle perspective view exterior.* **HL 188-10** *Lunar 'tracked' vehicle with excavation pipe. The production notes specified that there should be assorted 'lunar surface vehicles'.*

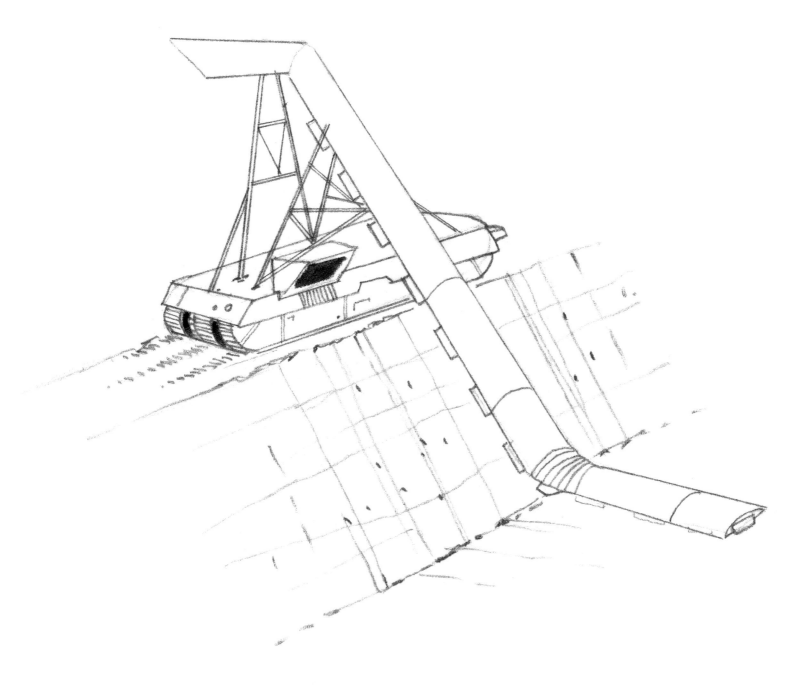

HL 188-10

MOON TRANSPORTATION

Early concepts

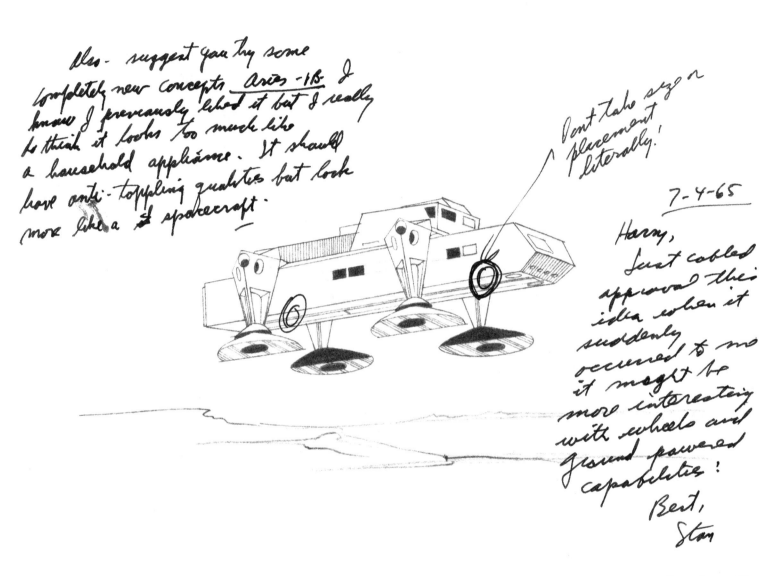

Also - suggest you try some completely new concepts. *Aries -1B* I know I previously liked it but I really to think it looks too much like a household appliance. It should have anti-toppling qualities but look more like a spacecraft.

Don't take size or placement literally!

7-4-65

Harry,

Just cabled approval this idea when it suddenly occurred to me it might be more interesting with wheels and ground powered capabilities!

Best,
Stan

MOON PIGGY-BACK LOADED

HL 190-01

Early concepts for lunar carrier vehicle, with annotations by Stanley Kubrick—and second thoughts about Aries-1B. In the production notes, Aries-1B would 'fly over the moon's surface... to TMA-1 cave site', and there would also be 'Passenger Bus with waiting driver, etc.'.

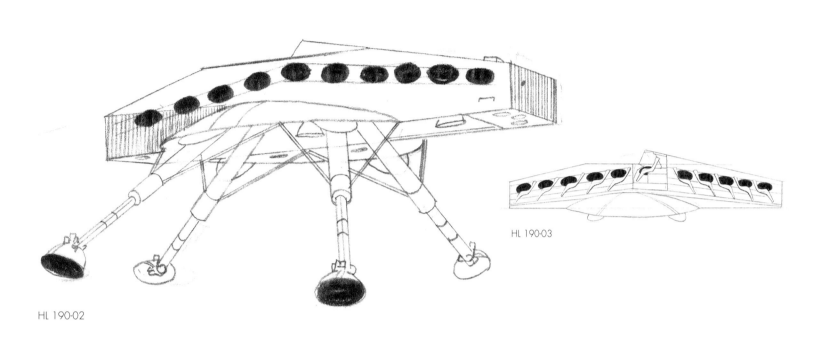

HL 190-03

HL 190-02

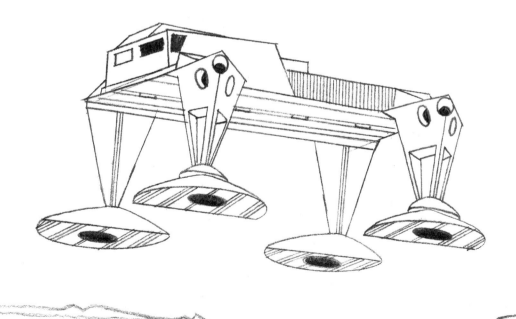

HL 190-04

MOON BUS

Early concepts with 'wheels and ground powered capabilities'

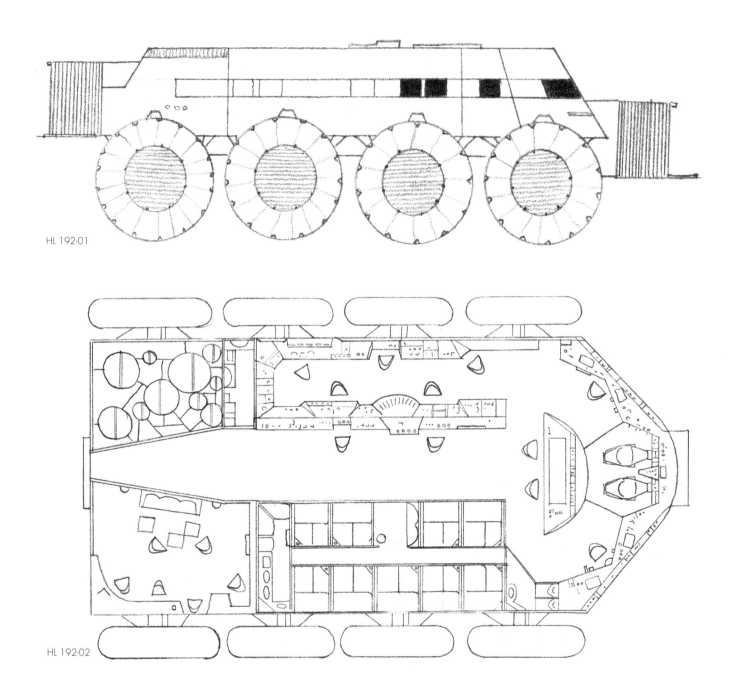

HL 192-01

HL 192-02

HL 192-01 *Early concept of Moon bus.* **HL 192-02** *Moon bus with interior plan view.* **HL 192-03** *Early concept of Moon bus in action (two views).* **HL 192-04** *Early concept of Moon bus with retractable wheels.* **HL 192-05** *Early concept of Moon bus (section view) with docking gantry at TMA-1.* **HL 192-06** *Early concept of Moon bus with large wheels.* **HL 192-07** *Early concept of Moon bus in action.*

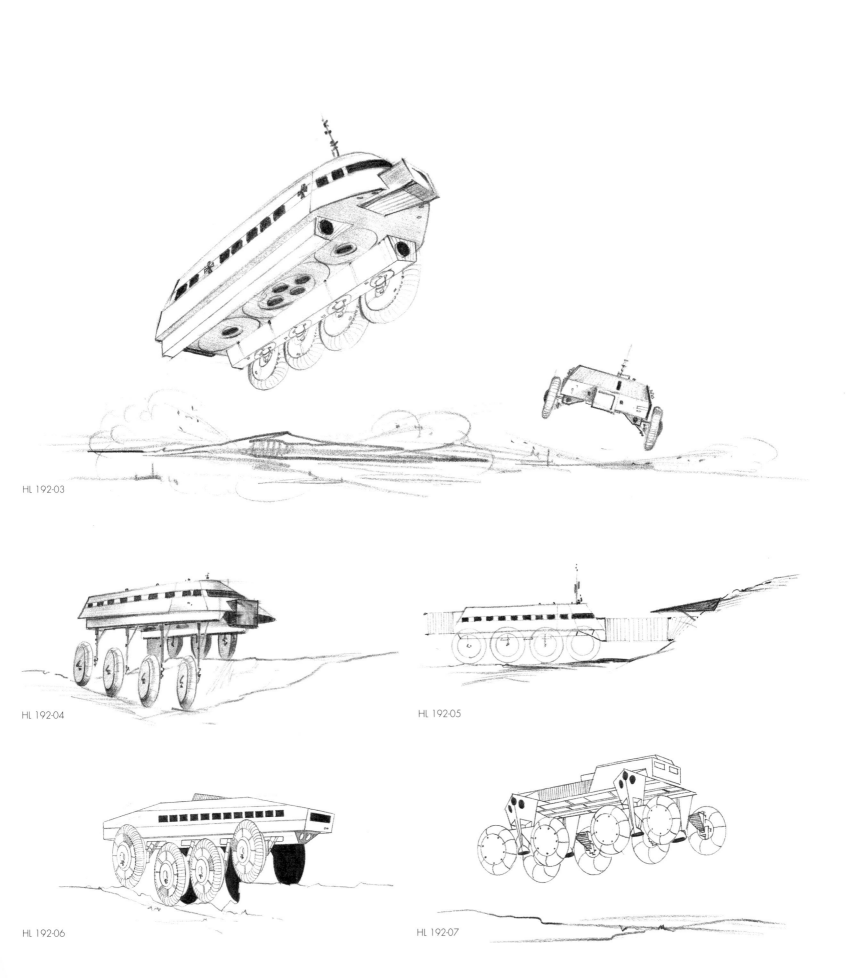

HL 192-03

HL 192-04

HL 192-05

HL 192-06

HL 192-07

MOON BUS
Developing concepts

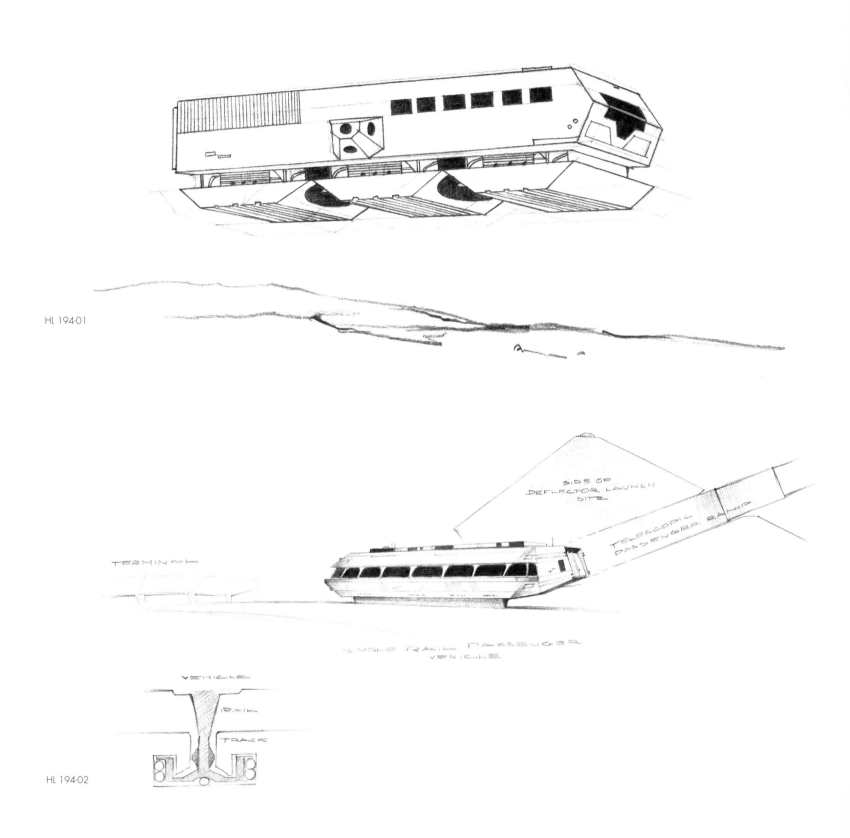

HL 194-01

HL 194-02

HL 194-01 *Early concept of Moon bus.* **HL 194-02** *Single rail passenger vehicle with telescopic ramp, terminal and side of 'deflector launch site'; plus section detail of vehicle, rail and track.* **HL 194-03** *Interior view of Moon bus.*

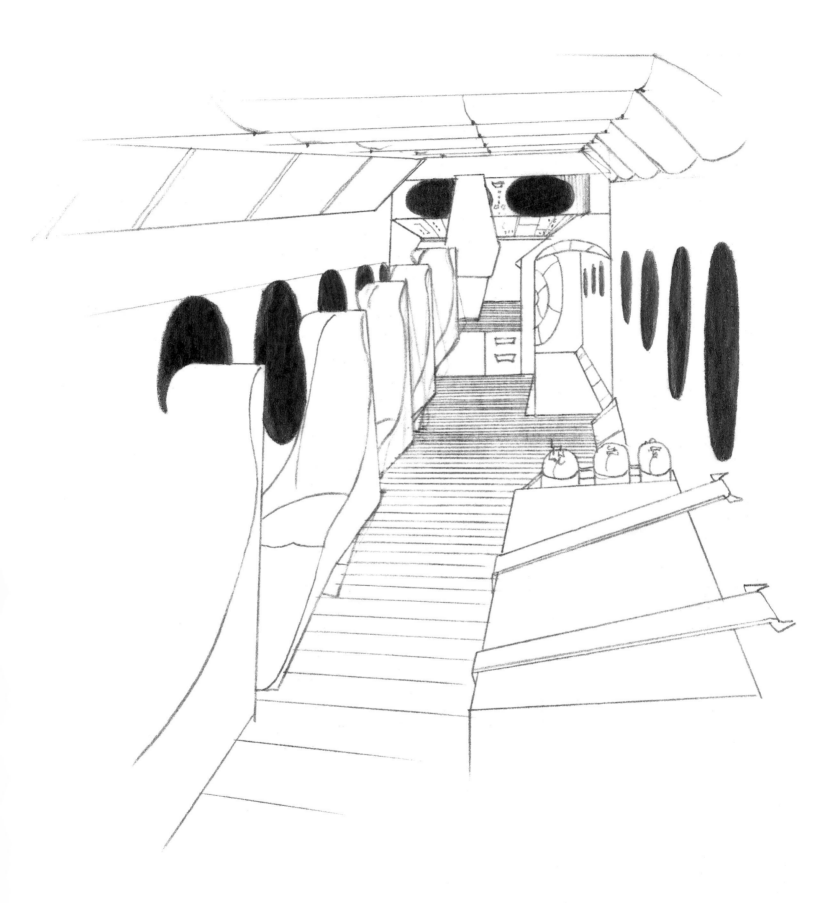

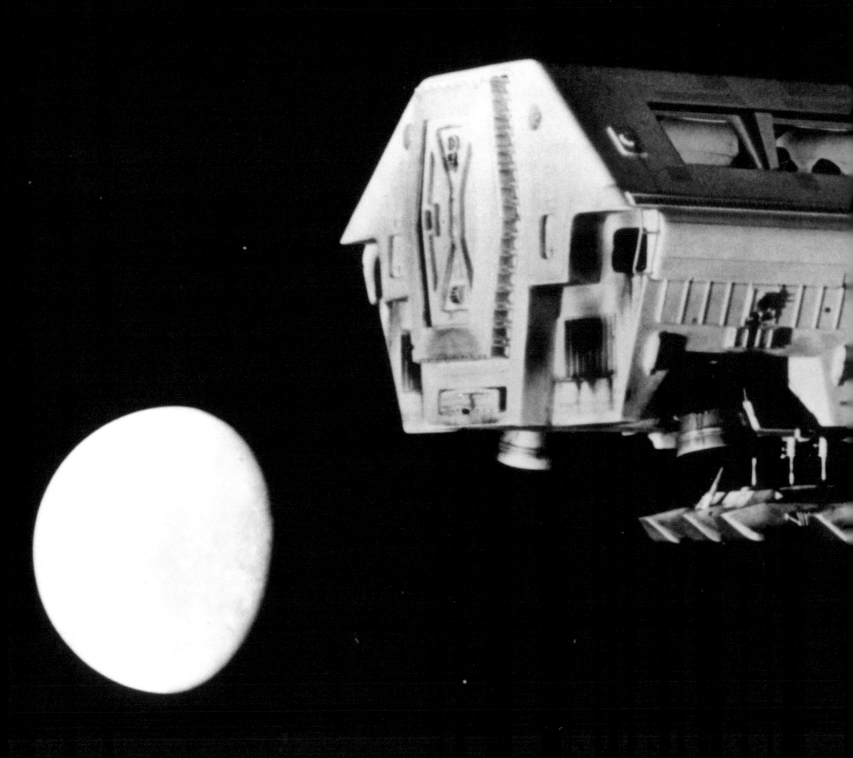

The lunar rocket bus—as seen in the finished film—which transports the scientists from Clavius base to the alien monolith within the crater ring of Tycho.

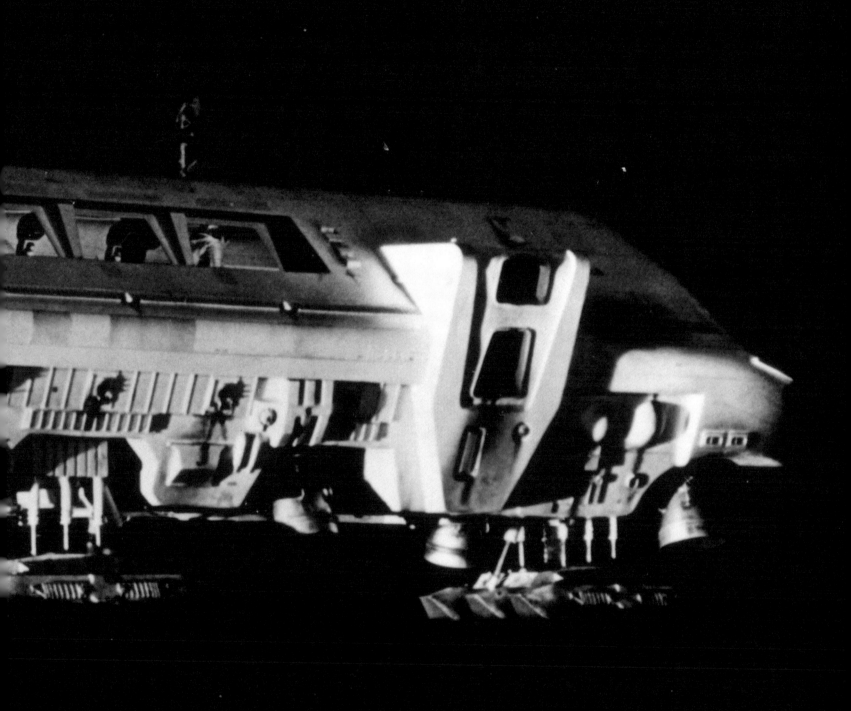

MONOLITH

Early concepts

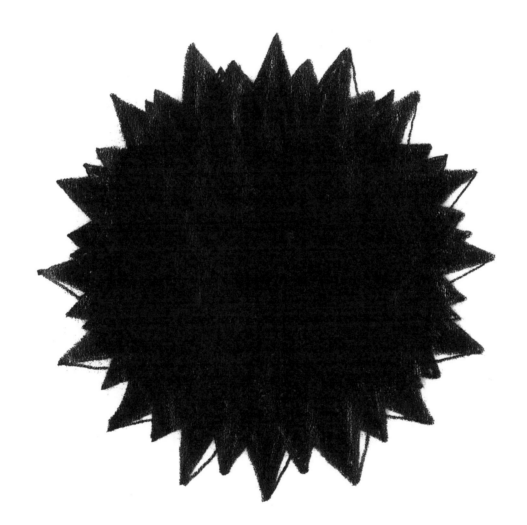

HL 198-01

HL 198-01 *Early monolith—geological design.* **HL 198-02** *Early Monolith—12 different geological/geometric designs, some of which were later transposed to 'beyond infinity'.*

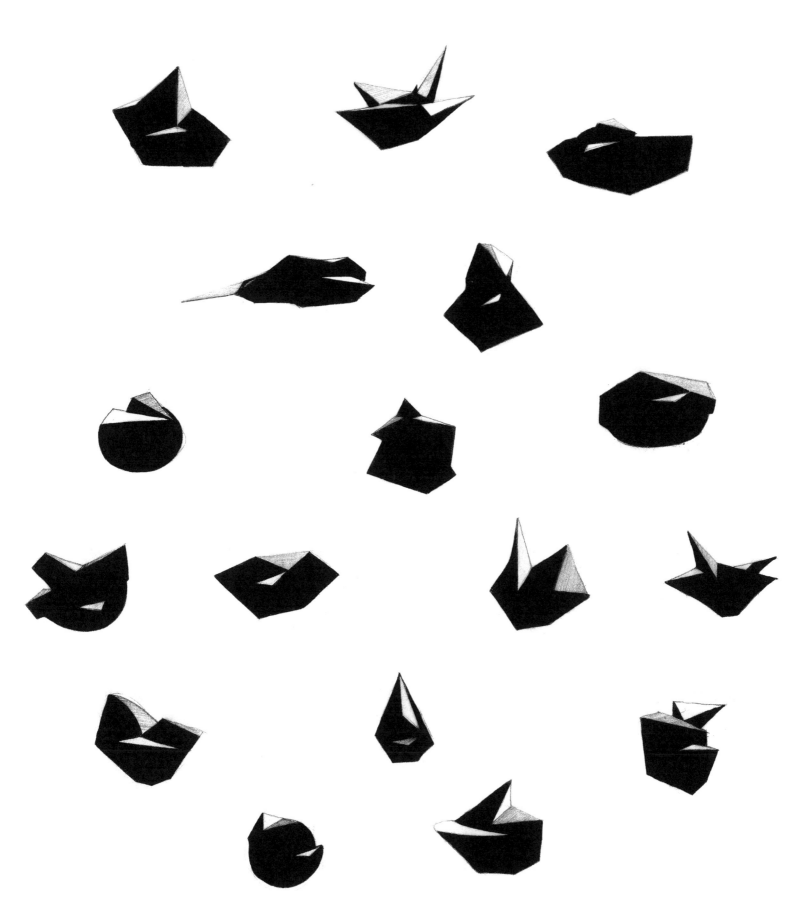

MONOLITH

Early concepts, in situ at TMA-1

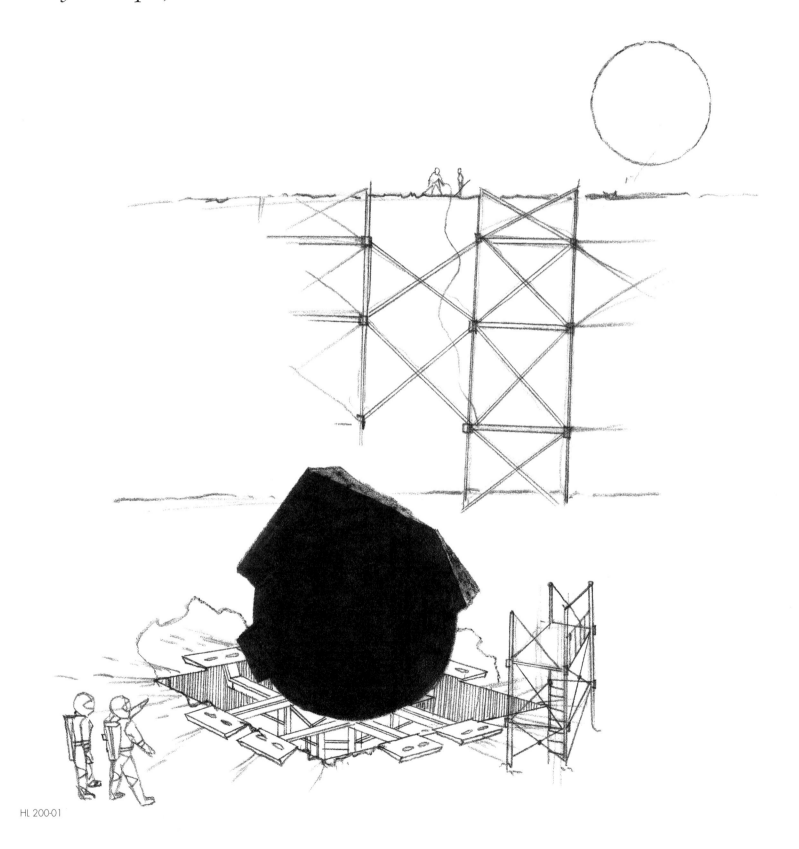

HL 200-01

HL 200-01 *Early concept for monolith, viewed by scientists.* **OPPOSITE:** *Early model shot of 'pyramid' monolith, in lunar trench.*

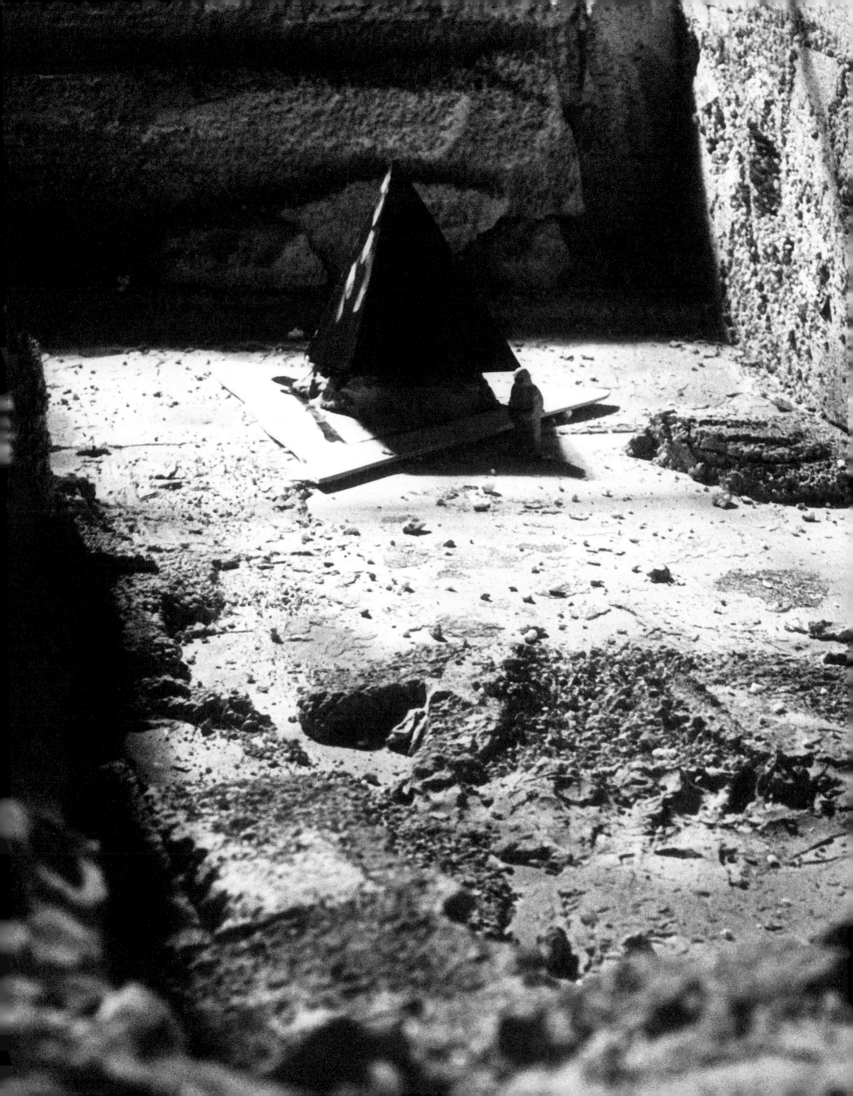

MONOLITH

Early concepts, in situ at TMA-1

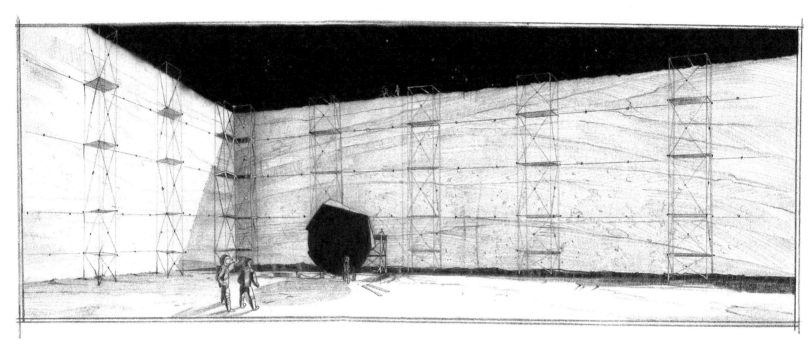

HL 202-01

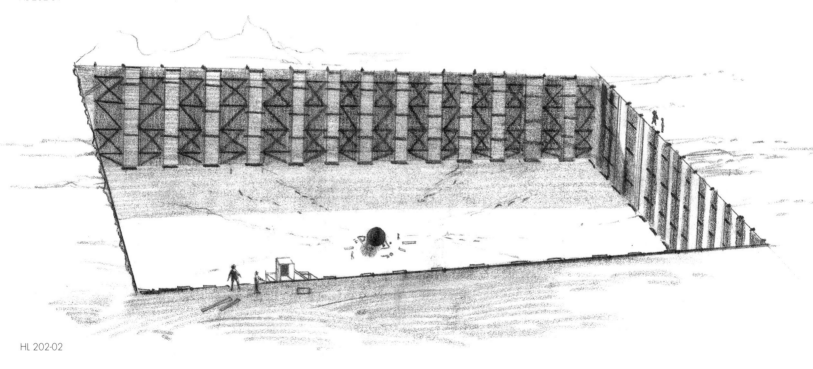

HL 202-02

HL 202-01 *Wider view of lunar excavated trench with monolith.* **HL 202-02** *Lunar excavated trench with monolith from above.* **HL 202-03** *Lunar excavated trench with monolith, and scientists viewing from above.* **OVERLEAF** *Full-sized lunar trench set being constructed, when the monolith was still a 'pyramid' shape.*

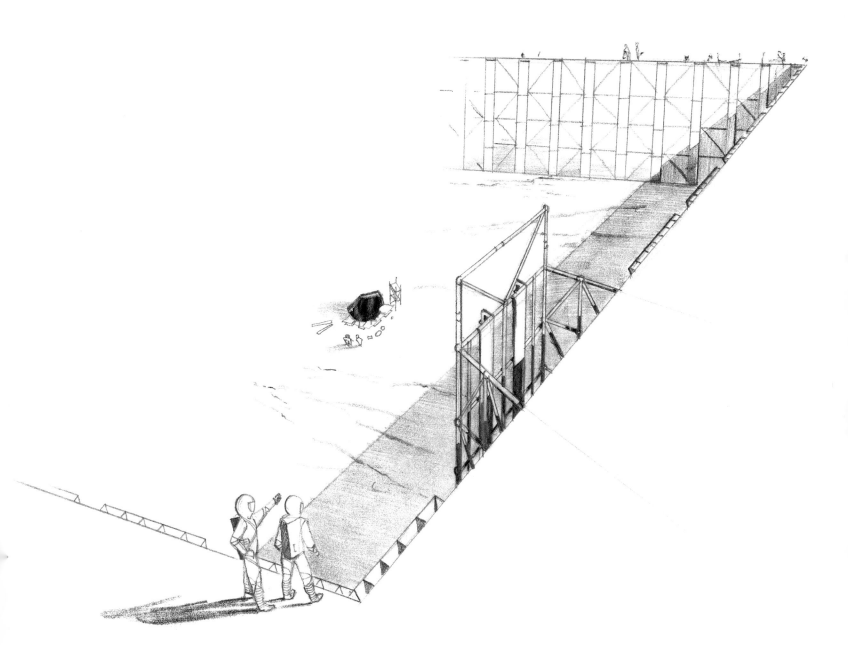

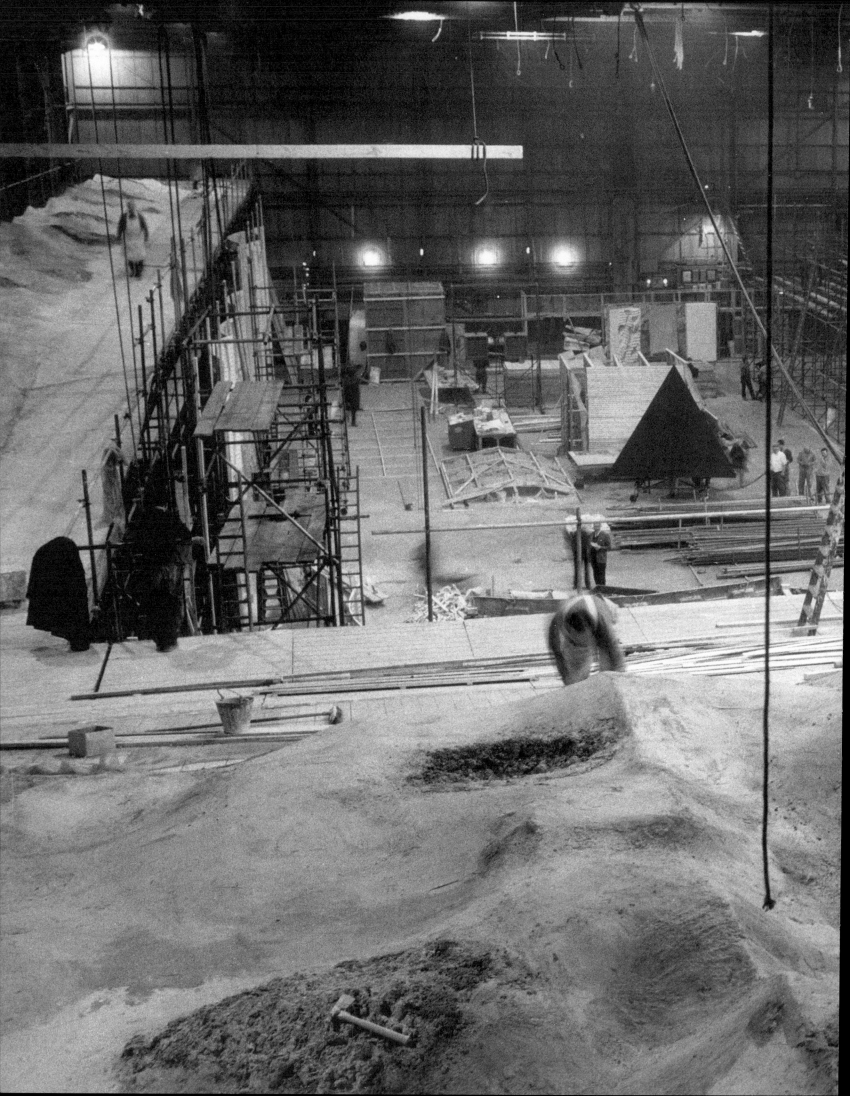

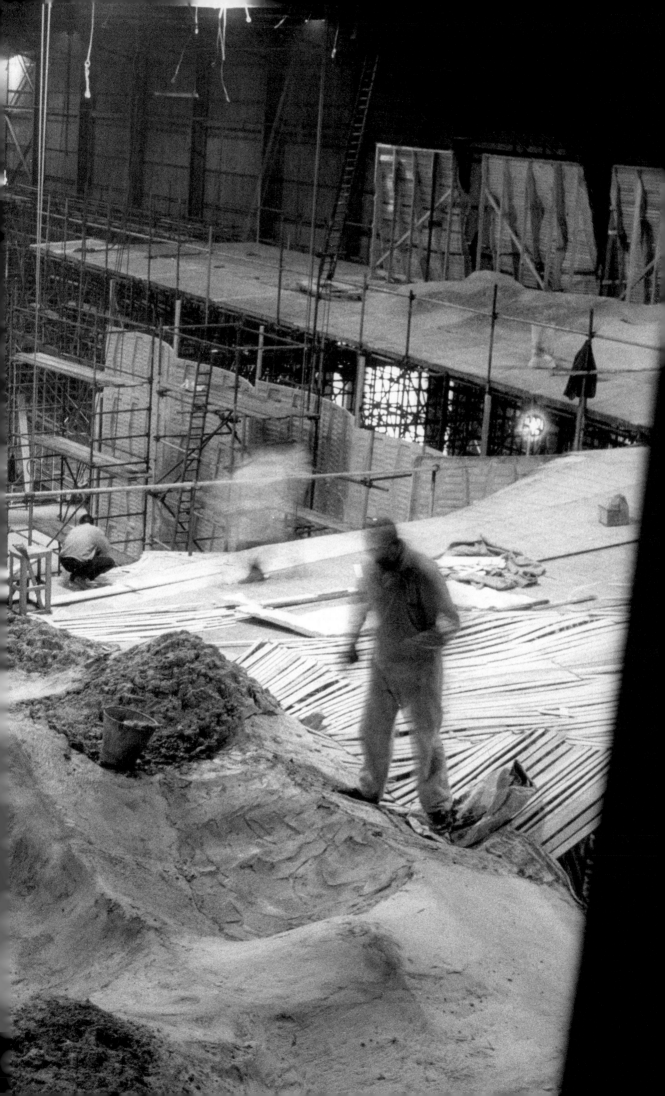

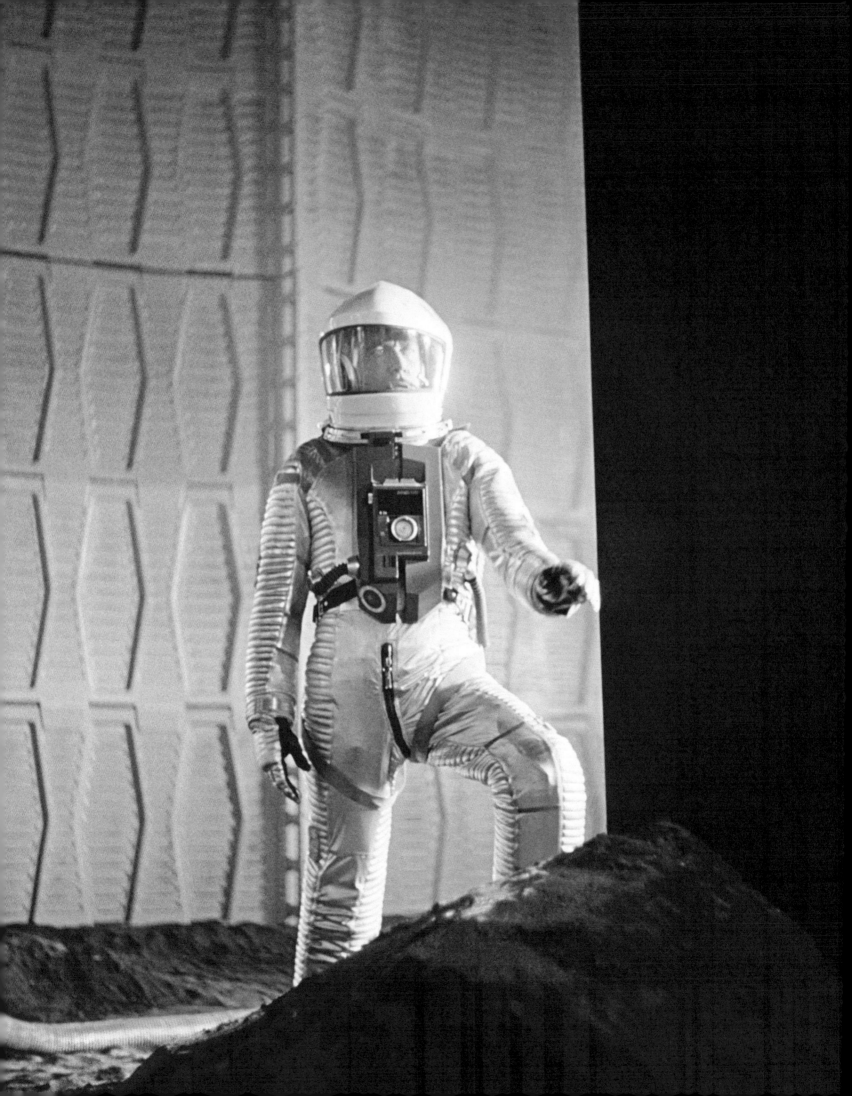

OPPOSITE: *The 12ft high matt blacker-than-black rectangular monolith, in the film, which Harry Lange called 'a very, very simple and basic idea—in perfect proportion'.*

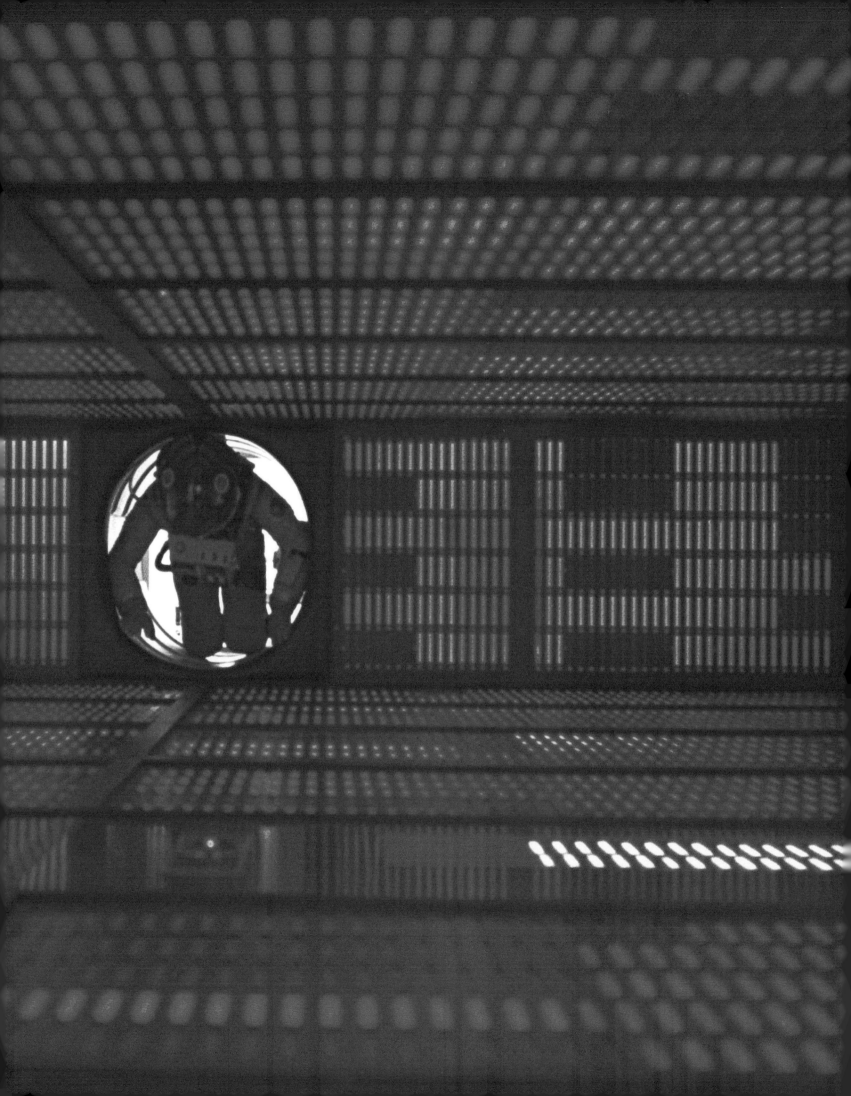

ODYSSEY III
TOWARDS JUPITER

Ten month secret mission towards Jupiter, on the 520 foot long manned Discovery interplanetary spacecraft, 'designed to travel four thousand times further than the distance from Earth to the Moon'.

DISCOVERY INTERPLANETARY SPACESHIP
Early launch concept

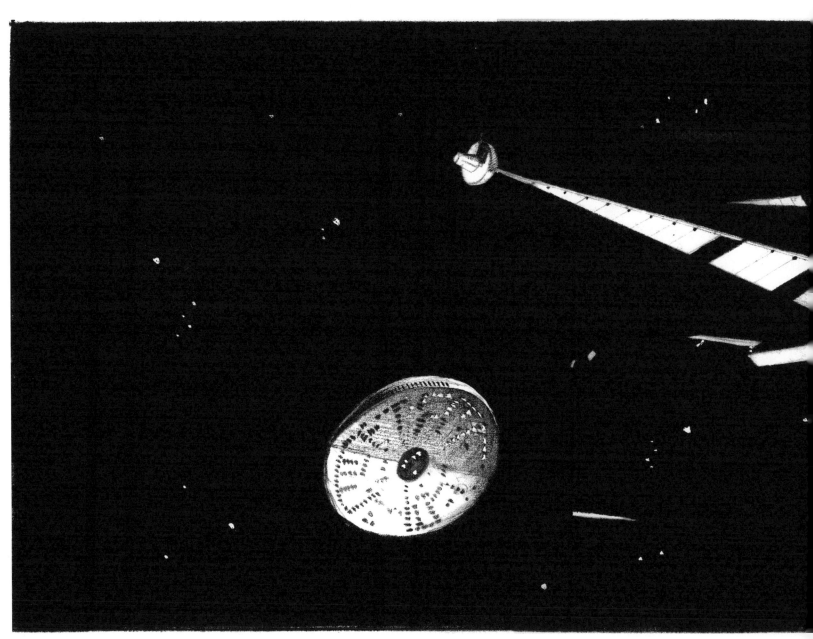

HL 210-01

HL 210-01 *Discovery spacecraft—with dragonfly configuration—being constructed with Space Station in background orbiting Earth. In the original treatment of **Journey Beyond the Stars**, Discovery was to 'pull out of her parking orbit' on Space Station One; then, in the later production notes, this sequence was to be omitted and 'we go directly from Jupiter Mission Briefing to the "Discovery" Spacecraft already on its way to Jupiter'. From the outset, the brief was to avoid traditional streamlined solutions to spacecraft design.*

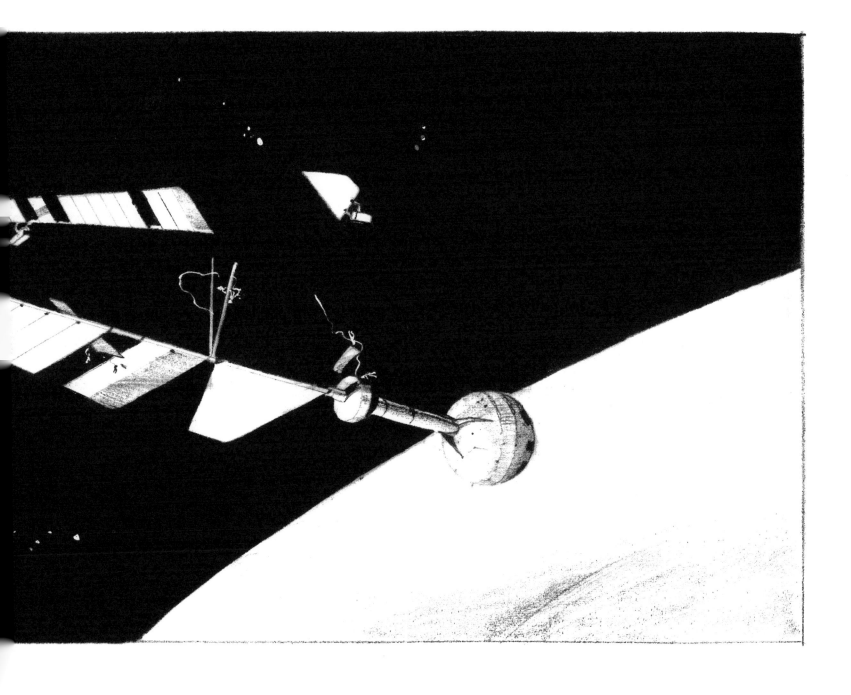

DISCOVERY
Early concepts

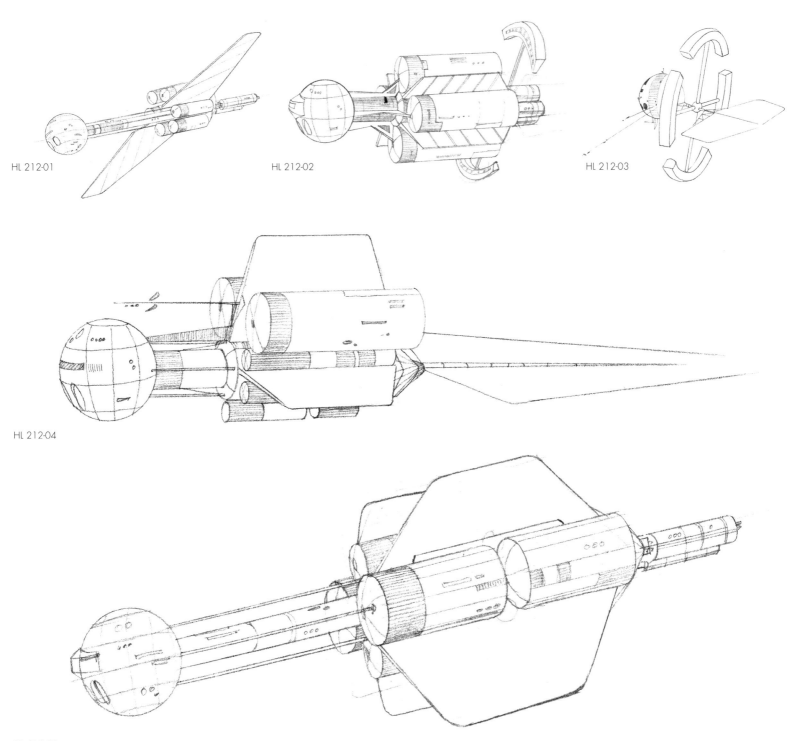

HL 212-01

HL 212-02

HL 212-03

HL 212-04

HL 212-05

HL 212-01 *Command module with heat radiator wings.* **HL 212-02** *Command module with fuel storage tanks, life support centrifuge and propulsion system.* **HL 212-03** *Very early version of Discovery—compare early versions of Space Station.* **HL 212-04** *Command module with cylindrical fuel tanks, life support, and dragonfly-shaped heat radiation panel.* **HL 212-05** *Command module with fuel storage, heat radiation panels, propulsion system.* **HL 212-06** *Discovery (7L) with cylindrical fuel tanks, centrifuge, life support systems and propulsion system.*

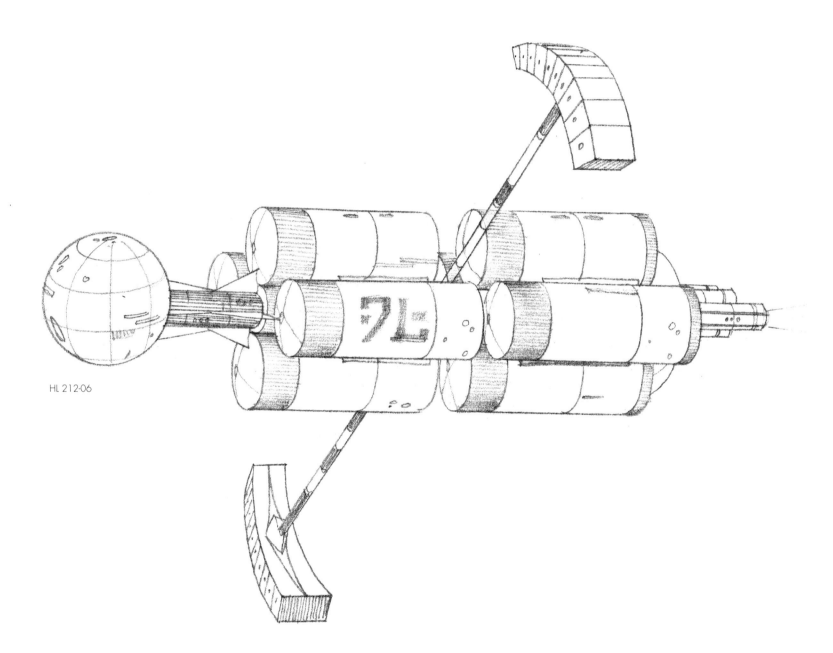

HL 212-06

DISCOVERY

Early concepts

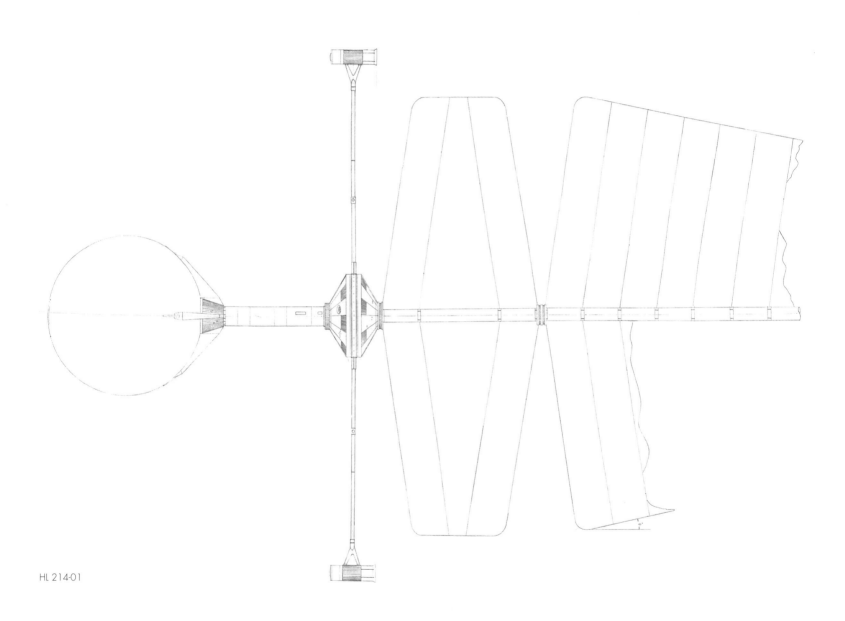

HL 214-01

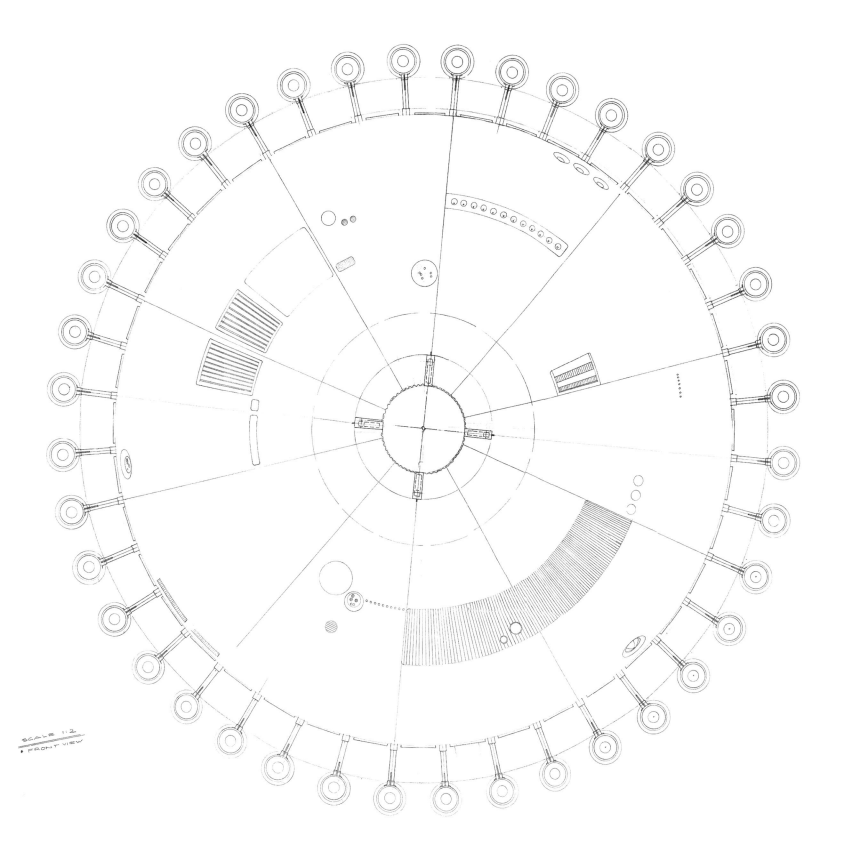

SCALE 1:2
FRONT VIEW

HL 214-02

DISCOVERY

Early 'Bell' or 'Saucer' shaped concepts

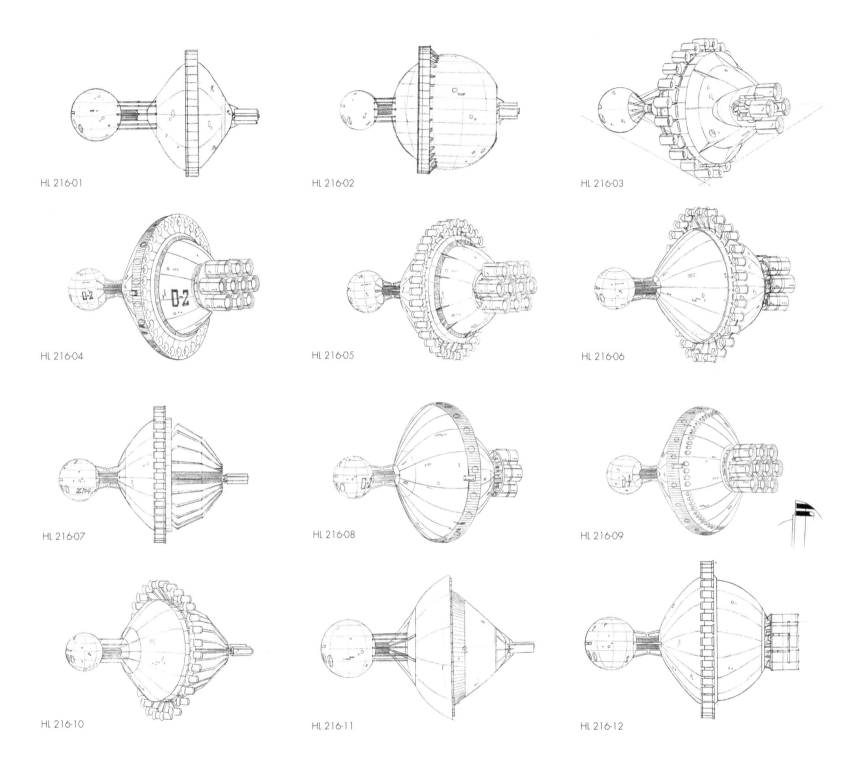

HL 216-01

HL 216-02

HL 216-03

HL 216-04

HL 216-05

HL 216-06

HL 216-07

HL 216-08

HL 216-09

HL 216-10

HL 216-11

HL 216-12

HL 216-01 *Command module with bell shaped configuration.* **HL 216-02** *Command module with bulbous fuselage.* **HL 216-03** *Command module with compressed bell shaped fuselage and propulsion system detail (rear view).* **HL 216-04** *Command module (D2) with bell shaped fuel storage and life support, and propulsion system details (rear view).* **HL 216-05** *Command module with bell shaped fuselage and detailed propulsion system (rear view).* **HL 216-06** *Command module with bell shaped fuselage, external storage tanks and propulsion system.* **HL 216-07** *Command module (Z34) with bell shaped fuselage, heat radiation fins, and propulsion system.* **HL 216-08** *Command module (D2) with enclosed bell shaped fuselage and propulsion system.* **HL 216-09** *Command module (D4), bell shaped fuselage with propulsion system and life support detail.* **HL 216-10** *Command module with bell shaped fuselage and external life support modules, radiated heat fins and propulsion system.* **HL 216-11** *Command module with compressed bell shaped fuselage and propulsion system.* **HL 216-12** *Command module with compressed bell shaped fuselage, life support system and propulsion system configuration.* **HL 216-13** *Command module with bell shaped fuel cell configuration, and heat radiation dragonfly design panels.* **HL 216-14** *Command module with integrated bell shaped fuselage, cylindrical fuel storage tanks and propulsion system.* **HL 216-15** *Command module (D4) reverse bell shaped fuselage and propulsion system.* **HL 216-16** *Command module (D2) with bell shaped fuel storage and life support, and propulsion system.* **HL 216-17** *Command module (D4) with reverse bell shaped fuselage and propulsion system.*

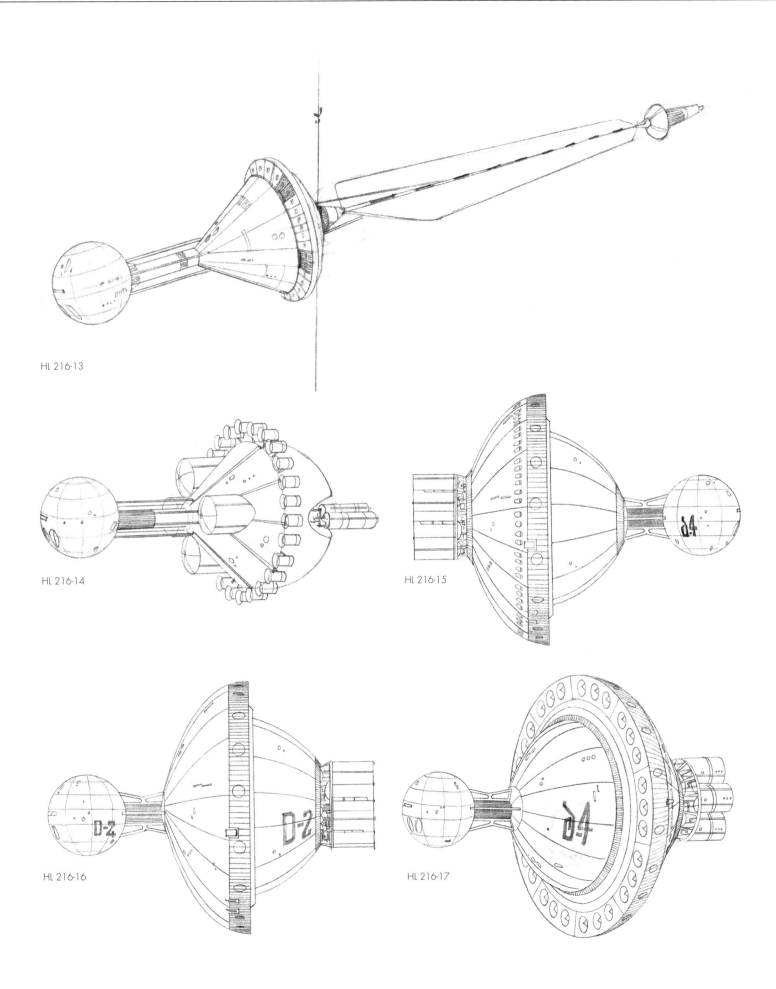

HL 216-13

HL 216-14

HL 216-15

HL 216-16

HL 216-17

DISCOVERY

Early 'Bell' or 'Saucer' shaped concepts

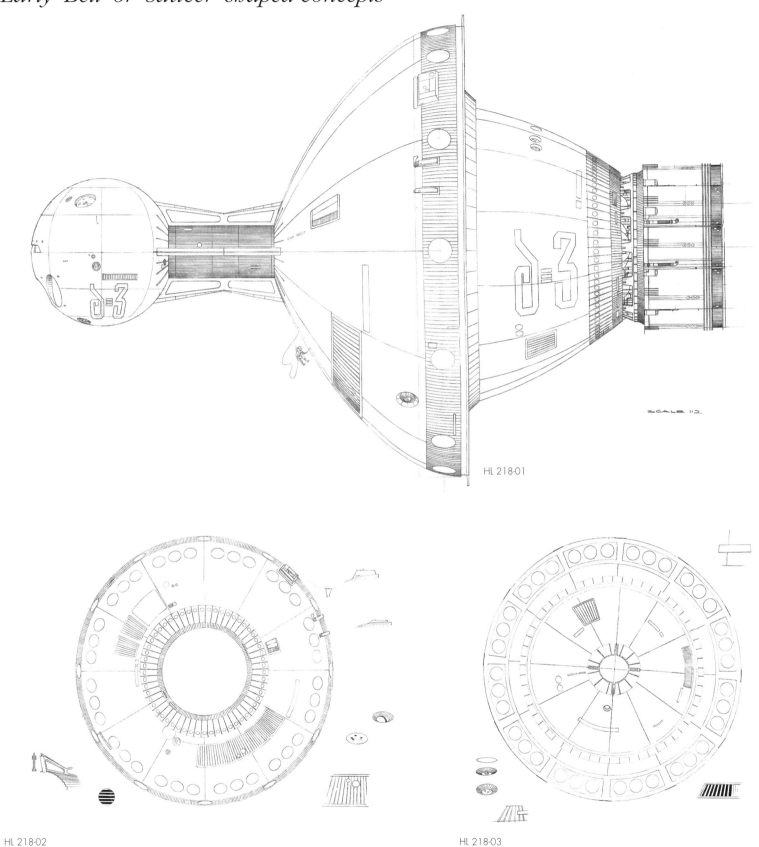

HL 218-01

HL 218-02

HL 218-03

HL 218-01 *Command module (D3) with bell shaped fuel storage and life support, and propulsion system details.* **HL 218-02** *Command module (D2) section with bell shaped fuel storage and life support, and propulsion system details.* **HL 218-03** *Discovery section view with surface construction detail.* **HL 218-04** *Discovery early concept showing command module and reverse bell shaped fuselage.* **HL 218-05** *Discovery propulsion system multiple views.*

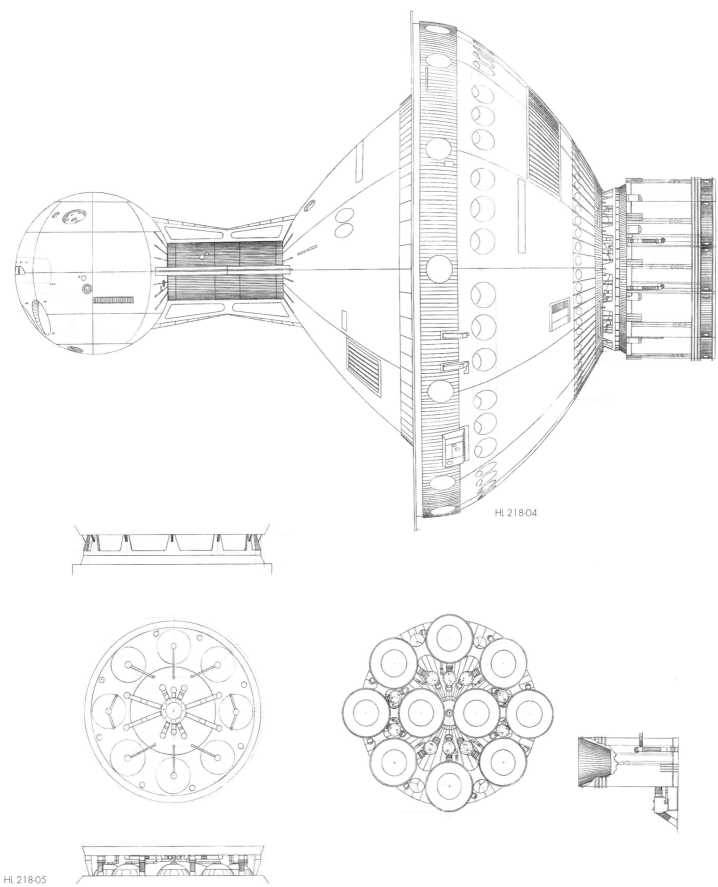

HL 218-04

HL 218-05

SCALE 1:2

DISCOVERY

Early 'Circular' shaped concepts

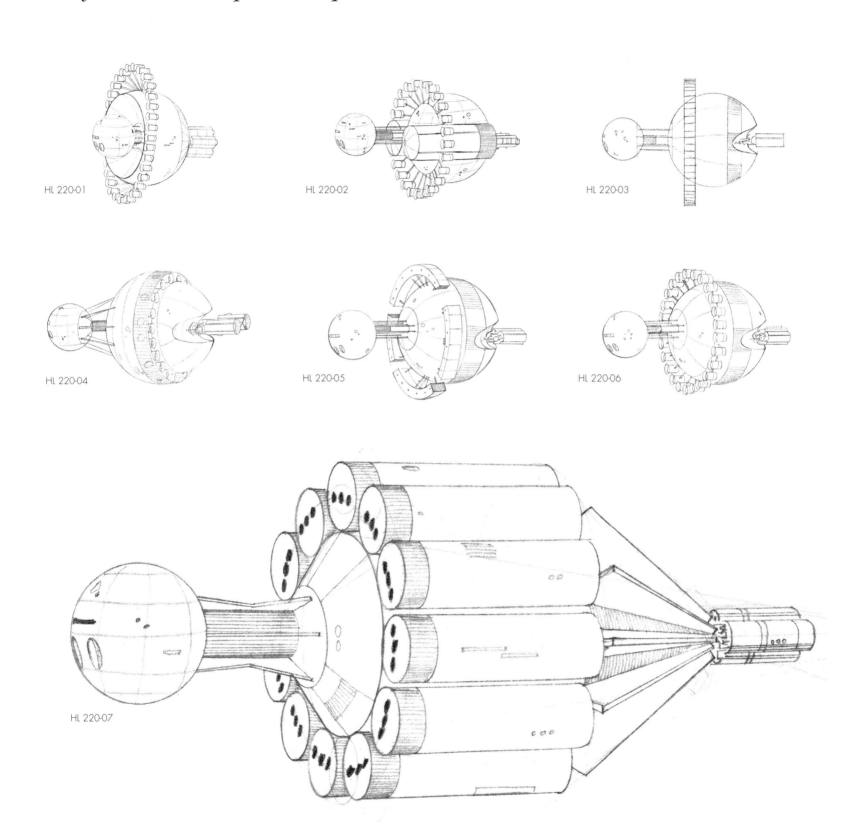

HL 220-01

HL 220-02

HL 220-03

HL 220-04

HL 220-05

HL 220-06

HL 220-07

HL 220-01 *Command module with concave circular fuselage and propulsion system.* **HL 220-02** *Command module with circular fuselage, twin fuel tanks, life support, storage and propulsion system.* **HL 220-03** *Command module with circular fuselage.* **HL 220-04** *Command module with circular fuselage and propulsion system detail.* **HL 220-05** *Command module with circular fuselage, external life support blocks and propulsion system.* **HL 220-06** *Command module with circular fuselage.* **HL 220-07** *Command module with cylindrical fuel storage, radiated heat dissipation panels and propulsion system.* **HL 220-08** *Command module with circular fuselage (front view).*

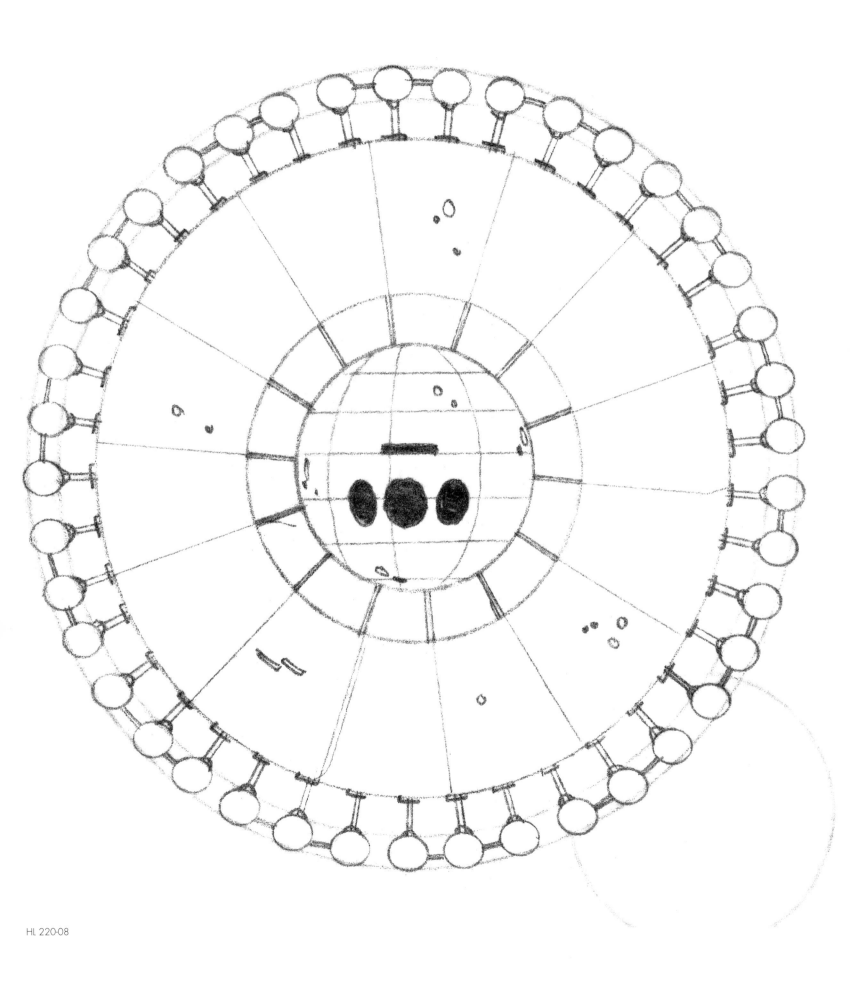

DISCOVERY

Early 'Cylindrical' concepts

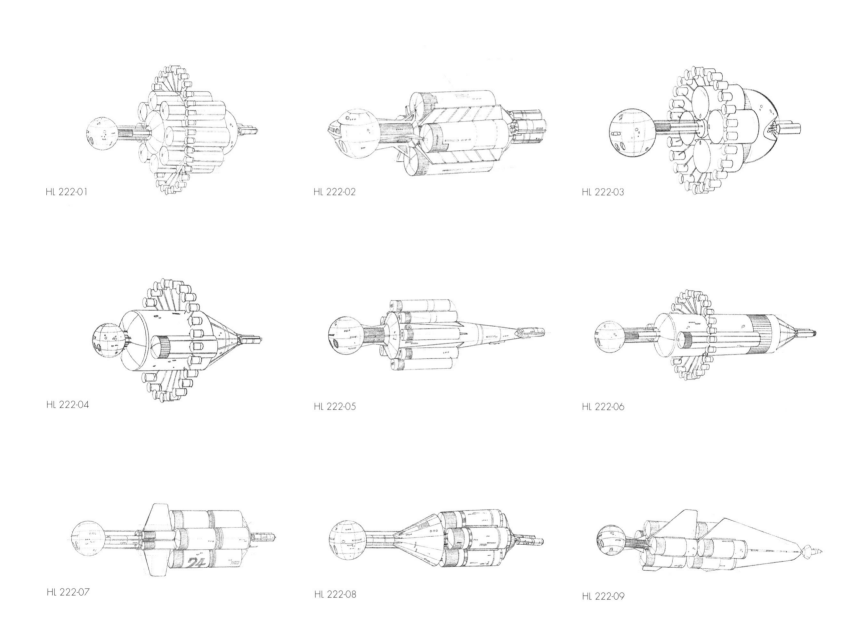

HL 222-01

HL 222-02

HL 222-03

HL 222-04

HL 222-05

HL 222-06

HL 222-07

HL 222-08

HL 222-09

HL 222-01 *Command module with cylindrical fuel storage, life support system and propulsion systems.* **HL 222-02** *Command module with cylindrical fuel tanks, propulsion system and heat dissipation fins.* **HL 222-03** *Command module with compressed cylindrical storage tanks and bell reverse-shaped propulsion system.* **HL 222-04** *Command module with compressed cylindrical fuselage and propulsion system.* **HL 222-05** *Command module with cylindrical fuel storage tanks and propulsion system.* **HL 222-06** *Command module with cylindrical fuselage and propulsion system.* **HL 222-07** *Command module with cylindrical fuel storage and radiation panels.* **HL 222-08** *Command module with bell shaped life-support system, cylindrical fuel storage tanks and propulsion system.* **HL 222-09** *Command module with cylindrical storage tanks and dragonfly heat radiation panels.* **HL 222-10** *Command module with cylindrical fuel tanks, life support systems and nuclear propulsion system.* **HL 222-11** *Command module with life support system and fuel storage.*

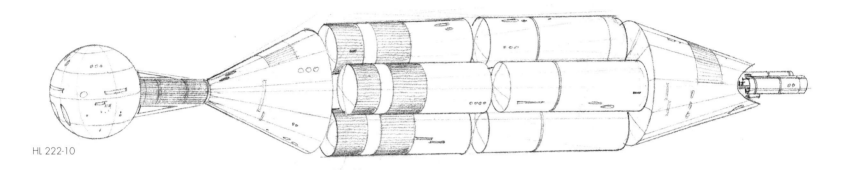

HL 222-10

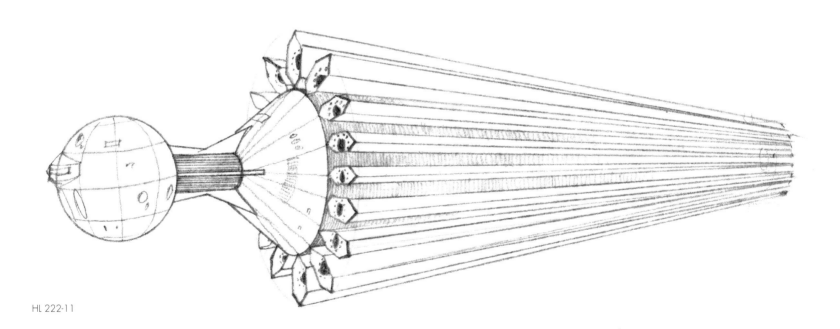

HL 222-11

DISCOVERY

Early blueprint with cylindrical fuel storage

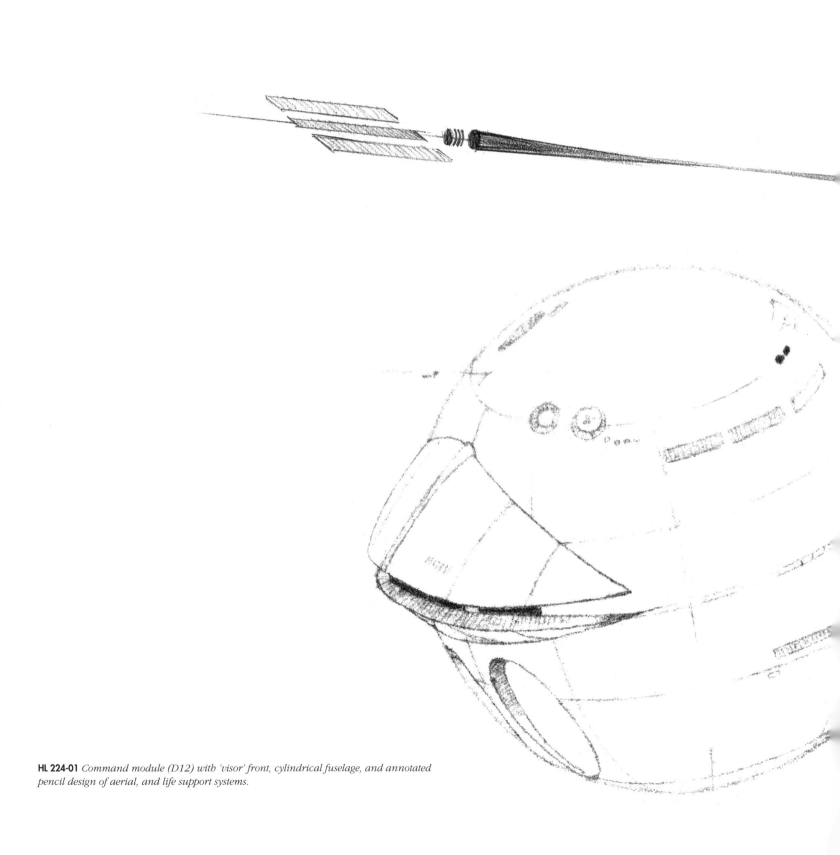

HL 224-01 *Command module (D12) with 'visor' front, cylindrical fuselage, and annotated pencil design of aerial, and life support systems.*

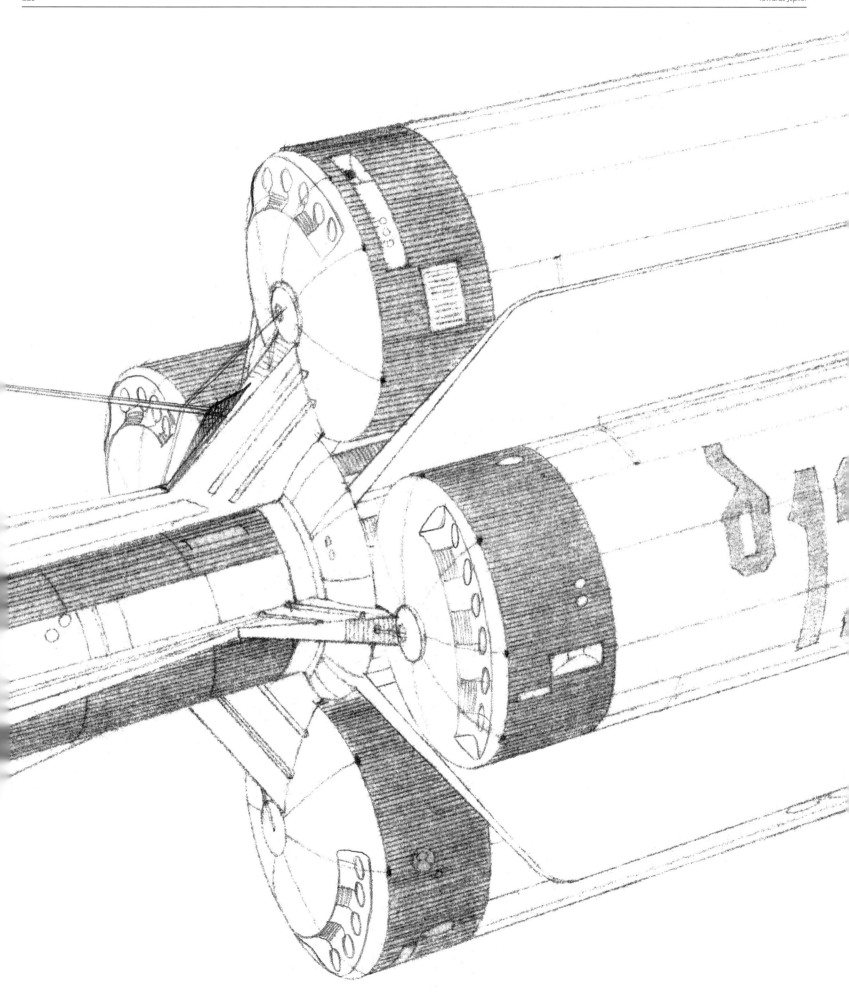

DISCOVERY

Early concepts with 'dragonfly' heat radiation panels

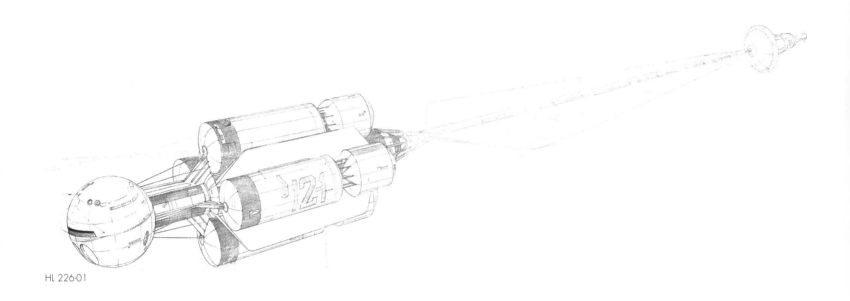

HL 226-01

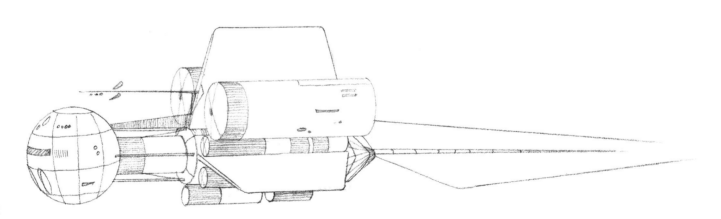

HL 226-02

HL 226-01 *Discovery, early concept (D12-1) showing fuel storage tanks, 'dragonfly' heat panels and propulsion system.* **HL 226-02** *Command module with cylindrical fuel tanks, life support, and 'dragonfly' heat radiation panel.* **OPPOSITE** *Test photograph of command module with dragonfly heat radiation panels and fuel storage tanks (polystyrene model).*

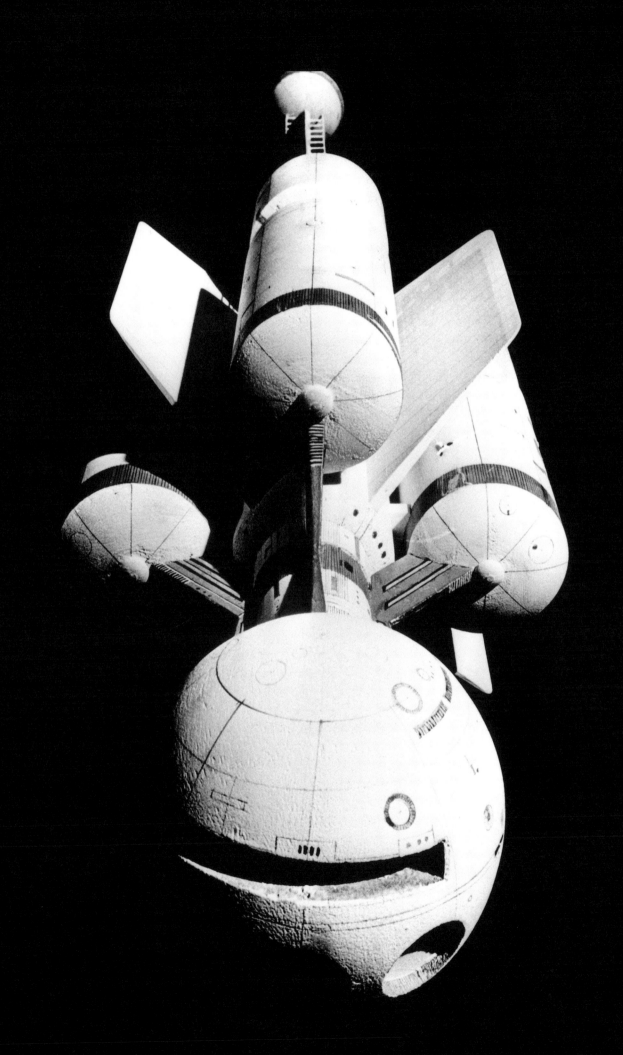

DISCOVERY

Early concepts with 'dragonfly' heat radiation panels

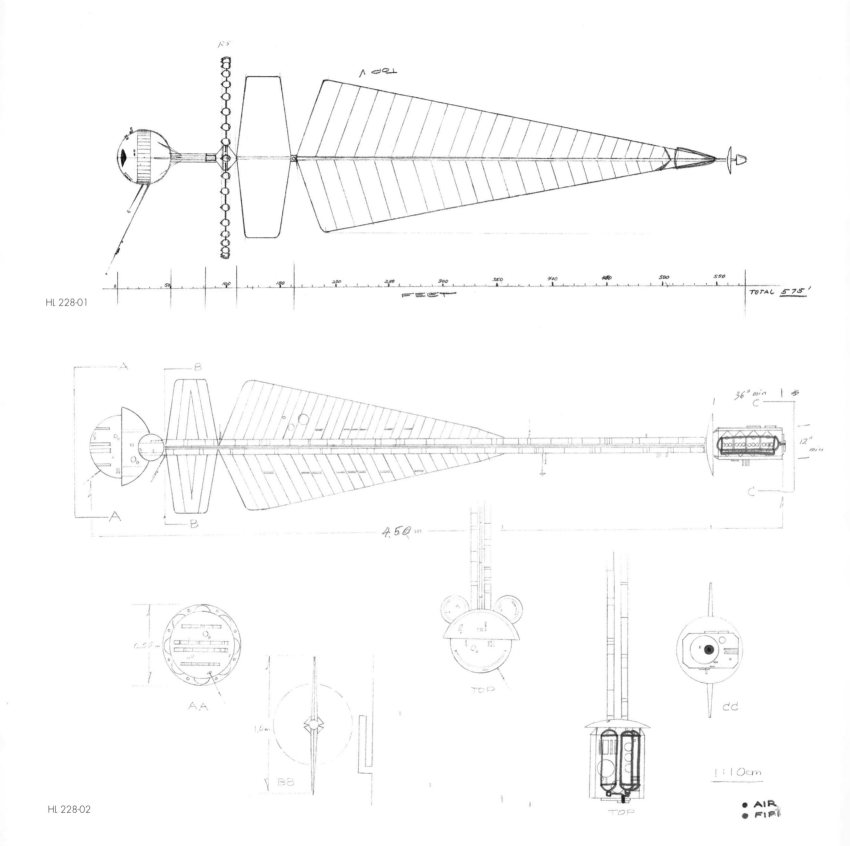

HL 228-01

HL 228-02

HL 228-01 *Discovery showing command module, fuel storage tanks, dragonfly heat panels and propulsion system, plus scale in feet.* **HL 228-02** *Blueprint: Discovery, early concept with cross section views, scale and blue & red design annotations.* **HL 228-03** *Command module with elongated fuselage, dragonfly radiation panels and propulsion system.* **HL 228-04** *Command module with cylindrical fuel tanks, and dragonfly heat radiation panels.* **HL 228-05** *Command module with life support system, fuel tanks and propulsion system, and dragonfly heat radiation panels.*

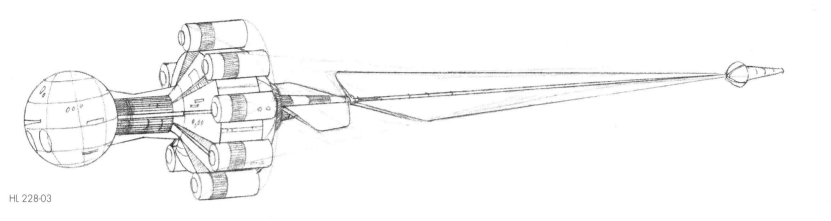

HL 228-03

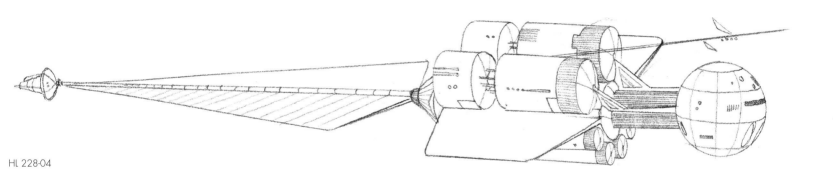

HL 228-04

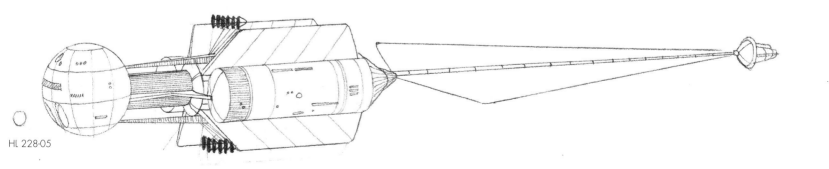

HL 228-05

DISCOVERY

Early concept with 'dragonfly' heat radiation panels

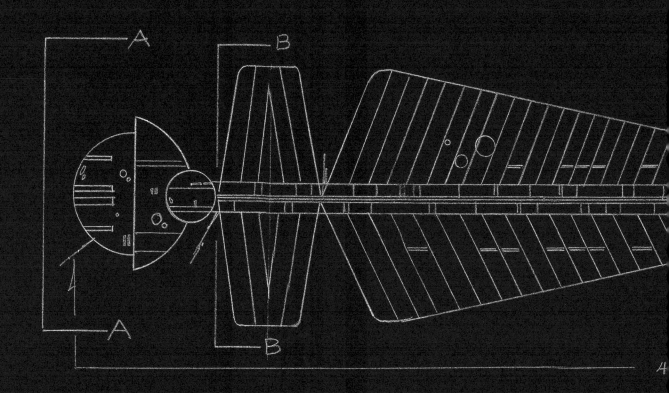

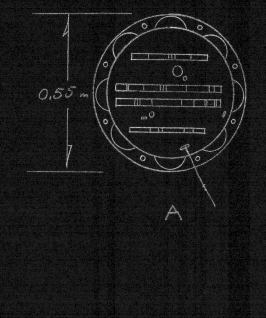

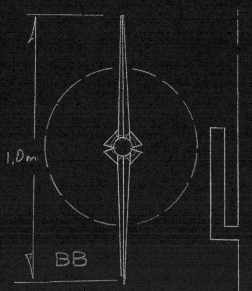

HL 230-01 *Early concept with 'dragonfly' heat radiation panels—cross section views, and scale in metres.*

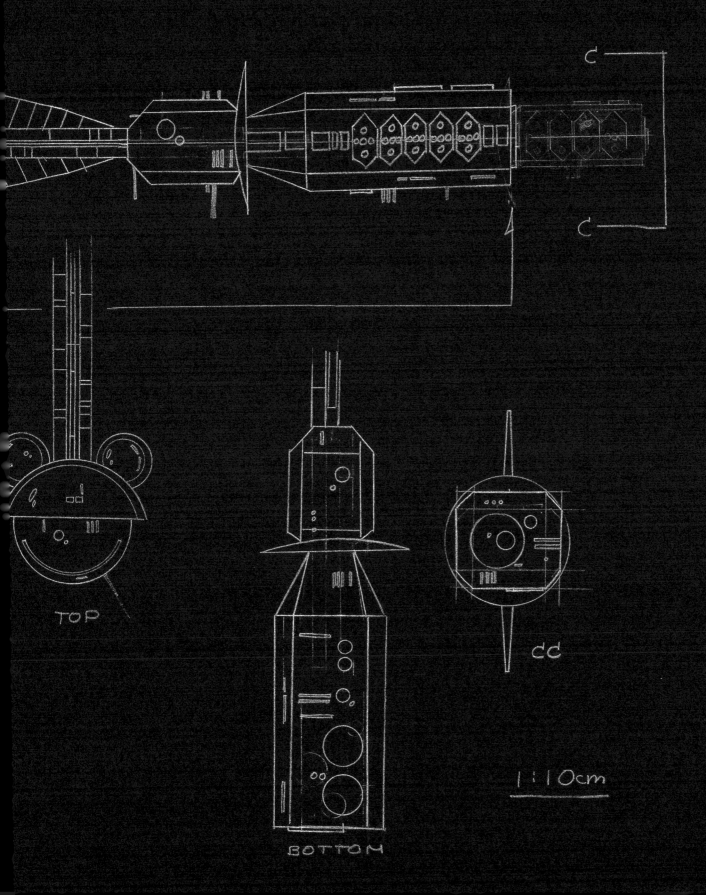

TOP

BOTTOM

CC

1:10cm

DISCOVERY

Propulsion systems and fuselage details

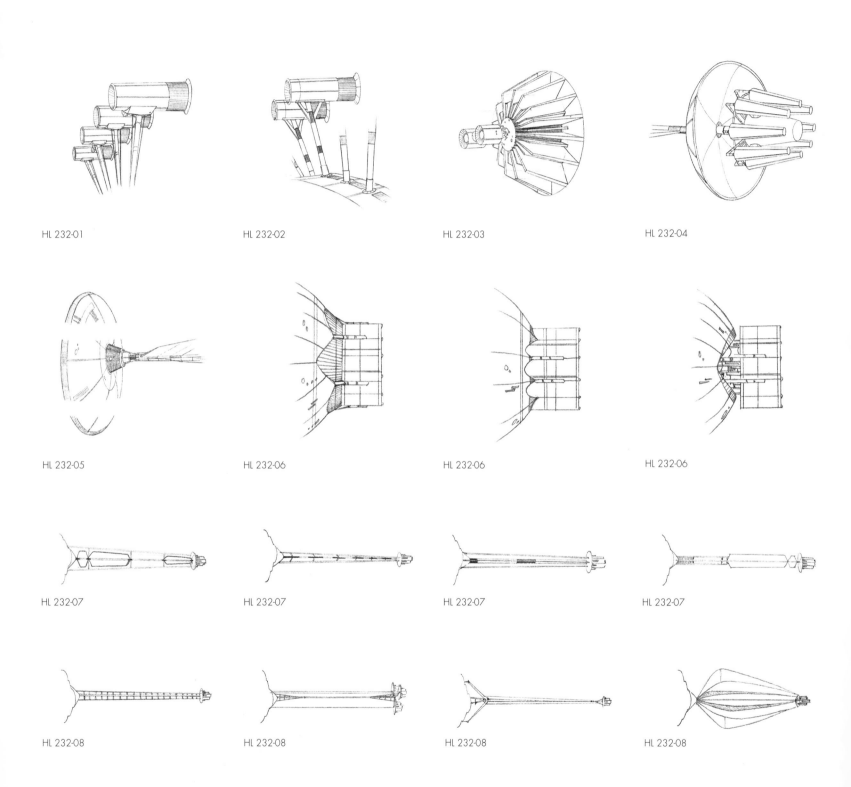

HL 232-01   HL 232-02   HL 232-03   HL 232-04

HL 232-05   HL 232-06   HL 232-06   HL 232-06

HL 232-07   HL 232-07   HL 232-07   HL 232-07

HL 232-08   HL 232-08   HL 232-08   HL 232-08

HL 232-01 *Life support system/fuel storage detail.* **HL 232-02** *Life support system/fuel storage detail.* **HL 232-03** *Propulsion system with heat radiation fins (rear view).* **HL 232-04** *Discovery propulsion system.* **HL 232-05** *Propulsion system with pusher plate and heat radiator for 'Project Orion' concept.* **HL 232-06** *Propulsion system (three views).* **HL 232-07** *Discovery propulsion system (four designs).* **HL 232-08** *Four designs of nuclear propulsion system for Discovery.* **HL 232-09** *Detailed propulsion system design for Discovery.* **HL 232-10** *Discovery fuselage linkage detail.*

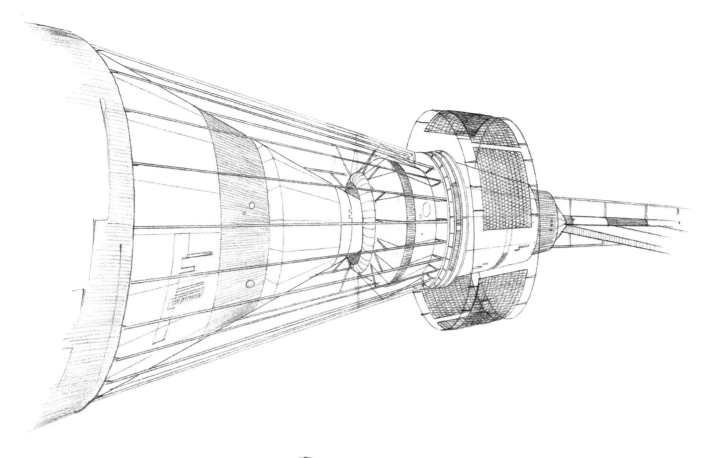

HL 232-09

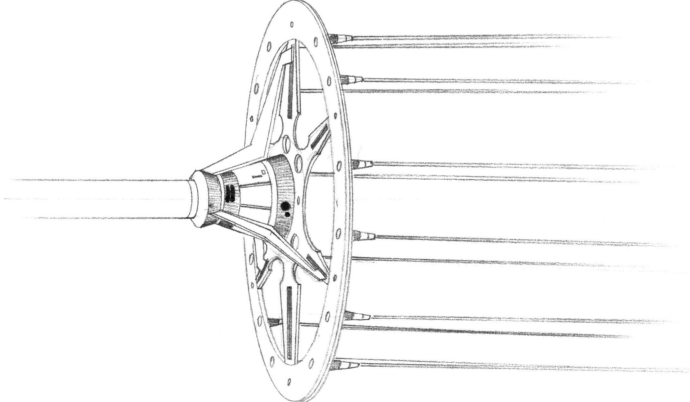

HL 232-10

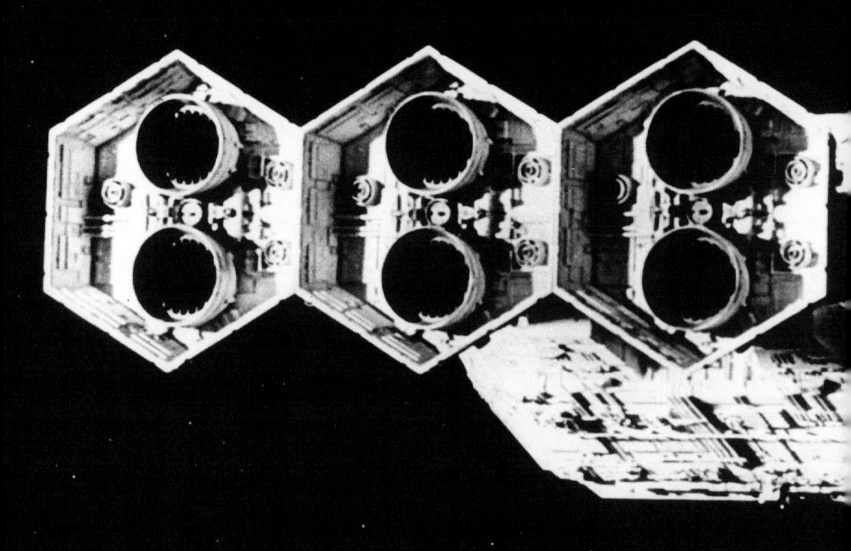

Discovery (final version) on its way to Jupiter, showing the three hexagonal propulsion units, each with two exhaust nozzles, with hundreds of feet of tankage separating them from the command module: the ship is propelled by 'cavradyne' gaseous-core nuclear reactor engines.

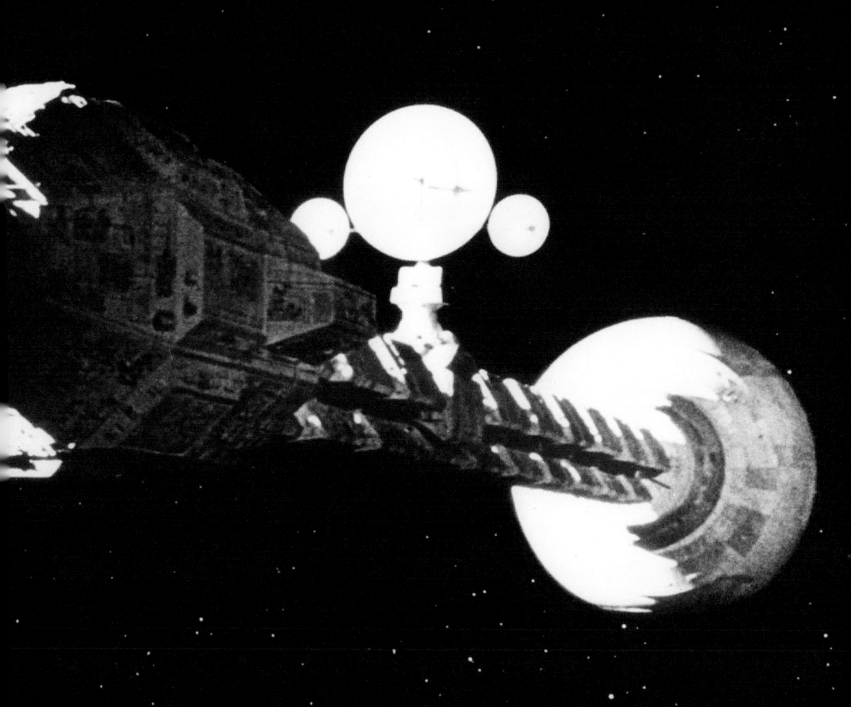

DISCOVERY
Towards the final design

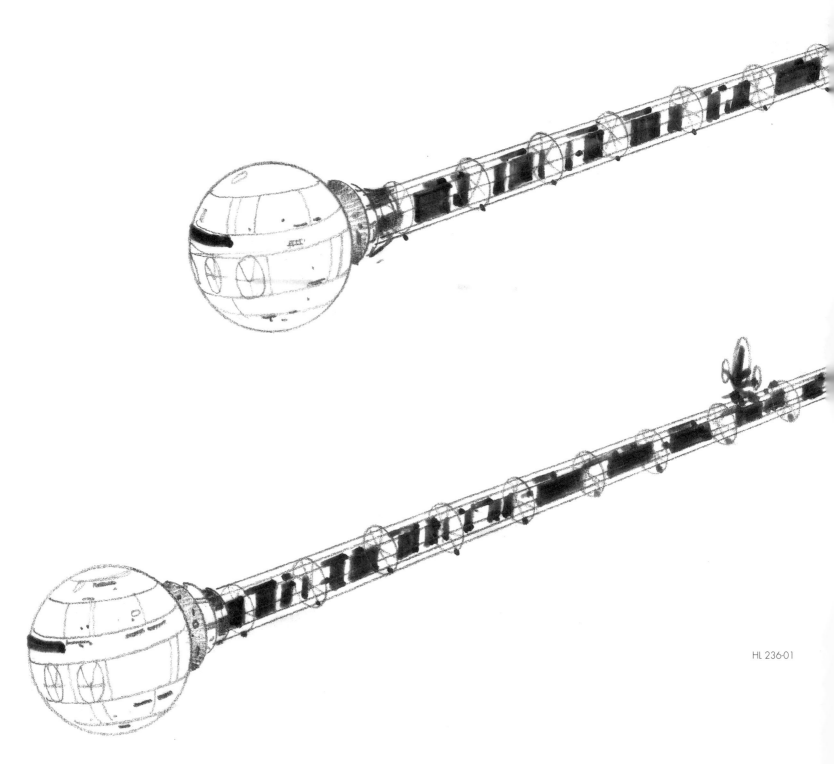

HL 236-01

HL 236-01 *Discovery with command module, fuel cells, propulsion system, and heat dissipation cooling panels (two views).* **HL 236-02** *Discovery with command module, fuel cells, propulsion system, and heat dissipation panels at different angles.*

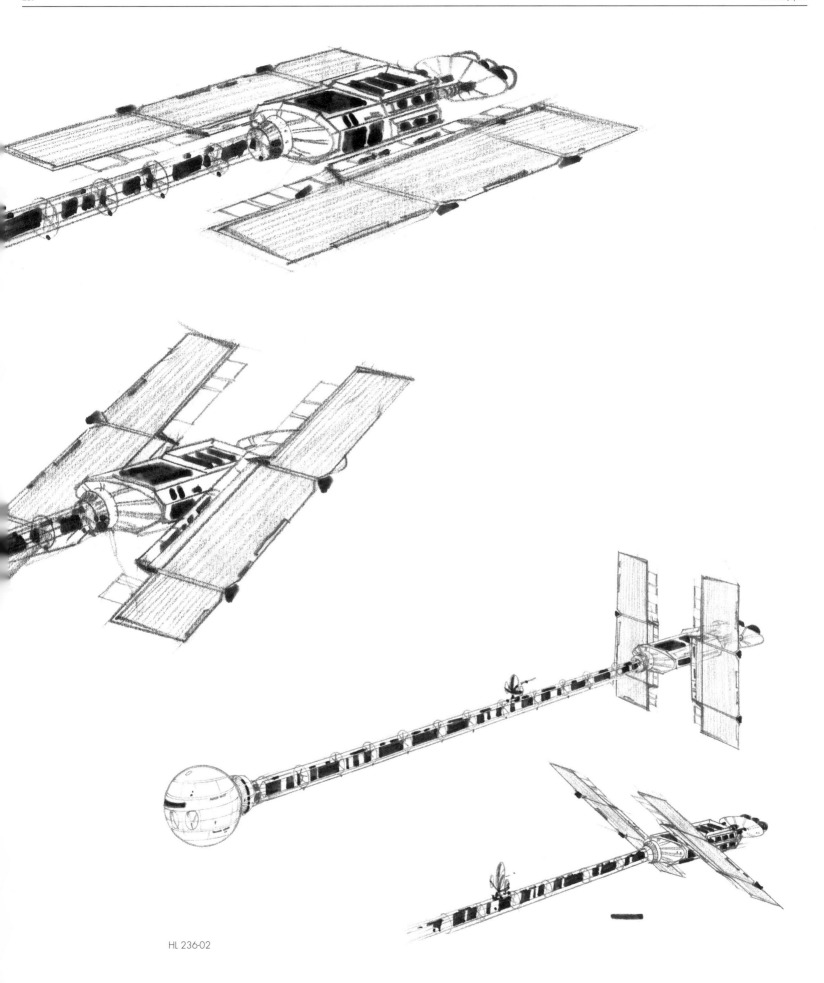

HL 236-02

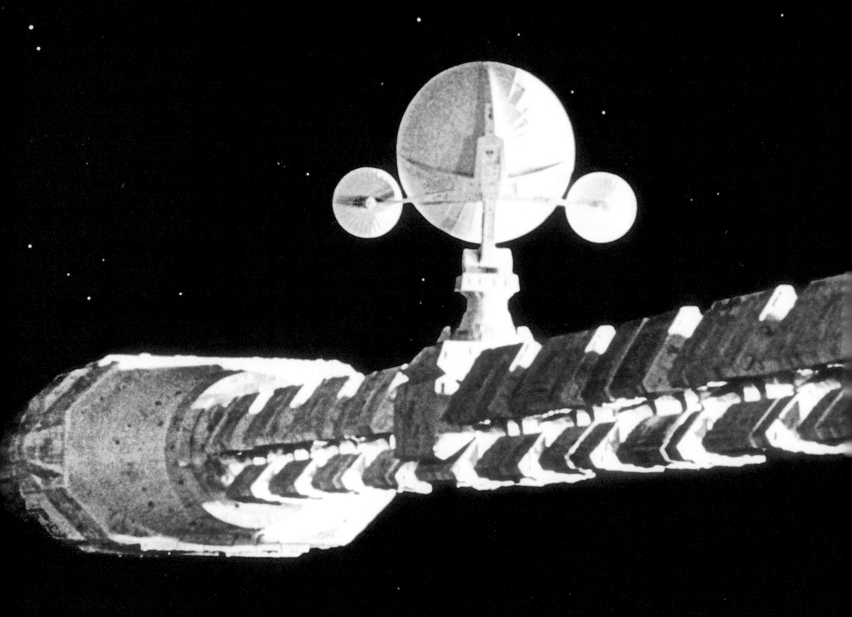

Discovery (final version), seen from the command module—complete with communications system and space repair pod.

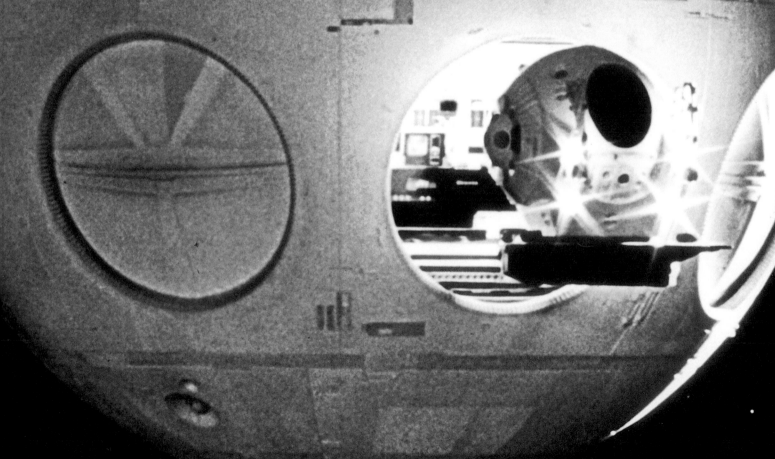

DISCOVERY

External communications systems

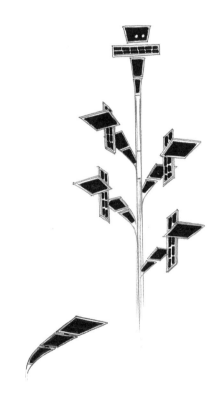

HL 240-01

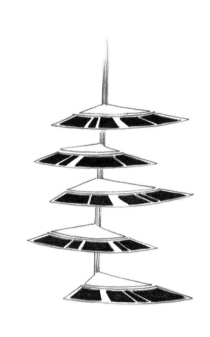

HL 240-02

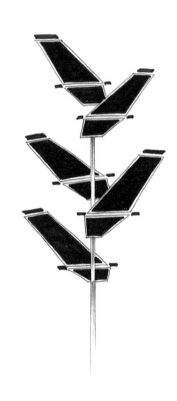

HL 240-03

ABOVE *Discovery communications aerials (pencil and ink)—three concepts.* **OPPOSITE** *Discovery communications detail.*

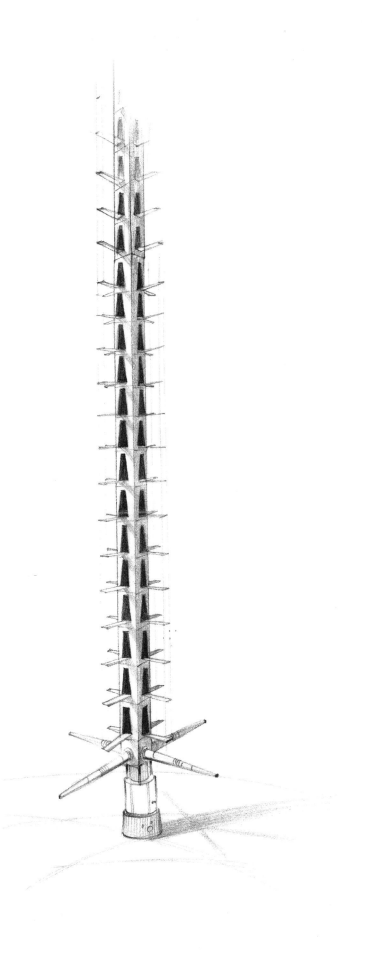

DISCOVERY
External communications systems

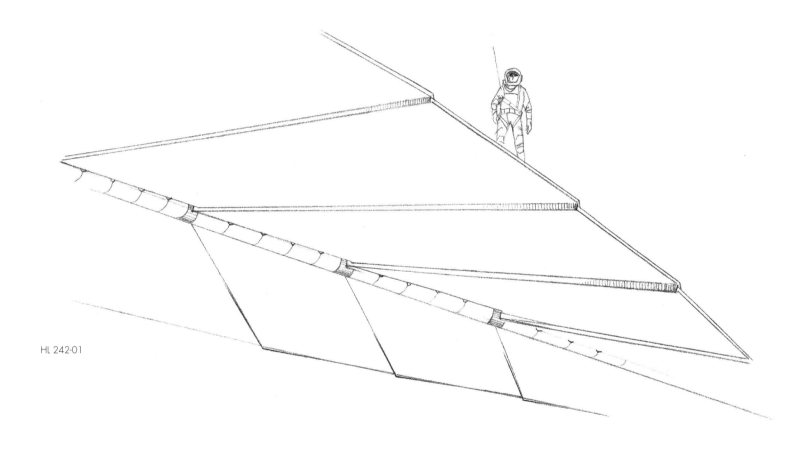

HL 242-01

ABOVE *Communications aerial with astronaut.* **OPPOSITE** *Various early concept drawings of Discovery communications equipment.*

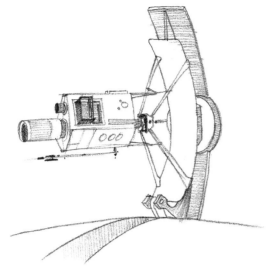

HL 242-02

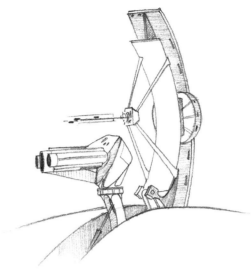

HL 242-03

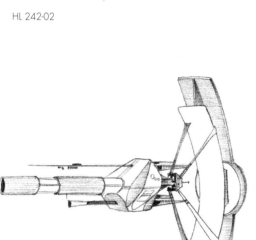

HL 242-04

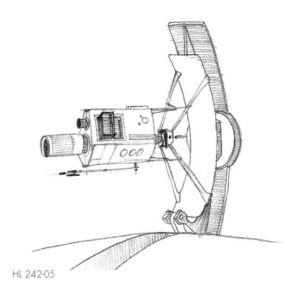

HL 242-05

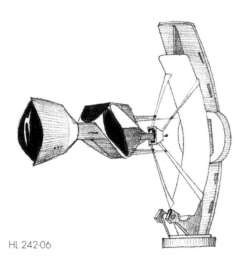

HL 242-06

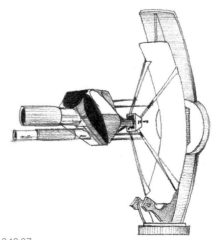

HL 242-07

DISCOVERY
External communications aerials

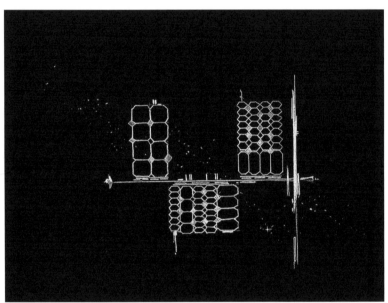

HL 244-01

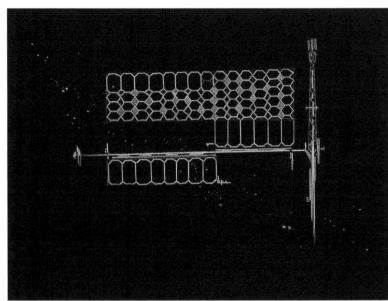

HL 244-02

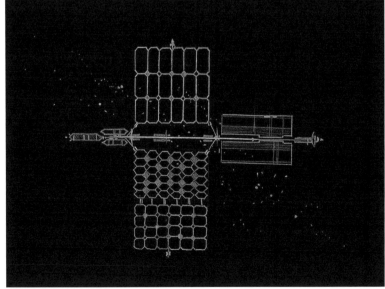

HL 244-03

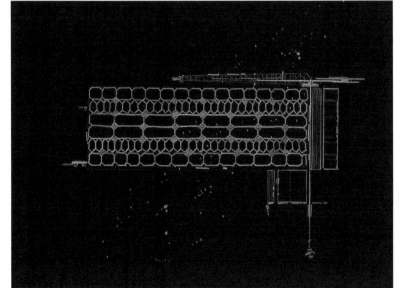

HL 244-04

ABOVE *Four concepts for Discovery communications aerials (pencil on black paper).* **OPPOSITE** *Two further concepts for Discovery communications aerials (pencil on black paper).*

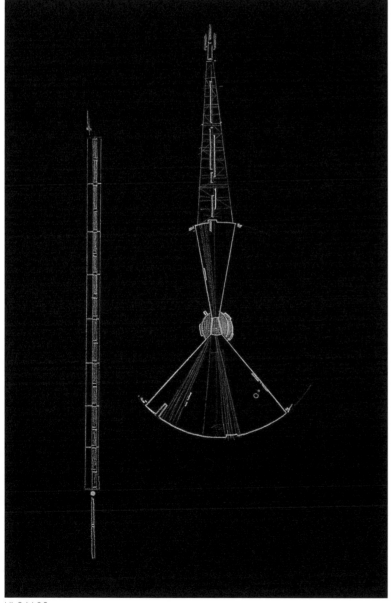

HL 244-05

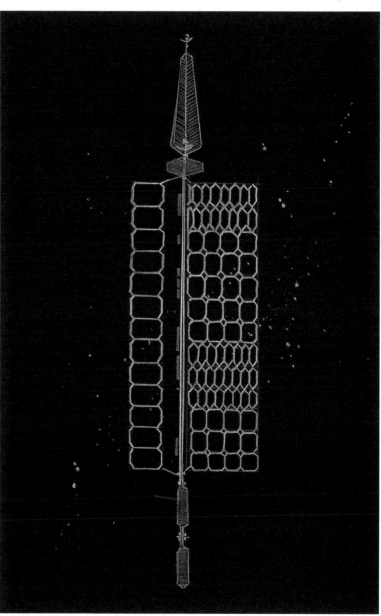

HL 244-06

DISCOVERY

External communications aerials

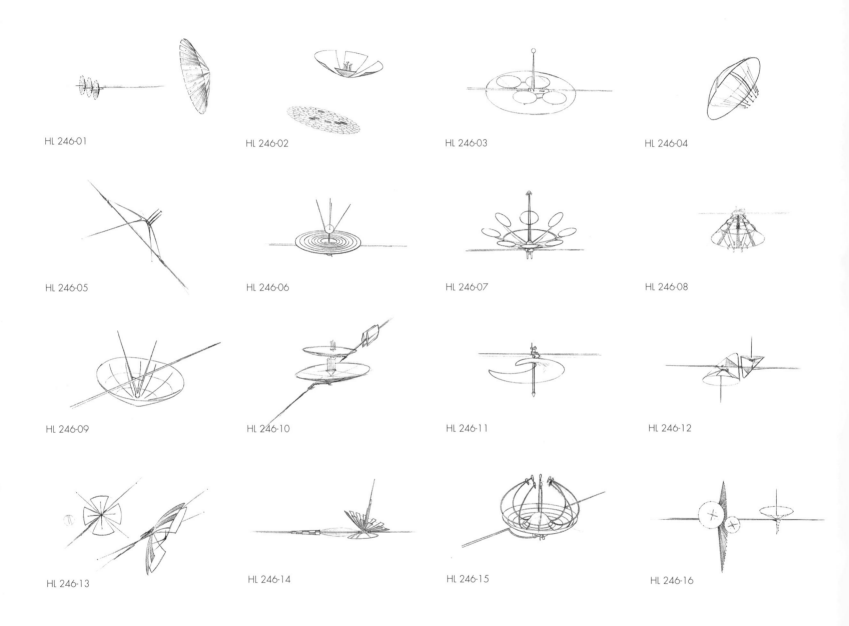

HL 246-01   HL 246-02   HL 246-03   HL 246-04

HL 246-05   HL 246-06   HL 246-07   HL 246-08

HL 246-09   HL 246-10   HL 246-11   HL 246-12

HL 246-13   HL 246-14   HL 246-15   HL 246-16

ABOVE *Various 'thumbnail' drawings of Discovery communications aerials.* **OPPOSITE** *Abstracted concepts for Discovery communications aerials (pencil on black paper).*

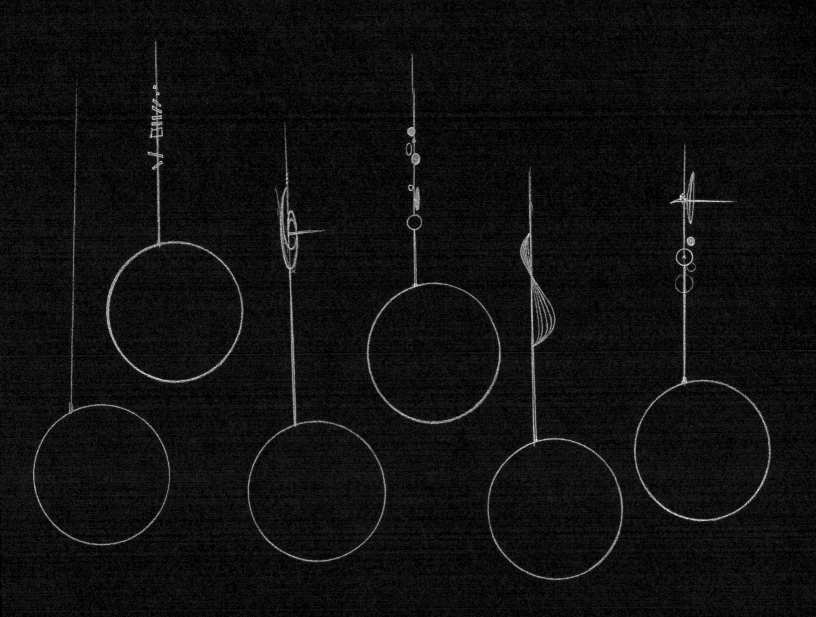

HL 246-17

DISCOVERY

External communications aerials

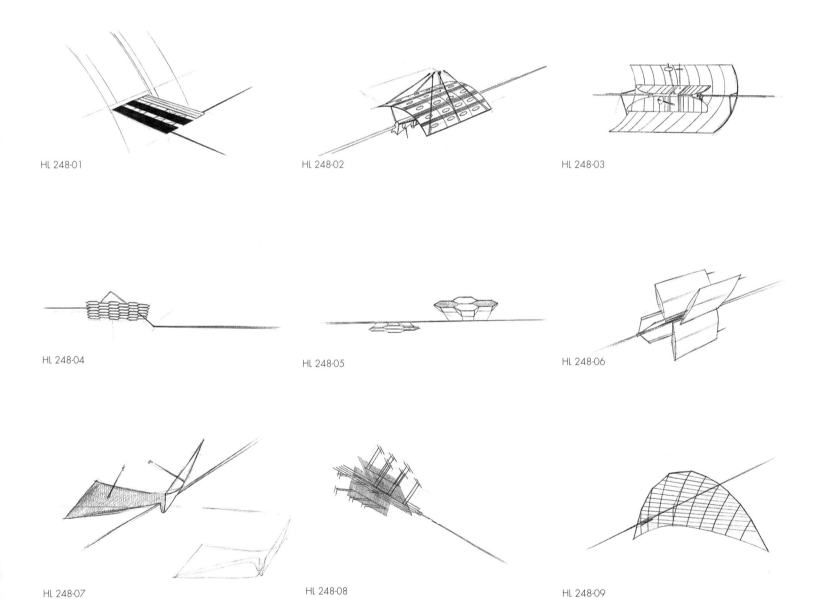

HL 248-01

HL 248-02

HL 248-03

HL 248-04

HL 248-05

HL 248-06

HL 248-07

HL 248-08

HL 248-09

ABOVE *Further 'thumbnail' drawings of Discovery communications aerials.* **OPPOSITE** *'Butterfly' concept for Discovery communications aerial.*

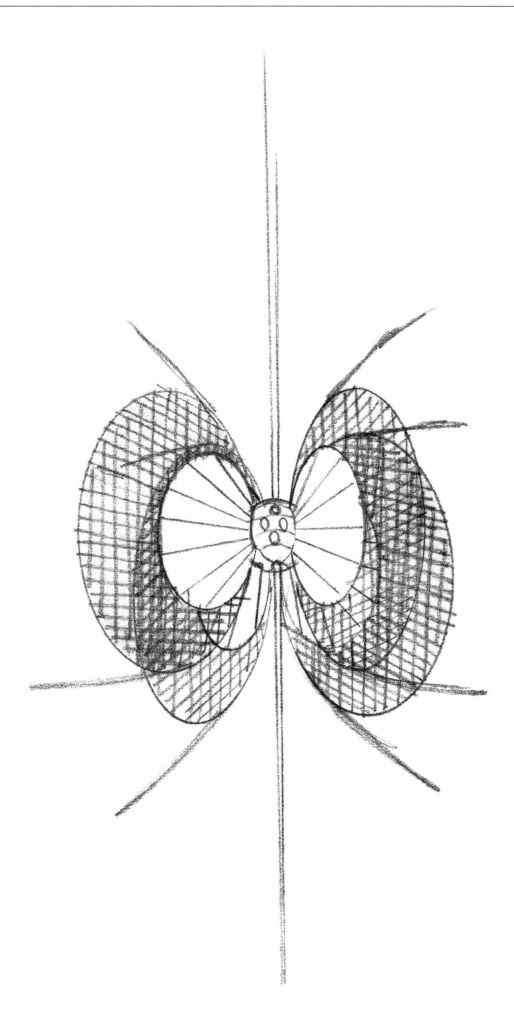

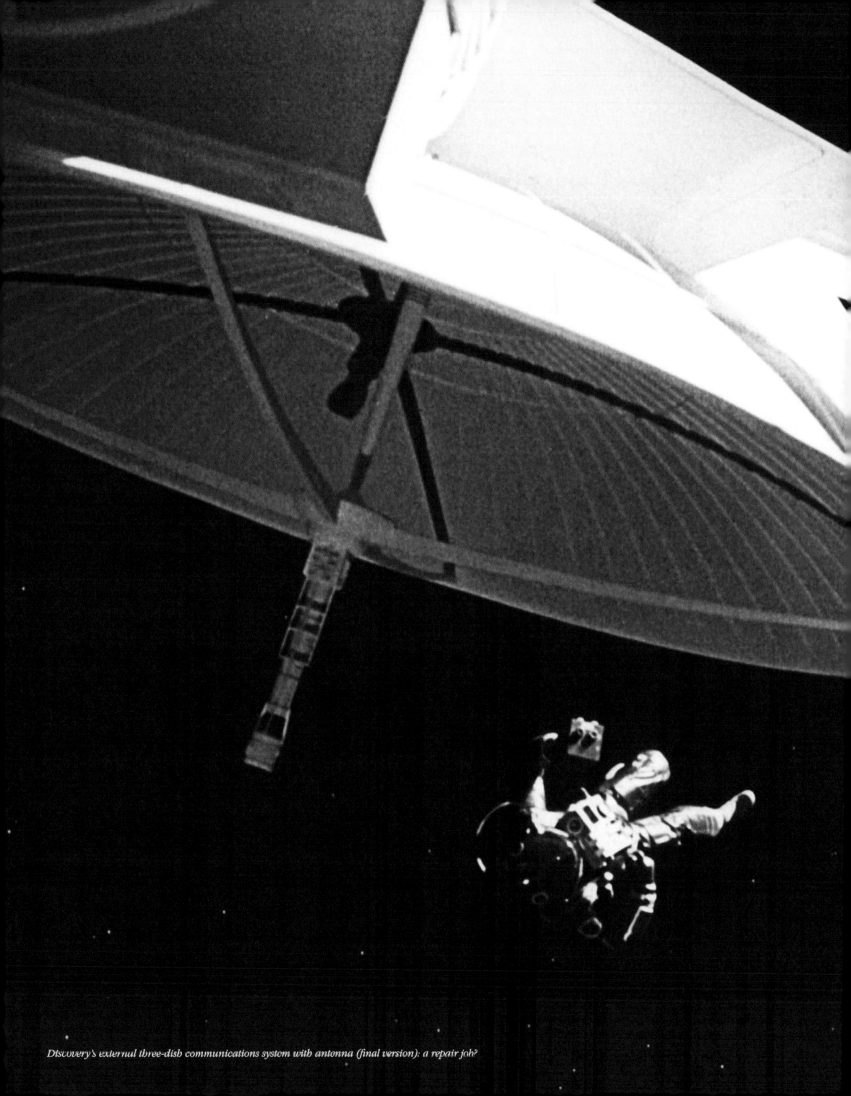

Discovery's external three-dish communications system with antenna (final version): a repair job?

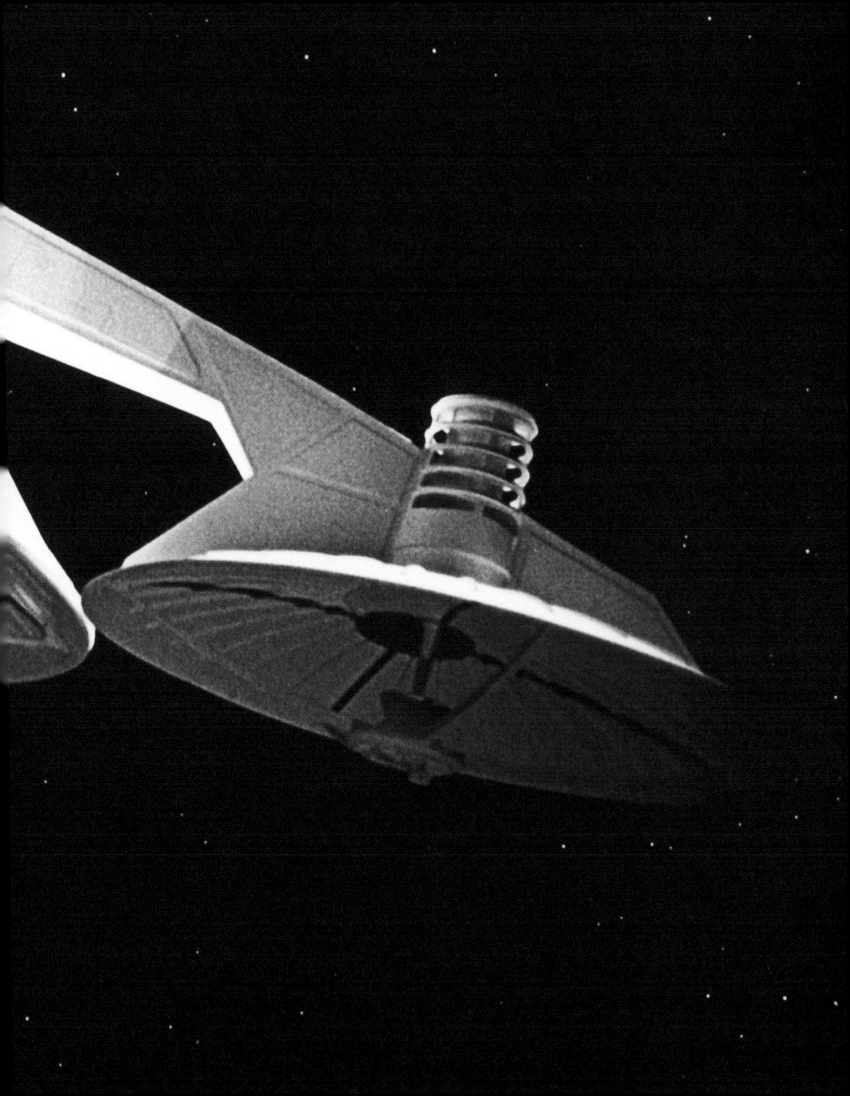

DISCOVERY
Command module and Centrifuge interior concepts

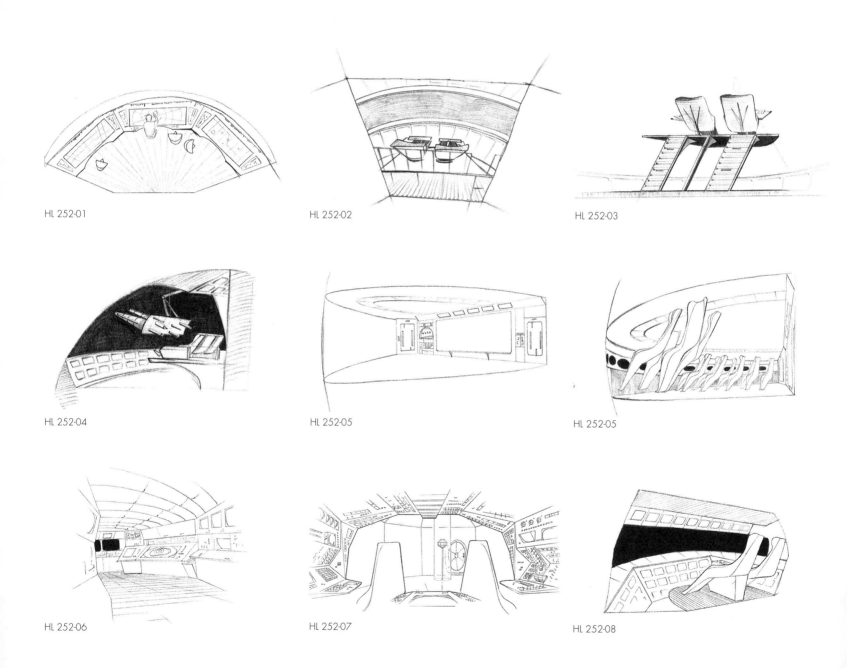

HL 252-01

HL 252-02

HL 252-03

HL 252-04

HL 252-05

HL 252-05

HL 252-06

HL 252-07

HL 252-08

HL 252-01 *Command module flight deck (top view) with navigation screens.* **HL 252-02** *Discovery interior command deck.* **HL 252-03** *Discovery interior command deck seating.*
HL 252-04 *Command module interior with observation telescope.* **HL 252-05** *Discovery interior command deck (two views).* **HL 252-06** *Discovery command module with computer instrumentation.* **HL 252-07** *Discovery command module with flight deck.* **HL 252-08** *Discovery work station.* **HL 252-09** *Discovery work station with seating. The Command Module was one of the four main sets for the interior of Discovery: 'means must be found to retain the Astronauts comfortably in their command positions in the cockpit'.*

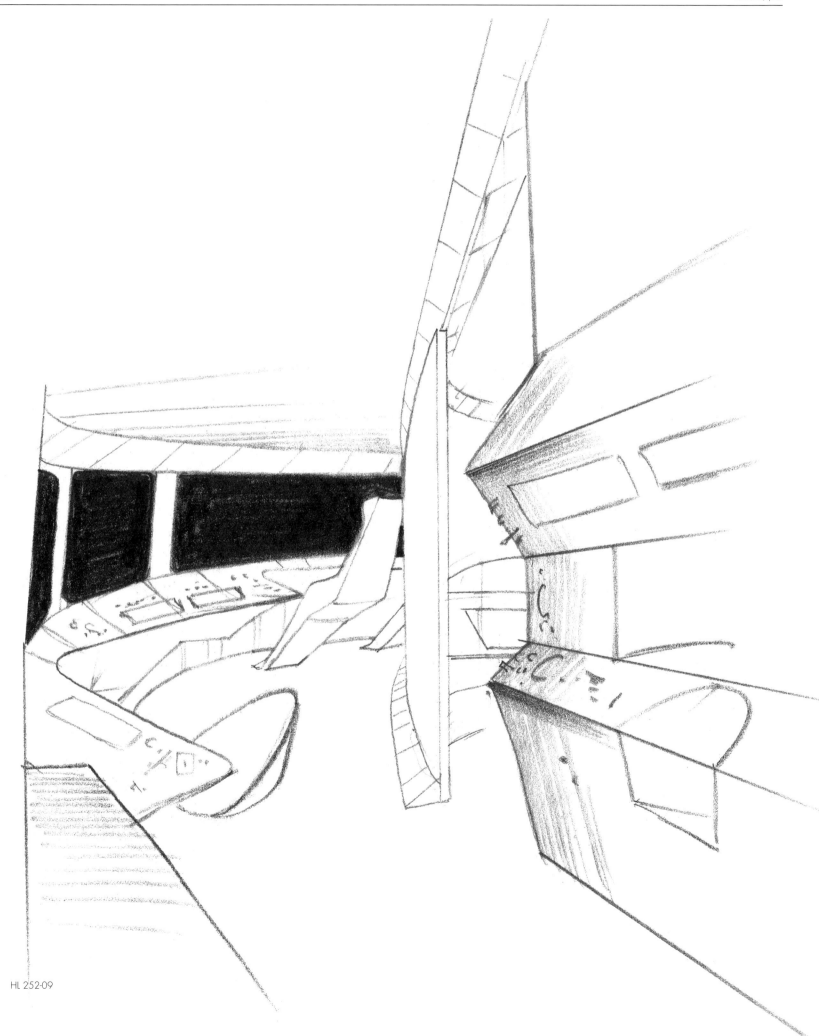

DISCOVERY
Flight deck instrumentation

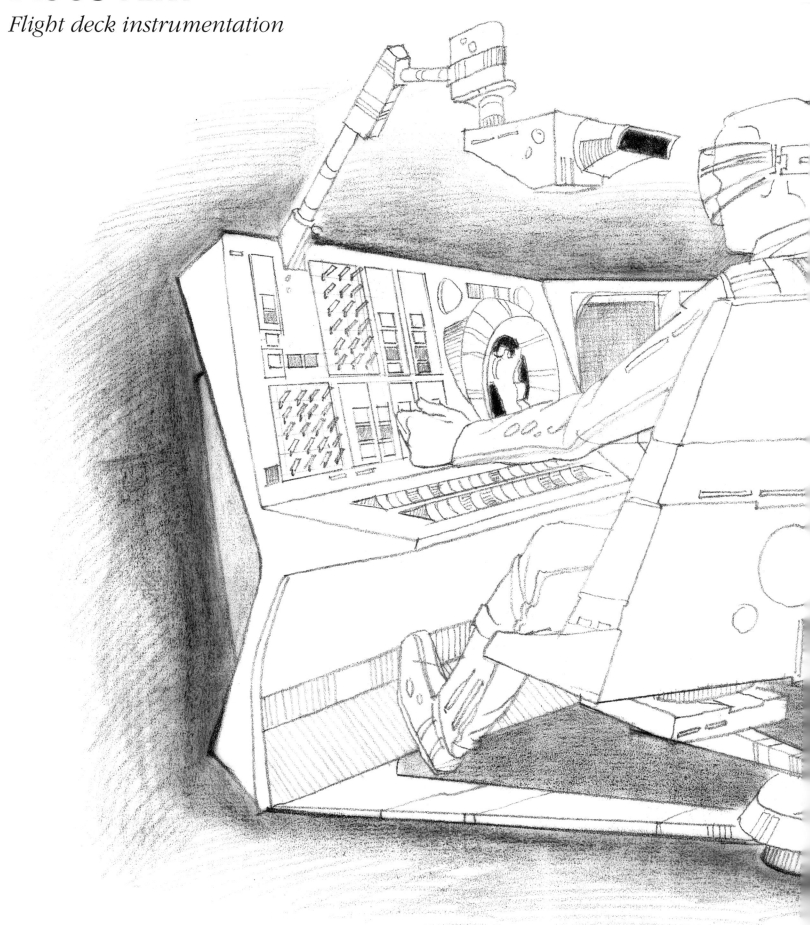

HL 254-01 *Interior flight deck instrumentation with two operators.*

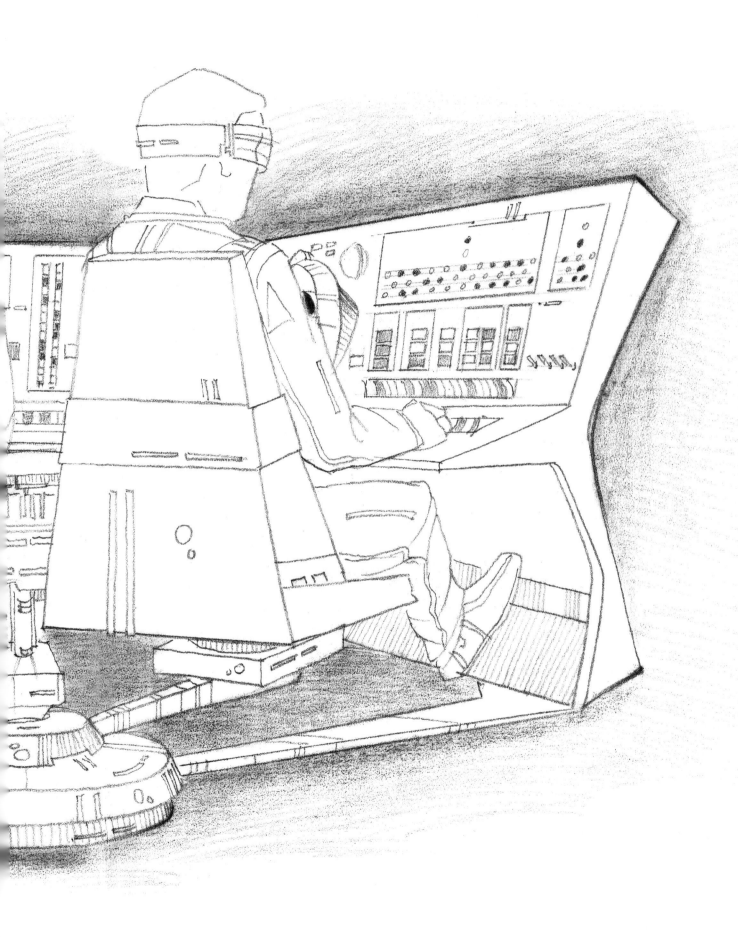

DISCOVERY

Command module and 'brain room'

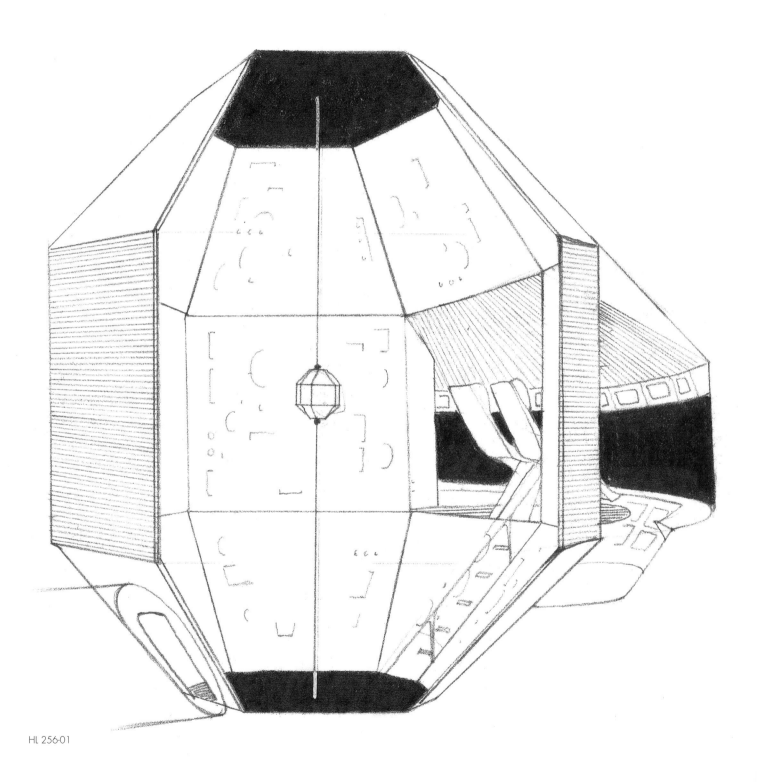

HL 256-01

HL 256-01 *Command module interior, with detail of brain room (early concept for the 'brain and nervous system of the ship').* **HL 256-02** *Early detail for 'brain room'.*

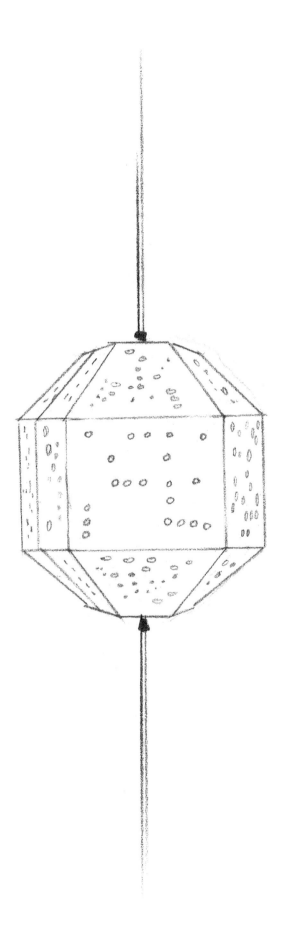

DISCOVERY

Command module cross-sections

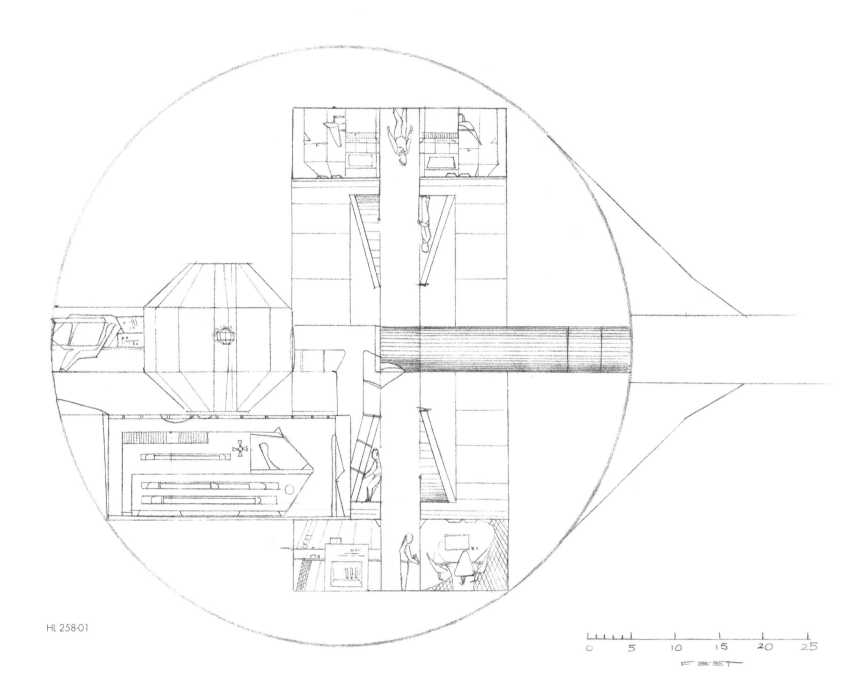

HL 258-01

0   5   10   15   20   25

FEET

HL 258-01 *Discovery command module section showing command deck, brain room, pod bay and centrifuge, with scale in feet.* **HL 258-02** *Discovery command module with interior cross section view, including brain room and pod bay.*

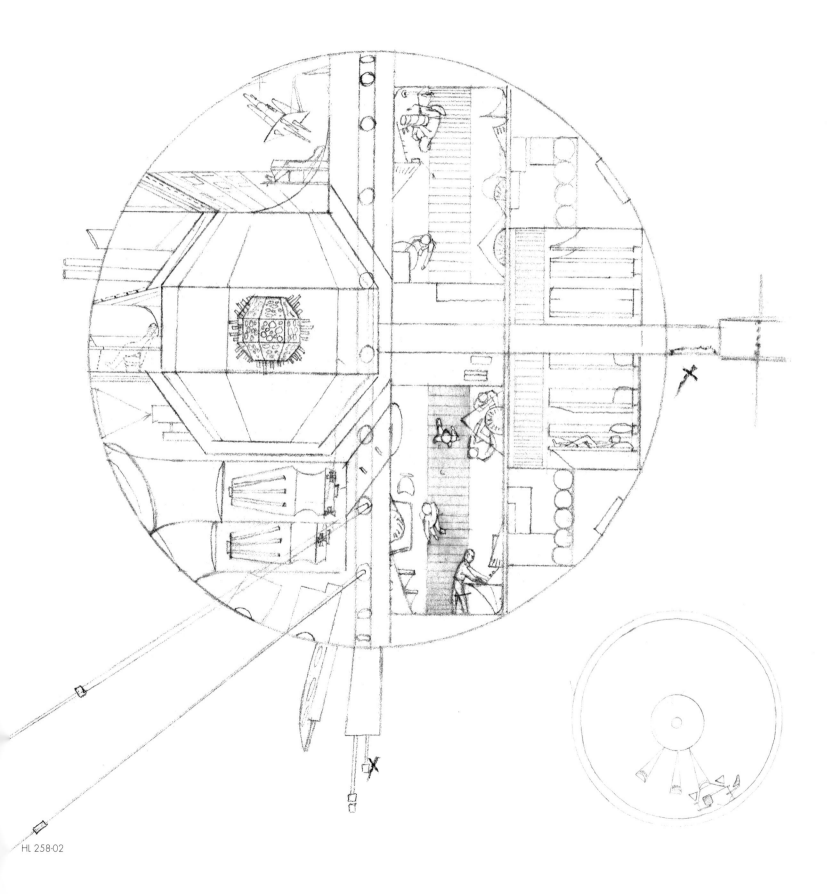

HL 258-02

DISCOVERY
Command module interior concepts

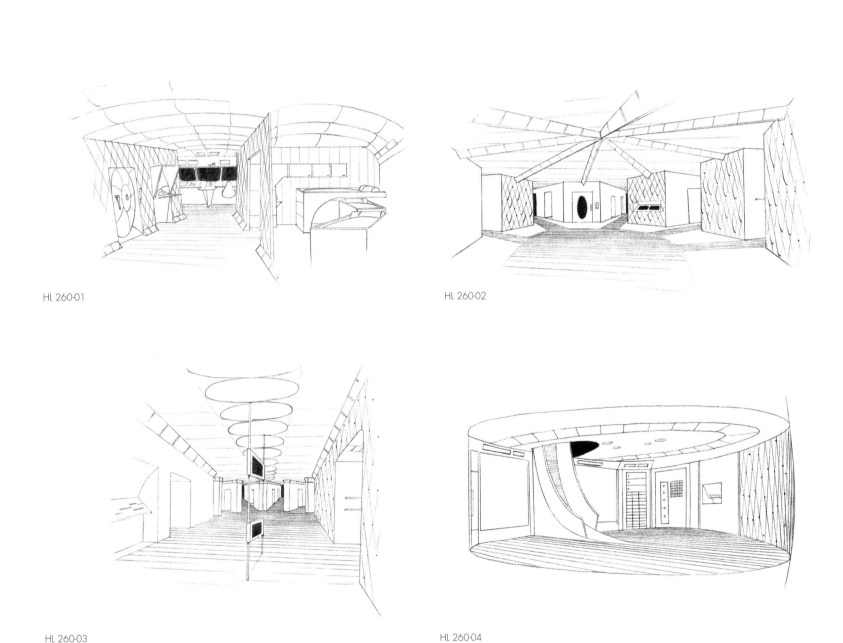

HL 260-01

HL 260-02

HL 260-03

HL 260-04

HL 260-01 *Command module accommodation block and flight deck.* **HL 260-02** *Discovery interior central access.* **HL 260-03** *Discovery interior access passageway.* **HL 260-04* *Discovery interior floor access slide.* **HL 260-05** *Discovery work station, with seating.*

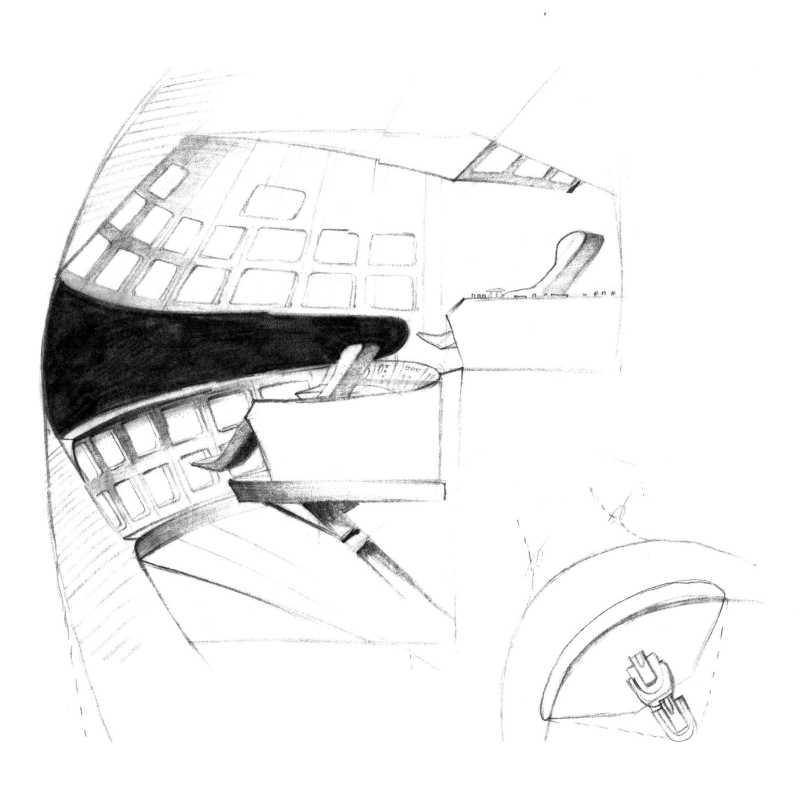

DISCOVERY
Interior blueprint

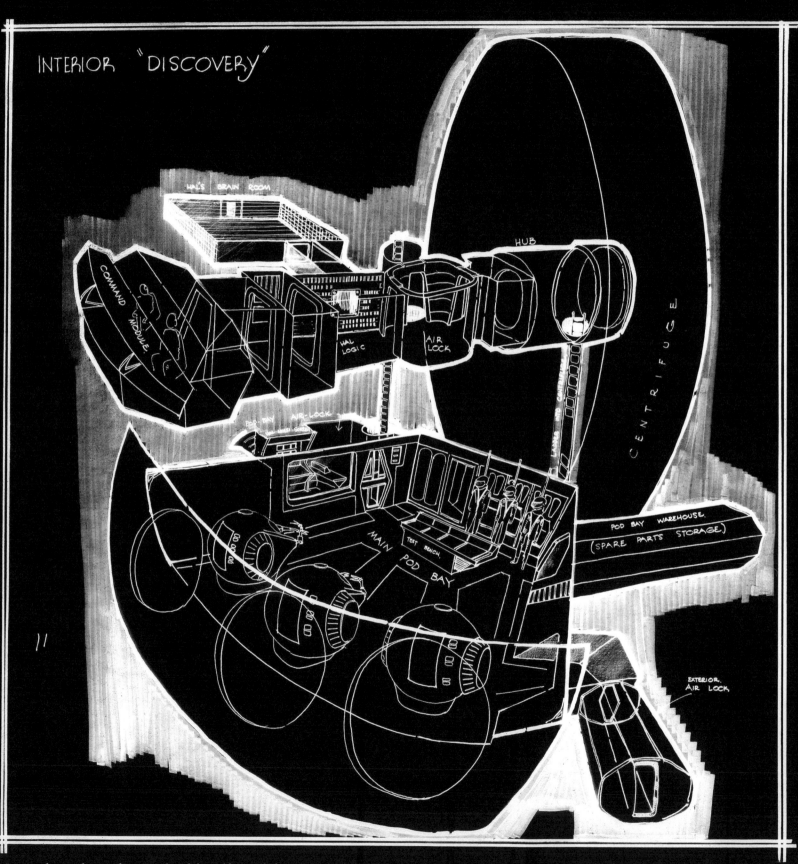

INTERIOR "DISCOVERY"

HAL'S BRAIN ROOM

HUB

COMMAND MODULE

CENTRIFUGE

HAL LOGIC

AIR LOCK

POD BAY AIR-LOCK

MAIN POD BAY

TEST BENCH.

POD BAY WAREHOUSE.
(SPARE PARTS STORAGE.)

EXTERIOR.
AIR LOCK

Interior showing layout of command module, pod bay, Hal's brain room and Centrifuge.

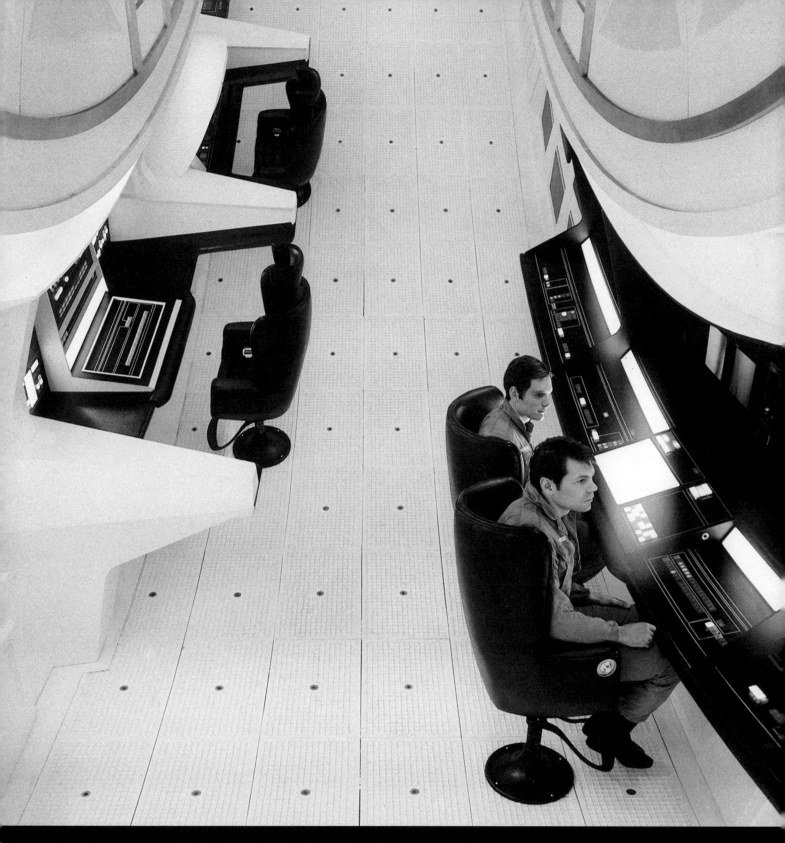

Interior of Centrifuge (final version) with Bowman (Keir Dullea) and Poole (Gary Lockwood) at their digital workstations. In the production notes, there were 13 pages of engineering details (design, construction, movement, lighting and electrical) on the Centrifuge alone.

DISCOVERY
Command module exterior concepts

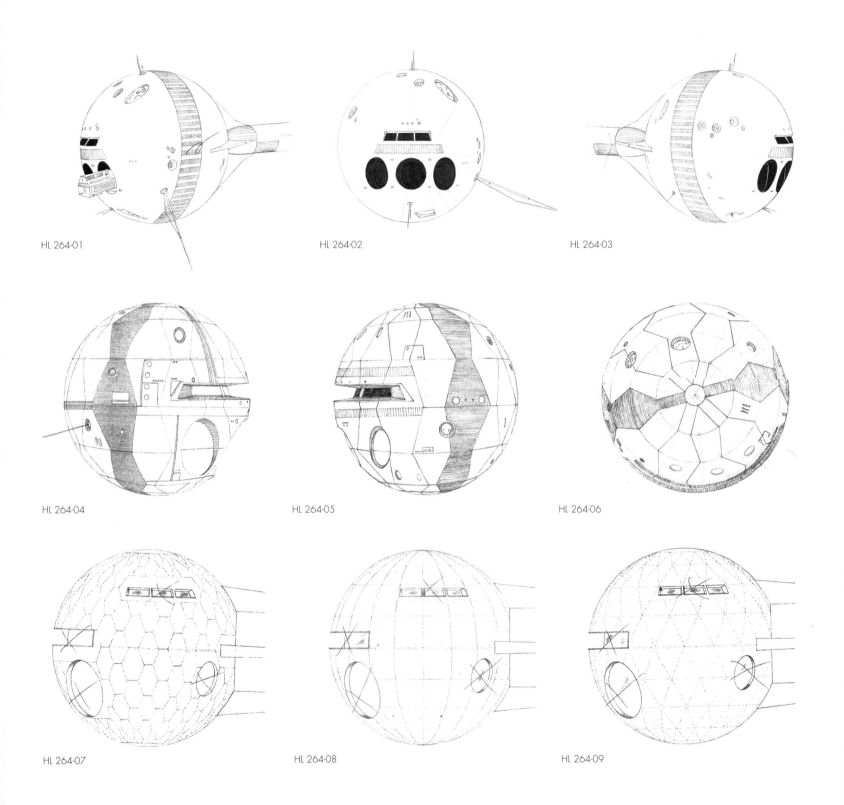

HL 264-01

HL 264-02

HL 264-03

HL 264-04

HL 264-05

HL 264-06

HL 264-07

HL 264-08

HL 264-09

HL 264-01 *Command module early concept with repair pod and aerials.* **HL 264-02** *Command module early concept (front view) with external surface detail.* **HL 264-03** *Command module early concept with external surface detail.* **HL 264-04** *Command module blueprint with pencil annotation.* **HL 264-05** *Command module detail drawing.* **HL 264-06** *Command module (view from below).* **HL 264-07** *Command module with window designs and ceramic tile surface design.* **HL 264-08** *Command module blueprint with window designs.* **HL 264-09** *Command module with window designs—blueprint.* **HL 264-10** *Command module (D-3) with surface and window details.*

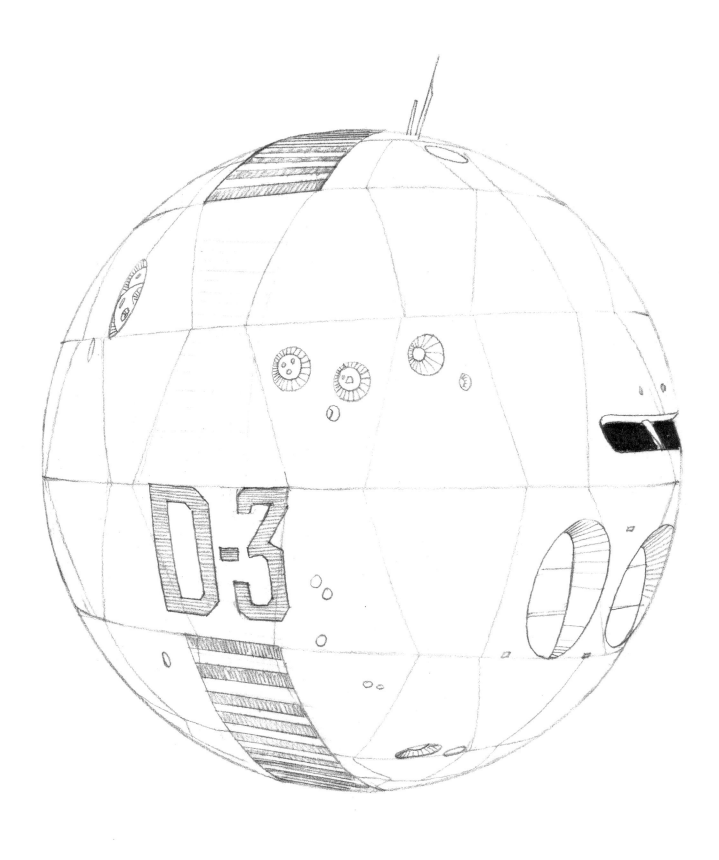

DISCOVERY

Command module exterior concepts

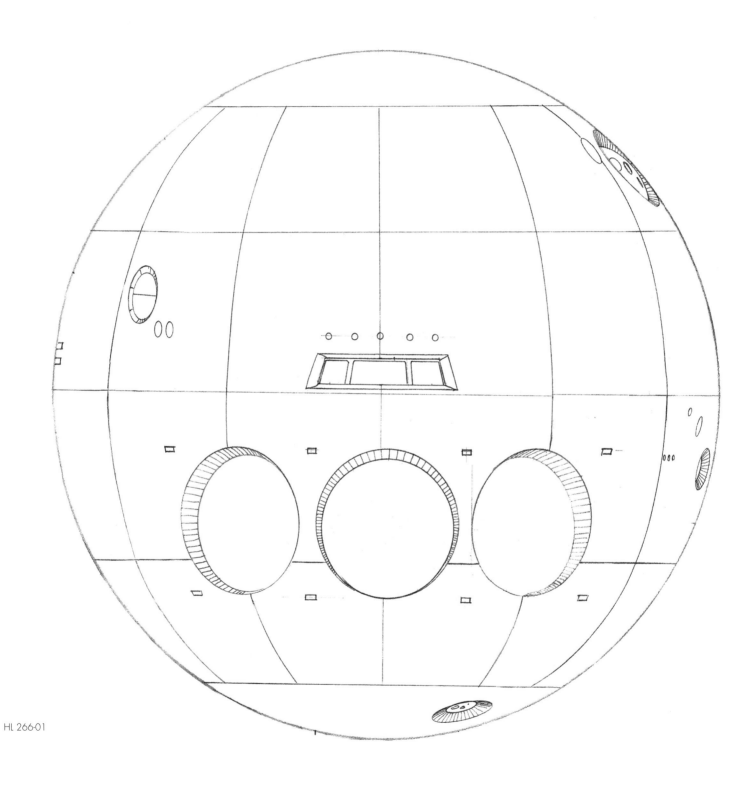

HL 266-01

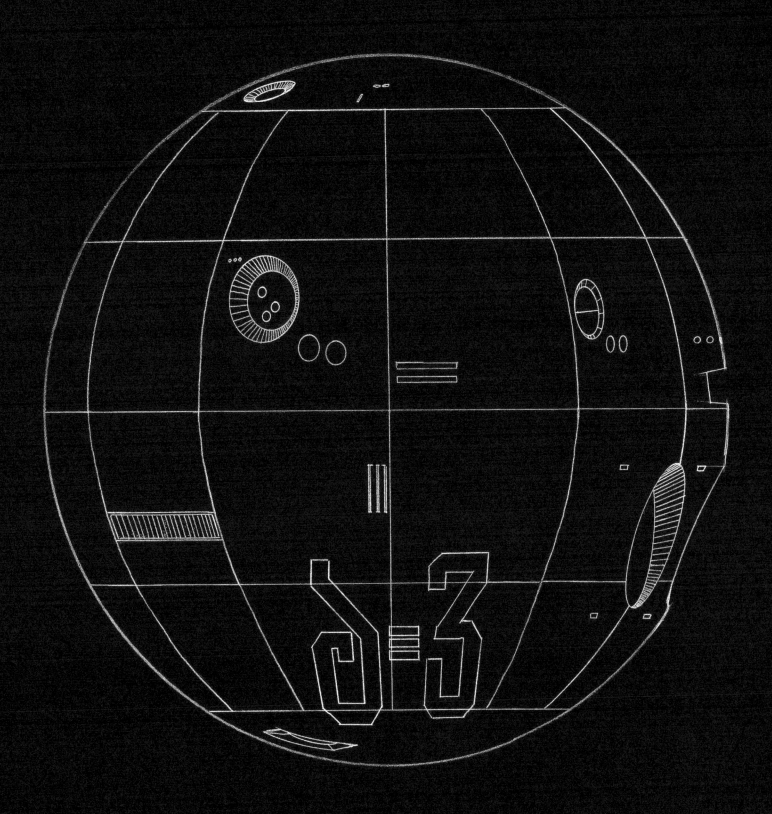

DISCOVERY

Fuselage links and details

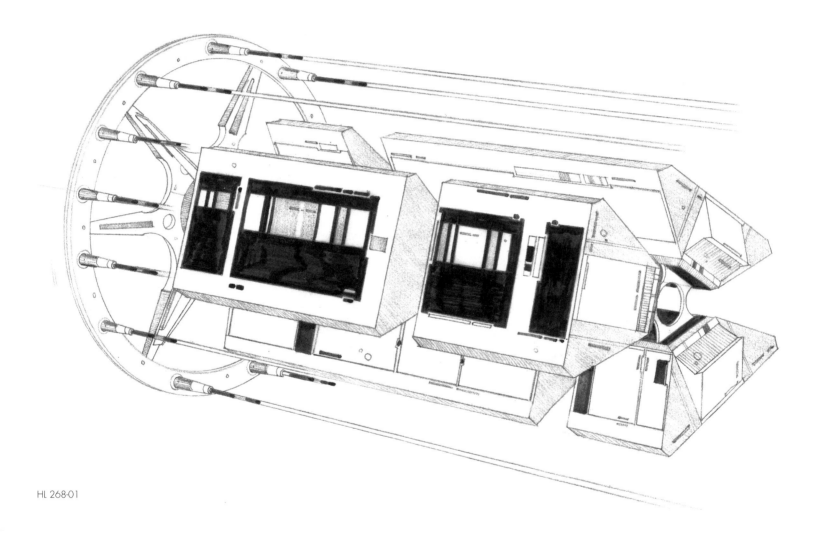

HL 268-01

HL 268-01 *Discovery exterior fuselage with segmented fuel and life support storage compartments.* **HL 268-02-HL 268-09** *Eight Discovery command module blueprints with pencil annotations of fuselage links.*

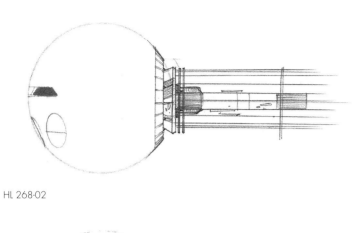

HL 268-02

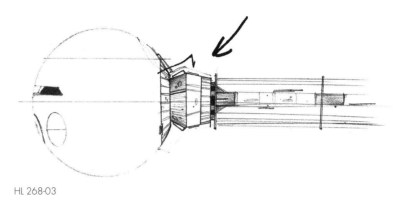

HL 268-03

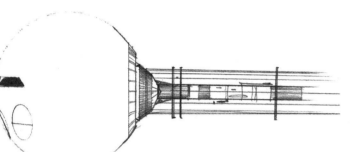
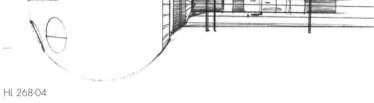

HL 268-04

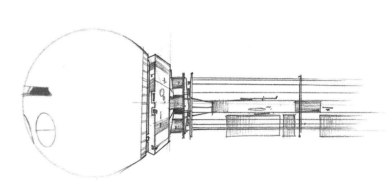

HL 268-05

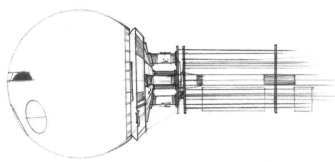

HL 268-06

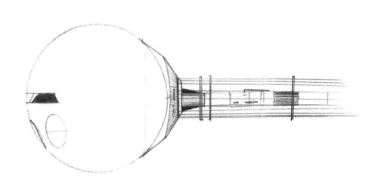

HL 268-07

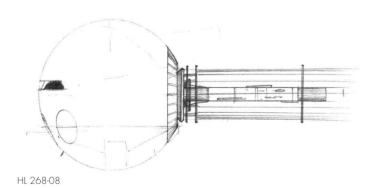

HL 268-08

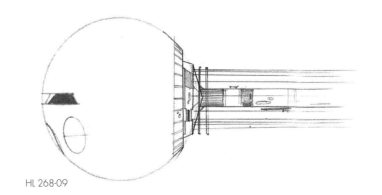

HL 268-09

DISCOVERY

Command module instrumentation and ceiling

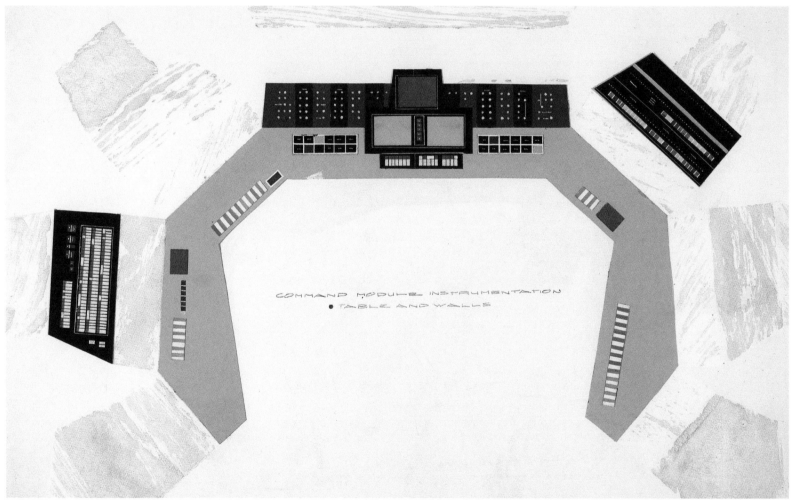

HL 270-01

HL 270-01 *Discovery command module instrumentation—table, workstations and walls.* **HL 270-02** *Discovery command module ceiling panels.*

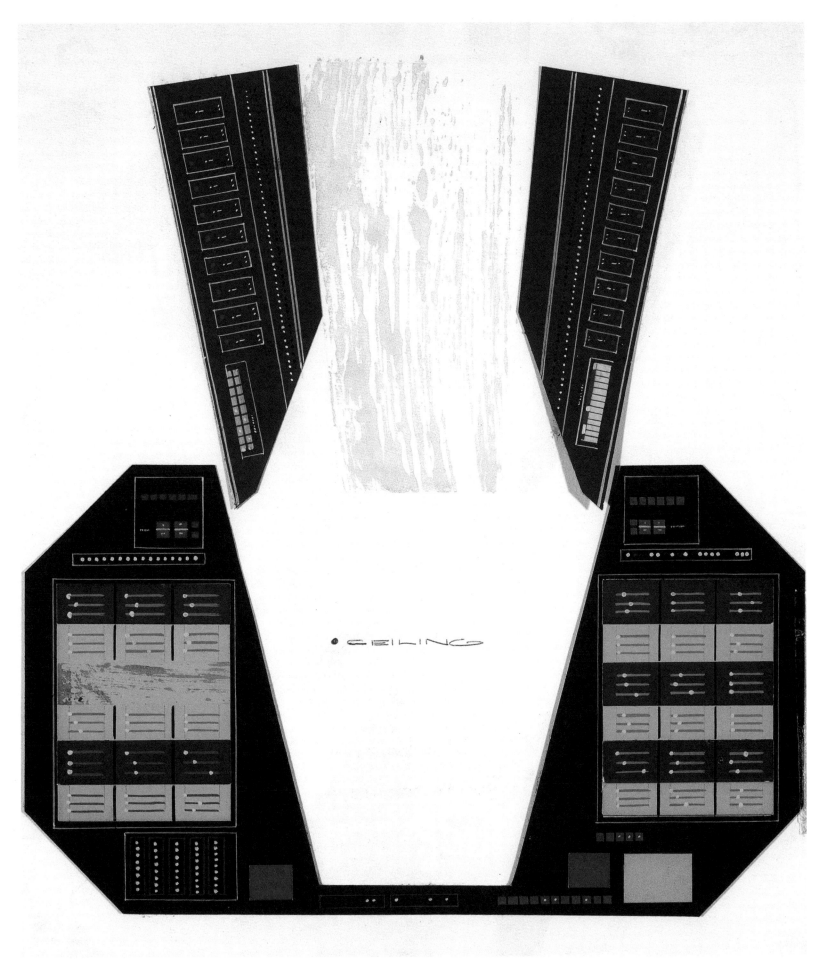

CEILING

DISCOVERY
Centrifuge concepts

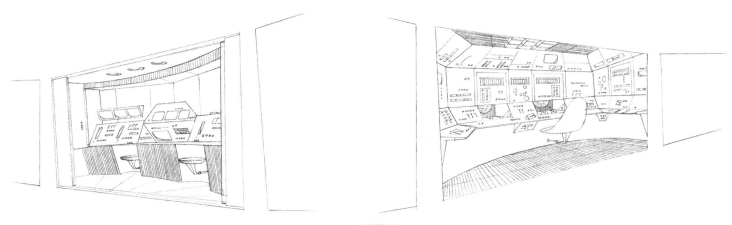

HL 272-01

HL 272-02

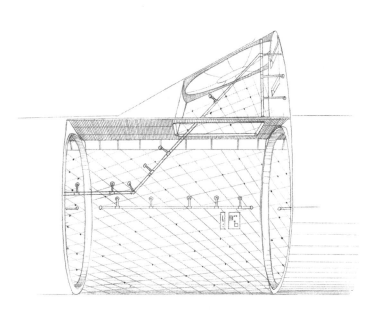

HL 272-03

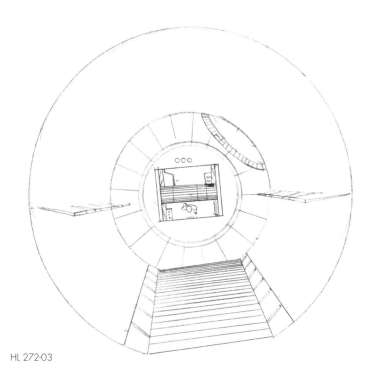

HL 272-03

HL 272-01 *Discovery Centrifuge console detail.* **HL 272-02** *Discovery Centrifuge with operational console.* **HL 272-03** *Discovery interior with view into Centrifuge entrance (two views).* **OPPOSITE** *Two views of Discovery Centrifuge.*

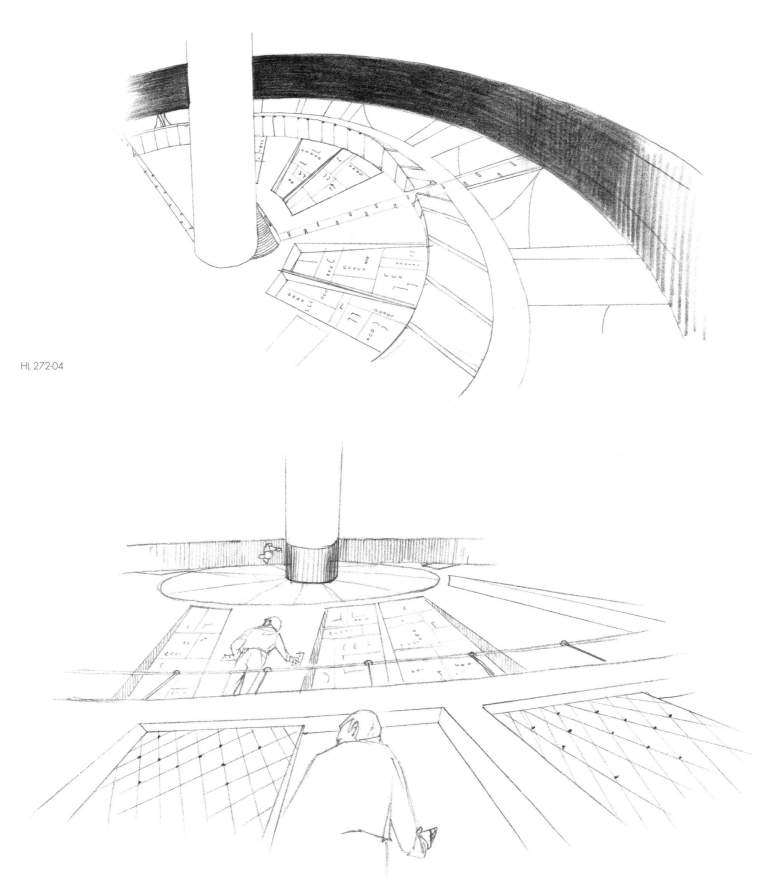

HL 272-04

HL 272-05

DISCOVERY
Centrifuge layout

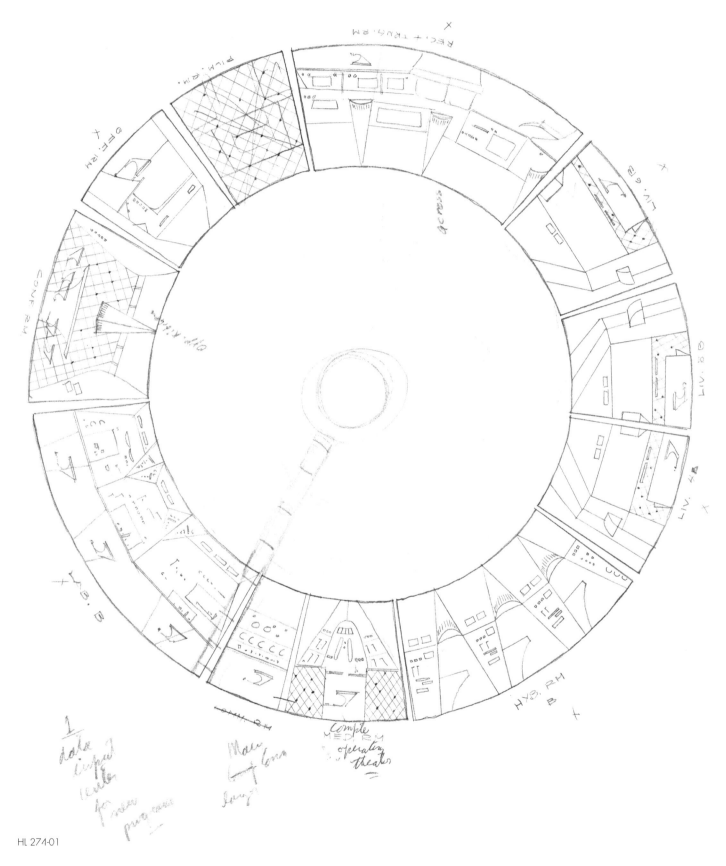

HL 274-01

HL 274-01 *Discovery Centrifuge area function layout with annotations by Stanley Kubrick.* **OPPOSITE** *The final revolving Centrifuge set, with its curved floor, brightly lit for filming of interiors.*

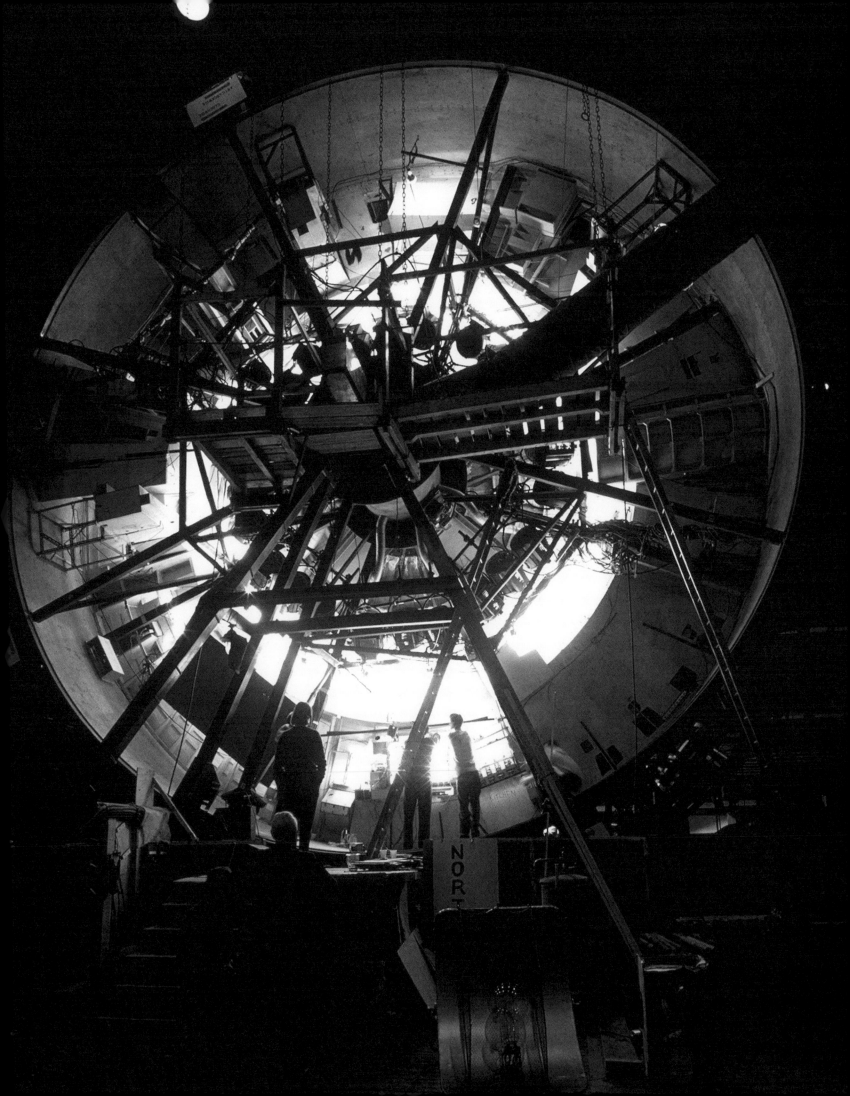

DISCOVERY

Centrifuge plan and cross-section

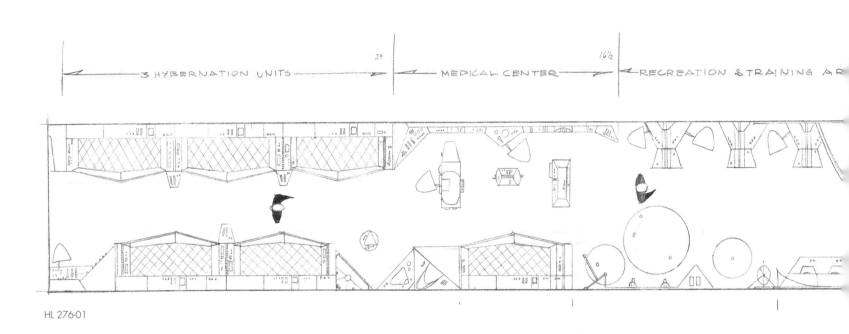

3 HYBERNATION UNITS · 24 · MEDICAL CENTER · 16½ · RECREATION & TRAINING AR

HL 276-01

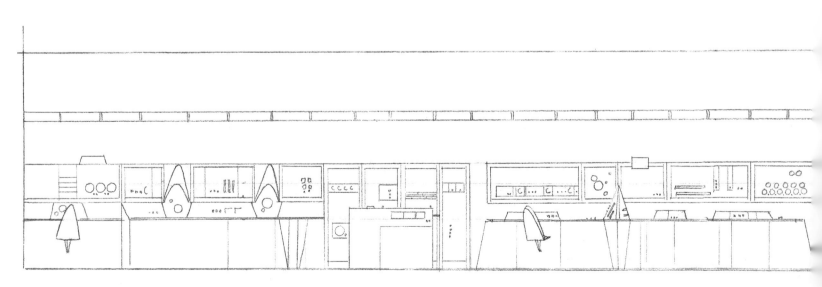

HL 276-02

HL 276-01 *Discovery Centrifuge plan view.* **HL 276-02** *Discovery Centrifuge cross-section view.*

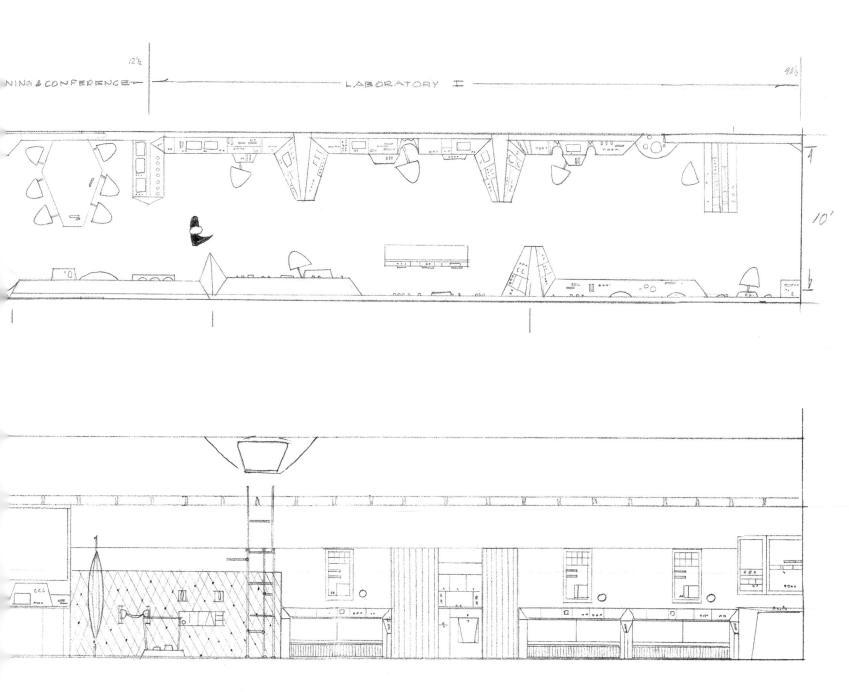

NING & CONFERENCE

12½'

LABORATORY I

48½'

10'

DISCOVERY

Space pod concepts

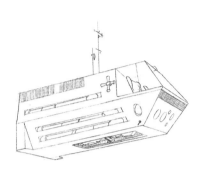

HL 278-01

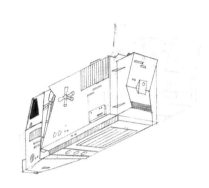

HL 278-02

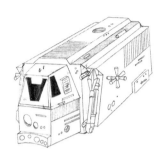

HL 278-03

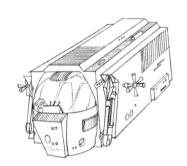

HL 278-04

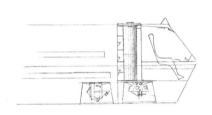

HL 278-05

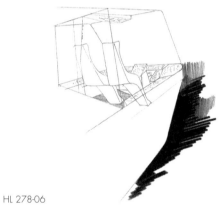

HL 278-06

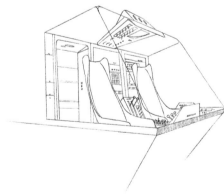

HL 278-07

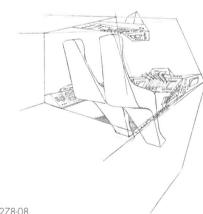

HL 278-08

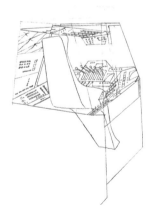

HL 278-09

ABOVE *Various 'thumbnails' of early space pod concepts—when the pods were rectangular, sometimes with room for two astronauts: they resemble the moon bus design.*
OPPOSITE *Early contextual drawings of space pods—in flight and in the pod bay: the apertures are round at this stage and the pods rectangular.*

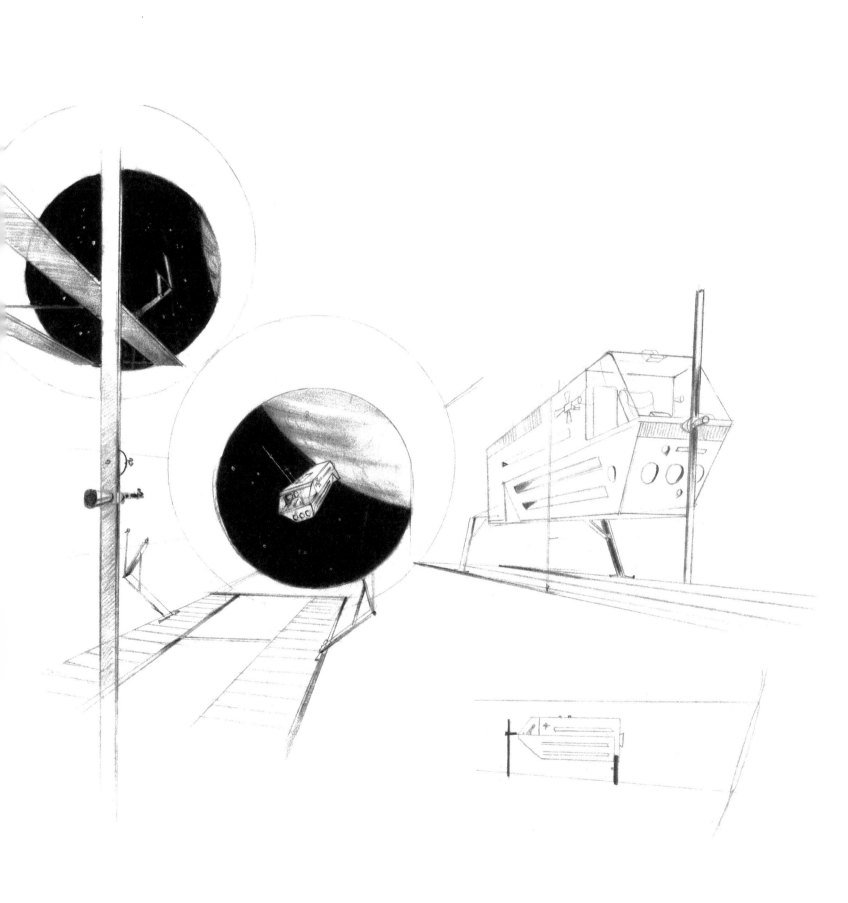

DISCOVERY
Space pod concepts

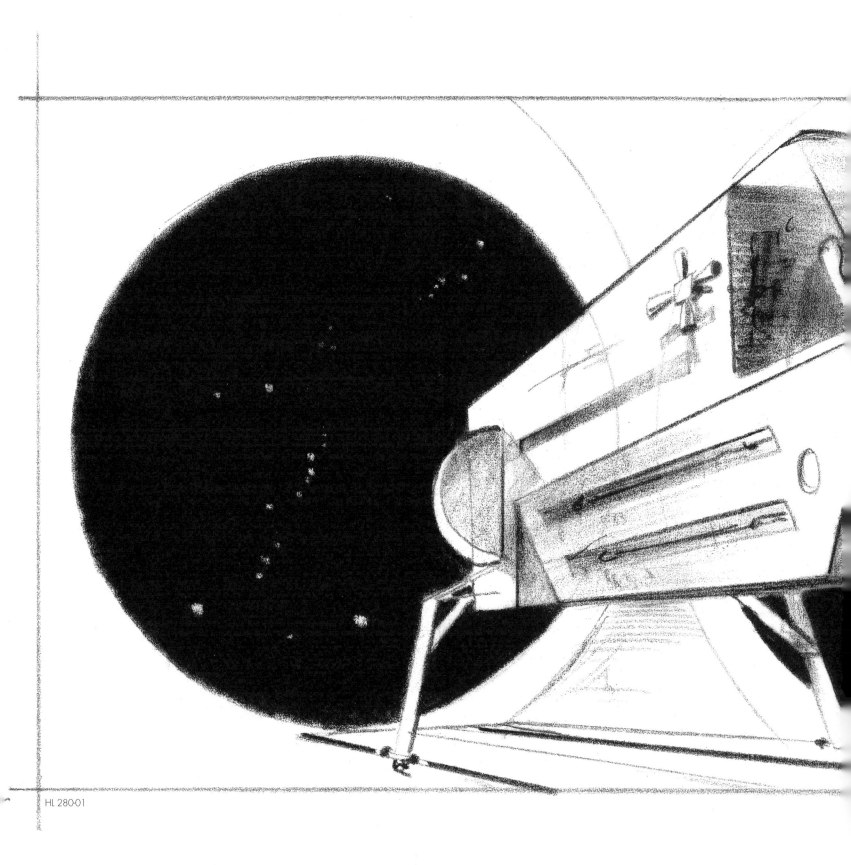

HL 280-01

HL 280-01 *Early Space pods—in the pod bay and in flight, with astronauts for scale.*

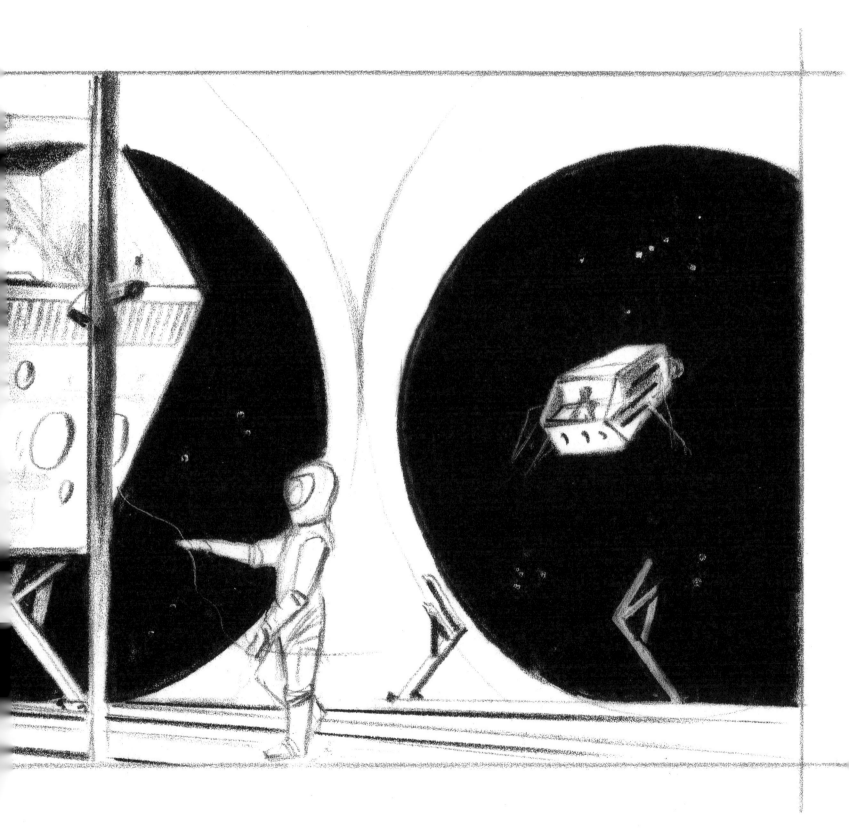

DISCOVERY
Pod Bay interiors

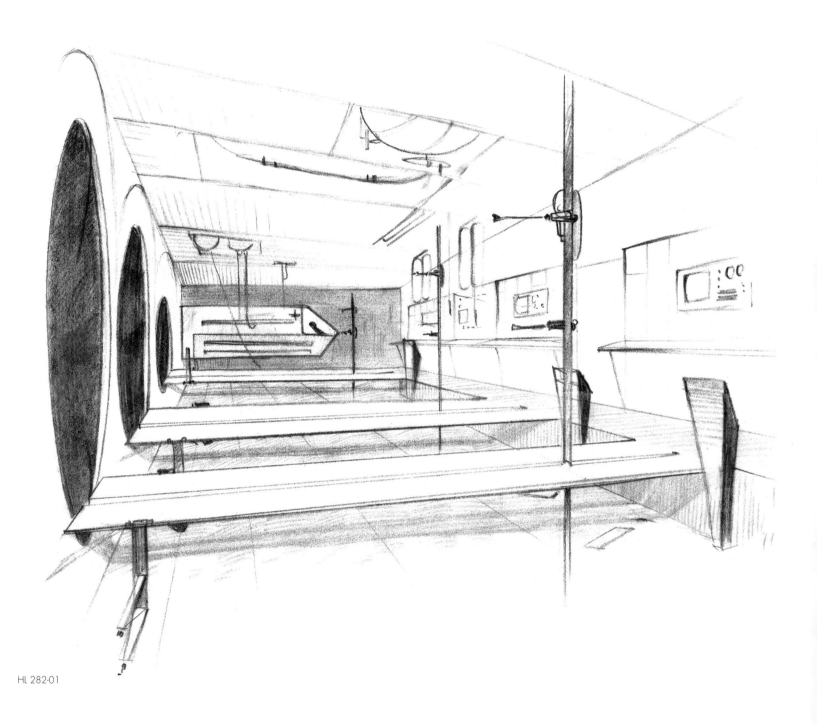

HL 282-01

HL 282-01 *Early concept design for pod bay.* **HL 282-02** *Pod bay workbench (two versions).* **OVERLEAF** *Final version of the pod bay interior, with spherical pod for 'repair and maintenance'.*

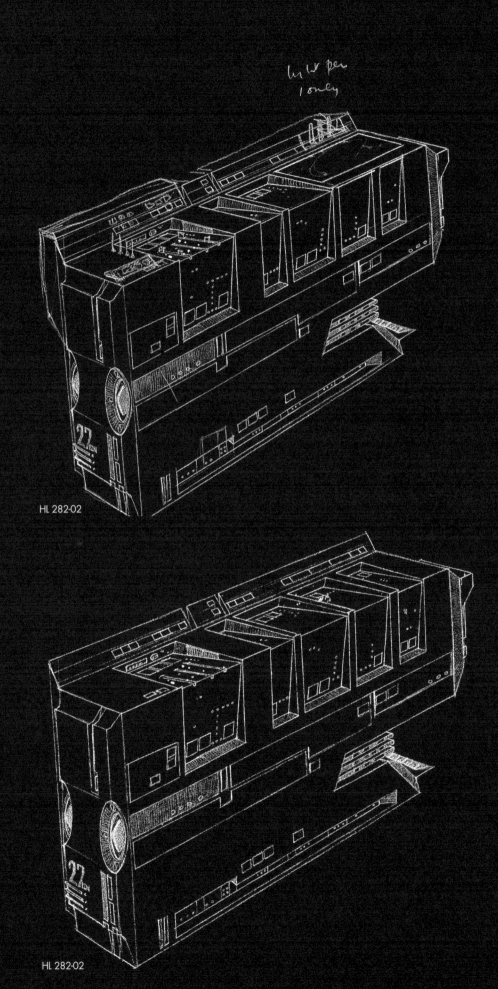

HL 282-02

HL 282-02

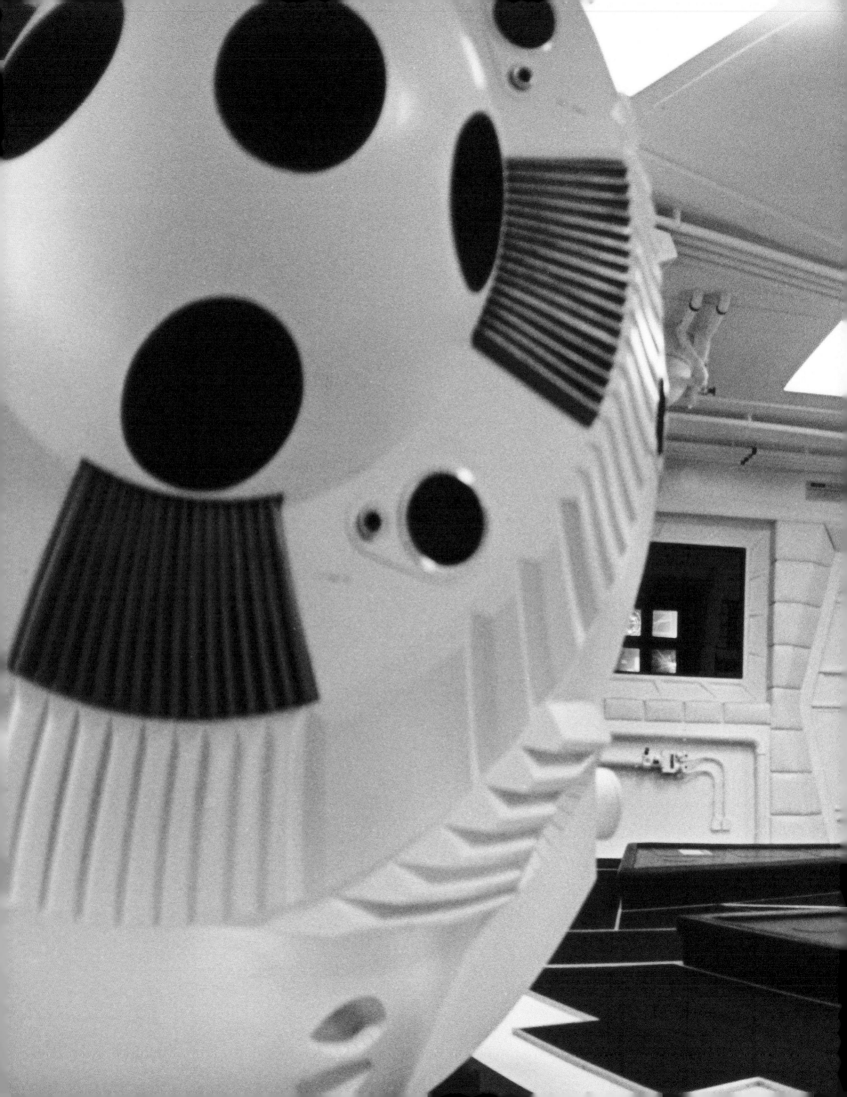

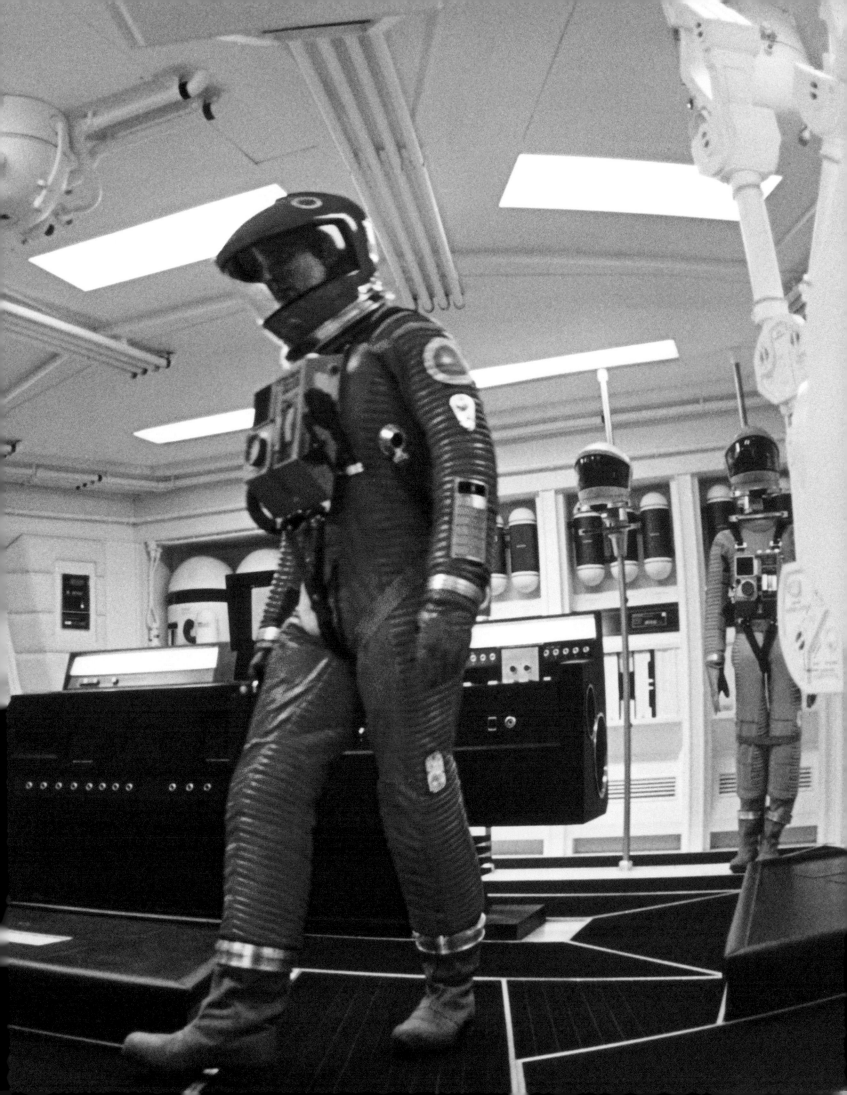

DISCOVERY

Pod robotic manipulator arm concepts

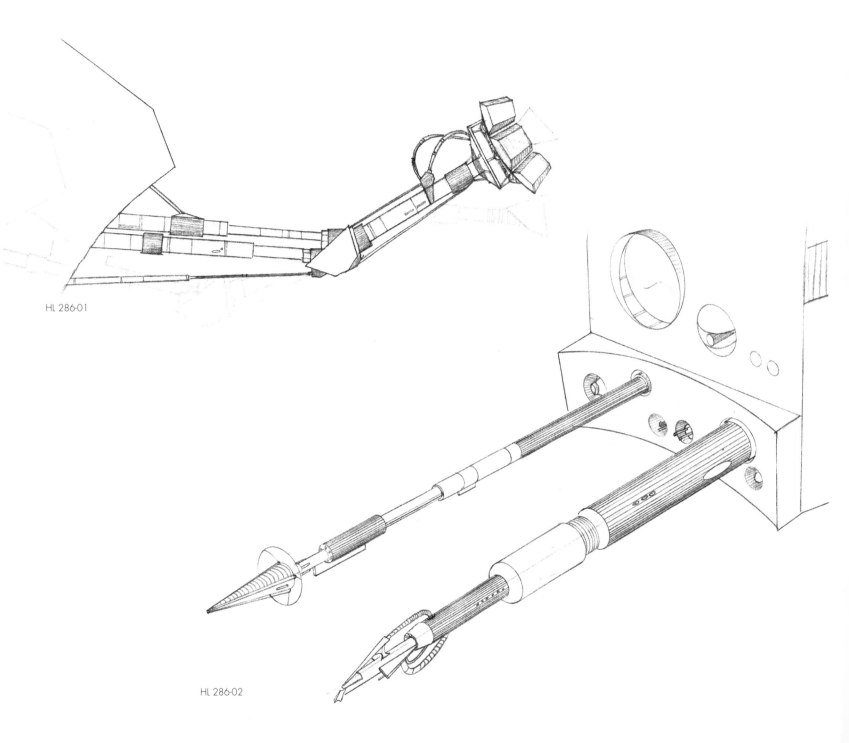

HL 286-01

HL 286-02

HL 286-01 *Side view of pod arm.* **HL 286-02** *Early concept of pod arms.* **HL 286-03** *Three side views of pod arms showing movement.* **HL 286-04** *Top views of pod arms with a variety of sensors.* **HL 286-05** *Detail of pod arm with a variety of probes.* **HL 286-06, HL 286-07 & HL 286-08** *Three side views of pod arm, with claw variations.*

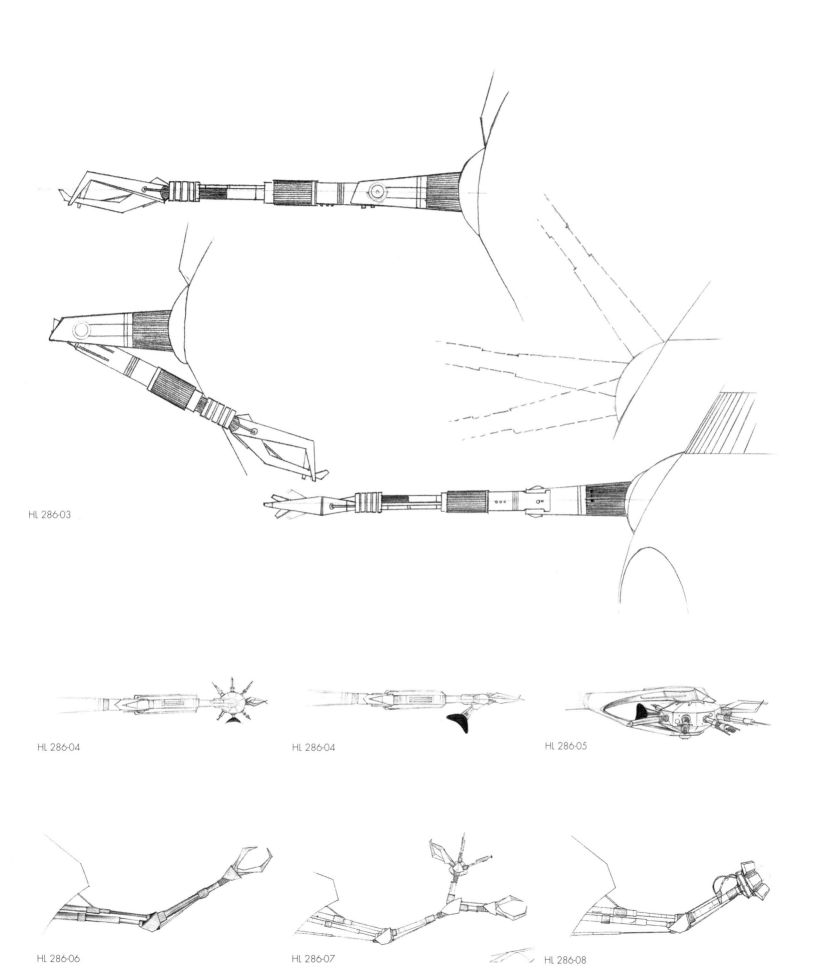

HL 286-03

HL 286-04

HL 286-04

HL 286-05

HL 286-06

HL 286-07

HL 286-08

DISCOVERY

Pod cockpit concepts

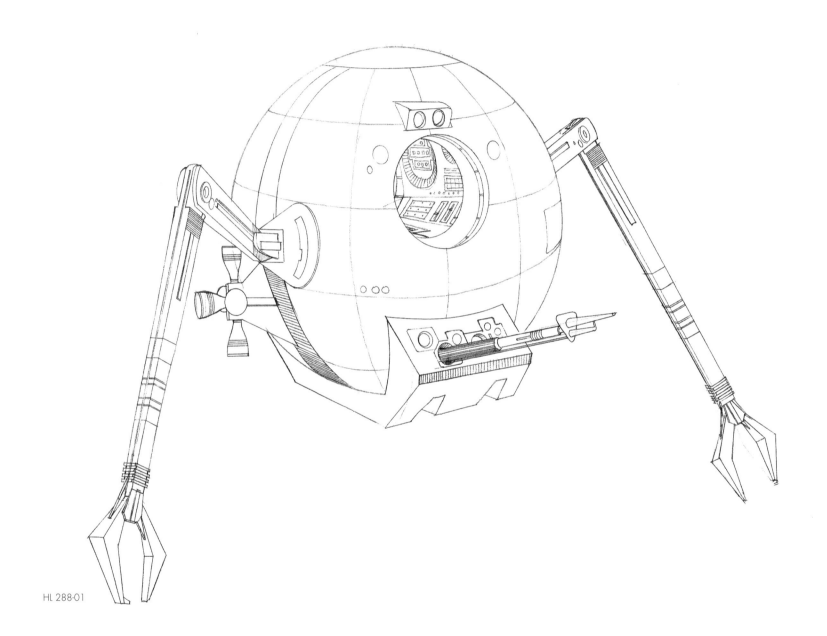

HL 288-01

HL 288-01 *Exterior view of round pod with extended arms and cockpit details.* **HL 288-02** *Interior pod cockpit with detailed instrumentation.* **HL 288-03** *Interior pod cockpit (section view) with instrumentation.* **HL 288-04** *Interior pod cockpit front elevation.*

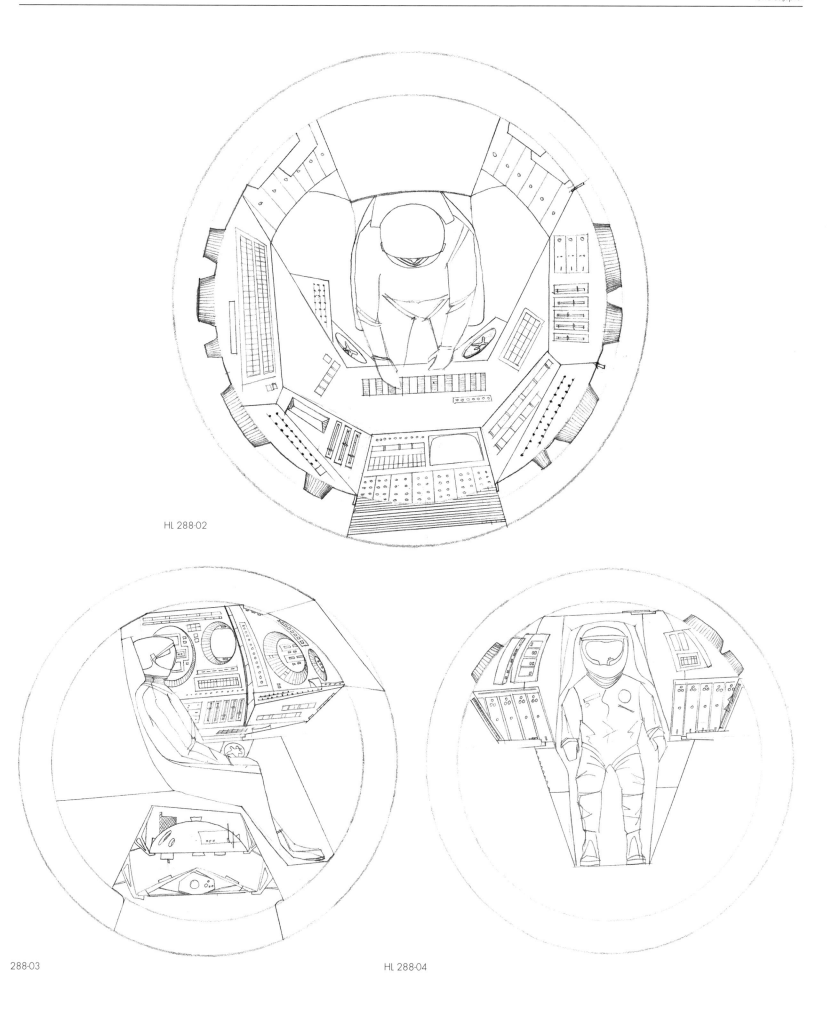

HL 288-02

288-03

DISCOVERY
Pod details

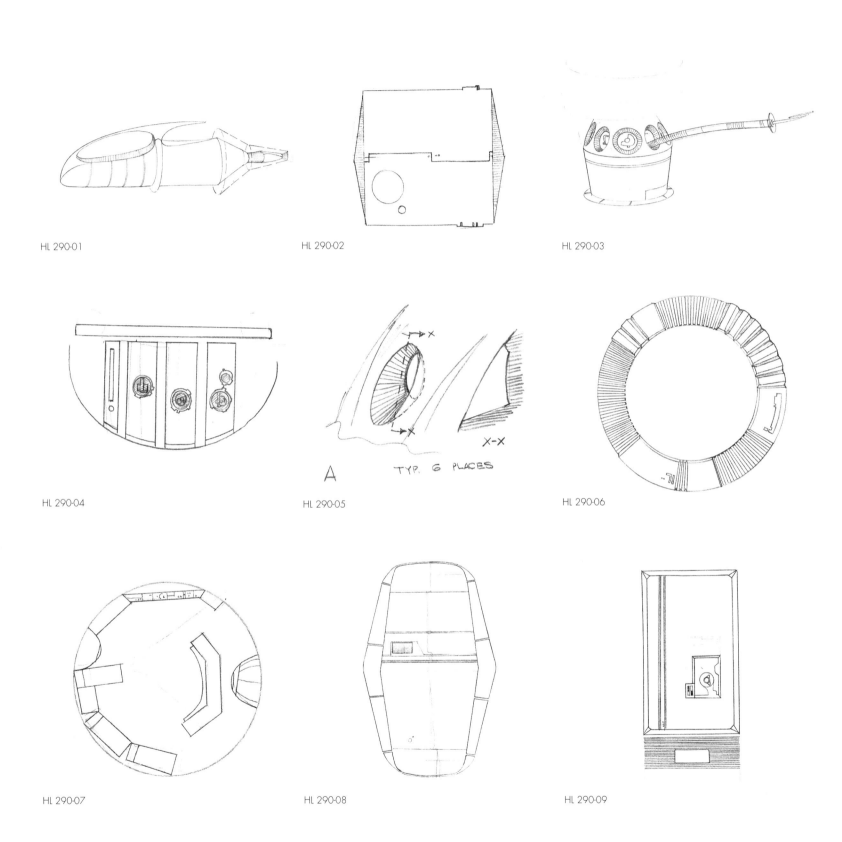

HL 290-01

HL 290-02

HL 290-03

HL 290-04

HL 290-05

A   TYP. 6 PLACES

X–X

HL 290-06

HL 290-07

HL 290-08

HL 290-09

HL 290-01 *Pod re-fuelling nozzle detail.* **HL 290-02** *Pod satellite bay.* **HL 290-03** *Re-fuelling nozzle.* **HL 290-04** *Exterior pod detail.* **HL 290-05** *Detail of pod re-fuelling aperture.* **HL 290-06** *Discovery pod surface detail.* **HL 290-07** *Discovery pod (top view).* **HL 290-08** *Discovery interior pod door.* **HL 290-09** *Discovery exit pod door.* **HL 290-10** *Discovery pod door with over-painted detail.*

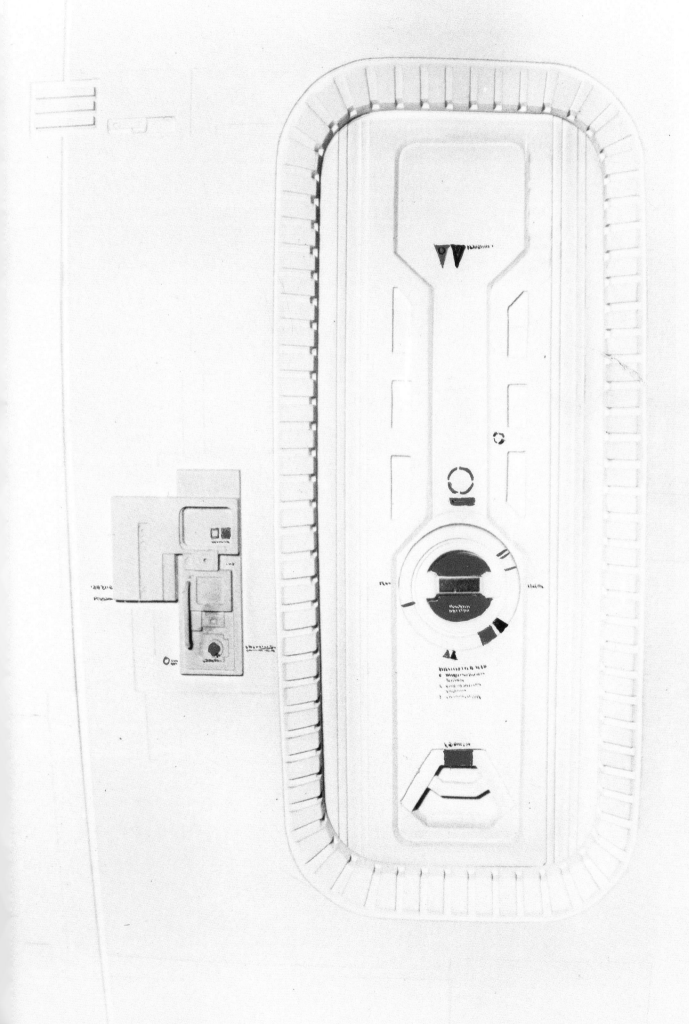

DISCOVERY
Final pod design

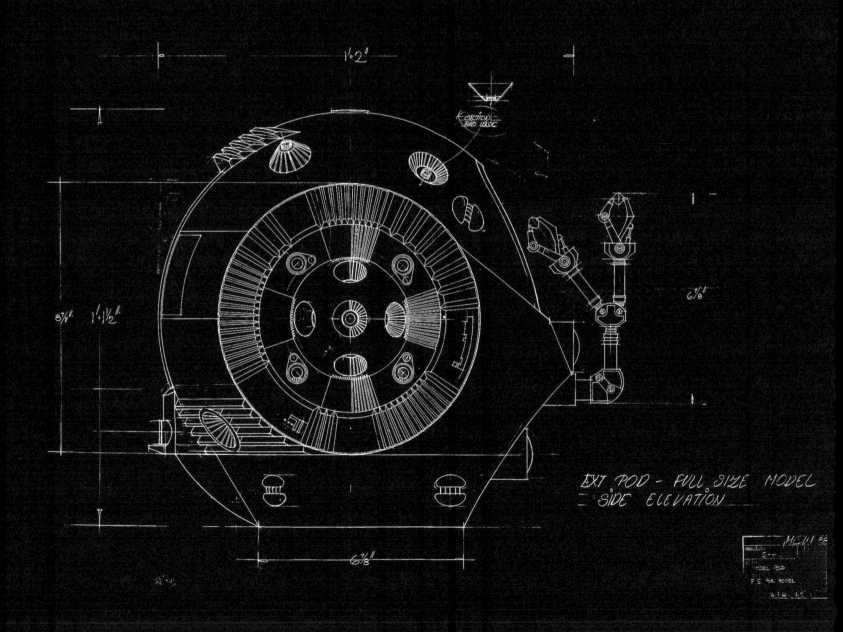

EXT POD - FULL SIZE MODEL
SIDE ELEVATION

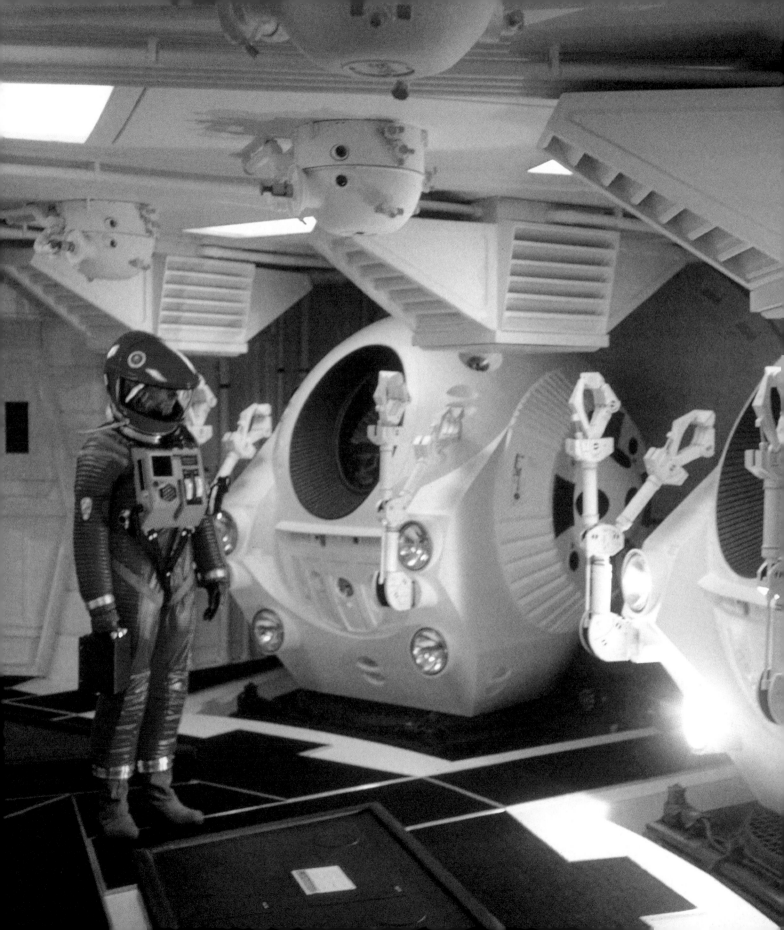

DISCOVERY

Details of keys, screens and communications devices

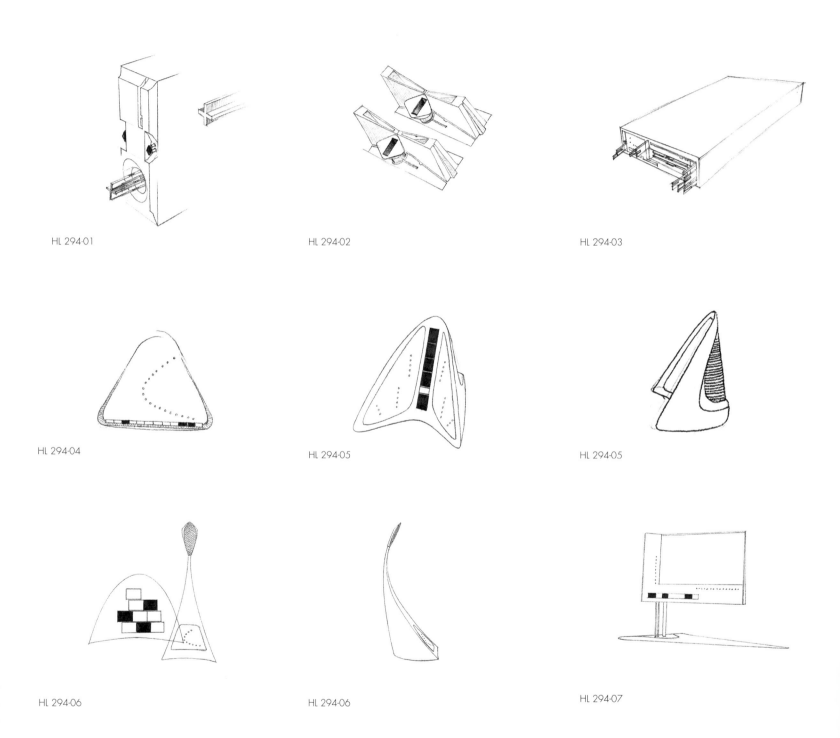

HL 294-01

HL 294-02

HL 294-03

HL 294-04

HL 294-05

HL 294-05

HL 294-06

HL 294-06

HL 294-07

HL 294-01 *Discovery computer room key socket detail.* **HL 294-02** *Discovery computer room key socket.* **HL 294-03** *Discovery computer room key device.* **HL 294-04** *Communications device.* **HL 294-05** *Communications device (two views).* **HL 294-06** *Discovery internal communications handset (two views).* **HL 294-07** *Television monitor.* **OPPOSITE** *Four concepts for Discovery information screen consoles.*

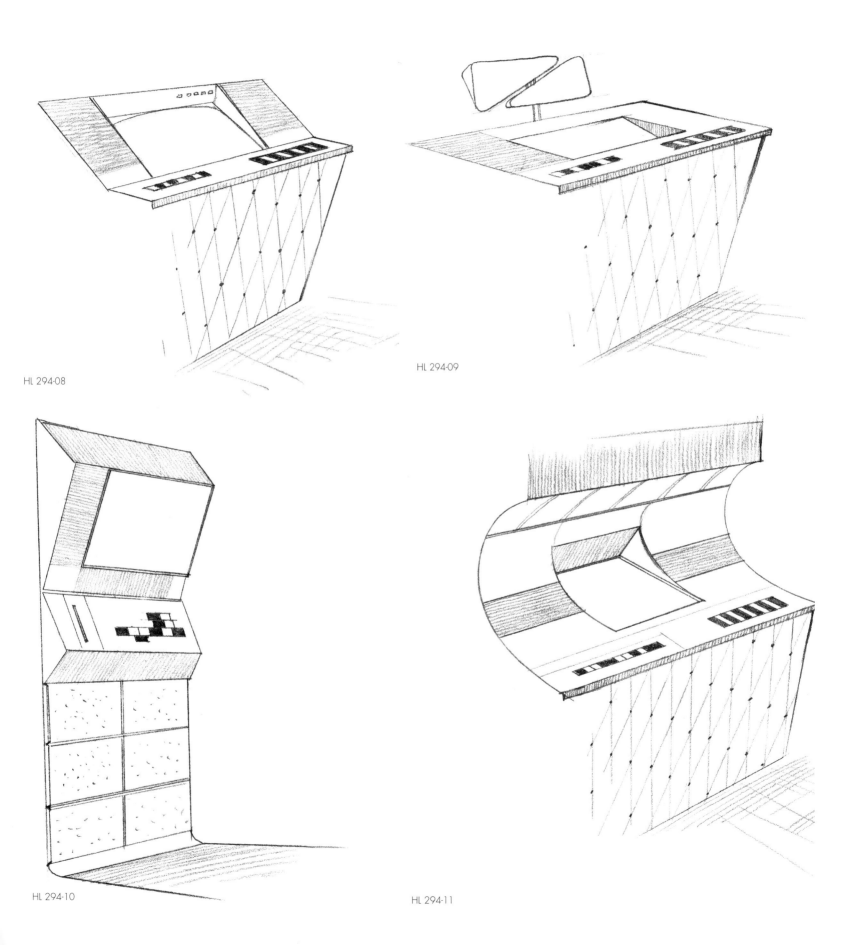

HL 294-08

HL 294-09

HL 294-10

HL 294-11

DISCOVERY
Instrument panels

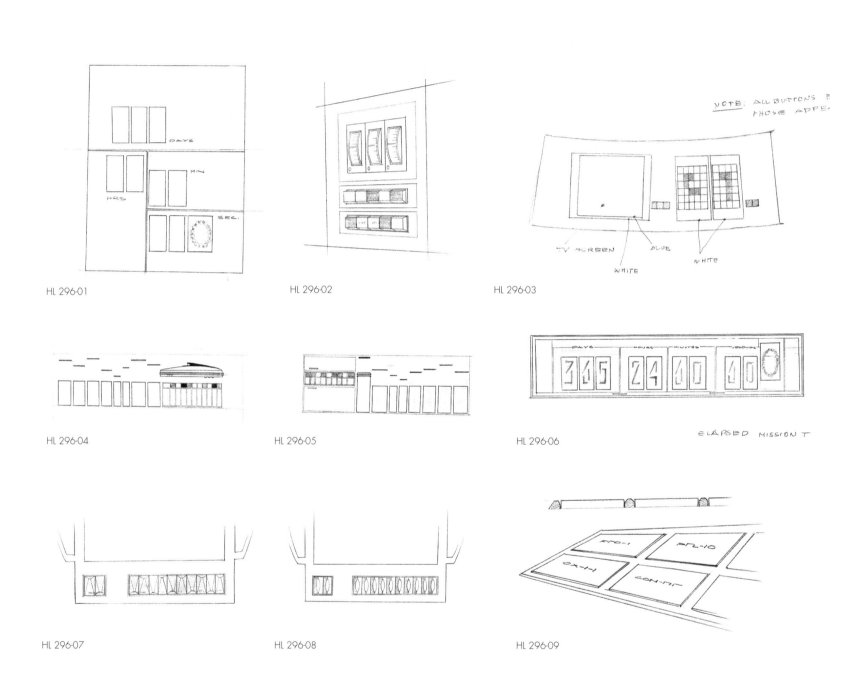

HL 296-01

HL 296-02

HL 296-03

HL 296-04

HL 296-05

HL 296-06

HL 296-07

HL 296-08

HL 296-09

HL 296-01 *Discovery time-keeping panel.* **HL 296-02** *Interior instrumentation.* **HL 296-03** *Cockpit interior instrumentation panel with annotations.* **HL 296-04** *Computer instrumentation panel.* **HL 296-05** *Computer instrumentation panel.* **HL 296-06** *Mission time counter for space vehicle.* **HL 296-07** *Instrumentation rocker switches.* **HL 296-08** *Variation of rocker switch design.* **HL 296-09** *Instrumentation buttons with cross section.* **HL 296-10** *Work station for Discovery.* **HL 296-11** *Left hand instrumentation panel for cockpit.* **HL 296-12** *Right hand instrument panel for cockpit.*

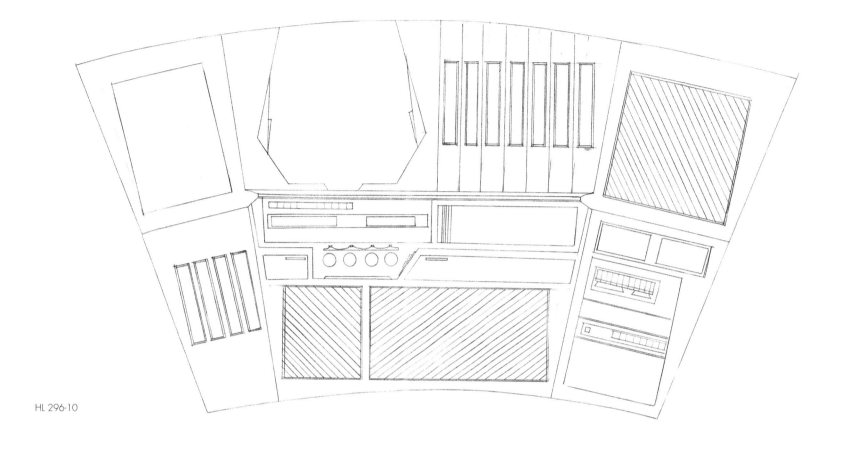

HL 296-10

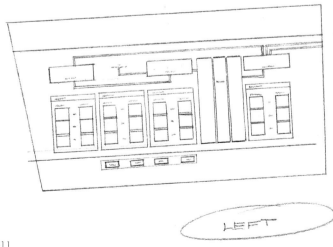

LEFT

HL 296-11

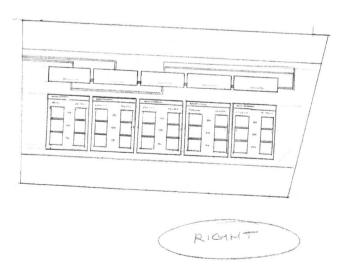

RIGHT

HL 296-12

DISCOVERY

Early concepts for interior of command module

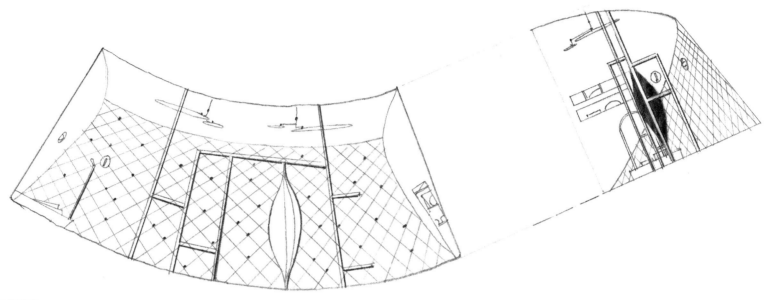

HL 298-01

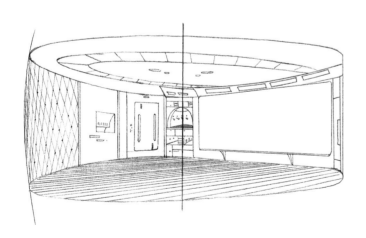

HL 298-02

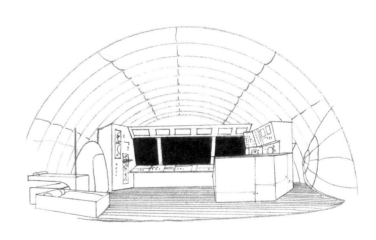

HL 298-03

HL 298-01 *Discovery Gymnasium—two views.* **HL 298-02** *Discovery interior recreation room* **HL 298-03** *Discovery sleeping quarters and flight deck.* **HL 298-04** *Discovery interior operating theatre.* **HL 298-05** *Discovery medical centre rotating operating table.*

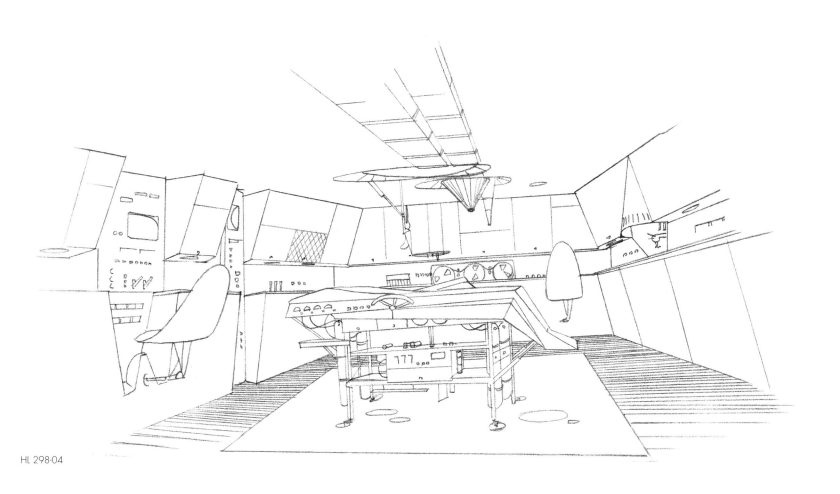

HL 298-04

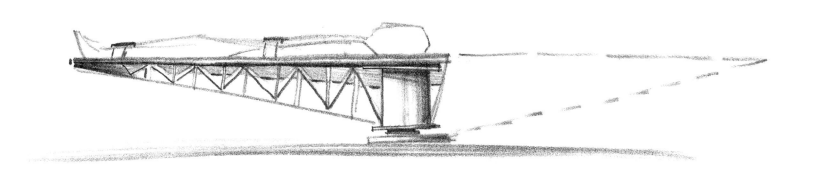

HL 298-05

DISCOVERY

Early concepts for interior of command module

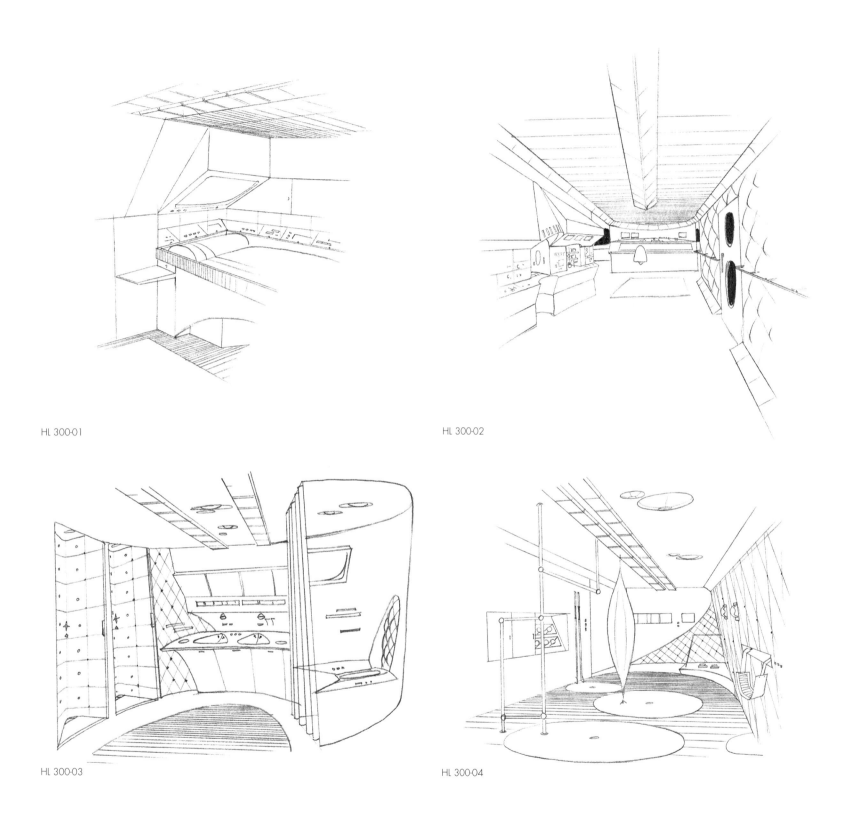

HL 300-01

HL 300-02

HL 300-03

HL 300-04

HL 300-01 *Discovery medical centre.* **HL 300-02** *Discovery operations room.* **HL 300-03** *Discovery bathroom and showers.* **HL 300-04** *Discovery Gymnasium.* **HL 300-05** *Discovery scientific apparatus.*

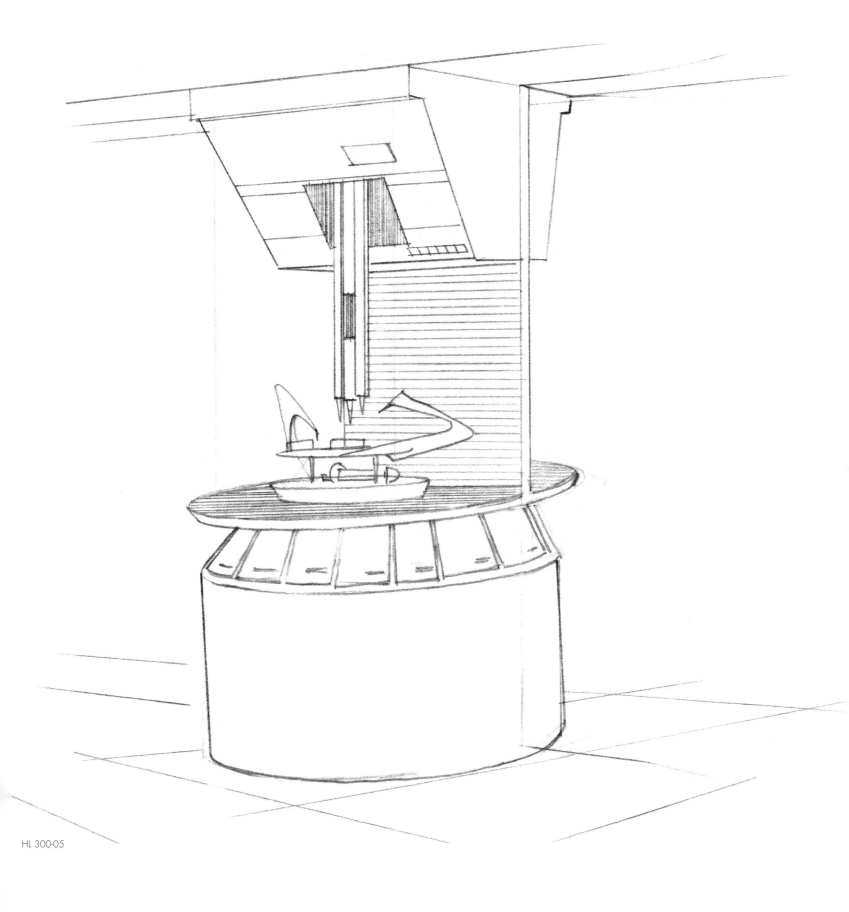

DISCOVERY

Concepts for interior

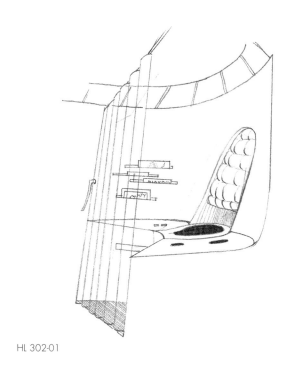

HL 302-01

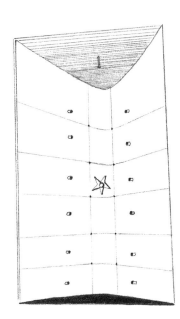

HL 302-02

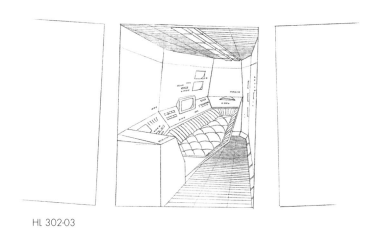

HL 302-03

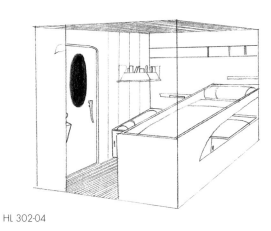

HL 302-04

HL 302-01 *Discovery toilet.* **HL 302-02** *Discovery shower.* **HL 302-03** *Discovery sleeping quarters with communications centre.* **HL 302-04** *Discovery sleeping quarters.* **HL 302-05** *Discovery sick bay.*

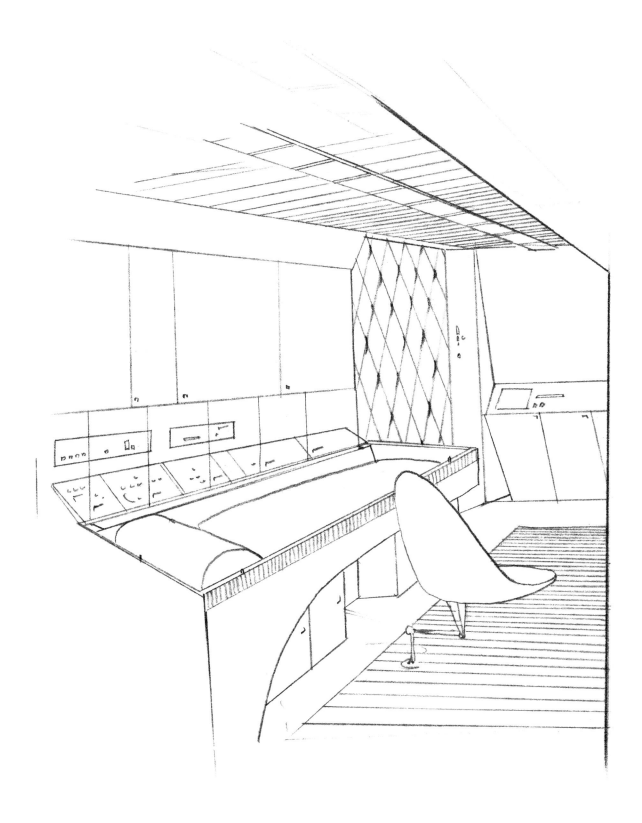

SPACE PROBES
Concepts for 'beyond Jupiter'

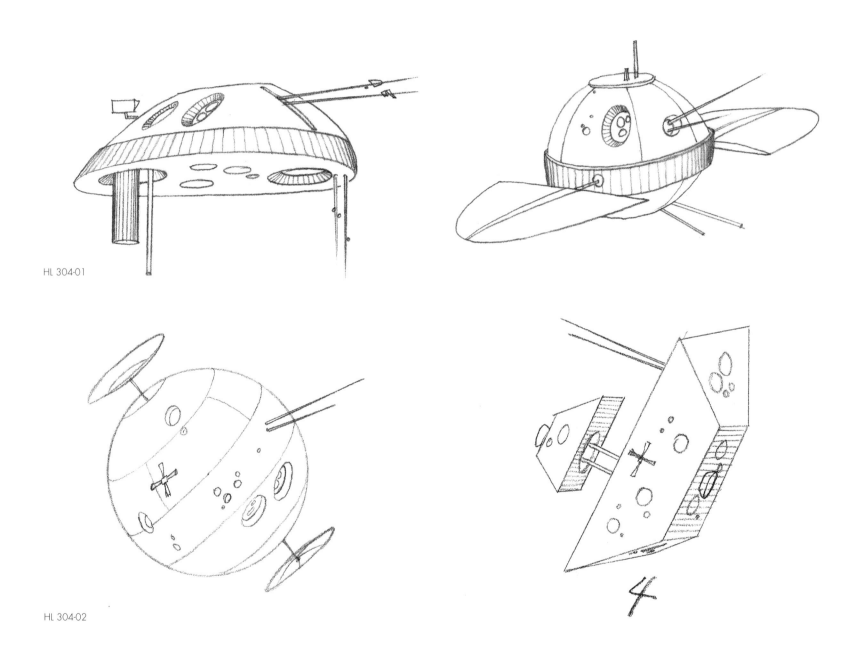

HL 304-01

HL 304-02

HL 304-01 *Two space probe designs.* **HL 304-02** *Two space probe designs.* **HL 304-03** *Four space probe designs.* **HL 304-04** *Two probes with fixed non-solar panels. These 'thumbnails' of space probes seem to have been originally intended for 'the final journey' section of the film, which included 'probes into space' in the original treatment. In some cases, they were interchangeable with the hardware designed for 'arrival in space'.*

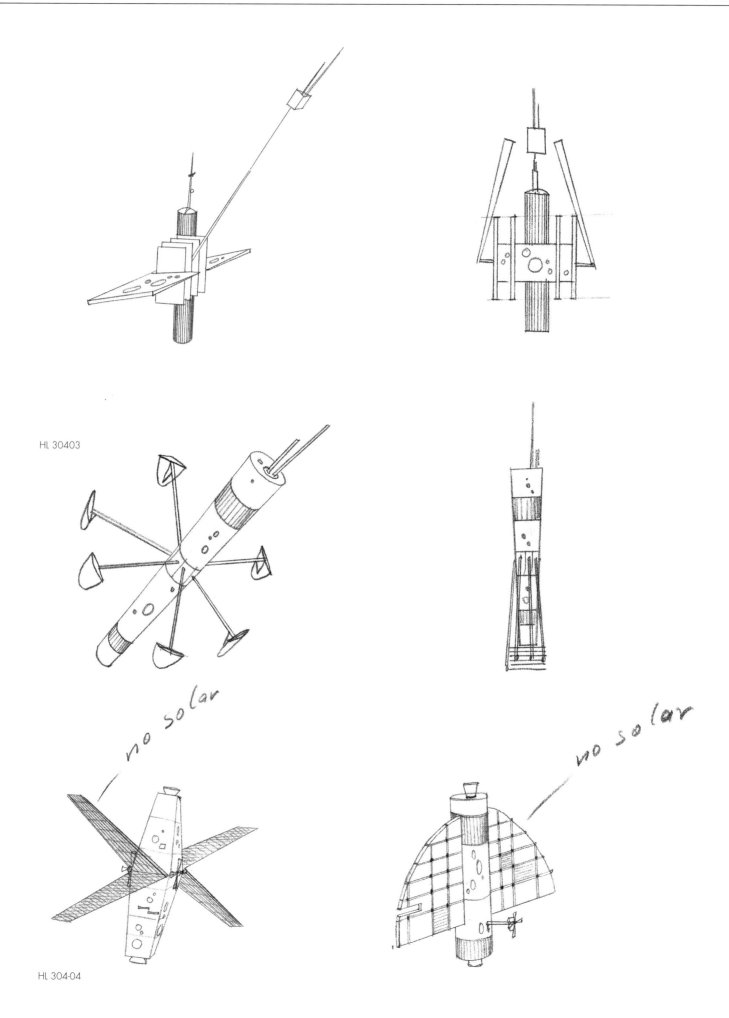

HL 30403

no solar

no solar

HL 304-04

SPACE SUITS AND HELMETS

Early concepts

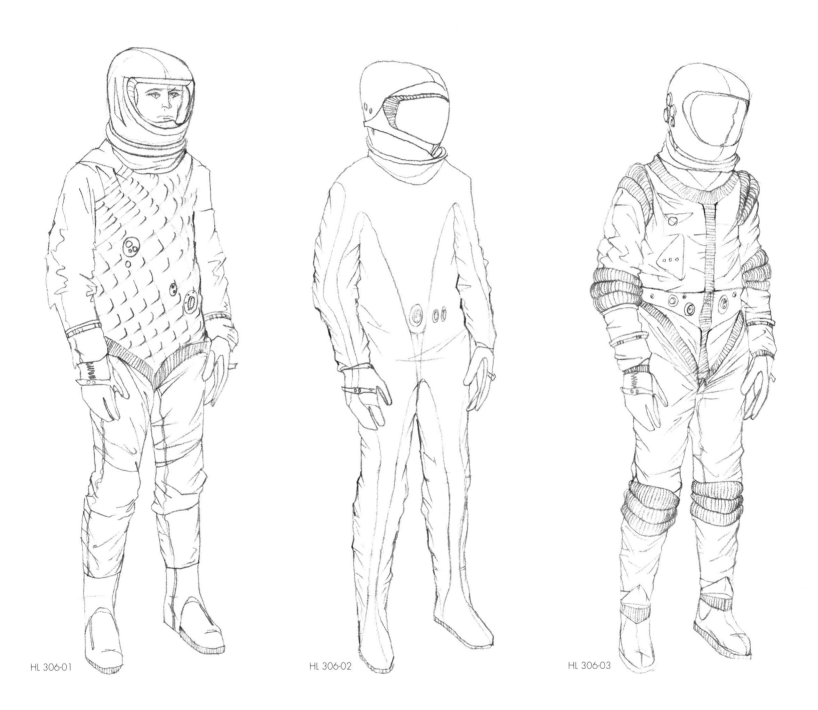

HL 306-01

HL 306-02

HL 306-03

HL 306-01 & HL 306-02 *Early space suit concepts—full figure front view.* **HL 306-03 & OPPOSITE** *More developed space suit concepts, with horizontal stitching to prevent distortion when the suit becomes inflated—an idea researched by NASA.*

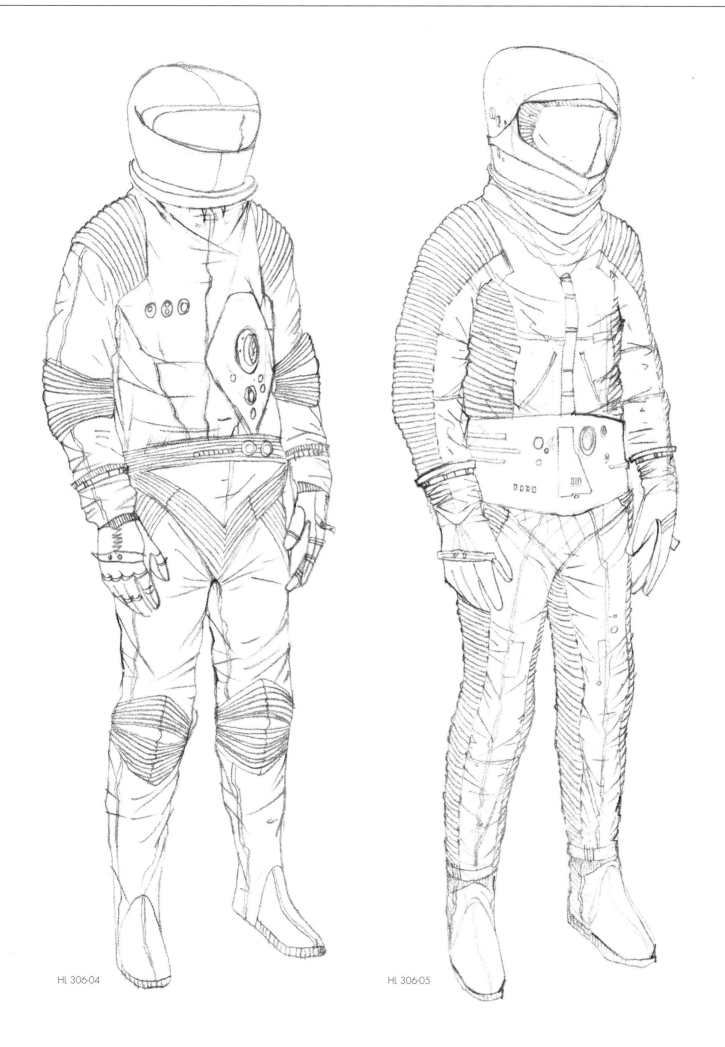

HL 306-04

HL 306-05

SPACE SUITS AND HELMETS
Early concepts

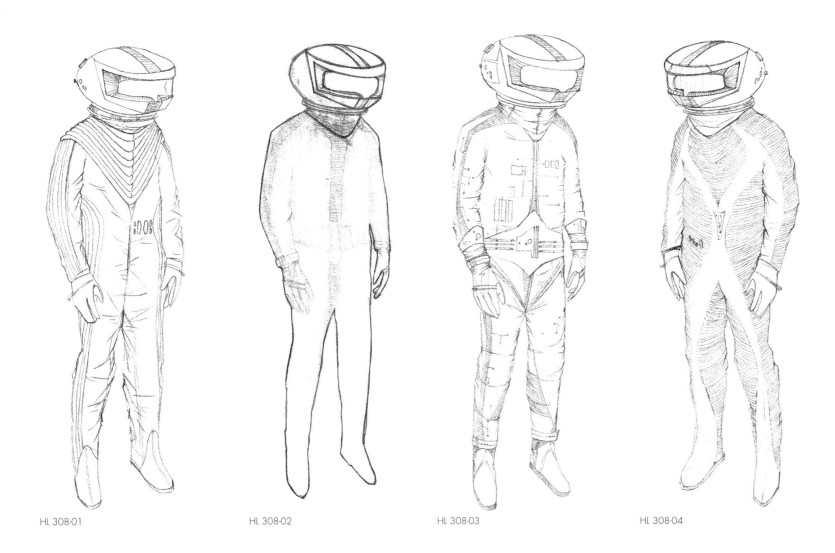

HL 308-01   HL 308-02   HL 308-03   HL 308-04

ABOVE *Early space suit concepts—full figure front view, working towards horizontal stitching.* **OPPOSITE** *Early space suit concepts—full figure front view—one with 'scales', one with horizontal stitching.*

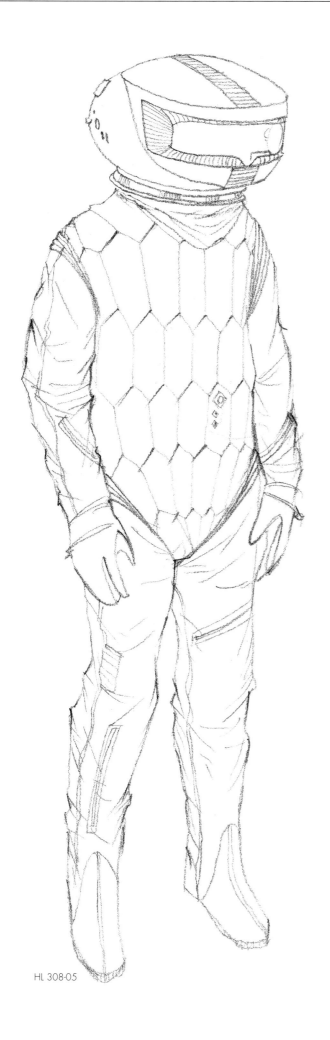

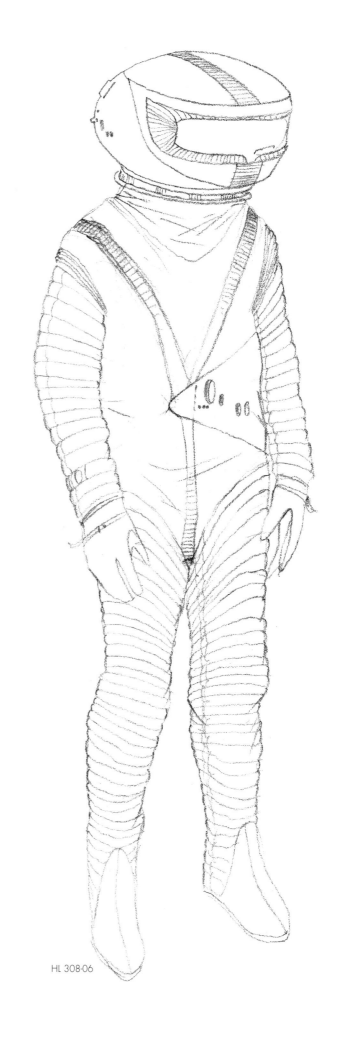

HL 308-05

HL 308-06

SPACE SUITS AND HELMETS

Concept for life support pack

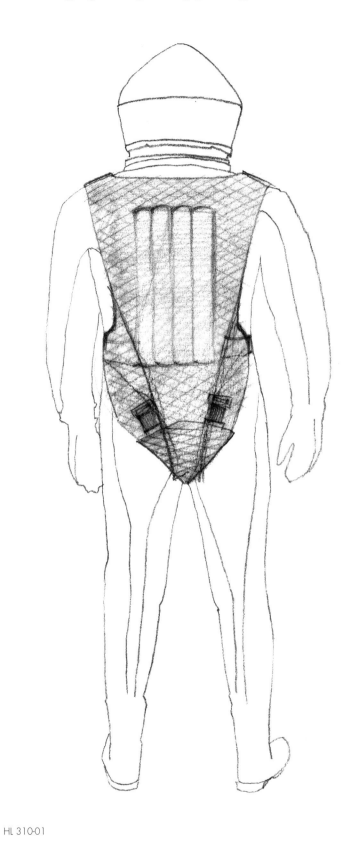

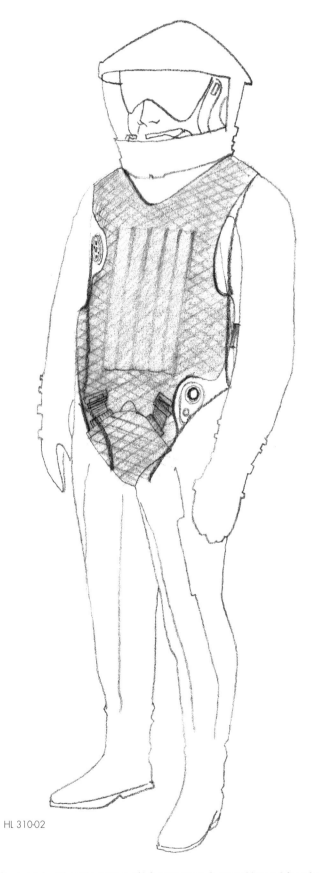

HL 310-01

HL 310-02

HL 310-01 *Space suit (rear view) with early version of life support pack.* **HL 310-02** *Space suit (front view) with early version of life support pack, resembling a life-jacket.*
OPPOSITE *Bowman (Keir Dullea) with one of the final versions of space suit and life support pack.*

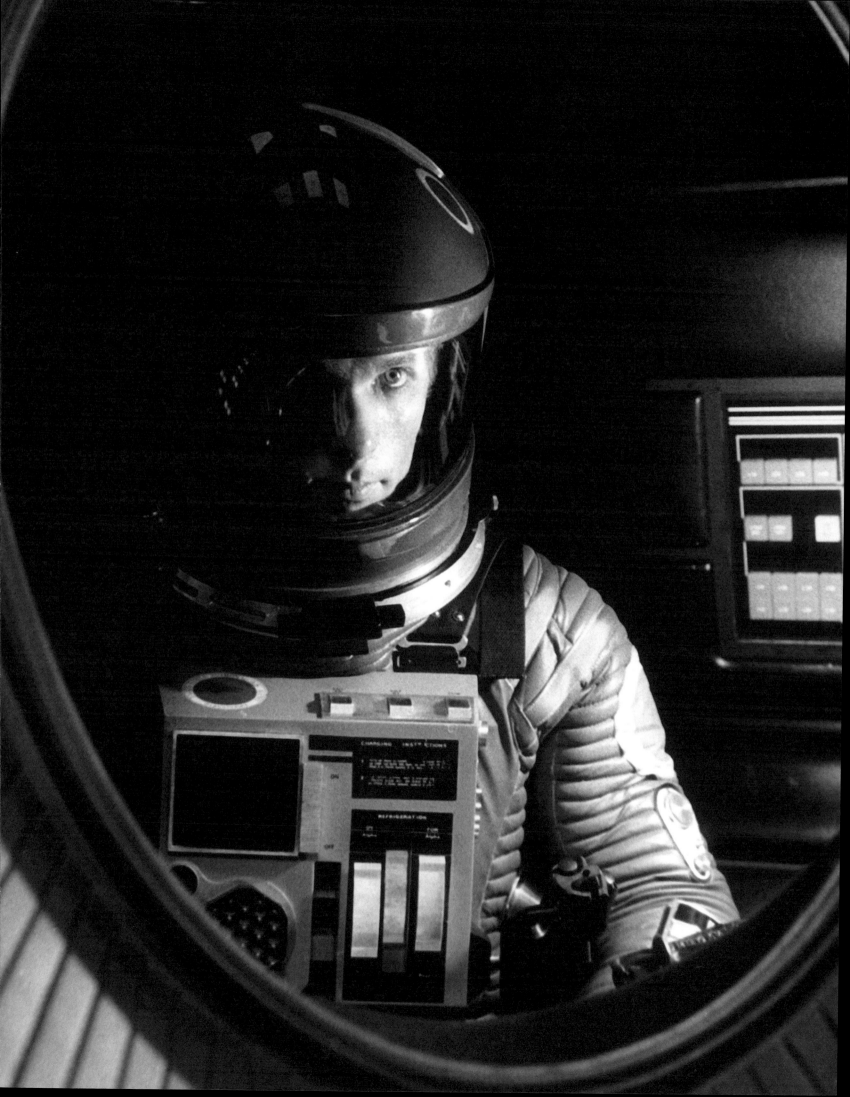

SPACE SUITS

Rectangular life support pack, and communication panel

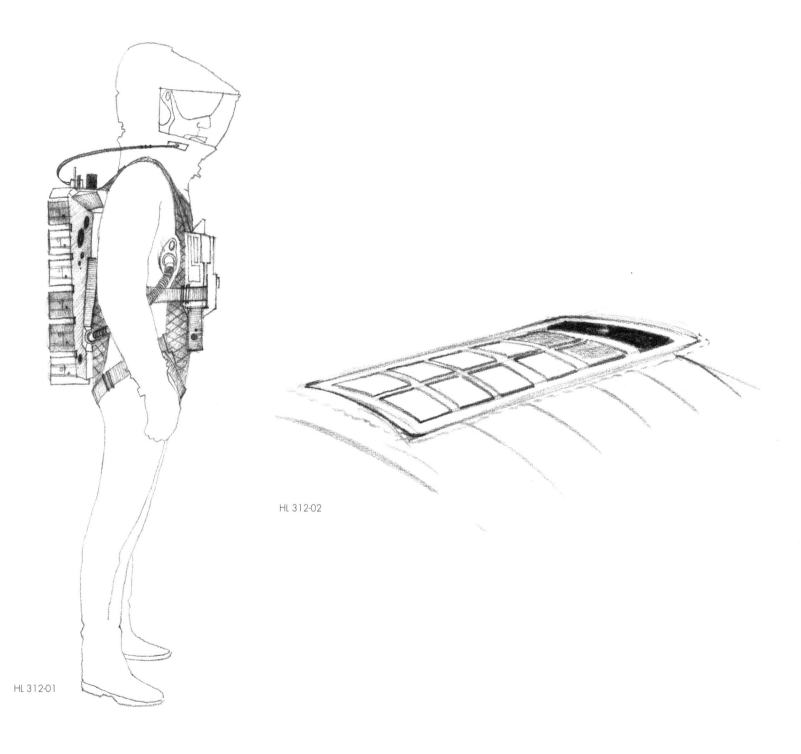

HL 312-02

HL 312-01

HL 312-01 *Full side view space suit with front and back life support pack.* **HL 312-02** *Space suit communication panel located on left arm.* **OPPOSITE** *Bowman (Keir Dullea) in space suit and helmet with life support pack on his chest.*

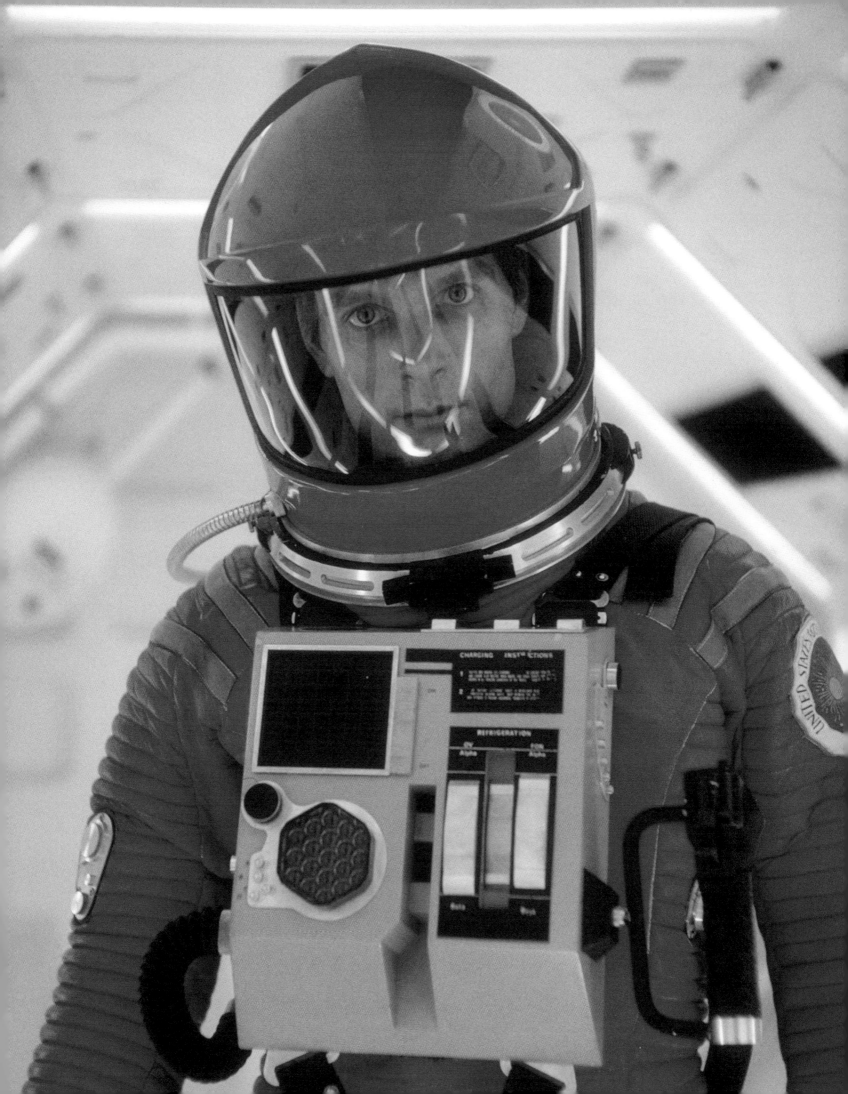

SPACE SUITS
Detailed blueprints

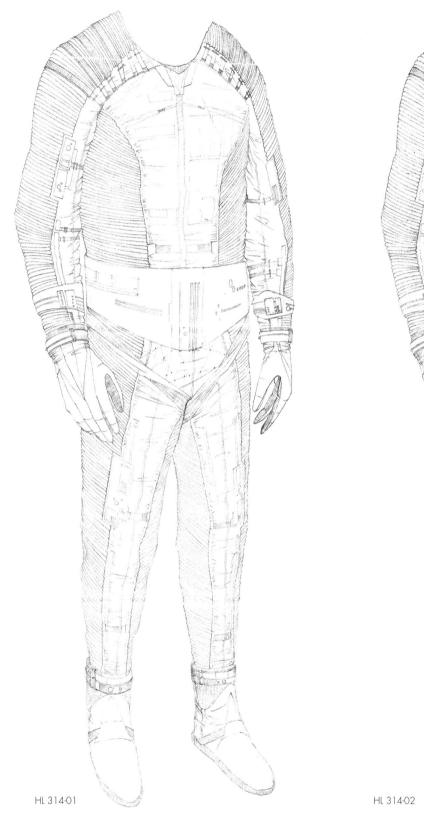

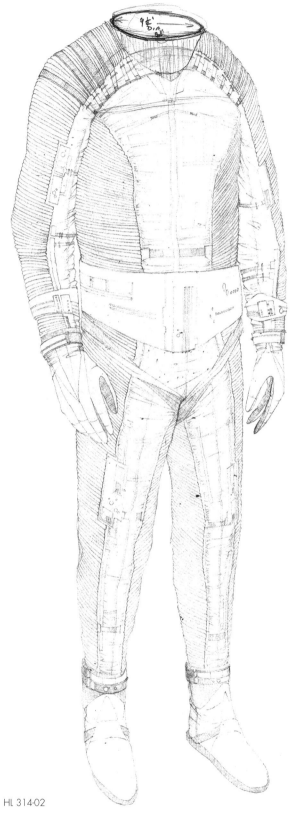

HL 314-01

HL 314-02

ABOVE *Space suit blueprints full figure (front view) with horizontal stitching.* **OPPOSITE** *Space suit blueprints full figure (rear view) with surface texture details and horizontal stitching.*

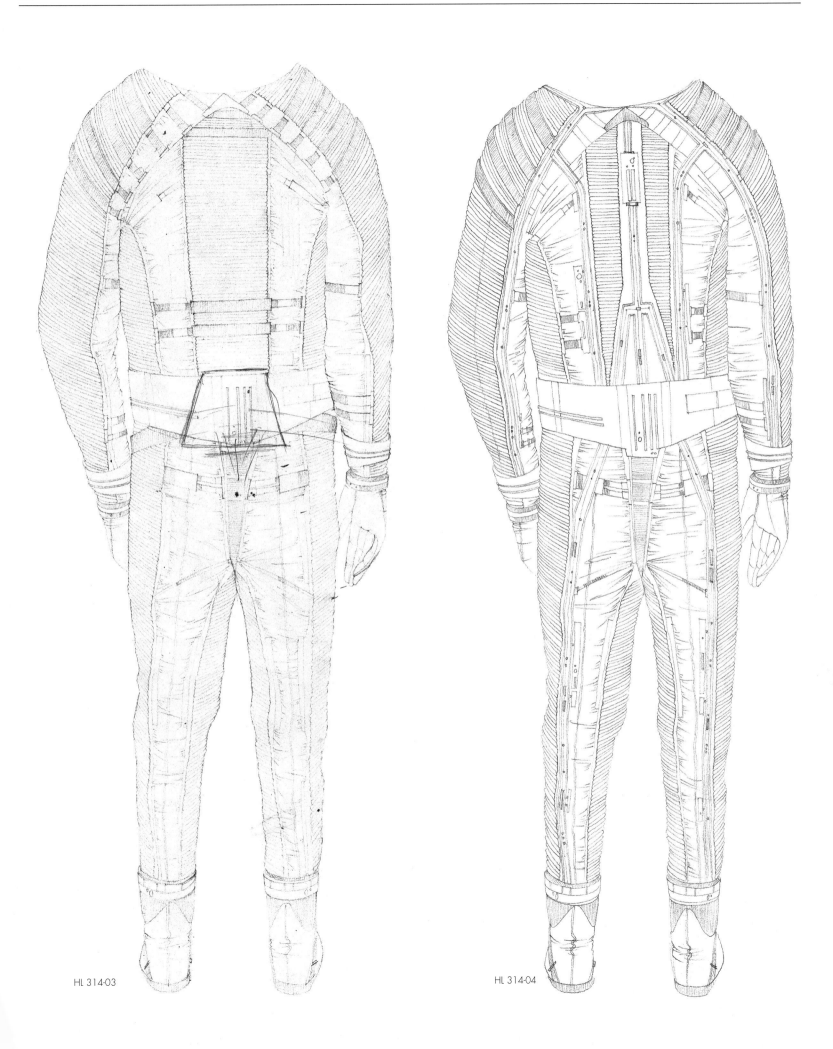

HL 314-03

HL 314-04

SPACE SUITS AND HELMETS
Towards the final design

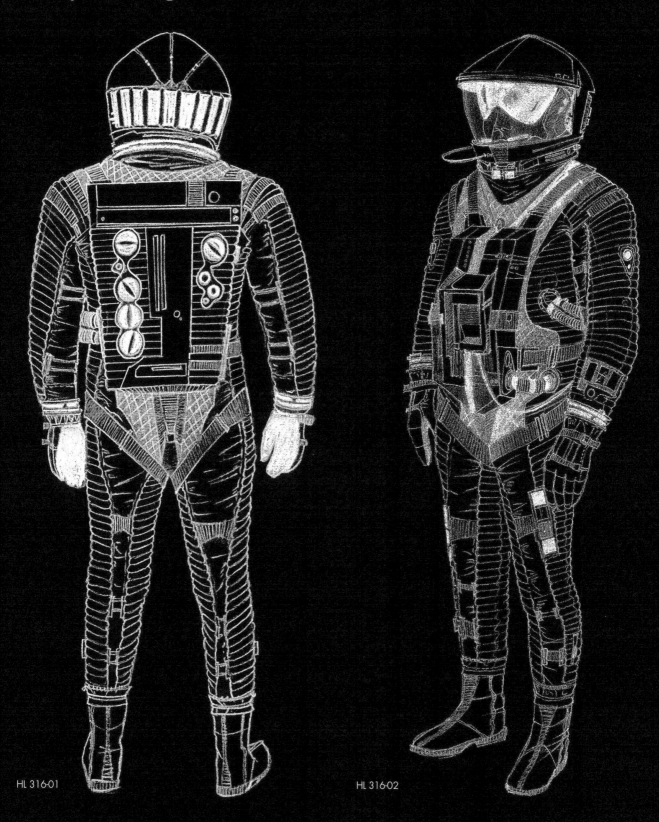

HL 316-01

HL 316-02

HL 316-01 *Full-length rear view with life support pack detail and mission packs on back of helmet.* **HL 316-02** *Final design for spacesuit, full figure (front view).* **OPPOSITE** *Poole (Gary Lockwood) in his space suit, walking on brightly lit interior set.*

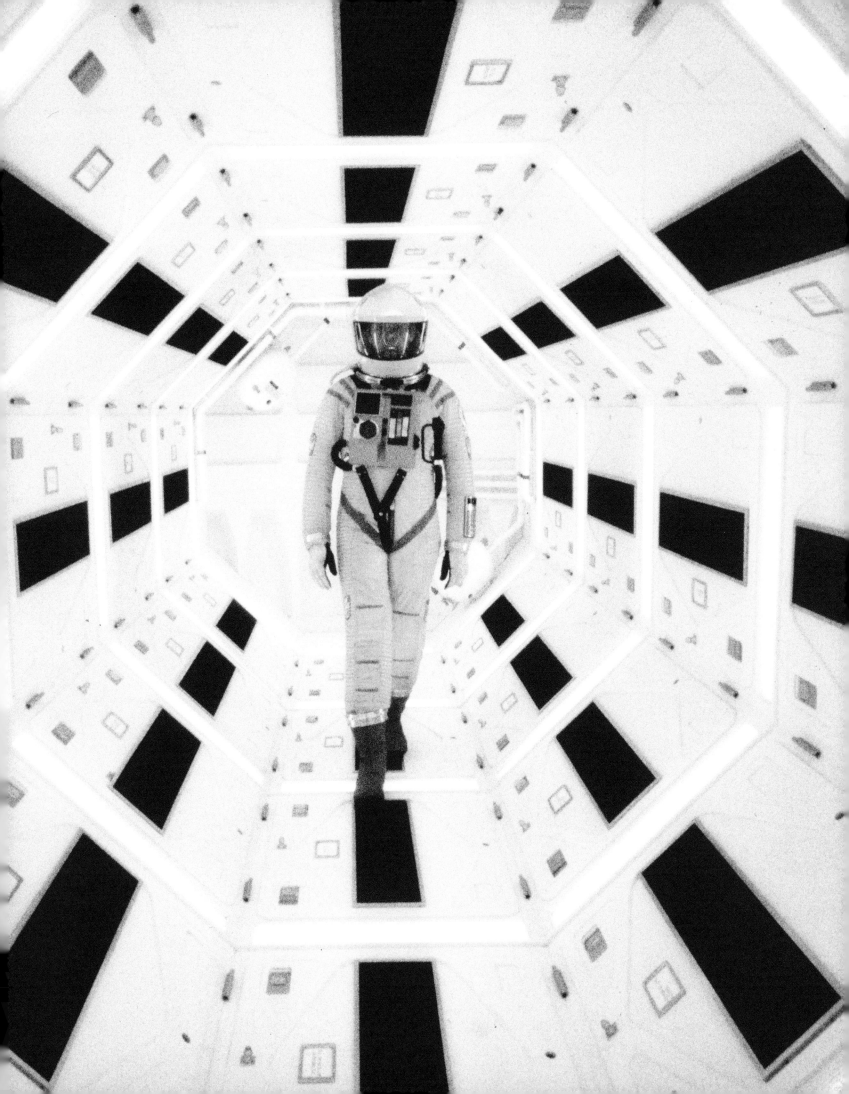

SPACE HELMETS
Early concepts

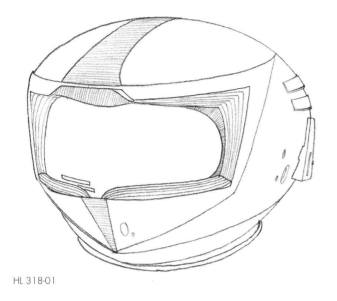

HL 318-01

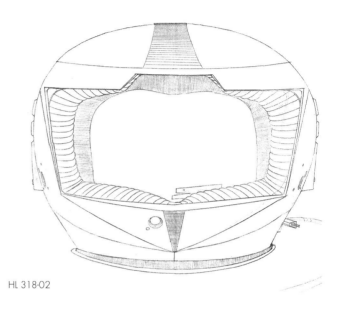

HL 318-02

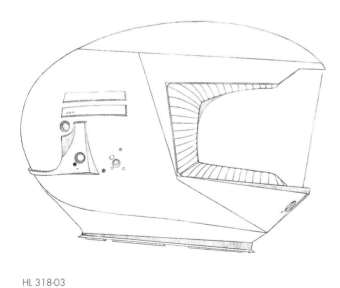

HL 318-03

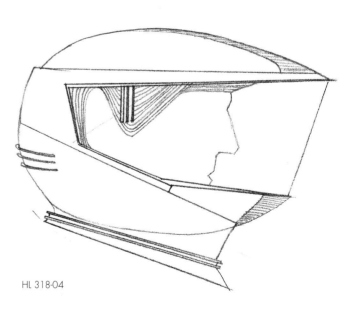

HL 318-04

HL 318-01 *Space helmet with surface detail and visor with mission pack (three quarter view).* **HL 318-02** *Space helmet front view of HL 318-03.* **HL 318-03** *Space helmet side elevation.* **HL 318-04** *Space helmet (profile view) with visor.* **OPPOSITE** *Space helmet concepts (profile view) with surface details and visors.*

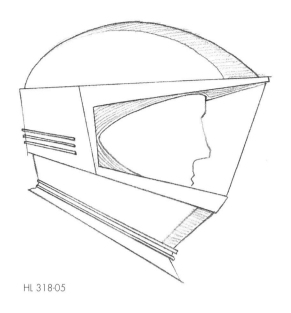

HL 318-05

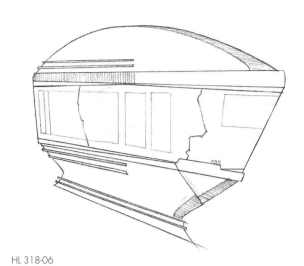

HL 318-06

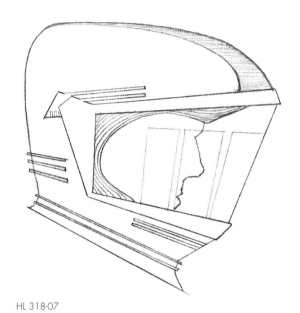

HL 318-07

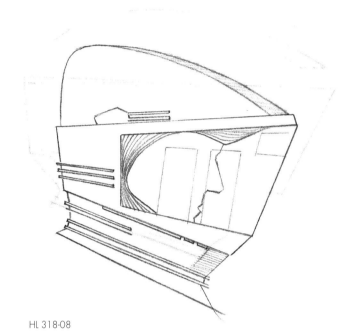

HL 318-08

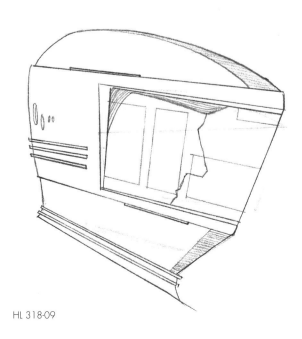

HL 318-09

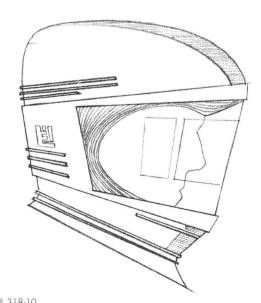

HL 318-10

SPACE HELMET
Visor slide mechanism

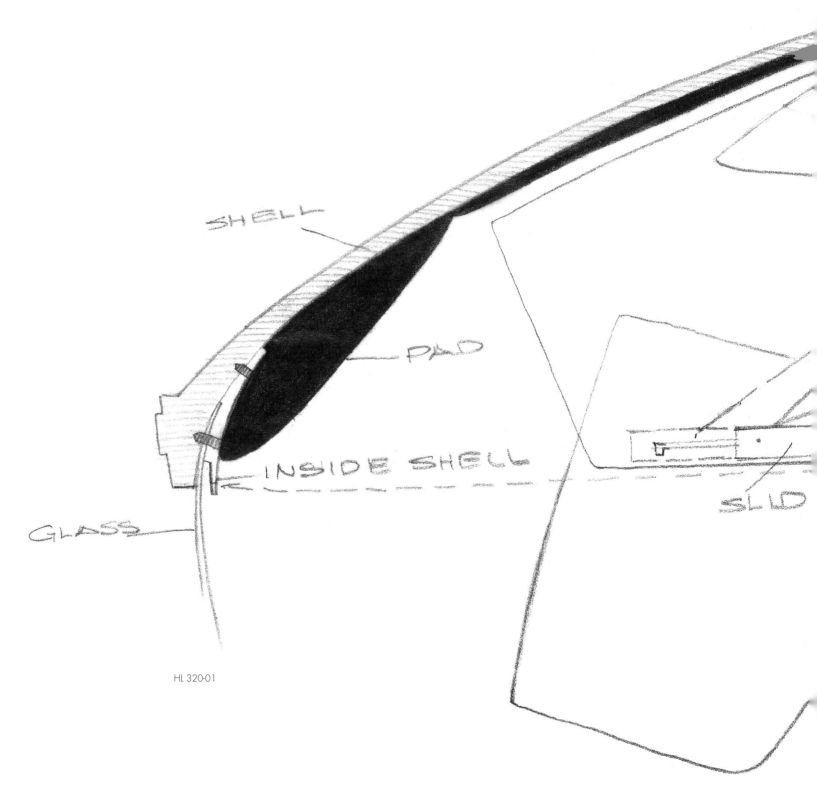

HL 320-01

HL 320-01 *Cross section of space helmet with visor slide mechanism.*

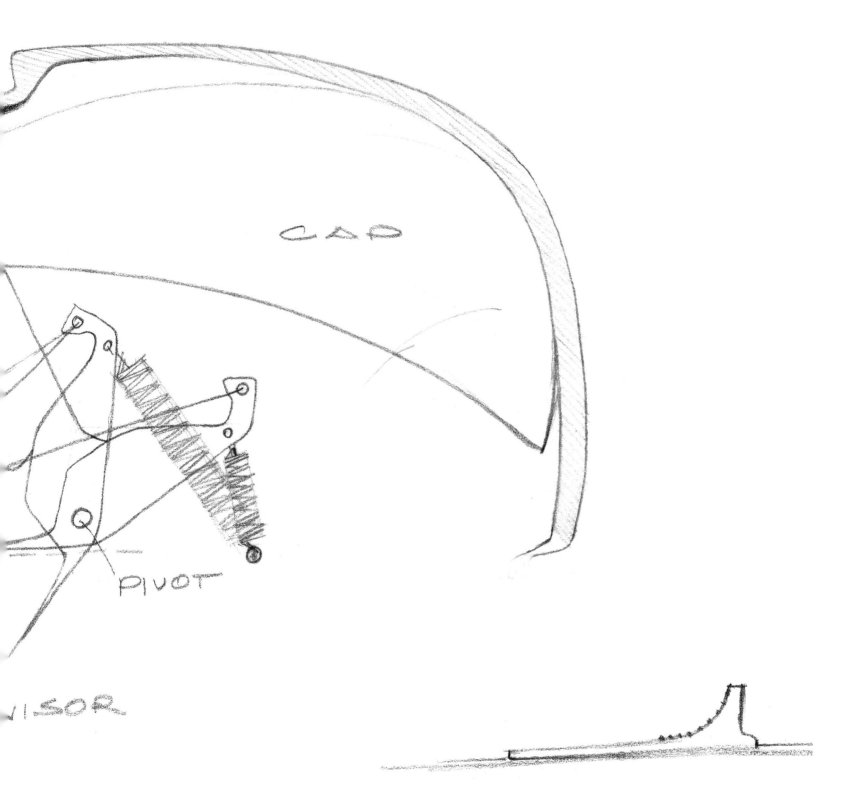

CAP

PIVOT

VISOR

SPACE HELMETS
Early concepts

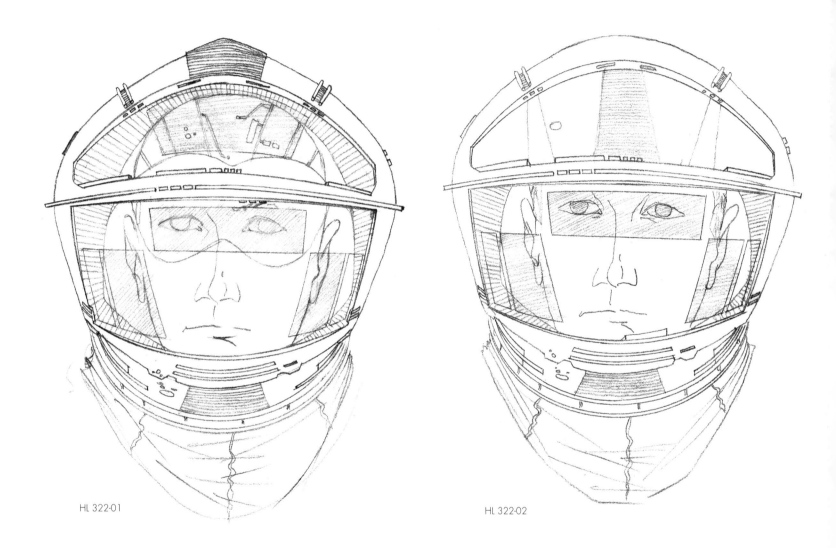

HL 322-01

HL 322-02

HL 322-01 *Space helmet (front view 'solar').* **HL 322-02** *Space helmet (front view 'moon').* **HL 322-03** *Space helmet (top view) with solar visor.*

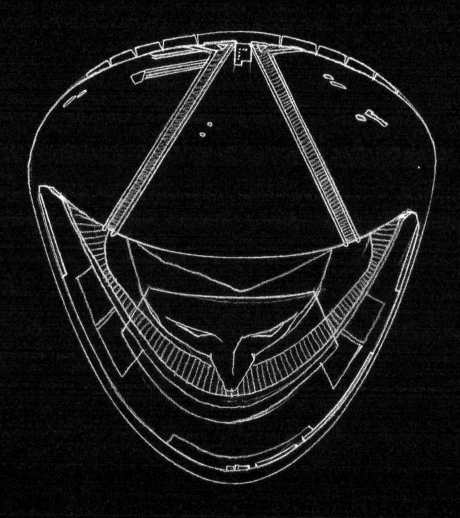

HL 322-03

SPACE HELMETS

Towards the final design

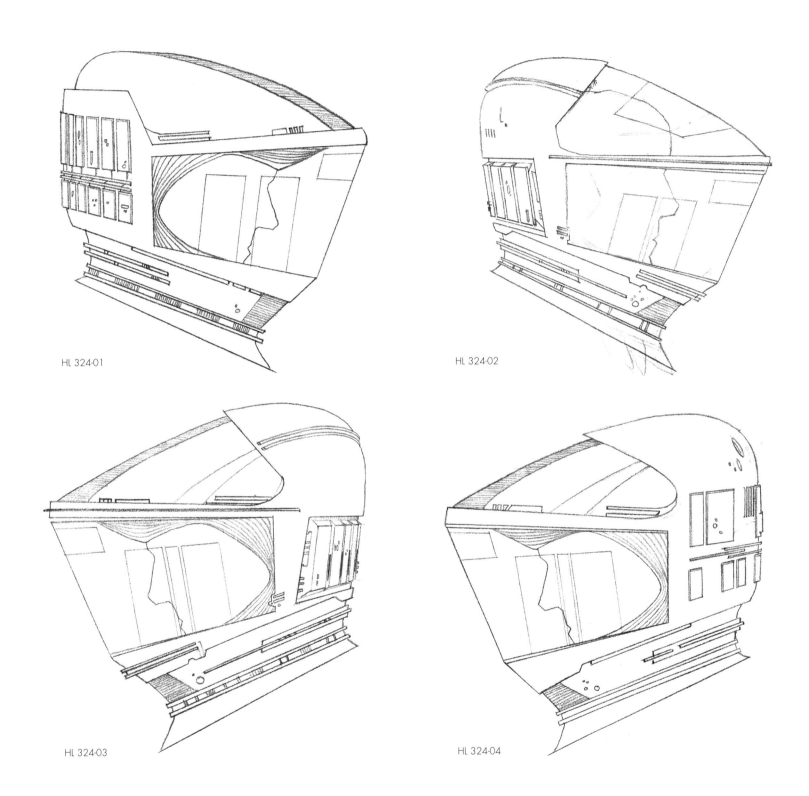

HL 324-01

HL 324-02

HL 324-03

HL 324-04

HL 324-01 *Space helmet with surface detail, visor and plug-in mission data module (profile view).* **HL 324-02** *Space helmet with surface detail, solar visor and plug-in mission packs (profile view).* **HL 324-03** *Space helmet with surface detail and visor with mission packs (profile view).* **HL 324-04** *Space helmet with surface detail, and visor with mission packs (profile view).* **HL 324-05** *Space helmet rear view with details of plug-in mission data/computer module.* **OVERLEAF** *The scientists in their space suits (final version), on the site of the Tycho Magnetic Anomaly.*

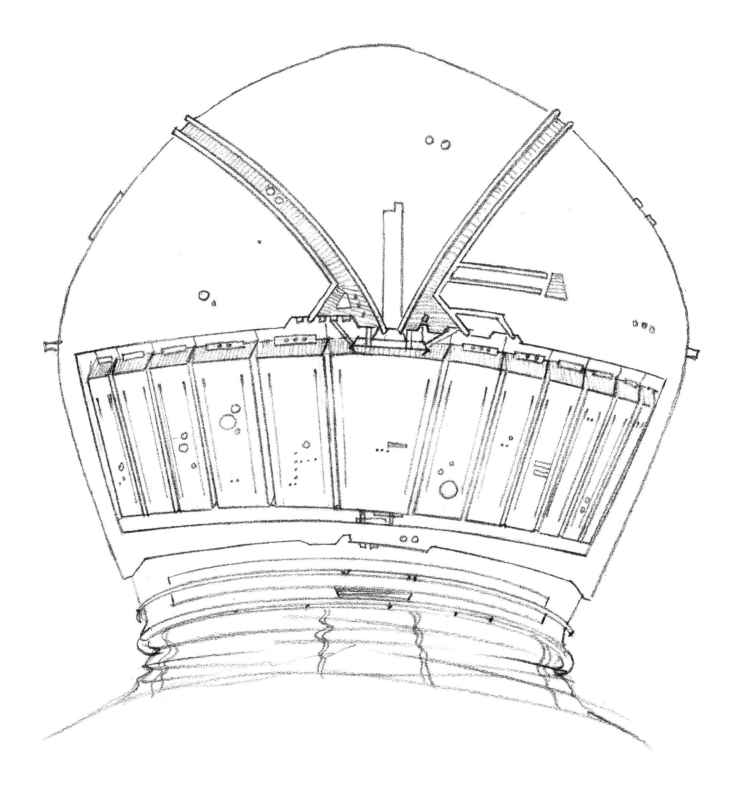

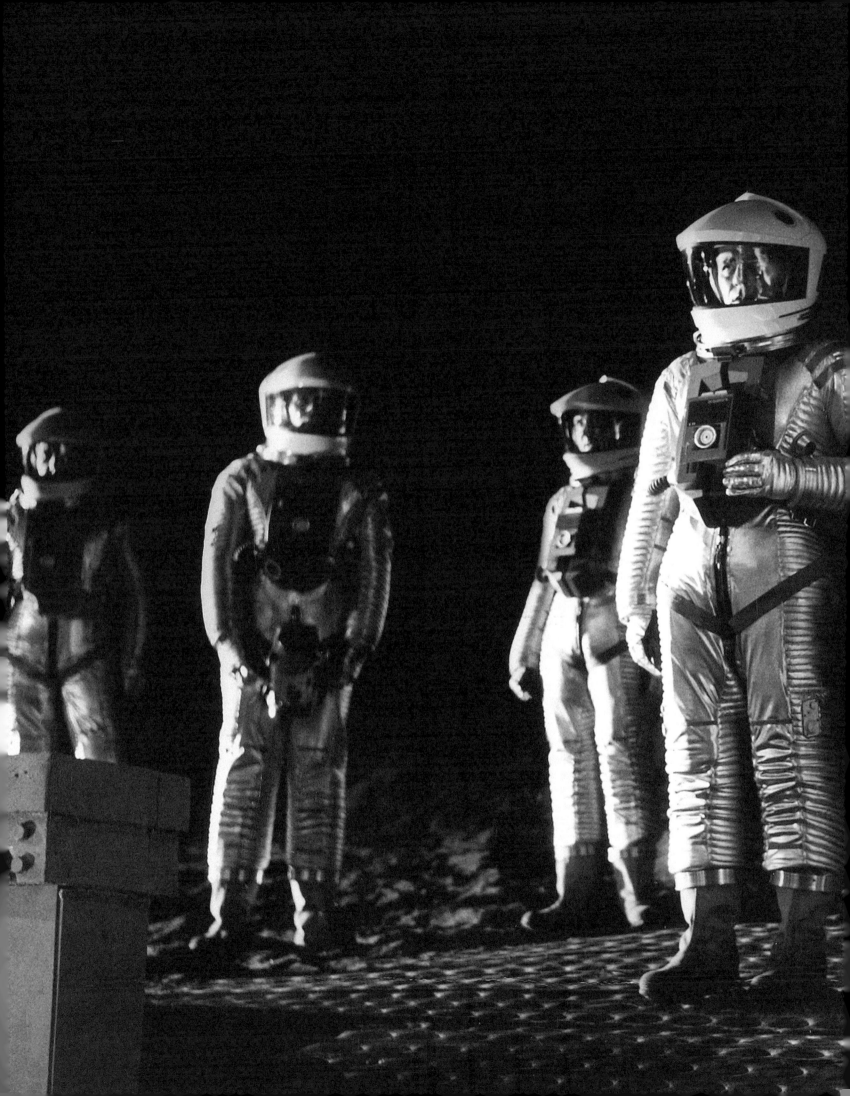

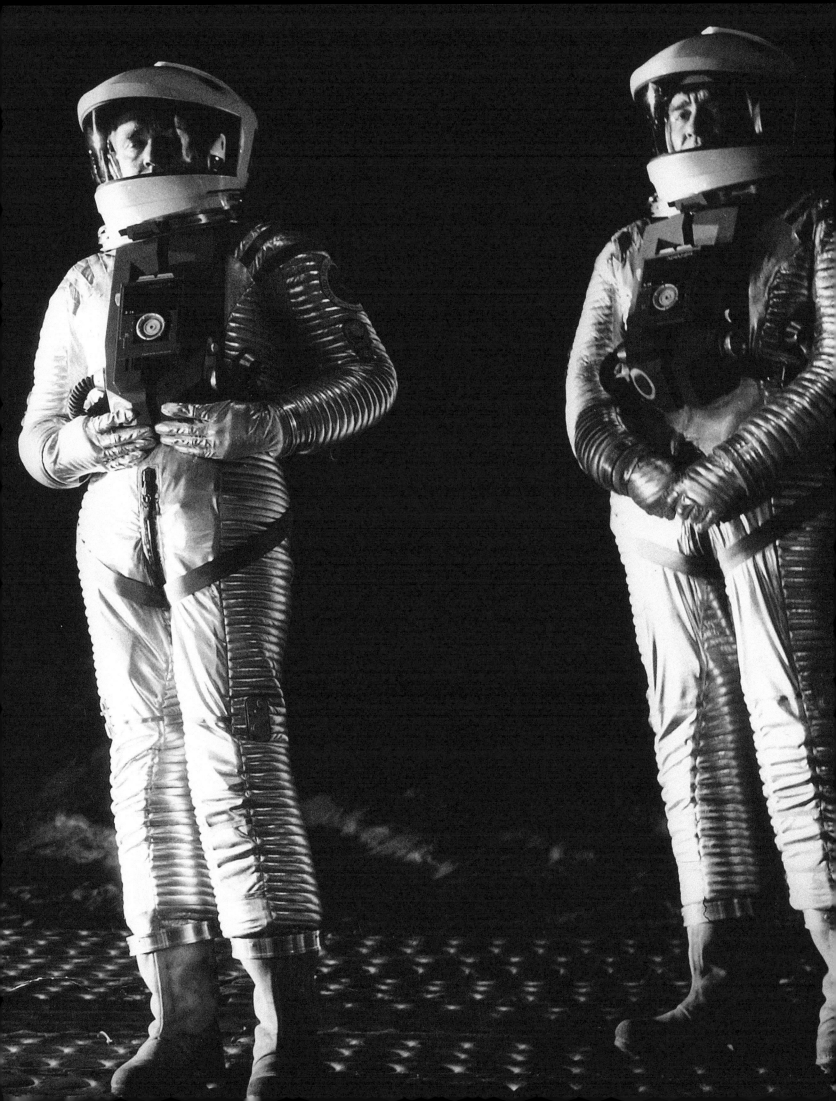

ODYSSEY'S END

Back Home

THE MOVIE POSTER CAMPAIGN

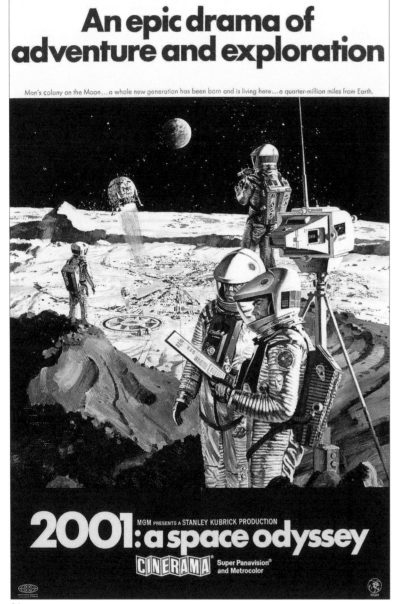

1A

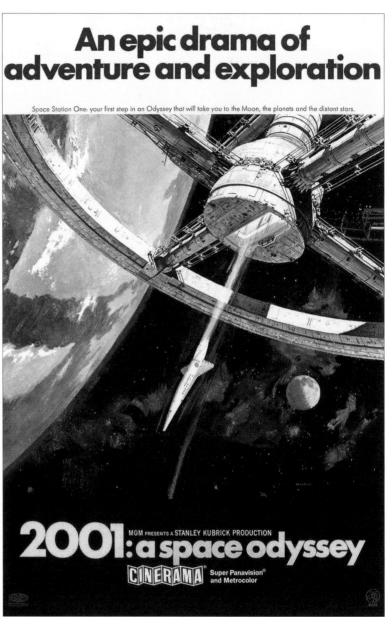

1B

*Robert McCall's artwork—based on Harry Lange's designs—was featured in the initial publicity campaign for **2001: A Space Odyssey**. **1A** Scientists surveying—on the heights above lunar colony. **1B** A spaceplane flies at speed out of the circular Space Station. **1C** Astronaut stands next to the hibernaculum inside the Centrifuge aboard Discovery. This visual style was only used for the film's initial Cinerama release.*

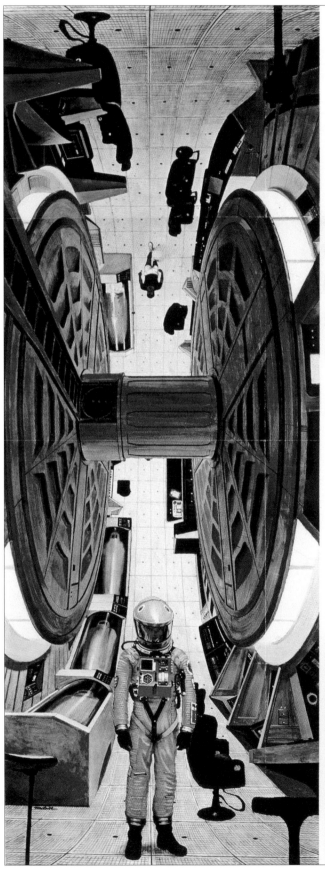

An epic drama of adventure and exploration

…taking you half a billion miles from Earth…
further from home than any man in history.
Destination: Jupiter.

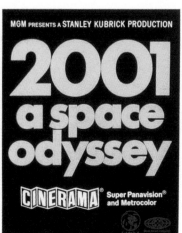

ACKNOWLEDGEMENTS

Warm thanks to Sir Ken Adam, the late Fred I. Ordway III, and Prof. David Watkins for long interviews in October 2013, November 2013 and January 2014 respectively—their still-vivid memories revealing how important the *2001* experience was to them; in the case of Ken Adam, he also shared his fascinating correspondence with Stanley Kubrick; to Jan Harlan, the Kubrick family and the archivists for giving me access to the Stanley Kubrick Archive within the University of the Arts, London; to Abraham Thomas, then of the V&A, for sending me his conference paper on product design; to John Lange and Tony Nourmand for sharing with me Harry Lange's amazing collection of drawings, designs, documents and photographs; to Piers Bizony, for his generosity and encouragement; to my design history students over the years, especially the ones who specialised in film design; to John Longhurst and The Boynett Collection. Unpublished letters are presented in italics. The prefix 'HL' followed by a number—in the detailed captions to drawings—shows that the image originated in the Harry Lange archive, for which I am also very grateful to the Lange family. Most of the HL images are being published here for the first time. The detailed caption descriptions are partly based on the archive's own identifications and wording. Thanks, too, to those who gave me extra information, after reading the first edition of this book.

SIR CHRISTOPHER FRAYLING

Professor Sir Christopher Frayling was until recently Rector of the Royal College of Art and Chairman of Arts Council England. He is currently Professor Emeritus of Cultural History at the RCA, Visiting Professor of Contemporary Arts at Lancaster University and a Fellow of Churchill College Cambridge. An historian, a critic, curator and award-winning broadcaster, he is the author of twenty-one books on the arts and design—four of them on design for film.

Opposite: Harry Lange's witty retrospective collage of elements from 2001, mainly re-arranging bits of the interplanetary spaceship Discovery.

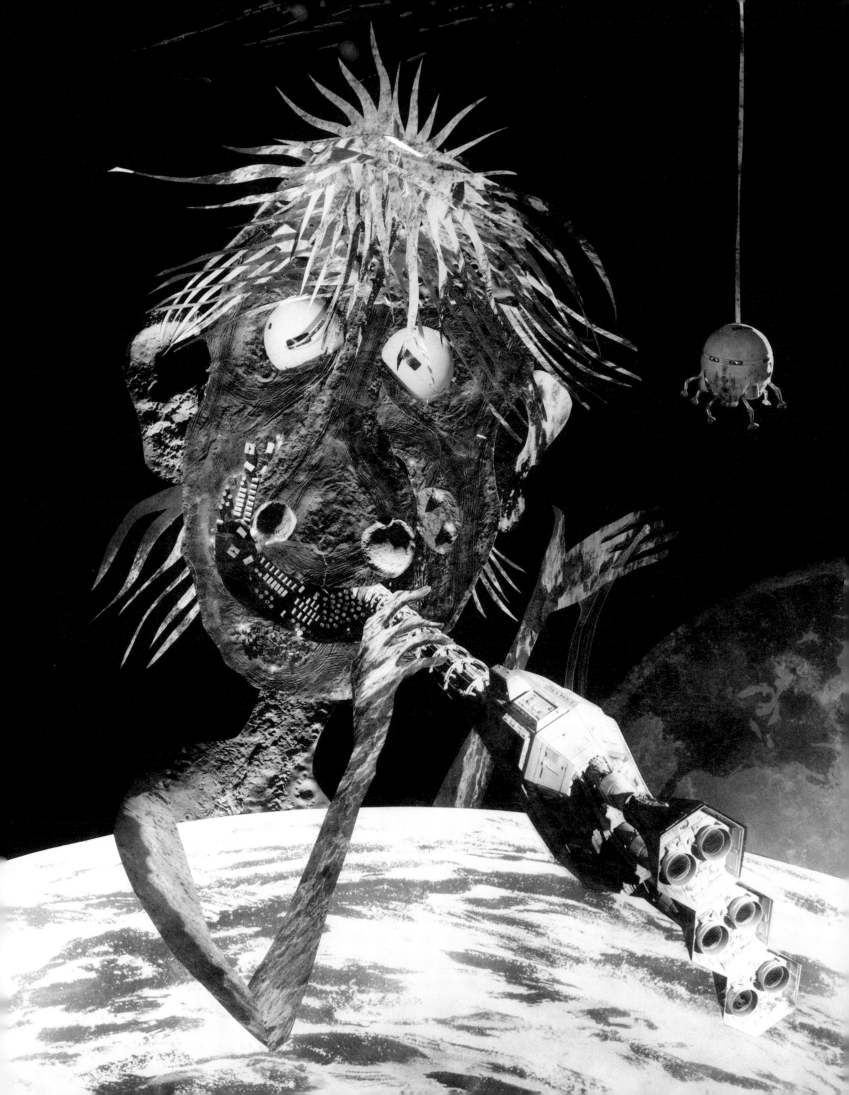

BIBLIOGRAPHY

*denotes an especially useful source

Ken Adam and Christopher Frayling: **Ken Adam Designs the Movies** (Thames & Hudson, 2008)

* Jerome Agel, ed.: **The Making of Kubrick's 2001** (New American Library, 1970)

John Baxter: **Stanley Kubrick – a biography** (Carroll and Graf, 1997)

* Piers Bizony: **2001 – Filming the Future** (Aurum Press, 1994)

* Piers Bizony: **Making of Stanley Kubrick's 2001** (Taschen, 2014)

* Elizabeth Boggis: **That Was Tomorrow – designing modernity in science fiction films** (unpublished M.A. thesis,

Royal College of Art, 1994; includes as Appendix III interview with Harry Lange)

John Brosnan: **The Primal Screen** (Orbit, 1991)

Michel Ciment: **Kubrick – the Definitive Edition** (Faber and Faber, 1980)

Arthur C. Clarke: **2001: A Space Odyssey** (Legend, 1990; with foreword)

* Arthur C. Clarke: **The Lost Worlds of 2001** (Sidgwick and Jackson, 1972)

* Arthur C. Clarke: **Report on Planet Three** (Gollancz, 1977)

Thomas Craven: **The Making of 2001** (documentary film, April 1966)

* Bernd Eichhorn et al: **Stanley Kubrick** (catalogue, Filmmuseum, Frankfurt, 2004)

* Eugene M. Emme, ed.: **Science Fiction and Space Futures** (American Astronautical Society, 1982)

Christopher Frayling: **Ken Adam – the art of production design** (Faber and Faber, 2005)

Christopher Frayling: **Mad, Bad and Dangerous? The scientist and the cinema** (Reaktion, 2005)

Clive James: **2001 – Kubrick versus Clarke** (in Cinema, Cambridge, No. 2 March 1969)

* Adam K. Johnson and Frederick I. Ordway III: **2001 – The Lost Science** (Apogee Press, 2012)

David A. Kirby: **Lab Coats in Hollywood** (MIT Press, 2011)

* Stanley Kubrick Archive: especially 12/2 **2001 preproduction**; 12/3 **2001 production**; 12/8 **2001 papers and letters**

and 12/9 **2001 photographs and slides**

* Harry Lange Collection: of **drawings, designs, typescript documents and photographs** (private collection)

Harry Lange: **Obituaries** (July-August 2008), especially in the **Daily Telegraph**, **Guardian** and **Independent**

Neil McAleer: **Odyssey – The Authorized Biography of Arthur C. Clarke** (Gollancz, 1992)

* Howard E. McCurdy: **Space and the American Imagination** (Smithsonian, 1997)

Frederick I. Ordway III and Mitchell Sharpe: **The Rocket Team** (Apogee Press, 2007)

Danny Peary: **Screen Flights, Screen Fantasies** (Doubleday, 1984)

Antoine Pecqueur: **Les écrans sonores de Stanley Kubrick** (Editions du Point d'Exclamation, 2007)

Stephanie Schwam, ed.: **The Making of 2001: A Space Odyssey** (The Modern Library, 2000)

Vivian Sobchack: **Screening Space** (Rutgers University Press, 1999)

David G. Stork, ed.: **HAL's Legacy** (MIT Press, 2000)

* Abraham Thomas: **Future proof – products in 2001: A Space Odyssey** (unpublished conference paper, 2013)

Andrew Utterson: **From IBM to MGM – cinema at the dawn of the digital age** (Bfi/Palgrave, 2011)

Alexander Walker: **Stanley Kubrick Directs** (Abacus, 1972)

Alexander Walker et al: **Stanley Kubrick, Director** (Weidenfeld and Nicolson, 1999)

Jim Wynovski: **They Came From Outer Space** (Doubleday, 1980)

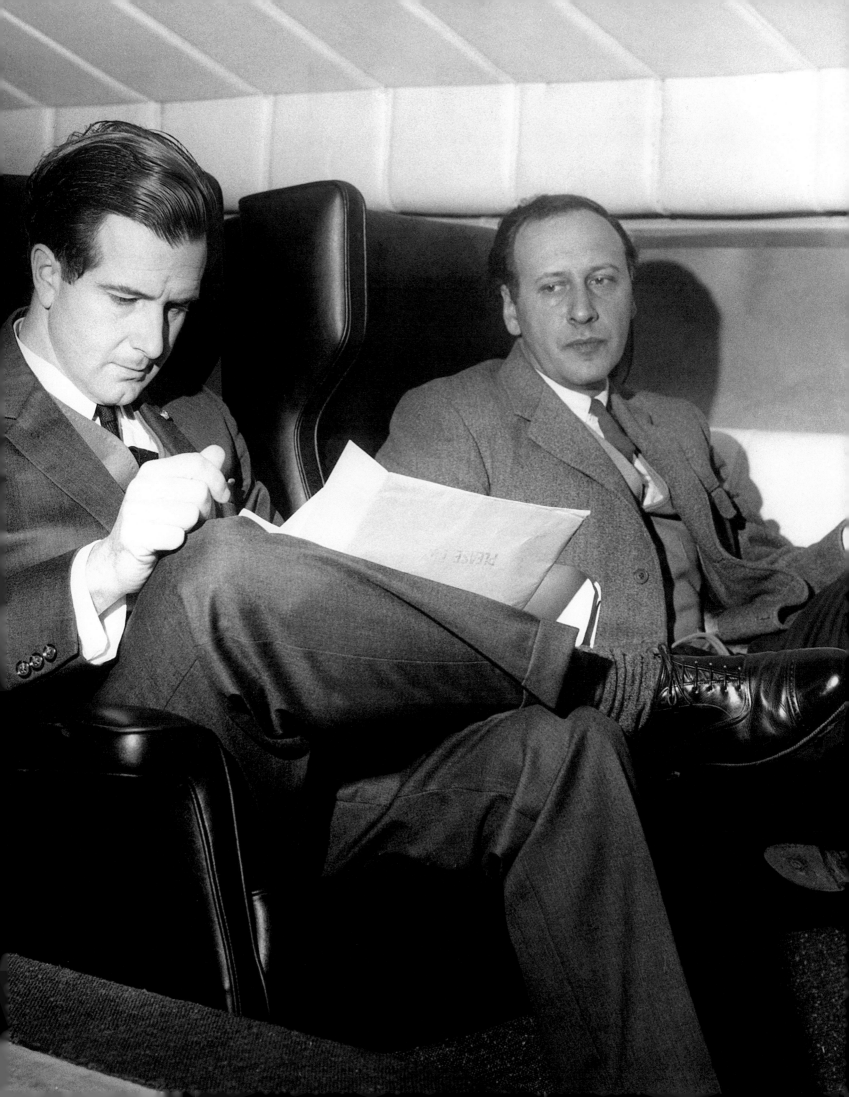

Text by Christopher Frayling
Edited by Christopher Frayling and Tony Nourmand
Art Direction and Design by Joakim Olsson
Project Co-ordination by Alison Elangasinghe
Production Assistance by Rory Bruton
Pre-Press by HR Digital Solutions

Published in 2019 by Reel Art Press, an imprint of Rare Art Press Ltd, London, UK

www.reelartpress.com

Third Edition
8 7 6 5 4 3 2 1

First published in 2015

ISBN: 978-0-9572610-2-0

All images from The Harry Lange Archive courtesy of The Boynett Collection except: p.10 mptvimages.com; p.27 Photo by Evening Standard/Getty Images; p.51 Photo by Jean-Philippe CHARBONNIER/Gamma-Rapho via Getty Images; p.54-55 MGM/The Kobal Collection; p.57 All "British Film Institute"; p.59 Top Photo by John Jay/mptvimages.com; p.64 "British Film Institute"; p.81 Photo by Jean-Philippe CHARBONNIER/Gamma-Rapho via Getty Images; p.98 Photo by John Jay/mptvimages.com; p.148-149 TCD.fr; p.150 Photo by John Jay/mptvimages.com; p.160-161 TCD.fr; p.178-179 TCD.fr; p.196-197 MGM/The Kobal Collection; p.206 TCD.fr; p.208 Photo by John Jay/mptvimages.com; p.224-225 MGM/The Kobal Collection; p.238-239 MGM/Archive Photos/Getty Images; p.250-251 MGM/The Kobal Collection; p.263 Photo by Dmitri Kessel/The LIFE Picture Collection/Getty Images; p.275 Photo by Dmitri Kessel/ The LIFE Picture Collection/Getty Images; p.282-283 mptvimages.com; p.293 Photo by Dmitri Kessel/The LIFE Picture Collection/Getty Images; p.311 Photo by John Jay/mptvimages.com; p.313 Photo by Dmitri Kessel/The LIFE Picture Collection/Getty Images; p.317 Photo by Dmitri Kessel/The LIFE Picture Collection/Getty Images

Printed by Graphius, Gent.